GERARD CHESHIRE

# 3

# MODERN
# HISTORY

## From World War Two to
## the World Wide Web:
## Great Stories in Modern
## History for Every Day
## of the Year

ICON BOOKS

Originally published in UK in 2008 by Icon Books Ltd

This edition published in the UK in 2009 by
Icon Books Ltd, Omnibus Business Centre,
39–41 North Road, London N7 9DP
email: info@iconbooks.co.uk
www.iconbooks.co.uk

Sold in the UK, Europe, South Africa and Asia
by Faber & Faber Ltd, Bloomsbury House,
74–77 Great Russell Street, London WC1B 3DA
or their agents

Distributed in the UK, Europe, South Africa and Asia
by TBS Ltd, TBS Distribution Centre, Colchester Road
Frating Green, Colchester CO7 7DW

This edition published in Australia in 2009
by Allen & Unwin Pty Ltd,
PO Box 8500, 83 Alexander Street,
Crows Nest, NSW 2065

This edition published in the USA in 2009 by Totem Books
Inquiries to Icon Books Ltd,
Omnibus Business Centre,
39–41 North Road, London N7 9DP

Distributed to the trade in the USA by
National Book Network Inc.,
4501 Forbes Boulevard, Suite 200,
Lanham, Maryland 20706

Distributed in Canada by
Penguin Books Canada,
90 Eglinton Avenue East, Suite 700,
Toronto, Ontario M4P 2YE

ISBN: 978-184831-069-8

Text copyright © 2008 Icon Books Ltd, Gerard Cheshire and John Farndon

Additional material by Nick Sidwell, Duncan Heath and Sarah Higgins

Typesetting and design by Hands Fotoset
Set in 11 on 12pt Garamond

Printed and bound in the UK by
Clays Ltd, St Ives plc

The publishers would like to thank Catherine Slack for her diligent research in aid of this book.

# Contents

# CONTENTS

# Preface

The world has changed dramatically since the end of the Second World War. Countries have risen and fallen; revolutionaries have come and gone. The world wide web has been invented, as have personal computers, the mp3 player and 3D cinema. And, of course, the bikini. Much has changed about the way we live our lives. Science and culture; conflict and resolution; politics and the environment have all had an effect on how we think about the world in the 21st century. But when did it all happen?

Bringing together a calendar year of the most significant events to have occurred in the post-war years allows us to see exactly what happened when, and in doing so it brings us closer to history itself as it has unfolded over the past half a century and more. So, as well as the aforementioned internet (13 November 1990), computer (19 January 1984), iPod (23 October 2001) and cinema (9 April 1953), you will come across momentous days which have shaped humanity – such as the deployment of the atomic bomb on Hiroshima (6 August 1945) or the first footsteps on the Moon (21 July 1969), as well as more diverse stories – including the launch of the Mini (26 August 1959) and indeed the bikini (5 July 1946) – that shed light upon us as human beings.

Amassing our collective modern history in this way also enables us to find out which years and decades have been the most eventful since the end of the war. 1945, perhaps unsurprisingly, takes the honour of being the most significant post-war year. But as well as bringing a close to the conflict, the same year also saw the US embark on their rocket programme, the origins of the myth surrounding the Bermuda Triangle, and the appearance of the prototype microwave oven. Two other years stand out as being particularly active in the course of recent history: 1953, which saw humans uncover the structure of DNA, conquer Everest and develop a vaccine for the dreaded polio; and 2003, which has given us moments such as the first draft of the Human Genome Project, the launch of the space probe, *Beagle 2*, and the 100th birthday celebrations of powered flight.

However, if the busiest individual years have come from the 1940s, 1950s and 2000s, the busiest decade was of course the 1960s. From the Cuban missile crisis and the assassination of JFK to the invention of the laser and the beginning of the space race, and encompassing too the introduction of the contraceptive pill, the debut of Bob Dylan and the crusade by Mary Whitehouse to clean up British society, as well as starker events such as the Cultural Revolution in China, the discovery of the link between smoking and cancer, and the Chilean earthquake, the sixties set the tone for much of what has followed over subsequent decades.

The contrast between achievement and devastation – the best of times and the worst of times – is a pattern from this decade that has been repeated across the face of our recent past. Reading these stories, you will encounter not just tales of war and peace, but the contrast between human good and human folly, the crippling effect of natural disasters and the indomitable human spirit that never gives up trying to invent, discover, accomplish and overcome.

And where does this all leave us now? The previous books in this series, *365 – Great Stories from History for Every Day of the Year* and *366 – A Leap Year of Great Stories from History for Every Day of the Year* (both available from www.iconbooks.co.uk and all good bookshops), recounted the rich tapestry of history from across the centuries and millennia. *365 Modern History – From World War Two to the World Wide Web: Great Stories in Modern History for Every Day of the Year* aims to bring history up to date and uncover its constant dynamism. The 2000s, not yet complete and almost too immediate to take their place alongside decades from the 20th century, are already promising to deliver some of the most significant events that will mould history for forthcoming generations. Who knows – what is taking place today, as you read this, might well find that it has its own place in the next book in this series. History, if nothing else, is constantly surprising.

# 1 January

## *The Euro becomes the common currency for much of Europe*

**2002** In the face of growing trade competition with other regions of the world, it began to make sense for European countries to pool their resources and present a united front for the sake of preserving their import/export businesses. The idea proposed was a common currency, effectively making all member countries a part of the same trading 'super-nation'. The units of common currency became known as euros (€), an allusion to the name Europe. Incidentally, the word Europe was itself derived from the Greek god of the east wind, who was also called Euros.

Some European countries began trading in euros on paper as early as 1999, but the currency was launched in its physical form in 2002. Twelve of the fifteen EU members at that time scrapped their traditional currencies to face a brave new world of oneness. Those countries that stood their ground were Britain, Denmark and Sweden. They argued that the only argument in favour of adopting the euro could be a guaranteed fiscal advantage. Without that guarantee they were unprepared to enter a common currency.

The twelve other nations took the view that the only way to find out was to embrace the experiment and face the consequences. So far there seems to have been no marked advantage or disadvantage for euro countries. However, they do share an allegiance of market convenience, which some analysts view as a progressive ethos that will serve them well in future decades. The euro is now the common currency of around 320 million people from thirteen countries – Slovenia was included on 1 January 2007. A number of territories not in the EU have also adopted the euro, among them Andorra, Monaco, the Vatican City and San Marino.

As a unit of currency the euro is subdivided into 100 cents. Coin denominations are €2, €1, 50c, 10c and 5c. The 2c and 1c coins have become virtually obsolete, although still legal. Paper notes are €500, €200, €100, €50, €20, €10 and €5. The coins usually possess common sides and national sides alluding to the countries in which they were minted. The notes have no national identity as not all countries print them.

# 2 January

## Peter Sutcliffe, aka the notorious 'Yorkshire Ripper', is finally arrested

**1981** Peter Sutcliffe was a lorry driver who developed a taste for murdering prostitutes by means of bludgeoning them over the head with a hammer. His criminal moniker – the 'Yorkshire Ripper' – arose due to similarities between his *modus operandi* and that of the infamous Jack the Ripper, who killed and mutilated a number of women in the Whitechapel area of Victorian London.

Sutcliffe's criminal career spanned a period when modern forensics and policing techniques were still in their infancy. DNA fingerprinting, for example, had not been developed and computers were not yet part of the infrastructure. Consequently, although Sutcliffe was brought in and interviewed, he managed to slip through the net on a number of occasions.

In addition, a hoaxer beguiled the police with letters and a tape purporting to have been created by the killer. Following the arrest of Sutcliffe himself, the hoaxer became known as 'Wearside Jack' as he had misled the police into believing that the Ripper was from Wearside in north-east England, rather than Yorkshire. Sutcliffe had initially evaded arrest because he had a different accent to the voice on the tape, and the police dismissed him as a suspect.

Wearside Jack remained at large for a quarter of a century until September 2005, when new DNA profiling of saliva on the envelopes containing the hoax letters found a match with a John Humble. He was convicted of perverting the course of justice and sentenced to eight years' imprisonment in 2006.

Peter Sutcliffe was found guilty of murdering thirteen women between 1975 and 1980, four of whom might have survived had Humble not played the hoaxer. Sutcliffe will be eligible for parole in 2011 but it seems unlikely that he will ever be released from prison, having such a high profile.

He admitted to seven counts of attempted murder, but he was never tried for them. The seven surviving women all wished to preserve their anonymity, so the police decided that a trial would not be in the public interest, since Sutcliffe was already behind bars for life.

It seems that Sutcliffe fitted the classic 'loner profile' that so often seems to go with deviant behaviour. He cultivated no friendships while at school, and his job meant that he spent a good deal of his time in isolation. He seems to have been happily married, but had no children.

# 3 January

## The USA breaks diplomatic relations with Cuba

**1961** Two years earlier, on 3 January 1959, Alaska had become the 49th state of the USA. It had been bought from Russia way back in 1867, but increasing tensions between the two countries prompted the US government to formally include the area in their national boundaries, as it would have been strategically vital had the Cold War boiled over into military conflict.

In the October of 1959 the president of Cuba, Fidel Castro, declared himself to be a communist sympathiser and therefore an ally of the Soviet Union (USSR). By March 1960 Castro had established diplomatic relations with the Soviets, by way of aid agreements, and had purged his government of those politicians with anti-communist sentiments.

The US government grew increasingly anxious at the prospect of having a potential Soviet point of missile attack so close to their own doorstep. A trade embargo imposed on Cuba in late 1960 failed to weaken Castro as they had intended. Instead, he simply turned his back on the Americans and embraced Soviet ideology all the more. The US government subsequently severed diplomatic relations with Cuba in January 1961.

By this time, many ousted and exiled anti-Castro politicians were planning to invade Cuba and dislodge Castro by military coup. In April 1961, with the promise of US assistance, they launched their attempt. The Bay of Pigs, as it is known, was a disaster. At the last moment, the US President Kennedy decided to withdraw air support, for fear of antagonising the USSR. The following month, Castro declared himself a fully fledged Marxist–Leninist communist and Cuba a socialist republic.

Now the scene was set for the very Cuban–Soviet alliance that the USA did not wish to see. Castro allowed the USSR to build nuclear missile silos on Cuba, under the pretext that they were there to protect Cuba from another invasion attempt. The Cuban missile crisis began on 16 October 1962 when US aerial reconnaissance photographs revealed the presence of a missile base on the island. Kennedy immediately opened lines of communication with the Soviet leader, Nikita Khrushchev.

Twelve days later the crisis was brought to an end when Khrushchev announced that the nuclear installation would be dismantled with immediate effect. It would, however, be another 27 years until the Cold War finally thawed with the collapse of the Berlin Wall.

# 4 January

## The first man-made satellite, Sputnik 1, comes back to Earth

**1958** The Sputnik programme began with the launch of *Sputnik 1* on 4 October 1957. There would be seventeen further satellites named *Sputnik*, with the last being launched on 10 November 1998. The eighteen were actually numbered 1–41 because the numerical sequencing was irregular.

*Sputnik 1* was a very basic satellite. It was essentially a polished aluminium sphere a couple of feet (600 mm) in diameter, with four whisker-like antennae. The design became the cliché for the appearance of satellites in mid-20th-century animated cartoons and the like. Inside the sphere, *Sputnik 1* was equipped with two simple transmitters which emitted radio signals for the duration of its orbit. The transmitters worked at different frequencies – 20 and 40 megahertz – so that Soviet scientists could compare the signals they received to find out information about the density and temperature of the ionosphere, which is the upper layer of the atmosphere. The sphere was also filled with pressurised nitrogen gas, so that punctures from meteoroids could be detected in changes to the radio waves caused by the resultant drop in pressure.

As it turned out, *Sputnik 1* was never struck during its orbit, but it was completely destroyed on re-entry. Air resistance simply caused it to burn up or decay, so that it actually returned to Earth in the form of airborne debris. Nevertheless, the Soviets had drawn first blood against the USA and the Space Race was on in earnest.

*Sputnik 2* had already been launched before *Sputnik 1* had retired itself from service. The second *Sputnik* had the distinction of being the first space vehicle, as it carried with it a female dog named Laika. The animal perished from overheating only a few hours after entering orbit. It would have died anyway, however, as no provision had been made for the satellite to safely re-enter the atmosphere. Even so, Laika had shown scientists that mammals could survive a rocket launch. The experiment became the first step on the way towards manned space flight.

Artificial satellites have come a long way since *Sputnik 1*. There are currently over 2,500 in orbit. Many thousands more have come and gone. Their purpose is varied. Many are communications satellites, used for dealing with the electronic signals of radio, television, telephones and the internet. Some are used to monitor the Earth's landmasses and oceans, while others look the other way into space. There are also weather satellites, spy satellites and space stations, where scientists carry out experiments in weightless environments. Satellites that move in relation to the Earth's surface are described as being in geocentric orbits. Those that remain still, above the equator, are said to have geostationary orbits.

# 5 January

## The American Civil Liberties Union wins a famous legal battle

**1982** In 1925 a trial took place in Tennessee, which became known as the Scopes Trial. It involved a teacher called John T. Scopes, who had the state of Tennessee take him to court for violating a new law – the Butler Act – that forbade him from teaching human evolution, in favour of the belief in the divine creation of humanity, as entertained by the Christian Bible.

The scientist Charles Darwin had published his theory of evolution in 1859. By the 1920s it had been widely accepted, by Christians, agnostics and atheists alike, as a commonsense explanation for the origins of animal and plant species. However, the southern states of the USA still harboured populations of fundamentalist Christians – evangelicals – who believed in a literal interpretation of the Bible.

Scopes was found guilty as charged, largely due to the influence these evangelicals were able to exert on the US government. Remarkably the Butler Act remained in force until 1967, when it was finally repealed by a more modernist Tennessee legislature.

It came as something of a surprise then, that the state of Arkansas should vote on a similar law as late as 1981, called the 'Balanced Treatment for Creation-Science and Evolution-Science Act'. When the American Civil Liberties Union decided to contest the law in court, it was dubbed the 'Scopes II Trial'.

The central argument between the two sides focused on the presentation of proof that the other was incorrect in their assertions. In essence it boiled down to irreconcilable differences in beliefs, so that a stalemate position arose, as it inevitably does in such situations. The federal judge, however, found in favour of the secular view. He declared the new law to be void on the grounds that it was 'unconstitutional to even imply the existence of a creator in a public school science class or to teach any scientific theory that is not purely naturalistic.'

This landmark ruling had a clear message: there was no room for any crossover between scientific and religious camps. Only secular science was to be taught in science lessons; Christianity was to remain within the remit of religious education.

# 6 January

### *The world-renowned Russian ballet dancer Rudolf Nureyev dies from an Aids-related illness*

**1993** His death served to highlight the very real risk of an HIV pandemic and helped in the campaign to make people aware of the need to be more cautious about having casual sexual encounters. To a large extent, the populations of more developed countries began to correct their behaviour over the coming years to ensure that the rate of infection for Aids-related illnesses reached a plateau and then declined, but many developing countries were subjected to catastrophic and rising rates of infection.

The origins of HIV (Human Immunodeficiency Virus) are unknown to science. The virus is found to be resistant to drugs, making a cure so far unattainable.

Those who are HIV positive are found to be able to carry the virus for years before it develops to a point where symptoms are detectable. When this does happen, it become known as Aids (Acquired Immune Deficiency Syndrome) and the outcome is invariably fatal. Sufferers do not die from the virus itself, but rather from the fact that the virus renders them defenceless against other diseases that the human body can normally combat very easily. In other words, their immune system closes down, making them susceptible to attack by other viral, bacterial and fungal infections.

HIV is actually a rather poor contagion, as it readily perishes outside of the body once it is exposed to desiccation and/or a drop in temperature. This means that it is relatively difficult to become infected as the virus requires warm blood or sexual fluids to act as a conduit from one body to the next. Furthermore, it requires access to the bloodstream in order to enter the new victim.

In the West infection rates are highest among homosexuals, although heterosexual intercourse is actually a more effective mode of transmission. Other carriers can become infected by blood transfusion and the sharing of hypodermic needles for drug use. Unborn babies also stand a high chance of being infected by their own mothers via the placenta.

In many African countries the HIV–Aids problem is sexually related. Poor education about the disease, a lack of available barrier contraceptives (such as condoms) and sores from other sexual infections have produced an environment perfect for the virus to flourish in. Needless to say, many millions of babies are born with the virus too, so that in some places there are more people infected than not. So far, drugs only serve to alleviate symptoms which ultimately lead to death.

An unlikely link between Aids and the drug Thalidomide has been formed in Africa over recent years. Thalidomide inhibits the growth of new blood vessels and this has proved effective in the treatment of tumours known as Kaposi's sarcomas, which are triggered by the virus. Unfortunately, this association has led to a new generation of 'Thalidomide children', as many of those who take Thalidomide are young females who don't understand the implications of taking the drug during pregnancy until it is too late. Thalidomide adversely affects the development of offspring in the womb, and babies are born with malformed limbs.

# 7 January

## The Khmer Rouge regime is ousted from power in Cambodia

**1979** Born as Saloth Sar, Pol Pot was a failed academic with political ambitions and social aspirations. When Cambodia gained political independence from France in 1954, Saloth Sar took advantage of civil unrest in the country to bring his newly formed communist party to the fore. Properly known as the CPK

(Communist Party of Kampuchea), the party adopted the French title *Khmer Rouge* after the predominant ethnic group in Cambodia, the Khmer, and the red of communism. Saloth Sar became Pol Pot as an abbreviation of the French *politique potentielle*, due to the 'political potential' seen in him by his fellow communists.

By 1968 the Khmer Rouge had begun an uprising against the Cambodian government. Then in 1970 Pol Pot formed an alliance with the neighbouring communist party of North Vietnam, the Viet Minh, which helped the Khmer Rouge take power after a five-year war.

Pol Pot's agenda turned out to be a blend of Marxist communist ideology and an expression of his own resentment towards the well-off and well-educated. Students and the middle classes were initially banned from joining the Khmer Rouge, in favour of those who came from the peasantry. But things were set to get a lot worse. Anyone who opposed the Khmer Rouge was tortured and executed. Then anyone deemed superfluous to requirements was exterminated.

Pol Pot developed the notion of a perfect communist state where all were equal. That meant that anyone with any form of education or other social advantage was killed. In effect he decapitated the population by removing all of those with the potential to see his nation progress on the world stage. But that didn't matter to Pol Pot, who imagined a totally autonomous and self-reliant nation, with him in charge.

Inevitably the infrastructure of Cambodia – renamed Kampuchea during Pol Pot's rule – began to fail and disintegrate, leading to widespread famine and social unrest. In 1978 his former ally, the Viet Minh, overthrew the Khmer Rouge in order to restore a semblance of normality to the country. Pol Pot and his most loyal followers were driven into hiding, never to return to power again.

The phrase that sums up Pol Pot's despotic hold over Cambodia from 1975–9 is the one the Khmer Rouge used in justifying the slaughter of an estimated 2 million people: 'To keep you is no benefit, to destroy you is no loss.'

# 8 January

## *David Bowie is born as plain old David Jones*

**1947** Due to the fact that there was already a famous David Jones, in the pop group The Monkees, he changed his surname to Bowie, pronounced to rhyme with 'showy'. Bowie's initial forays into pop music were tinged with a certain level of amateur theatricality. He hadn't properly formulated an image or persona when he had an early hit single in the shape of 'Space Oddity' in 1969, in part due to the fact that the US had put the first men on the Moon in that same year.

Following that success, Bowie then released a whole sequence of singles that flopped over a three-year period. Finally, having recorded the album *The Rise and Fall of Ziggy Stardust and the Spiders from Mars*, he struck gold in the form of the eponymous Ziggy Stardust, an alienesque figure with outlandish clothing, hair and makeup.

Through the mid to late 1970s, David Bowie cultivated a reputation for an avant-garde and inventive genius. He had a string of albums and singles which saw him continually evolving creatively, both in terms of his music and his public image. This extraordinary run of success earned him the nickname 'The Chameleon of Rock', such was his ability to reinvent himself time and time again. In addition to his career as a rock star he also forged sideline careers as a producer of other people's music, and as an actor and artist.

It has been said that Bowie has an 'art school mentality', which essentially means that he perceives any type of creativity as one and the same thing, since they are all forms of self-expression. Consequently he has never been afraid to try anything new. For the most part he has enjoyed success on his own terms, but inevitably his fans have sometimes thought differently. Nevertheless, Bowie has always seemed to maintain an air of coolness, no matter what he has attempted.

Since the 1970s and early 1980s it would be fair to say that David Bowie's star has fallen slightly in terms of his musical consistency. This is not least because Bowie has insisted on pursuing a non-conformist agenda, taking him into areas that are not necessarily aurally accessible to a mass market. In his later years he has become something of a guru and sage to younger musicians with similar creative ideals.

# 9 January

### The, as yet, only supersonic airliner makes its first test flight

**1969** Concorde saw commercial use from 1976–2003, until a single disaster saw it taken out of commission. So few Concorde planes were made, that just one crash saw the aeroplane go from having the best safety record to the worst safety record of any airliner. Its days were numbered.

The term 'supersonic' means faster than the speed of sound waves, which travel at a speed of roughly 761 mph (1,224 kph). This speed does vary with altitude and atmospheric conditions, but not a great deal. The idea of exceeding the speed of sound was very attractive to the designers of Concorde as it seemed to hail a new age in global transportation. However, it had its problems.

For one thing, supersonic aircraft carry a pressure wave, which is an accumulation of sound energy that cannot escape the machine due to its velocity. This results in a loud sonic boom as the pressure wave travels along with the aeroplane. The boom was found to be disruptive to people and animals on the ground, so Concorde was only allowed to travel supersonically when flying over oceans.

Secondly, travelling at and above the speed of sound puts enormous stresses and strains on a vehicle. Air friction causes the entire aircraft to heat up and stretch in length, so that the components are tested to their limits. Also, supersonic aircraft can never be very large, as they require a dart-like shape and enormous engines to push them through the air at high speeds. This in turn makes running a supersonic airliner a very expensive business because it can carry relatively few passengers, who have to cover high maintenance and fuel costs.

In the end it became apparent that only the privileged few could afford to fly on Concorde, and that the advantages of arriving at a destination a few hours earlier weren't enough to entice other passengers to spend the extra money. The super-wealthy often preferred to own personal small jet aircraft anyway, or to fly by private charter.

By the time of the crash, near Paris on 25 January 2000, Concorde was an obsolete aircraft eking out a living largely by giving luxury pleasure flights. As soon as it was deemed to be unsafe in the public consciousness, its death knell was sounded. When Concorde 203 fell from the sky, the bottom of the market for supersonic passenger flights fell out too.

# 10 January

## The United Nations holds its inaugural meeting

**1946** Following the Second World War, the United Nations was properly formalised and had its first General Assembly to discuss reparations. The term 'United Nations' had been coined in 1941 by US President Roosevelt and UK Prime Minister Churchill to describe those countries that were allied in the fight against the Axis Powers.

The prototype to the UN had been the League of Nations, which was formed in 1919, following the end of the First World War. Ironically, both Germany and Japan had been members of the League of Nations – but this hadn't precluded them from nurturing ideas of territorial conquest and preparing for war against other members The idea behind the United Nations was to create an international organisation that brought more stability to the political world.

Following the Second World War, many countries, including those that had been defeated, had to repair the damage done to their infrastructures. Social, political and economic problems had to be discussed and dealt with in the aftermath, which was where the UN came to prominence. In addition to this, there was the problem of dealing with war criminals. Those accused of atrocities between 1939 and 1945 were ultimately put on trial in Nuremberg, Germany and in Tokyo, Japan.

In the post-war years, the purpose and aims of the United Nations became more honed as the organisation matured. It now has different organs that make up the body. The UN General Assembly is an annual forum in which representatives from all member states have an opportunity to discuss details of international relations and law, as well as the role and function of the UN itself.

There is also the UN Security Council which deals with matters of peace and security among nations. It has just fifteen member states. China, France, Russia, the US and the UK are permanent, while ten memberships are given temporarily to other states for periods of two years.

A fundamental flaw in the UN Security Council is that it has no true power over nations that rock the boat. There is no consequence for nations that violate the rules and of the five permanent members that oversee activities two – namely France and the UK – are no longer in the positions of power and influence that they once enjoyed in the post-war environment. The true efficacy of the United Nations is therefore called into question when it comes to heavyweight issues.

# 11 January

## The US administration officially links smoking tobacco with ill health

**1964** Remarkably, during the First and Second World Wars cigarettes had actually been given to service men and women as they were seen as an essential supply. At that time in history 80 per cent of adults smoked in most countries, and tobacco was viewed as a mild form of medication – a pick-me-up and stress reliever for the common man. Somehow, the enormous number of deaths due to smoking-related diseases, such as emphysema and lung cancer, were either overlooked or simply not connected with smoking. Besides, the world had other things to worry about; not least the tens of millions lost in warfare.

Tobacco was originally used by Native American tribes in rituals and ceremonies. When European settlers arrived they took to smoking, chewing and sniffing tobacco (in the form of snuff). Tobacco became popular in Europe itself during Elizabethan times and demand was met by tobacco plantations in the southern US – Virginia and the Carolinas – which also played a part in promoting the slave trade. For the next 350 years, tobacco became as familiar to the world as potatoes, tomatoes or any other produce originating from the Americas.

In the 1950s scientists began to suspect that smoking wasn't that good for health after all, but governments were earning enormous sums from the taxation of tobacco. Quite apart from any ethical concerns about social welfare, there was a clear fiscal conflict between gaining revenue and covering the cost of dealing with those dying from smoking-related illnesses. Consequently little was actually done to discourage people from smoking, not least because many in power were smokers themselves.

In addition to this it was apparent that smoking entered people into a lottery of illness, rather than inevitably causing premature death. Everyone knew someone who had lived to a ripe old age yet smoked every single day of their adult life, so it was human nature to prefer to think that illness would visit the other man rather than oneself.

It wasn't until the evolution of the litigious society in the late 20th century that governments began to take smoking-related illness seriously. The term 'passive smoking' entered the vernacular. Suddenly it was possible for a non-smoker to legally claim that their illness had been caused by other people's smoking. Soon it became illegal to smoke in public spaces and places of work. Added to this, a heightened awareness of self-preservation and healthy lifestyle choices catalysed a change in people's overall attitude towards smoking. The seesaw of public opinion on smoking had tipped the other way.

# 12 January

## *Air travel enters a new age*

**1970** The first purpose-built airliners flew in 1949; they were the de Havilland Comet and the Avro C102 Jetliner. By the 1960s, international air travel was becoming popular and manufacturers were experimenting with ever-larger designs in order to carry more people. By 1966 Boeing was experimenting with the idea of a double-decked airliner, although the idea of the wide-bodied airliner eventually took precedence. Ultimately the design of the 747 turned out to be a compromise between the two – wide-bodied but with the forward section of the fuselage double-decked. The design was radically different to what had gone before and gave the airliner an immediately recognisable profile.

Most remarkable at the time was the idea that such a seemingly non-aerodynamic and cumbersome machine should be able to fly at all, let alone be a commercially successful aircraft. Nevertheless, on this day in 1970, the Boeing 747 – known affectionately as the jumbo jet – made its first flight across the Atlantic Ocean. In doing so, it became the first in a long line of wide-bodied airliners to grace the skies around the world. Since 1970 there have been many variations of the 747 as the basic design has caught up with advances in technology and been adapted for different uses.

In more recent times there has been a recognised need for super-airliners – superliners or superjumbos – capable of carrying many more passengers. In response to this Boeing is introducing a stretched version of the 747, which will be known as the 747-8 I (International). It will be nineteen feet longer than the standard 747, at a record breaking 251 feet (76.4 metres), and be able to carry 467 passengers in its three-class internal configuration.

In 1977 the world's worst air disaster occurred on the island of Tenerife, involving two Boeing 747s. On 27 March a taxiing plane was hit by another in the process of taking off. The death toll was 583, including passengers and air crew. It remains a stark reminder of the kinds of tragedies that can result from transporting hundreds of people *en masse* in aircraft.

The superliner Airbus 380 is able to carry a remarkable 853 passengers when in economy configuration. It is shorter than the 747-8 I, but larger in overall size. One can only imagine the outcry when one of those falls from the sky or collides with another airliner. Even though such aircraft are equipped with highly advanced computerised telemetry to take off, fly and land safely, it doesn't eliminate all potential causes of catastrophic failure, whether natural or man-made.

# 13 January

## The Fab Four begin their assault on America

**1964** John Lennon, Paul McCartney, George Harrison and Ringo Starr had already established themselves in Britain the year before, so their manager Brian Epstein decided that the time was right for The Beatles to go for world domination of the popular music industry. Their debut single in the US, 'I Want to Hold Your Hand', duly reached the top slot in the charts.

By 1966 the band had become so popular worldwide that John Lennon flippantly remarked that 'Christianity will go. It will vanish and shrink. I needn't argue with that; I'm right and I will be proved right. We're more popular than Jesus now; I don't know which will go first – rock 'n' roll or Christianity. Jesus was all right but his disciples were thick and ordinary. It's them twisting it that ruins it for me.'

His words were quoted from an interview and published in Britain on 4 March in the *London Evening Standard*. Sensibilities on religion in Britain were such that the piece was barely noticed, but US evangelical fervour meant that propagandists found the story and let it run in a teen magazine called *Datebook*. The angry reaction of the American public – particularly in the Deep South –

saw radio stations ban the playing of Beatles records, and outraged Christians burn vinyl in the streets.

When asked about his thoughts on the destruction of so many Beatles records, Paul McCartney addressed the situation with the sarcastic Liverpudlian wit that gave the band their endearing charm: 'They have to buy them to burn them!'

Lennon, on his next visit to the United States, made a rather meandering speech by way of an apology for offending the people of the land of free speech. It was 11 August in Chicago, the eve of the first concert of The Beatles' final US tour. On their return to Britain, fears for their safety prompted them to become a studio-based outfit and they never toured again.

In December 1980 Lennon was assassinated by a born-again Christian who had singled him out as the ideal target for garnering notoriety. Despite his troubled relationship with America, Lennon had settled to live in New York following the split of The Beatles in 1970.


# 14 January

## US scientists publish work on an enzyme found to slow the ageing process in organisms

**1998** The process of ageing happens fundamentally because organisms reach a point where their reproductive usefulness has passed. Beyond that point cell renewal and maintenance fall away, so that physical and mental decline is characteristic until death occurs.

Many cells relinquish their 'lives' as part of a natural process. They allow themselves to die off in the process of sculpting the functional shape of an organism. In vertebrates this process, which is called apoptosis, allows the differentiation of body extremities from an initial mass of cellular material. For example, the fingers and toes on the ends of our arms and legs separate due to apoptosis of the tissue in between.

Apoptosis is part of the healthy upkeep of the body and mind right from birth, so that children lose up to 25 billion cells per day. Obviously these cells are replaced more quickly than they are removed, enabling children to develop into adults. But the situation changes in adulthood. Initially the cell death–renewal ratio reaches equilibrium so that growth halts. Eventually, though, the stability shifts off-centre so that fewer cells are replaced than lost.

As many as 80 billion cells are lost each day by an adult human, but it becomes progressively more difficult for the body to counter the loss. The result is shrinkage of the body and organs, as it has to use component chemicals in dying cells to manufacture others. Also, many cells have to live longer than they would in a younger specimen, increasing the likelihood of cell malfunction and disease.

Where apoptosis is excessive it is described as hypotrophy. Vital organs can become so diminished that they fail in their bid to sustain life. Where apoptosis is insufficient it is described as hypertrophy and can lead to malfunctions such as carcinomas or cancers, where old cell nuclei codes become corrupted and unchecked proliferations ensue. Both are due to diminished anti-apoptosis (cell replacement).

It is evident, therefore, that to inhibit the ageing process, it is necessary to target the slowing of cell replenishment, so that apoptosis can continue at a healthy pace, as it does in organisms on top of their game. The enzyme discovered by the scientists catalyses new cell production by promoting the intake of new cell-building material from food, so that old material can continue to be discarded or recycled by apoptosis beyond the normal threshold.

# 15 January

### President Nixon orders a halt to offensive actions in Vietnam

**1973** The US entered the Vietnam War fully in 1965, with the confidence of a nation that had never before been defeated. However, jungle warfare turned out to be the undoing of the American army. Before long, fallen soldiers in body-bags were being delivered home with growing frequency. Despite the loss of life, the situation in Vietnam indicated that the enemy wasn't about to be beaten any time soon.

By 1973 more than 50,000 US combatants had died and public opinion had swayed heavily against continued involvement. 'Tactical withdrawal' became the only route open to the US administration. The very last US troops to leave Vietnam did so in 1975.

The reasons for the success of the adversary were several. For one thing the opposing Vietnamese soldiers, the Viet Cong (VC), were fighting in their native lands, while the Americans were on foreign soil. They therefore had the home advantage as they knew the terrain, the climate and the habitat so well that they coped far better than the US troops. The VC also had an uncanny ability to conceal themselves in the jungle. Out of uniform, they were impossible to distinguish from US-supported civilians and it was a simple matter to hide among them in villages. In addition the Viet Cong developed underground encampments, which linked together like rabbit warrens and had camouflaged entrances.

Perhaps most importantly the VC comprised battle-hardened guerrilla fighters, while the US army comprised new and naive recruits who famously had an average age of just nineteen years. The jungle conditions were intolerable for these inexperienced soldiers. Many of the American combatants resorted to smoking drugs just to get through each day, having resigned themselves to an inevitable death. This became a self-fulfilling prophecy, as they rendered themselves devoid of the faculties that might have saved their lives.

The US military resorted to some questionable tactics in their attempts to overcome the Viet Cong forces. Carpet-bombing areas of jungle with napalm was a strategy designed to eradicate the hidden enemy, but it did little other than decimate crops and kill innocent villagers. Petrified US troops committed massacres, such was their paranoia that they were about to be ambushed.

In the end the US offensive was a mess. At best, the Americans had failed to secure victory, losing many military lives as they did so. At worst, they were in retreat and had lost their first war.

# 16 January

*The last shah of Iran flees his country into exile*

**1979** The Persian Empire had been established in 559 BC and it lasted in one form or another for 2,538 years. Persians began adopting Islam following the death of the prophet Muhammad in AD 632, and the Islamic Golden Age began in AD 750. This marked the point where Islam took proper hold within the Empire and began to spread outside of Persia too. Even though the Persian Empire eventually diminished in size, until it became Iran, its legacy was to leave Muslim enclaves all over its former territory.

A year before the shah fled, in January 1978, a revolution had begun in Iran. The general population had decided that their days of living in a monarchy were numbered. Iran had been ruled by royalty since the heyday of the Persian Empire. An Islamic state, however, offered a more egalitarian, as well as spiritual, way of life and was therefore a very attractive proposition. The Ayatollah had been exiled from Iran in 1964 because of the threat he posed to the monarchy. More and more Iranians, however, became devout Muslims in the years that followed and they inevitably thought of him as their rightful leader. Even though he was absent in body, he was ever-present in mind.

Despite the enormous wealth of Shah Mohammad Reza Pahlavi, he could do nothing to halt the tide of change in his people. He was a Muslim himself, but he was a moderate who wished to westernise Iran. He also recognised Israel as the homeland of Judaism, which gave oxygen to the flames of Islamic fundamentalism in the religious right. There was also an influential communist movement in Iran, which served to stir up resentment towards the divide between the rich and the poor. All in all it became a bad situation for the monarchy and the Shah left Iran after 37 years in power.

Both the Muslims and communists had played their parts in the revolution of Iran, but such was the religious fervour of the population, it soon became clear that the country was to become a theocracy. On 1 April 1979 Iran officially became an Islamic state with the returned Ayatollah Khomeini as its head.

The last shah of Iran spent his exile in Egypt, Morocco, the Bahamas, Mexico, the US and Panama. He returned to Egypt in December 1979 and died of cancer in July 1980. Anwar Sadat, the president of Egypt, was assassinated the following year under a fatwa related to his sympathies towards Shah Pahlavi and the US.

# 17 January

## The Palomares Incident

**1966** Palomares is a fishing village on the Mediterranean coastline of Spain. In 1966 it became the scene of the worst radiation contamination accident not involving a nuclear power station. On the fateful day a B-52 bomber carrying nuclear weapons collided with a KC-135 tanker from which it was receiving fuel in mid-air. The collision caused the tanker to explode into smithereens with the loss of all four crew. The bomber broke apart as it plummeted to the ground. Four of its crew members were lucky enough to survive.

The bomber had been loaded with four hydrogen bombs, all of which spilled from the aircraft as it was sent earthbound. Three of the weapons struck land near to the village, while the fourth plunged into the Mediterranean and settled on the seabed at a depth of 2,500 feet (760 metres). The detonating devices in two of the bombs that made landfall exploded on impact with the ground. They were powered by conventional explosives, but the explosions caused considerable radioactive contamination of the area because quantities of uranium and plutonium were sent into the air. In effect, they became 'dirty bombs'.

An area of 2 km² was assessed to contain the worst of the contamination and the recovery team removed 1,750 tonnes of topsoil in their clean-up operation. Having removed the three terrestrial bombs, the recovery team set their sights on locating and dealing with the submerged bomb. It was brought to the surface eight days later.

A local fisherman happened to see the fourth bomb splash into the water and the US recovery team was able to use this as their starting point. They then employed probability based on the calculated direction and speed of the bomb's entry into the water to produce a search grid. This was superimposed on to the seabed, and a process of elimination eventually led them to the resting place of the weapon.

Interestingly the fisherman, Francisco Simó Orts, claimed salvage rights to the bomb for his part in locating it. He claimed that 1–2 per cent of the value was customary in such cases. The bomb happened to be worth $2 billion, giving him a claim to $20–40 million. The US Air Force eventually settled with him out of court, so no one knows how much he actually received.

In 2006 the Spanish and US governments agreed to fund a new clean-up operation of the area. A new study had shown that soil radiation levels were still unnaturally high. Fauna and flora have been shown to be contaminated too, suggesting that uranium and plutonium deposits still lie below ground and are being brought into the surface environment by the actions of root growth, burrowing and so on.

# 18 January

## US–USSR treaty on control of nuclear weapons

**1968** By the late 1960s it became clear that the balance of nuclear power between enemy nations was such that annihilation was a certain outcome for all concerned should there be a nuclear war. As a result, someone coined an appropriate acronym for this insane state of affairs: MAD (Mutually Assured Destruction). Under such a cloud it was decided that humanity might benefit from a silver lining and so it was that a treaty was drawn up to control the worldwide spread of nuclear armaments. It became known as the Treaty on the Non-Proliferation of Nuclear Weapons.

In terms of 'making a difference', however, the treaty was, and still is, worth essentially very little. Despite the fact that the nuclear nations have markedly reduced their arsenals in accordance with the agreement, they continue to possess enough nuclear weapons and component materials to destroy the world several times over.

The treaty itself covered three fundamental themes or 'pillars' as they were described. The first was non-proliferation, the second was disarmament and the third was the right to peacefully use nuclear technology. It was this third pillar that essentially balanced the equation, and in doing so cancelled out any intended benefits. In other words, nations were allowed to continue producing the ingredients for nuclear weaponry even if they had agreed to disassemble existing weapons and to cease the manufacture of new ones.

Of course the key problem is that nuclear technology can be put to use in a number of ways that are both constructive and destructive. The benefits from using nuclear power as an energy source are so clear that it has always been easy to argue in favour of its continued use. Consequently it has never been possible to prevent nations from mining and refining the radioactive elements necessary for this application of the technology.

There is only a small difference between nuclear power and nuclear weapons. Nuclear power utilises the heat that is gradually given off when radioactive material is encouraged to undergo a fission reaction under controlled conditions. Nuclear weapons explode because the fission reaction is allowed to go out of control, leading to the sudden release of energy in one hit. It is easy to see, then, that preparing raw materials for use in nuclear power stations and nuclear-powered sea vessels is only a short step away from using them in nuclear weapons. This is why 'rogue' nations are dealt with suspiciously when they develop supposedly benign nuclear technologies of their own.

# 19 January

### *The first computer with a graphical user interface and mouse tool is unveiled*

**1984** Today we take computers so much for granted that we forget that they had to start somewhere, and that someone had to come up with the fundamental format upon which they are now based. Before 1984, computers were rather mysterious machines that displayed sets of green coded numbers and letters that meant nothing to the layperson. Only those trained in computer language could understand them and put them to any useful purpose. As tools they had rather limited employment, literally 'computing' data for obscure applications.

Then, someone had the bright idea of designing computers as tools for the masses. That someone was Steve Jobs, the man behind Apple Computers. The first machine was called the Macintosh 128k. The user no longer had to understand computer language; instead they were presented with a graphical interface and a mouse with which they could select what they wanted.

It was on this day in 1984 that Apple unveiled the new computer. The first machines were sold to the general public on the 24th for $2,495. If this still seems like a considerable expense, bear in mind that prior to this the only other computers with a graphical user interface – huge machines designed for specialised industrial use – cost upwards of $10,000 each. What Apple had achieved with the Macintosh 128k was, for the first time, to put computing into the hands of middle-class consumers.

These figures, however, pale in comparison to what Apple paid for the television advert that announced their new product to the world. Directed by the famed Hollywood helmsman Ridley Scott, and screened during a break in the Super Bowl XVIII on 22 January (a game estimated to be watched by up to 2 billion people around the world), it cost an impressive $1.5 million. It paid dividends for Apple though; in less than four months the Macintosh 128k had sold some 72,000 units.

The first industries to really recognise the potential of the Apple Macintosh were those in publishing, advertising and graphic design. Eventually, supply and demand meant that people at home were able to set themselves up as desktop publishers, and the development of the internet meant that computers could be linked up from any location.

The graphical interface, along with the mouse tool, ultimately became standard for all personal computers, or PCs as they are now known. In addition, other brands of computer effectively caught up with Apple and there was little to distinguish one from another. Inevitably different computer manufacturers had to put their heads together and ensure that their electronic languages were compatible with one another. Today, PCs are virtually identical in the way they appear and operate, but we have the original Apple Macintosh to thank for it all.

# *20 January*

## *The first pulsating star is detected by astronomers*

**1967** The British astronomers Jocelyn Bell and Antony Hewish made their discovery by detecting radio waves arriving in pulses from outer space. The pulses were so regular that it seemed possible that they may have been a communication signal arriving from extra-terrestrials on a far-off planet. The codename given to the emission location was LGM-1, which stood for 'Little Green Men-1'.

However, a third astronomer, Fred Hoyle, identified the source of the radio signals as a neutron star and proposed that the celestial body must be rotating in such a manner that it was sending a beam of electromagnetic radiation past Earth at intervals of 1.337 seconds. It was proposed that such phenomena should be known as pulsating stars or pulsars, and this one was given the official code CP1919.

A neutron star is a collapsed star with a very high density and mass. It is surrounded by an electromagnetic field, just as the Earth and the sun are, only far stronger. At the poles of the electromagnetic fields, beams of electromagnetic radiation manage to escape the gravitational pull of the neutron star. It is this electromagnetic radiation that can be detected as radio waves, which, along with light, ultraviolet, infrared, microwaves and so on, are a part of the electromagnetic spectrum.

The reason they arrive at our planet in pulses is due to the so-called 'lighthouse effect'. Again, as on Earth, the magnetic poles are not in the same position as the geographical or physical poles which mark the axis points of rotation. This means that the beams of electromagnetic radiation scan space in funnel shapes as the neutron star rotates. It follows, then, that Earth just happens to be in the path of one of the beams emitting from CP1919 as it spins.

It is likely that pulsars had been detected before 1967 but that they were dismissed as radio interference. Since 1967 many new pulsars have been identified and listed. Some are more complex than CP1919, involving twin or binary stars. Others emit electromagnetic radiation at X-ray frequencies, while others pulse so quickly that they seem to produce a constant signature until the recorded signals are slowed down to increments of thousandths of a second. One pulsar – PSR B1257+12 – is the centre of the system containing the first extrasolar (not of our solar system) planets discovered.

# 21 January

## The world's first nuclear-powered submarine is launched, the USS Nautilus

**1954** Nuclear-powered submarines work on the same principle as nuclear power stations do on land. Onboard nuclear reactors are used to super-heat water into steam. The steam is then used to drive turbines which provide a mechanical means of propulsion. The turbines also generate electricity for other uses. As the radioactive fuel lasts for a long time, it means that nuclear submarines can remain at sea for extended periods without needing to refuel. However, nuclear reactors are very expensive to both build and run. Added to this, they are also extremely large and heavy, so can only be fitted into appropriately sized vessels.

USS *Nautilus* demonstrated the advantages of nuclear power as soon as she departed on her maiden voyage. She broke all records for the speed and endurance of a submersible vehicle, showing that nuclear power was the way forward for larger submarines and warships. She was able to remain underwater for weeks at a time without surfacing and although she was never called into action, this offered a clear strategic advantage with regard to marine warfare.

The submarine really made a name for itself in 1958 when it became the first craft to reach the geographical north pole below the pack ice. This was no easy voyage as the ice was over 60 feet thick in places, offering no egress should anything go wrong during the journey. Traditional compasses and other navigational equipment lose their effectiveness at latitudes above 85°, north or south, due to the proximity of the magnetic poles, and special equipment had to be designed for the job. Nevertheless, the submarine passed over the north pole on 3 August and continued on its way. The voyage took the submarine from the Bering Strait, between Alaska and Russia, to the coast of Greenland in the North Atlantic Ocean.

At the time this was an important achievement for the US because the USSR had been ahead in the Cold War technology race since the launch of *Sputnik 1* into space in 1957. USS *Nautilus* remained in service until March 1980 when she was decommissioned. She had sailed in excess of 300,000 miles (555,000 km), which is equivalent to circumnavigating the globe about twelve times. She now serves as a floating museum of submarine history in Groton, Connecticut, USA.

# 22 January

### Bjorn Borg, tennis ace, hangs up his racquet

**1983** Björn Borg put himself in the record books in the summer of 1980 when he won the Wimbledon Men's Singles Championship for the fifth year in a row. Borg's star had begun to ascend in 1974 when he won the French Open for the first time. His run then lasted until 1981 with his sixth victory in the same competition. In all, he won eleven Grand Slam championships and was runner-up an additional five times.

Before Borg's rise to dominance, the tennis world had been a rather straight-laced and conservative environment. It was very much the preserve of the wealthy upper classes, simply because they were the ones who could afford to build their own tennis courts. But by the late 1960s things were beginning to change. Working- and middle-class children were using municipal courts to learn the game, and this growth in popularity led to an inevitable sea change within the game itself.

Borg had a reputation for being silent and undemonstrative on court. This apparent 'coldness' seems to have played its part in the defeat of his opponents, because he was difficult to read and therefore difficult to beat. When the stakes are high, keeping a cool head can be vital to clinching victory. In addition to his supremacy as a tennis player, Borg was also a highly skilled tactician and athlete.

When he began to lose his touch he decided to cut his losses and retire gracefully rather than slowly fade from view. He missed the limelight, however, and made an unsuccessful comeback attempt between 1991 and 1993, by which time he was too old and racquet technology had superseded his preferred wooden frames.

Even though other tennis players have now equalled and even surpassed his achievements, Borg retains a certain reverence among the tennis fraternity. His private nature has fed the Borg myth, unsullied by the familiarity that comes with frequent media exposure. Also, Borg seems to personify the essence of a great tennis player, and his appearance and personality lent him a level of charisma and sex appeal that seem to have been lacking in other champions, both before and since his heyday. The long hair and headband made him the first 'rock star' of the tennis scene, just as George Best was the first of the soccer scene.

# 23 January

*Sweden leads the way in environmental concern by*
*becoming the first to ban aerosols with CFC propellants*

**1978** Chlorofluorocarbons (CFCs) are harmful to the ozone layer because they release halogen (chlorine and fluorine) atoms when exposed to ultraviolet light from the sun. The halogen atoms react with the ozone and deplete the layer in the stratosphere that protects the Earth's surface from overexposure to ultraviolet-B, which is harmful to both plants and animals, including humans.

Ultraviolet light also has a generative effect, converting normal oxygen molecules – $O_2$ – into ozone molecules – $O_3$ – so there must clearly exist a balancing mechanism anyway that prevents the ozone layer from becoming too thick. One might think of the ozone layer as being similar to a film of oil on water. It is relatively thin, so that it doesn't take much of a discrepancy in this cycle of production and decay to cause a hole.

Back in 1973, scientists named Frank Rowland and Mario Molina had theorised that halogens sourced from CFCs could play a significant role in the diminishment of the ozone layer. Their work was published in 1974 and set the wheels in motion for the modern view on environmental pollution. Rowland, Molina and another scientist named Paul Crutzen, who had shown that nitric oxide can have a similar effect, jointly won the Nobel Prize for Chemistry in 1995 for their efforts.

On 16 September 1987, a treaty for the protection of the ozone layer was inaugurated and became known as the Montreal Protocol. This was two years after the hole in the ozone layer was first detected over Antarctica. It was seen as scientific proof of the threat posed to the ozone layer due to human industrial activity, although no one knows for certain that there wasn't always a hole there naturally. Measurements suggest that industrial pollutants do play a significant part in the depletion of ozone, but it has also been proven to decay in super-cool temperatures, such as those found above the poles. The importance of the Montreal Protocol is to ensure that the hole – natural or man-made – doesn't get so large that UV-B begins to become a problem for the planet's life forms.

In the case of humans, the immediate effects could be rapid increases in skin cancers and similar ailments. On a larger scale, the UV-B could kill off terrestrial plants and phytoplankton (planktonic plants), thereby upsetting the global food chain and leading to environmental disaster on an unimaginable level. To date, nearly all of the world's countries have signed the Montreal Protocol.

# 24 January

### Second-to-last Japanese soldier is captured in Guam, believing that the Second World War was still being fought

**1972** The Second World War in the Pacific and south-east Asia was fought on a great many islands. Thousands of Japanese soldiers found themselves defending territory in remote locations. When the end of the war came in 1945, the authorities did the best they could to let the outpost soldiers know that hostilities had ceased. This was done by air-dropping leaflets over islands and jungle areas. A good many soldiers, however, took the leaflets to be a ruse to capture them, so remained in hiding for years after the war. The Japanese adherence to notions of honour meant that dying in battle was preferable to capture or surrender – so it suited them to stay put.

Shoichi Yokoi had survived in a jungle cave on the island of Guam for 27 years when he was finally discovered and overpowered by two local fishermen. Upon his return to civilisation he said to the Japanese media, 'It is with much embarrassment that I return alive'.

He became something of a celebrity in Japan as a kind of real-life Robinson Crusoe figure, admired for his strength of character. In later years he admitted that he had found the leaflets but had felt a strong desire to remain in the jungle simply because he felt at peace with the world. His childhood had been an unhappy one, so he had decided to wait until his tormentors had died of old age.

The very last Japanese soldier to hang up his rifle was Hiroo Onoda, who was holed-up on Lubang Island in the Philippines. His story was quite different, as the locals knew very well that he was living on the island. In fact he was originally accompanied by three other soldiers, one of whom surrendered in 1950, and the other two were killed in gun battles in 1954 and 1972. Onoda refused to believe that Japan had lost the war and continued to defend his territory until 1974, having killed about 30 islanders since 1945. He was contacted by an intrepid Japanese student who returned to Japan to locate his retired commanding officer, Major Taniguchi. The major travelled to the Philippines and ordered Onoda to lay down his arms, which he duly did without any fuss. He was pardoned for the post-war killings on the grounds that he believed the war was still being fought and that the islanders had been trying to trick him and his comrades into capitulation.

# 25 January

## Scientists get the measure of time down to one second in 300 years

**1955** It may seem unlikely, but units of time were not defined properly until 1967. Everyone agreed that there were 60 seconds in a minute, 60 minutes in an hour and 24 hours in a day. However, the length of a second wasn't an absolute. The trouble was that time was based on the rhythm of the Earth, and the Earth was not all that constant in its movements. In scientific terms this was a problem, even if it worked perfectly well in everyday life.

The first atomic clock used an element named caesium-133 ($^{133}$Cs) as a 'frequency standard'. Caesium-133 has two 'ground states' which means that the electron energy comes from the element itself, rather than an outside source. Electron transition between these two ground states is almost constant. In fact it strays

31

by just one second over a 300-year period. This is why caesium-133 was used in the first atomic timepiece. Caesium is a non-radioactive, alkali metal, which is liquid at room temperature.

In 1967 the International System of Measurements based the unit of time – the second – on the caesium-113 clock. Officially an SI (*Système International*) second is now equivalent to 9,192,631,770 cycles of the radiation which corresponds to the transition between two electron spin-energy levels of the ground state of the $^{133}$Cs atom. Needless to say, this means nothing to the layperson, but it is a necessary definition enabling scientists to accurately measure times and distances; especially useful in astronomy, for example.

The odd thing about time is that it can slow down or speed up in relative terms due to velocity. For example, when a CD is playing, the outside edge ages less rapidly that the centre, although the difference is too small to be detected. It follows that the centre of the Earth is older than the surface, and that the sun is older than the Earth, although only by miniscule amounts. Albert Einstein showed this effect as part of his Theory of Relativity. Light itself cannot age, because the speed of light is the 'universal constant' – the fastest-moving component of the universe.

If it were possible for astronauts to journey away from Earth for a few years at truly enormous speeds (approaching the speed of light), then they would return to find that the people back on Earth had aged more rapidly than they had. It follows that an atomic clock onboard would also disagree with one left behind on Earth.

# 26 January

## Australia celebrates its bicentenary as a Western nation

**1988** 1788 was the year that the first fleet of Europeans arrived to establish a European colony in Australia. The fleet was headed by Captain Arthur Phillip, and a large number of the white colonists were British convicts, sent to the other side of the world as punishment for their crimes. Australia was to become a penal colony, a remote prison camp. America had declared its independence from British rule in 1776, so the British government turned to Australia as the most suitable place to send its ne'er-do-wells. Legitimate settlers would use the labour of prisoners to establish the city of Sydney. When the convicts had served their time and become free men they were then able to return to Blighty or establish new lives for themselves in Australia.

The name 'Australia' means 'southern land' and was not adopted until 1824, following a suggestion by Captain Matthew Flinders in 1804. Before then the new country had been known as New Holland. The Dutch had mapped the western and northern coastline and Abel Tasman, after whom Tasmania is named, coined the name New Holland in 1644. Despite this, the Dutch failed to make a proprietorial claim to the continent as they saw no value in it. The British explorer, Captain James Cook, mapped the eastern coast of Australia in 1770. He made landfall at Botany Bay, which is now immediately south of Sydney, and recommended it as a good place to establish a new penal colony when he returned to England. His name for the region was New South Wales, which is still used today.

Inevitably the former convicts paired up and had children, so that by the turn of the 19th century Australia had begun to propagate its own Caucasian population. There were already tens of thousands of Native Australians, or aborigines, present when Sydney was first established, but they were treated like savages just as the Native Americans were. The British brought with them a sense of land ownership that was alien to the Native Australians, who lived a nomadic lifestyle. This meant that large swathes of territory suddenly became out of bounds to the Native Australians and they were forced to settle on ranches, virtually as slaves. Robbed of their traditional way of life and treated like second-class citizens due to their lack of Western education, it has taken a long time for the aborigines to receive any social compensation for their plight.

# 27 January

*Germany officially acknowledges the Holocaust by holding the first International Holocaust Remembrance Day*

**1996** 27 January was chosen because it was the day in 1945 that Soviet troops liberated the Auschwitz-Birkenau extermination camp in Poland, thereby revealing the full horror of the Nazis' 'final solution' to the world. The exact number of victims who perished at the camp will never be known, but estimates put the figure at between 1 and 2 million.

Most of the victims were Jewish and they originated from countries all over continental Europe. Anti-Semitism was central to the philosophy of the Third Reich under Adolf Hitler and the extermination camps became the ultimate expression of its prejudice. Many of the victims died from exhaustion, neglect, disease and human experimentation, but thousands more were systematically executed. Some were shot, while others were asphyxiated and poisoned with engine fumes or with a pesticide gas known as Zyklon-B.

The roots of anti-Semitism go back to Biblical times. The Jews were driven from their homelands by invading and occupying forces – firstly the Assyrians and then the Greeks and Romans after them. The result was the so-called diaspora, which meant a dispersal of Jews across the Middle East and Europe.

Due to their reluctance to assimilate into other cultures the Jewish populations historically tended to become ghettoised, and lived on their wits to get by. This invariably meant running businesses and money-lending, which brought them considerable wealth, as its profits tended to circulate only within their own segregated communities. This financial autonomy meant that Jewish populations were not subjected to the same economic fluctuations as the populations surrounding them. The inevitable result was resentment in the non-Jewish populations towards the Jews, who appeared avaricious and antisocial because they were seemingly better-off during times of hardship. Added to this, the Arabs adopted Islam as their homogenising religion in the 7th century. Islam forbids the lending of money for profit, so the Jewish people were seen as immoral as well as unfairly successful.

It was this pervading and deep-rooted prejudice towards the Jews that convinced Adolf Hitler and his cronies that they were directly responsible for the economic ruin of Germany following the First World War. As a citizen, he recalled how his fellow Teutonic neighbours had helped him get by, while his Jewish neighbours had kept themselves to themselves. It is perhaps human nature to harbour resentment towards those who fail to extend the hand of friendship in times of need, but Hitler learned to truly despise all Jews. When he rose to power, he used anti-Semitism to fan the flames of ambition in the Nazis by giving them a cause on which to focus their unifying anger.

# 28 January

### The space shuttle SS Challenger disintegrates less than two minutes after launch

**1986** The space shuttle programme had been a glorious US achievement. The global community had watched as test flights were made in previous years and had been enthralled by the maiden launch made in April 1981. The remit of the shuttle programme was to build a space craft that could be reused by returning to Earth as a conventional aircraft. As well as saving on resources, it meant that the shuttle could be used as a proper vehicle, capable of carrying equipment back and forth.

In order to spread the economic benefit of the shuttle programme, it was decided that different US companies should be used to construct the different components of the spacecraft. This is where things went inadvertently wrong.

The company assigned the responsibility of manufacturing the solid rocket boosters had opted to design them in parts, so that they could be transported more easily and then assembled on-site. One of the joins turned out to be the point of failure. O-rings were incorporated to seal the joins where cylindrical sections were pushed together. The material used for the o-rings should have been rubberised to form an effective seal, but low temperatures had rendered them inflexible. The stresses and strains of launch had shaken the joint loose, leading to catastrophic failure. SS *Challenger* started to break apart at an altitude of 48,000 feet and began to fall from the sky at 65,000 feet. The cabin section of the shuttle itself was not destroyed as there hadn't been an explosion, so the seven crew members lost in the disaster would have been aware of their plight for some time before they perished.

In 2003 a second shuttle disaster occurred, involving SS *Columbia*. On this occasion the orbiter broke up on re-entry to the Earth's atmosphere. Special heat-resistant tiles had been damaged during launch. They allowed the heat created by air resistance to burn holes through the fuselage of the shuttle. Eventually the vehicle lost its integrity and broke apart. The crew knew what was happening as they remained in radio contact with the ground until the last moment.

Despite these two horrific disasters, the shuttle programme has been a great success overall. As well as *Challenger* and *Columbia*, there are three other operational shuttles: *Discovery*, *Atlantis* and *Endeavour*. Between them they have made around 120 flights and paved the way for the new space programme, named Orion, which is set to begin in 2010.

# 29 January

## China starts to open relations with the West

**1979** Deng Xiaoping was the Chinese politician responsible for initiating the reforms that have led to China's incredible economic growth in recent years. Until 1979 the Chinese administration had adhered to a strict communist policy, the core of which meant avoiding political relations with capitalist nations. Deng was a moderate, however, and believed that it should be possible to uphold communist principles but still open trade routes with the West. This led him to sign diplomatic accords with then-US President Carter as an inaugural step forward.

Despite this apparent open-mindedness, Deng remained suspicious of the West, especially when the younger generation in China began to express a desire for more rapid modernisation in the following decade. This tension culminated in the massacre of around 2,000 students in Tiananmen Square in Beijing in June 1989. Deng had overreacted when the students began a demonstration and interpreted it as a threat to the government and its ideology. He sanctioned a military response which led to the murders. Deng retired from his position shortly afterwards in the face of worldwide condemnation for his actions.

Following his retirement, Deng still expressed his support for the market-orientated economic reforms that have since thrust China onto the world stage. The country is still run by the Communist Party of China, yet it has adapted to the modern world very effectively. In a way it has learnt from the mistakes of other communist regimes that have failed and seen that the way forward is to maintain the communist blueprint as a general way of structuring society, but to allow free trade with the outside world. So far it seems to be working well as China is the fastest-growing economy in the world.

It remains to be seen whether the inevitable divide between rich and poor will eventually become problematic for the government. That is, after all, the reason why communism took hold in the first place – in an attempt to force a more egalitarian society. In the end it may all come down to a resignation that communism doesn't work in practice and that democracy is the better option for the future. The intention behind capitalism has always been to allow a healthy flow of wealth in the world so that disparity is avoided, thereby removing the agents that lead to hostility and warfare. We can only hope that China manages its internal affairs as successfully as its external affairs.

# 30 January

## Mahatma Gandhi is assassinated

**1948** The Partition of India, in August 1947, was devised by the British as a solution to rising ethnic tensions in former India following the end of the Second World War. The Hindus, Muslims and Sikhs had managed to live alongside one another for centuries before, but Britain had lost its grip on much of its Empire in south-east Asia during the war years. This was because countries temporarily occupied by the Japanese had tasted a degree of freedom and Britain didn't have the finances or the troops to reassert itself in the post-war climate.

Sensing impending independence in other countries, India wanted a piece of the action too. Anticipating a new native government, the different religious factions consequently began fighting among themselves. Neither the Hindus nor the Muslims wanted the other in charge, so the British decided that it might be best to partition the country. They did this by demarking new borders and dividing the country into India, West Pakistan and East Pakistan (Bangladesh). India would house the Hindus and Sikhs, while Pakistan would be home to the Muslims.

Gandhi was deeply opposed to the partitioning of his nation. When the British announced their plan to partition India, the violence grew steadily worse, not least because the exact delineation of the borders was not revealed. Killing parties began murdering former neighbours in frenzied massacres, which only led to revenge attacks. When the British finally announced where the borders would be it meant that millions of people on each side became refugees and began mass migrations to places of safety. It is reckoned that somewhere between 1 and 2 million people lost their lives – if not from slaughter, then by starvation and disease. Undoubtedly the British could have managed the situation far better, but they no longer had a vested interest so they largely left the population to sort things out for themselves.

The assassination of Gandhi came about because India owed

money to the new Pakistani government. It had refused to pay up because Pakistani rebels were causing problems in the area of Kashmir which was still disputed territory. Gandhi insisted that the Indian government settle the debt because he saw it as a means of accelerating the peace process. Gandhi's killer, Nathuram Godse, was a radical Hindu who became so incensed by this that he shot Gandhi three times for, as he saw it, betraying his beliefs.

# 31 January

## The island of Nauru declares independence from Australia

**1968** It may not seem a particularly significant event, but Nauru is officially the smallest independent republic in the world, so it deserves some recognition. Nauru is a single egg-shaped island located in the middle of the South Sea Islands of the Pacific. There are thousands of islands but its nearest neighbour is some 300 km away, making it a rather remote place. The island was originally colonised by people of Asian descent approximately 3,000 years ago. European explorers discovered it in 1798 – the first white visitor was a British whaler named John Fearn. He was evidently impressed by the place, as he called it Pleasant Island.

Nauru is only 8.1 square miles (21 km²) in area. It is also a rather flat land, comprising a limestone plateau with a freshwater lake, called Buada Lagoon. If it weren't for the lake, the island would be unable to support a human population. As well as using the lake for water, the original inhabitants used the lake to farm *ibiji*, or milkfish. Although these are saltwater fish, they can be acclimatised to fresh water when juvenile. The Nauruans also harvested coconuts and pandanus fruits.

In 1878 there was a civil war on Nauru. The islanders used weapons traded from Europeans and managed to reduce their population from 1,400 to 900 over a ten-year period. The war was halted only because Germany annexed the island in 1888 and renamed it Onawero, an interpretation of the native name and that subsequently evolved into Nauru.

At the turn of the 20th century a British prospector found rock phosphate on the island. It was a valuable commodity at the time, used as a fertiliser in the same way as guano (the mineralised excrement of seabirds). With the outbreak of the First World War in 1914, Australia seized Nauru from Germany. Phosphate mining then brought wealth to the island until it was captured by Japan during the Second World War. In 1945 the island was liberated and fell under the trusteeship of New Zealand and Australia. The island became self-governing in 1966 and independent in 1968.

For a couple of decades the Nauruans enjoyed the highest living standard in the Pacific, but then the phosphate ran out. In recent times the island has required financial aid from Australia. It has also received compensation for the physical damage to the island from the phosphate mining, including a programme to rehabilitate the landscape.

# 1 February

## *The rotary piston engine is successfully ignited by Felix Wankel in Germany*

**1957** Conventional internal combustion engines use circular pistons that move up and down inside tubular cases. The linear energy produced is then translated into circular motion via a crankshaft. The German inventor Felix Wankel hit on the idea that it should be possible to design a far simpler engine, where the piston produces circular motion directly. If he succeeded, it would mean lighter engines with far fewer parts, making them more economical to manufacture and more reliable to use. He developed and perfected the 'rotary piston engine', not to be confused with the 'radial piston engine', which uses conventional pistons arranged around an axle. The conventional combustion engine is known as the 'reciprocating piston engine'.

The design of the Wankel engine, as it is now usually known, involves a trianguloid piston that has an eccentric rotation within an oval chamber. As it rotates, the three faces of the piston form cavities, which enlarge and reduce in sequence. This enables the drawing in of fuel and air; the compression and ignition of the fuel mix; the explosive expansion of the ignited mix; and finally, exhaust exit. The three faces run through this sequence of four operations in rapid and continuous succession, causing perpetual circular motion of the piston.

Although the principle is simple, maintaining perfect seals between each piston face has proved problematic due to wear. This is partly because the point of contact with the casing is small, so that any leak is pronounced. In addition, there is no oil reservoir to keep the seals lubricated, so the fuel requires oil to be included in the same manner as a two-stroke engine.

Nevertheless, Wankel engines have been refined over the years as better materials have been made available for their construction. A number of automobile manufacturers have incorporated Wankel engines into their vehicles, notably Mazda, from the 1967

Cosmo to the modern day RX-8. Wankel engines have also been used in aircraft, boats, motorbikes and powered models.

As they can be made very small, Wankel engines have also been used as peripheral engines inside vehicles that use conventional engines. They can be used to power compressors and seat belt tensioners, for example. Felix Wankel was inspired by his work on rotary valves during the Second World War, and was an old fashioned inventor who just kept on experimenting until he got it right.

# 2 February

## Punxsutawney Phil turns 100

**1987** Near the town of Punxsutawney in Pennsylvania, there is a mound called Gobbler's Knob. On top of the mound is a small coppice. Dug into the mound, however, there is a heated burrow – and in this burrow lives Punxsutawney Phil, the groundhog. And if this doesn't seem strange enough then consider that on this day in 1987, Phil turned 100 years old ... and that on the same day every year, nearly 40,000 people descend upon Punxsutawney, a town of just over 6,500 people, to see Phil come out of his burrow.

This, of course, is all part of the American tradition of Groundhog Day. Falling every 2 February, the day is a public holiday in the United States and Canada. On this day, Punxsutawney Phil emerges from his burrow and casts his eye upon the ground. If he can see his shadow, then there is to be another six weeks of cold weather before spring comes around, but if no shadow is present then the sun is believed to be just around the corner. Once Phil has made his assessment, he apparently relates it to a master of ceremonies in 'groundhogese', who then translates the meteorological prediction for the amassed crowd.

The origins of this cherished practice lie in the fact that 2 February, also known as the Feast of Candlemas, is positioned almost exactly six weeks before the spring equinox. Added to this, there is an old Scottish poem, popular in the United States, which claims among other things that:

> If Candlemas be fair and bright,
> Winter will have another flight.
> If Candlemas be cloud and snow,
> Winter will be gone and not come again.

The groundhog, which is a rodent belonging to the *Sciuridae* family along with squirrels and chipmunks, and also known as the woodchuck, has a more obscure role in the tradition. The first mentions of Groundhog Day, however, originate from Punxsutawney itself, where common belief held that the groundhog was so timid it could be frightened by its own shadow. Presumably the connection between this and the Candlemas poem grew up over the years until a groundhog was officially enshrined as Punxsutawney Phil in 1887.

Of course Phil is not alone when it comes to making prognostications. All across the US and Canada, there are rival groundhogs making their own forecasts. Buckeye Chuck, for example, lives in Marion, Ohio and then there is Wiarton Willie in Wiarton, Ontario and Dunkirk Dave in Dunkirk, New York to name but a few. Put together, these rodents are supposed to be an accurate bunch – some groundhog fans put their accuracy rate at between 75 and 90 per cent, although a study by the National Clinical Data Center claims that it is actually in the region of 39 per cent.

Despite the presence of his fellow groundhogs, however, Punxsutawney Phil remains the best-known and best-loved of all of them. Just six years after he turned 100, a film in which he starred alongside Bill Murray and Andie MacDowell was released. *Groundhog Day* has since been rated as one of the top 50 comedies of the 20th century, and it has ensured that Phil's name has stretched around the world.

# 3 February

*The Soviet helicopter Mil Mi-26 lifts the heaviest load ever made airborne by a vertical takeoff aircraft*

**1982** The weight lifted was 56,888 kg (56.9 metric tonnes) or 125,417 lb (56 long tons or 63 short tons). That is equivalent to, say, 50 small cars or over 700 men. Clearly a very large and powerful helicopter would be required for such a task and that is exactly what the Mil Mi-26 was. In truth, that weight included the weight of the helicopter itself, but that takes nothing away from the achievement – it was still an immense load. The empty weight of the aircraft is 28,200 kg or 62,170 lb, so the machine can lift twice its own weight from the ground.

The Mil Mi-26 was the first helicopter to operate with eight rotor blades, to optimise lift. The rotor is powered by two engines, so that in the event of single engine failure it can still fly. The Americans and British use a heavy helicopter with twin or tandem rotors – the CH-47 Chinook – which is more vulnerable in this respect, as the loss of one rotor would mean certain disaster.

There are a number of different versions of the Mi-26 in use, adapted for various purposes. Most are military transporters for troops and army equipment. Others are civilian airliners, used to haul people and cargoes to and from places where runways are not available for winged aircraft. Still others are adapted to carry water as 'fire-copters' for dealing with forest fires and infernos in tall buildings. There are also 'medi-copters' adapted into functional operating theatres for dealing with all manner of injuries, either *in situ* or while travelling to hospitals.

The helicopter's maximum speed is 295 kph, or 160 knots (184 mph). The range of the aircraft varies according to the fuel tanks fitted, but it can be between 800 km and 1,920 km. That is 432–1,036 nautical miles (497–1,192 miles). The service ceiling of these helicopters is just over 15,000 feet (4,570 metres). That is the altitude they can reach before the air becomes too thin to produce lift. Incidentally, that is the reason why mountaineers cannot be rescued by helicopter from high mountains. Mount Everest, for example, is 29,029 feet (8,848 metres) high, so helicopters can only get halfway up.

# 4 February

## The first World Cancer Day is held in an effort to raise international awareness

**2000** The last quarter of the 20th century saw a marked rise in the occurrence of cancers in human populations, leading to a campaign to increase awareness of the problem and encourage people to avoid carcinogenic agents.

Until the 17th century the term used for any ulcerous growth was 'canker'. The word was derived from the Latin word for crab – *cancer* – as such tumours were often surrounded by swollen veins, giving the appearance of a crab beneath the skin. Eventually the word 'cancer' was used to distinguish malignant cancerous tumours from those that are benign or caused by infections. The word 'carcinogen' is derived from the Greek word for crab – *karkinos* – and is used to describe an agent that is scientifically shown to cause cancers.

Two major causes of cancer in the latter half of the 20th century were identified as smoking tobacco and sunbathing. In the case of smoking there was an interesting historical perspective to the habit.

During the world wars governments had actually issued cigarettes to their troops as part of their essential rations. The proportion of smoking adults was as high as 80 per cent in Europe and America. Consequently both men and women began developing cancers of the airways – lung, throat and mouth – in huge numbers in their later years. It wasn't particularly difficult for the boffins to realise that smoking must have been a significant contributing factor. Since that era smoking has dramatically reduced in Western nations due to administrative measures and a general shift towards healthier living.

Sunbathing was a trend that caught on in the post-war years, when having a tan became something of a status symbol. Up until that time, the tanned body belonged to the farm labourer or fisherman, and was something to be avoided by the middle and upper classes. With the introduction of flights and package holidays to hot countries, the tan suddenly developed a cachet due to its association with wealth and affluence. Suddenly people looked healthy and attractive with tanned skin. Only with the turn of the 21st century did people pay the price for their vanity by dying in increasing numbers from skin cancer – malignant melanoma.

Treatment of cancers is improving all the time, as research reveals why and how they happen. However, there are no sure-fire ways of dealing with them and they are usually terminal. With no cure the onus is on prevention. There are too many cancer-causing agents in the world to completely avoid the risk, but a good starting point is to avoid carcinogens wherever possible. As is so often the case, education is key ... and that is the point of World Cancer Day.

# 5 February

### Genetically modified foods go on sale in the United Kingdom for the first time

**1996** The notion of genetic modification is a misleading one that has led to all sorts of confusion. Historically any plants or animals that have been improved by selective breeding are, by definition, genetically modified. Indeed, one could even say that we are all genetically modified, as our genetic coding differs from that of our parents. The only difference between breeding and the modern understanding of 'genetic modification' is that the latter is conducted under laboratory conditions and often termed 'genetic engineering' to distinguish it.

On this day in 1996, Sainsbury's and Safeway supermarkets began stocking tomato puree made from genetically modified fruit. The tomatoes in question had been grown in California and had been specially created to remove the gene that could cause them to rot. By reducing the risk of the tomatoes going bad, puree producers do not have to incur as much waste fruit as with conventionally grown tomatoes, and so the genetically modified puree is subsequently cheaper.

Although genetically modified products have now been on the supermarket shelves for well over a decade, genetic engineering is still perceived as a potentially dangerous scientific development by opponents for two key reasons. Firstly, it greatly accelerates and amplifies the process of genetic modification. Secondly, it can introduce genetic coding into plants and animals that wasn't there to begin with.

These two factors, it is argued, might result in strains of organisms that could cause havoc if introduced, deliberately or otherwise, into the natural environment. In addition, food products containing modified genes, it is suggested, might cause untold harm to humans due to reactions to 'unnatural' agents.

So far, neither scenario has become a reality, for one further reason. Ecological systems are so finely balanced that it is already very tough for existing organisms to maintain their foothold. That is to say, when mutations occur in nature they fail to survive and proliferate because there are too many environmental factors to cope with; the same is true of genetically modified organisms.

In truth we have far more to fear from existing pests and pathogens than any imagined ones. It seems that it boils down to belief systems. Humans are very good at using their imaginations to conjure beliefs that they then adhere to, even though the power of reason and empirical science provide evidence to the contrary. However, it is invariably best in the long run to think about things thoroughly before jumping to conclusions.

# 6 February

*British and French administrations agree to build a
tunnel beneath the stretch of sea known as the
Channel in English,* la Manche *in French*

**1964** The very first suggestion of the possibility of constructing a tunnel was made by a Frenchman, Albert Mathieu-Favier, in 1802. The idea was to have two sections of tunnel linked by a man-made island. In the latter part of the 19th century, French and British engineers made a number of boring tests, but work ceased in 1882 due to military objections. In other words, relations between France and England were uncertain, and a tunnel was perceived as a threat to national security.

Another attempt at tunnelling was made in 1922, following the First World War, but political unrest on the continent prompted similar objections. Had these not been acted upon, then Hitler might have succeeded in reaching England.

It took ten post-war years before the British government was in a position to seriously consider a tunnel again. A committee named the 'Tunnel sous la Manche Study Group' assessed the best approach and recommended the design now in place, which features two railway tunnels, and a third service tunnel. Work actually began in 1974, but financial difficulties led to cancellation only a year into the project.

Eventually, in 1986, a new project was set in motion under the banner of the Franco-British Channel Fixed Link Treaty. Constructing the tunnel took seven years and involved a total of around 13,000 people working in both directions. Enormous tunnel-boring machines were constructed within the initial shafts and then used to carve their way along a continuous stratum of chalk. The tunnels were lined with rings of reinforced concrete assembled in sections as the boring machines moved forwards. The two sections of the service tunnel met in 1990, and those of the rail tunnels a year later. The project was more or less complete by 1994.

At the centre there is a crossover chamber so that sections of rail tunnel can be closed for maintenance purposes, in case of fire, etc. The chamber is the largest man-made subterranean cavern in the world. Due to the fact that seawater permeates the limestone rock above, it has to be allowed to seep though to prevent an insurmountable build-up of pressure, which would crush the cavern. It therefore has a lining within the outer shell, so that the water can flow down into sumps and then be pumped away.

# 7 February

## The EU – European Union – becomes a reality as the original member states sign the Maastricht Treaty

**1992** There were several motives for forming the EU. A major factor was pursuit of the spirit of globalisation. The two world wars had devastated Europe, and been caused principally by economic instability and disparity. It therefore seemed an eminently sensible move to unite the European nations and allow a flow of people, trade and money between them, in order to prevent this from happening again.

One might liken it to the metapopulation of a species, which prevents isolation and promotes homogeneity. The EU would ensure that all of Europe had a common mindset and so didn't develop proprietorial notions of conquest by warfare.

Another strong incentive was born out of the Cold War. Tensions between the West and the Soviet Union meant that it was strategically advantageous for Western Europe to be seen as a political and ideological whole. Although the Soviet bloc had actually disintegrated by the time the EU came into effect, between 1957 and 1992 the EU had been preceded by the EC (European Community), and the psychology of this was carried into the new body.

The third catalyst for the EU was simply ideology and progression. It seemed only right that in the modern age we should forget our differences and view all European cultures as members of the same family. The legacy of the world wars was fear of another caused by prejudice and intolerance – xenophobia – so a spirit of bonhomie was born from the rubble of conflict.

Euro-sceptics argue that a free flow of people and cultures will lead to a loss of national identity as the whole of Europe becomes homogenised – an amalgam of traditions and tongues. If anything, people's sense of national identity has become accentuated in many respects, but as a positive thing rather than a form of differentiation.

One evident problem, though, with the opening of borders, has been that of immigration. Had the whole of Europe already reached a point of fiscal equilibrium, then there wouldn't have been such a strong incentive for migration in pursuit of wealth. As it is, the wealthier nations in Western Europe are hosting increasing numbers of Eastern Europeans who come to work. In a way, this is actively encouraged by industrialists, as it ensures that Western European industries remain healthy and well-resourced.

Those same industrialists tend to be the conservative Euro-sceptics, so it seems that one cannot have it both ways. They have had to learn to live with acculturation for the sake of maintaining power and influence on the world stage.

# 8 February

## The Allende meteorite strikes the Earth at Pueblito de Allende, Chihuahua, Mexico

**1969** Weighing in at several tons in total mass, the Allende meteorite hit the planet at five minutes past one o'clock in the morning. It had a created a bright flash of light as it hit the atmosphere and exploded a few minutes before it hit the ground.

Having disintegrated, the meteorite came to the ground in a shower of fragments and smithereens, which covered an area of about 60 square miles (roughly five miles wide by twelve miles long). So far over two tons of fragments have been recovered, but new pieces are discovered every year.

Upon scientific analysis, the Allende meteorite was found to be a very rare type, known as a carbonaceous chondrite (CV3). Such meteorites comprise the most chemically primitive rocks in the universe, as they are leftovers from the nebulae that formed the stars, planets and moons following the Big Bang. They pre-date, by 0.6 billion years, the oldest rocks found in the Earth's crust. As such they can tell us a great deal about the state of the universe during its genesis.

CV3 means 'Chondrite Vigarano-like 3', which is used for chondrites that have remained unaltered since their formation. Numbers lower than three indicate aqueous alteration – the effects of water – while numbers higher than three indicate thermal alteration – the effects of heat. Vigarano was the name given to a similar meteorite which fell on Italy in 1910.

The Allende meteorite was found to contain relatively complex carbon compounds and fullerenes, which are unusual carbon molecules that take the form of spheres and spheroids, unlike those that comprise graphite and diamond, which are layered into strata. Crystalline minerals were formed into chondrules or grains, set in a general cement known as matrix, rather like the composition of concrete. Overall the meteorite would generally be described as olivine, which is a greenish rock, rich in iron and magnesium.

Six months after the Allende meteorite fell, *Apollo 11* reached the Moon and returned with 45 lbs of lunar rock. Basalts found on the Moon displayed similar radiation damage to the meteorite, suggesting that both were almost as old as the universe itself, which is somewhere in the region of 4.7–4.8 billion years.

# 9 February

*Halley's comet reaches the point in its orbit closest to the sun – perihelion – for the first time in 76 years*

**1986** First, it should be pointed out that 'Halley' rhymes with 'valley', for the comet is named after the English astronomer

Edmond Halley (1656–1752) and not the US rock 'n' roller Bill Haley (1925–81), whose surname rhymes with 'daily'. Unfortunately the latter chose 'Comets' as the name for his backing group due to the similarity between his surname and the real thing. Since then the mispronunciation has stuck. Oddly enough, Bill Haley also died on 9 February.

Edmond Halley famously predicted the return of the comet, having observed it himself in 1682. He noted that it seemed to fit descriptions of comets made in 1531 and 1607, so he surmised that it would reappear in 1757. It was spotted in 1758. Since then it has been noted that the period of orbit varies between 75 and 76 years due to the gravitational influences of other astronomical bodies, which differ each time.

One of the most interesting things about Halley's comet is that it has marked the passage of human history. Due to its lucidity and size, its appearance has caught the attention of people since antiquity. As early as the 1st century AD, Halley's comet was known to return with regularity, simply because old folks had seen it twice during their lifetimes. Of course in those days, scientific explanations for comets hadn't been suggested, so its presence was seen as holding symbolic significance – a harbinger of either good or bad tidings, depending on circumstances.

Perhaps the most famous example of this was in England, in 1066. The comet was interpreted as an omen of bad fortune, and later that year Anglo-Saxon King Harold lost his life at the Battle of Hastings, allowing the Normans to conquer Britain. Such was the power of the comet's symbolism, it potentially became a self-fulfilling prophecy, making the Anglo-Saxons convinced that they were destined to lose to William the Conqueror.

Halley's comet wasn't a spectacular sight in 1986, simply because it didn't travel very close to our planet. Its historical appearances were far more spectacular and awe-inspiring. Astronomers have calculated that in AD 837, the comet passed by at a distance of only 3.2 million miles. It would have been as bright as the Moon and have had a tail stretching halfway across the sky. No wonder it freaked people out.

Incidentally, the tail of a comet doesn't trail behind it as intuition might conclude. Instead it always points away from the sun, as it is generated by solar radiation.

# 10 February

## Computers become more intelligent than human beings when Deep Blue defeats Garry Kasparov at chess

**1996** There is a difference between thinking more quickly than humans, and being more intelligent. Computers have always been able to think more quickly than humans, because that was their original purpose – to compute information at speed and in volume. In essence, they were intellectual labour-saving devices, designed to perform complex mathematical tasks, decipher codes or collate data.

Playing chess presented a whole new challenge to computer boffins. It was no longer about just thinking more quickly. It was about strategy – making choices when several options are available. That meant designing a machine that was more 'human' than ever before. IBM was the company that rose to the challenge by developing Deep Blue.

The genius behind Deep Blue was a computer whiz-kid named Feng-hsiung Hsu, who joined IBM in 1989. In 1996 the machine beat the reigning grandmaster in its very first game, but went on to lose the match. Deep Blue was upgraded to twice its former processing power, and in 1997 managed to win an entire match against Kasparov 3.5–2.5.

The secret behind Deep Blue was in understanding how human chess players think. They have an incredible capacity for imagining scenarios in their minds, involving variations of moves and the probability of countermoves being made against them. Deep Blue had to be able to 'imagine' the possible future permutations in a chess game, and select the most appropriate moves based on calculations of chance. In this way, it seemed to acquire a human-like personality – although it has been said that Kasparov is not all that human-like himself. He is so chess-intelligent that he actually thinks somewhat like a computer, with a kind of pure logic that is beyond the abilities of most people.

In a way then, Deep Blue and Garry Kasparov met in the middle. They revealed that intelligence is an intuitive process, based on reason born from considering options and calculating likelihoods. Computers are mechanical brains, while brains are biological computers. We'll really be in trouble when computers develop emotions and an ability to care about what people think of them. Imagine having to cultivate a relationship with a PC to get it to do what you'd like it to.


# 11 February

## Global Flyer, *a lightweight fixed-wing aircraft, manages to fly an incredible 25,766 miles without refuelling*

**2006** The problem the Wright brothers solved with their inaugural powered flight in 1903 was how to design an aeroplane capable of lifting itself, the pilot and the engine off the ground. It may not seem an incredible feat in this day and age, but there were people who doubted it was even possible at the turn of the 20th century.

At the time there were no lightweight composite materials available for building the aircraft itself, which meant having to design a plane in the manner of a kite, using wooden struts, canvas and cables. To generate enough lift, the wings had to be of enormous size, so there was always a conflict between lift potential and weight. In addition to this, internal combustion engines were heavy and unrefined machines that provided little propulsive thrust relative to their weight. It meant that the first successful aeroplane was the result of a finely-balanced equation, only just able to get itself airborne.

As power-to-weight ratio improved in engines, it became possible to refine the design of aeroplanes until the typical shape evolved in the 1920s and 1930s. Because they could go faster, they no longer needed as much wing area to generate lift: smaller wings could do the same job. It also meant that the functionality of aeroplanes was improved as they became more stable and manoeuvrable in flight.

The introduction of jet engines in the 1940s took the evolution of aeroplanes further still, so that the wings became positively vestigial, only requiring very small surfaces to maintain flight. However, jet engines use enormous amounts of fuel, so there was always a trade-off between the performance of an aircraft and its workable range, because carrying more fuel means a heavier load.

This is why designing an aeroplane that could fly very long distances without refuelling became such an attractive challenge at the turn of the 21st century. With modern materials it should have been possible to construct both an aircraft and an engine capable of surpassing all previous distance records, and it was.

*Global Flyer* was constructed from carbon fibre-reinforced plastic to make it highly robust, yet extremely lightweight. It was fitted with a single lightweight turbofan jet engine, called a Williams FJ44. The pilot for the record-setting flight was Steve Fossett who, along with the aircraft, accounted for just 17 per cent of the take-off weight. The other 83 per cent was fuel. The aeroplane remained airborne for 76 hours and 43 minutes. It took off from Kennedy Space Centre, circumnavigated the globe once and then flew on to land at Bournemouth Airport on the south coast of England.

# 12 February

*Diamond, the hardest substance known to man, becomes the second-hardest substance known to man*

**1985** In 1985 scientists discovered a hitherto unknown allotrope, or form, of carbon. It was found to have molecules arranged in the manner of a football, with twelve pentagons surrounded by twenty hexagons. In other words, it had hollow, spherical molecules.

The new molecule was scientifically coded as carbon-60 ($C_{60}$), due to the number of junctions making up the molecular structure. Its common name is Buckminsterfullerene, after Richard Buckminster Fuller, an architect who had developed the geodesic dome, which employs the same pentagon–hexagon structure. The $C_{60}$ molecules are now known casually as 'Buckyballs'. Since then, other fullerene variants have been discovered – $C_{36}$, $C_{50}$, $C_{70}$, $C_{72}$, $C_{76}$, $C_{84}$ – which use different combinations of junctions to form their molecules, and therefore come in varying shapes and sizes.

Ultrahard fullerite (UHF) is a form of $C_{60}$ that has been polymerised – the molecules have been bonded together to form a cohesive mass. Due to the stability of the carbon atoms in UHF, it has been found to have a surface hardness greater than that of diamond, which was traditionally thought to have been the hardest substance.

The Mohs scale of mineral hardness ranks diamond as 10 and talc as 1, so that all other minerals fall somewhere between the two. Since UHF is harder than diamond either it should be accorded number 11, or diamond should be demoted to 9. So far it has only been possible to synthesise UHF as microscopic crystals, so as yet it has no practical application. When larger crystals are developed, they could be used to make 'everlasting' saw blades and may be found to have other, less obvious uses.

Scientists are working on materials even harder than UHF. One is another allotrope of carbon known as ADNRs (aggregated diamond nanorods), which has been made in minute quantities by compressing and heating $C_{60}$. Another is a complex material named beta carbon nitride (BCN) which comprises crystals of densely packed carbon and nitrogen atoms. After significant research, it was finally synthesised by scientists at China's Shandong University in 2002.

Although it may seem strange that scientists can pinpoint their studies so accurately when it comes to discovering so-called 'theoretical materials', this is actually one of the properties of the periodic tables. Constructed by Dmitri Mendeleev in 1869, it ranks elements in a way that enables researchers to predict all possible variants, whether they exist in nature or not.

However, when it comes to diamonds and similar substances,

hardness is one thing, but strength and toughness account for a lot when using new materials for fabrication purposes. The carbon nanotube (CNT) – another type of fullerene – has been found to be harder, stronger and lighter than steel. As yet it has been prohibitively expensive to produce CNTs in sufficient quantities for anything other than experimental use, but they seem set to have a bright future.

# 13 February

## SS Discovery *captures the Hubble Space Telescope for its second service since its launch in 1990*

**1997** Named after British astronomer Edwin Hubble, the Hubble Space Telescope (HST) was launched into orbit around the Earth to overcome the problem of looking at space through the atmosphere. Even in locations where there is no light pollution, the image achieved by ground-based telescopes is blurred as photons bounce about among the air molecules and lose their coherence. Sitting in orbit above the atmosphere eliminates this problem entirely.

The first service mission to the HST took place in 1993. The mission was a matter of urgency because the telescope was found to be faulty. The main lens of the telescope had been ground and polished with an inaccuracy that meant distant galaxies and other celestial phenomena appeared blurred, when they should have been sharply in focus. Unfortunately the error hadn't been detected prior to launch, as it was not possible to test the telescope by looking through the atmosphere.

The solution was a corrective optics package, which had to be installed into the telescope by crew members of the SS *Endeavour*. The repair was a complete success, rendering the telescope fully functional and providing the astronomical and cosmological communities with the best images of outer space ever seen.

Subsequent visits have been for purposes of maintenance, and to change peripheral equipment devices, such as spectrographs and infrared cameras, which are used to view images in an extra-optical way. This enables scientists to see that which lies outside the normal scope of the human eye. In 1999, an onboard computer was installed, so that the telescope could process some of its data before transmitting it down to Earth. The electronics of the computer and other electrical devices are powered by photovoltaic solar panels.

Between 2003 and 2004 the HST was used to make an intimate study of a particular part of space, now known as the Hubble Ultra Deep Field. From Earth the area is about a hundredth the size of the Moon, or one thirteen-millionth the size of the entire sky – yet it contains 10,000 galaxies. The light from the farthest is 13 billion years old, making the universe incomprehensibly big and ancient.

# *14 February*

*The last chemical element in the actinide series – lawrencium – is 'discovered' or rather 'created' at the University of California*

**1961** Lawrencium (Lr) is element number 103 on the periodic table. It was named after Ernest Orlando Lawrence (1901–58), who founded the experimental facilities in which the chemical was synthesised – now called the Lawrence Berkeley National Laboratory. He invented the cyclotron, a type of particle accelerator used in nuclear physics.

The element is described as a radioactive synthetic element, as it doesn't occur in nature. This is because it undergoes rapid radioactive decay. The most stable isotope has a half-life of four hours, meaning that every four hours half of the remaining material decays into lower elements. Not enough of the element has ever been created to tell very much about its physical properties. It is probably a silvery-white metal en masse. As lawrencium has only existed briefly, and in such infinitesimally small amounts, it has no known uses.

To create lawrencium a device called a Heavy Ion Linear Accelerator was used. Another actinide element – californium (Cf) – was bombarded with boron ions, thereby promoting the californium atoms to a higher atomic number. Californium itself can only be acquired by synthesising it from curium, which in turn has to be synthesised from plutonium. Plutonium can be found in extremely small quantities in nature, but workable amounts are synthesised from uranium. Thus a synthesis chain, uranium–plutonium–curium–californium–lawrencium, had to be achieved.

All elements with atomic numbers higher than 92 are known as transuranic elements. This is because they exceed uranium – element 92 – in the periodic table. There are 24, with element 117 theoretically named as ununseptium (Uus). Only plutonium (94) and neptunium (93) occur in nature. That is 'nature' on Earth. It may be possible that others are created in extraterrestrial nature by the formation of stars. It follows then, that they may have been created as part of the genesis of our solar system, but have long since decayed into stable non-radioactive elements.

Dmitri Mendeleev, was the first person to realise that the chemical elements bore a relationship to one another. He devised the periodic table to show that different elements could be arranged according to their atomic structure. In so doing, he was able to demonstrate that certain elements were yet to be discovered, as their positions on the table were vacant. Ever since then scientists have striven to discover new elements. Element 101 is called mendelevium in his honour. The periodic table currently runs from element 1 (hydrogen) to element 118 (ununoctium).

As all recent additions to the periodic table have been created in the laboratory it may seem odd to say that they have been 'discovered', but that is because they can theoretically exist elsewhere in the universe. The same goes for mathematical formulae, as they are considered to exist in nature, so that mathematicians discover rather than invent them.

# 15 February

## The imperial monetary system is replaced by the decimal system in Britain

**1971** It may seem counter-intuitive now, but people used to count their money in twelves rather than tens. Perhaps not surprisingly, Britain eventually opted to conform to the standard used by most of the rest of the world.

The imperial system used monetary units of pounds, shillings and pence. Oddly this system was known by the abbreviation l.s.d. The 'l' stood for 'librae', the 's' for 'solidi' and the 'd' represented 'denarii'. This was an indication of the antiquated nature of the system, for *librae* was Latin for 'pounds', although it actually referred to the units of weight, hence 'lbs'. *Solidi* and *denarii* were the names of Roman coins. Ironically, the literal meaning of *denarii* is 'containing tens'. Nevertheless, the imperial system was used for 1,200 years, from medieval times until 1971.

In old money, as it is often termed, a shilling comprised twelve pennies, and a pound comprised twenty shillings (or 240 pennies). There were other denominations too: the florin was worth 2s (two shillings); the farthing was ¼d (a quarter of a penny); the sixpence was ½s; the ha'penny was ½d; and the threepenny-bit was 3d. There were also crowns and half-crowns. The crown was equivalent to 5s and the half-crown to 2s 6d. Additionally there used to be the groat, which was used until 1662 and was worth 4d, or ⅓s. Given that the metric or decimal system was far simpler in concept, it didn't take a great deal of imagination to see that Britain would benefit from decimalisation.

To save on the expense of minting an entirely new circulation of coins and notes in 1971, the solution was to promote the value of the penny, so that 100 new pence now made up a pound sterling. The shilling was demoted to five new pence, so that it was still worth a 20th of a pound.

Money, though, was only one area of imperial incrementalism. British measurements of weights, volumes, lengths and distances were equally out of kilter with the rest of Europe. Since 1971 there have been failed attempts to convert the British from the ounce and the pound to the gram and the kilogram, from the pint and the gallon to the millilitre and the litre, and from the inch, the foot and the mile to the centimetre, the metre and the kilometre. It's a wonder that someone hasn't yet attempted to decimalise time, so that there are, let's say, 100 seconds in a minute, 50 minutes in an hour and ten hours in a day. Come to think of it …!

# 16 February

## The Kyoto Protocol pledges to reduce greenhouse gas emissions

**2005** No one is denying that the world's climate is getting warmer, but the contentious issue is why this is so. There are three distinct camps in this regard. Firstly, there are those who suggest that the phenomenon is a man-made one, caused by the emission of industrial pollutants into the atmosphere. Secondly, there are those who claim it is an entirely natural phenomenon, cause by a fluctuation in the emission of solar radiation. Thirdly, there are those who span both arguments, suggesting that the phenomenon is caused by a combination of man-made and natural agents.

Greenhouse gases are so called because they trap solar radiation inside the atmosphere, causing a rise in temperature of both the air and the surface of the planet, much like the glass roof of a greenhouse. A good deal of solar radiation is naturally reflected away from Earth, but greenhouse gases effectively allow the radiation to pass into the atmosphere and then prevent it from leaving.

The trouble is that the greenhouse effect is necessary for life to exist on Earth in the first place. The concern is about the greenhouse effect increasing above normal levels. Furthermore, greenhouse gases are entirely natural gases, including water vapour, carbon dioxide, methane and ozone. It is therefore very difficult to measure the ratios between natural and man-made production of these gases.

This is why sceptics point to a natural cause for global warming. They suggest that the planet is simply entering a warm age, as opposed to an ice age – a perturbation from what we have come to regard as 'normal'. The idea is that increased solar radiation due to sunspots warms the oceans, which are then forced to yield their absorbed carbon dioxide. This subsequently warms the atmosphere, which in turn forces the ocean temperature higher, releasing more $CO_2$, so that global warming spirals upwards.

Since we know that human activity certainly produces more carbon dioxide than it is possible for plants to absorb, then we must be playing our part, even if the process is a primarily natural one.

It seems that our only realistic hope is to reduce the pace of global warming, but otherwise accept that the world is set to get cosier and hope that it doesn't lead to the next great extinction. The dinosaurs were extinguished by an atmosphere that banished light and warmth. We may be brought to our end by an atmosphere that invites too much in.

# 17 February

## The Beatles release their seminal double A-side single, 'Strawberry Fields Forever/Penny Lane'

**1967** The Beatles were at the very height of their powers going into 1967. They were in the middle of recording one of the most influential albums of all time: *Sergeant Pepper's Lonely Hearts Club Band*, which was released on 1 June of that year. Their double A-side was timed to keep fans happy while the band was holed up at Abbey Road Studios. It proved to be the perfect aperitif for it was, in many respects, a condensed version of the album even though neither song would appear on it.

Although John Lennon and Paul McCartney shared credits for their Beatles songs, whoever performed the lead vocal was generally the primary composer. This wasn't just a matter of ego; it made perfect sense from a performance point of view because song writers tend to produce songs that suit their own style and range of voice.

John Lennon's track was 'Strawberry Fields Forever', while Paul McCartney's was 'Penny Lane'. They were markedly different songs, yet they both described places and experiences remembered from their youth in their home town of Liverpool. 'Strawberry Fields Forever' was a psychedelic record, with strange modern instruments helping to evoke a sense of other-worldliness to suit a voice treated to give it a trebly radio quality. 'Penny Lane' was a bounding melodic record that used brass instruments and a plodding bass guitar to evoke a sense of tradition. The chirpy lead vocal was backed by falsetto voices to give it a carefree feel.

The songs are now regarded as having complemented one another perfectly, coming from opposite ends of the spectrum, yet equally matched in perfection. More importantly they expressed the different personalities of the two musicians. Lennon was inclined towards introspection, writing lyrics that voiced his feelings about things. McCartney was more inclined to compose outward-looking songs about his observations. *Sergeant Pepper* was largely cast in the same mould, so that every catchy McCartney melody was countered by one of Lennon's darker experiments. In a way it was a comment on reality, where life is mapped out by a mosaic of moments that possess different textures and colours.

# 18 February

*Pluto's 50th birthday, although it is no longer a planet but a planetoid*

**1980** It was the astronomer Percival Lowell who supposedly predicted the existence of Pluto in 1915, due to perturbations in the orbit of Uranus. They could only be explained, he claimed, by the gravitational pull of an undiscovered planetary body. He termed it 'Planet X' in anticipation of its being eventually found and identified.

Unfortunately for Lowell he died in 1916, some fourteen years before Planet X showed itself. As it turned out, Pluto was too small to cause the perturbations in Uranus' movements. The truth was that Neptune, discovered in 1846, was much denser than had been originally calculated. The prediction and subsequent discovery of Pluto, therefore, were quite accidental and coincidental.

Pluto is so far away from the sun that it takes over 248 of our Earth years for the planetoid to complete one orbit. Put another way, a Plutonian year is 248 times as long as a Tellurian (Earth) year. That means that it will actually celebrate the first anniversary of its discovery in the year 2178.

When Clyde Tombaugh announced his observation in 1930, there was much debate about the status of Pluto, due to its size. Nevertheless, it became a planet and remained so until 2006 when the IAU (International Astronomical Union) got round to defining a 'planet'. As a result Pluto was demoted from being the ninth planet in the solar system, to being the first lesser planet or planetoid. A bit like being relegated from the bottom of the First Division to the top of the Second Division, to use a sporting analogy.

Pluto actually has an eccentric orbital path – it doesn't orbit the sun in a circle, like the Earth. Instead it does so in an ellipse. Consequently its distance from the sun varies between about 7,376 million km and roughly 4,437 million km. This means that it periodically comes closer to the sun than Neptune during its travels. This, of course, means that there is potential for the two to collide, but it hasn't happened so far, simply because such vast distances and orbital times are involved. The chances of it happening are many billions to one.

# 19 February

*A rocket-powered sled on rails reaches four times the speed of sound on a test track in New Mexico*

**1959** The actual speed of the sled was 3,089 mph (4,972 kph), which is Mach 4.1, or 4.1 times the speed of sound. That record has since been beaten, doubled in fact, but it stood until 1982. The sled was unmanned and ran on a track known by the acronym SNORT (Supersonic Naval Ordnance Track) at the Holloman Air Force Base, New Mexico.

Between 1947 and 1954 manned tests were conducted. Their purpose was to experiment with the effects of extreme acceleration, high speeds without protection and sudden deceleration. The data were needed by the US Air Force with regard to the safety of jet and rocket planes, which had been in development since the Second World War.

A number of 'guinea pigs' were initially used, but one man eventually took on the challenge as the tests got more dangerous. He was Dr John Stapp, the man charged with the responsibility of conducting the experiments. He evidently felt that as he was accountable for any injuries, he should put only himself at risk. In addition, it enabled him to experience the effects first-hand and have a better insight into necessary improvements.

On 10 December 1954, Stapp earned himself the nickname 'Fastest Man Alive' when he achieved an incredible 632 mph (1,017 kph), which is just over 0.8 Mach. As if the speed wasn't remarkable enough, he reached it in just 5 seconds and stopped in 1.25 seconds, subjecting his body to incredible forces. In fact his deceleration exerted over 40 Gs (gravities) on him. It was so severe that the capillaries in his eyeballs burst and filled them with blood. He thought he would be blind for life, but his eyesight was returned to him within a couple of days.

Following that ride, the project focused on unmanned tests. Stapp went on to pioneer work into road safety. He played a vital role in the safety design of new cars by developing tests using crash test dummies and high-speed stop-frame photography to examine the processes involved when human bodies are involved in RTAs (road traffic accidents). Stapp was never surprised by human disregard for safety issues and once made a remark that became humorously known as Stapp's Law: 'The universal aptitude for ineptitude makes any human accomplishment an incredible miracle.'

# 20 February

*The Soviets launch their* Mir *space station into orbit around the Earth*

**1986** The purpose of the space station was to conduct all kinds of experiments in weightless conditions and to see what effects a lack of gravitational force would have on the human body. *Mir* was a great success and existed until March 2001 when it was decommissioned. It was forced out of orbit and destroyed by air resistance when it hit the atmosphere above the Pacific Ocean.

Between 1986 and 1996 several modules were launched and then connected together, allowing the space station to become gradually more complex, with different rooms for different purposes. It was so well designed for human habitation that it was manned by at least one person for a period of almost ten years.

Following the collapse of the Soviet Union, relations between the US and Russia improved and international cooperation led to Americans visiting *Mir* between 1995 and 1998. Thankfully they did their homework and were able to safely dock their space shuttles with *Mir*. The words 'What do you mean "metric"? We work in inches!' weren't used when the two came together.

Since the demise of *Mir*, an International Space Station has been under construction. It is now quite large and has a relatively low orbit, so that it is visible from Earth, given the right conditions. A clear sky with low light pollution is good, but the space station also needs to be reflecting light from the sun to show up against the night sky. It travels at 17,240 mph (27,750 kph). That means it completes each full orbit in about 1.5 hours and can clearly be seen scudding steadily across the firmament as a white dot.

Returning to the subject of weightlessness, scientists consider it vital to understand how organisms respond under such conditions. This is not least because it will be necessary for astronauts to cope with a lack of gravity if they are to travel to Mars in the foreseeable future. As well as the physiological effects on the body, there are the practicalities of living and working in weightless environments. Simple tasks such as visiting the toilet, eating and washing are hazardous because detritus and drops of fluid become airborne.

On the physiological level, our bodies have evolved to function on the basis that gravity is an ever-present force. Our bones, muscles and organs respond to there being a constant pull towards the ground, so a lack of gravity can affect growth and development. Even our sense of balance relies on gravitation, so that humans have no sense of what is up or down when gravity is lost. In point of fact, gravity is actually present aboard the International Space Station, but it is exactly matched by the centrifugal force, so that overall it is neutralised.

# 21 February

## *The structure of DNA is discovered, opening the way for modern genetics*

**1953** Ever since Charles Darwin had unleashed his theory of evolution in 1859, scientists had been trying to understand the mechanism that allowed traits to be inherited and blended together to produce the genetic variety necessary for natural selection to operate. Mendel showed how characteristics are passed to new generations in mathematically predictable ways and, in so doing, laid the ground rules for the modern approach to scientific empirical experimentation. Even so, the inner workings of heredity had yet to be revealed.

Then microscopy led to the discovery of chromosomes in cell nuclei, which were seen to cross over and pair up during the process of meiosis (a form of cell division). It was reasoned that chromosomes must be further divided into smaller units, which became known as genes. However, a physical explanation for the structure and storage of genetic information was still lacking. In 1929 a scientist named Phoebus Levene identified the gene chemical as DNA (deoxyribonucleic acid). The race was on to work out the structure of the DNA molecule, so that scientists could figure out how it stores its information.

Levene had already shown that the DNA giant molecule comprises the sub-molecules adenine, cytosine, guanine, thymine, deoxyribose and phosphate, but the physical structure of DNA needed to be discovered. Eventually X-ray studies of DNA showed that it had a twisted columnar shape. This gave scientists James Watson and Francis Crick a starting point to begin modelling a section of DNA molecule, using balls and rods to represent the sub-molecules involved.

A process of elimination and reasoning ultimately led to what is now described as the double-helix DNA molecule. On this day in 1953, Crick and Watson found that the molecule essentially resembled a twisted ladder. The rungs of the ladder are each made from base pairs of sub-molecules in four possible combinations: guanine–cytosine, cytosine–guanine, adenine–thymine and thymine–adenine. The deoxyribose and phosphate molecules make up the struts and joints of the ladder.

It was realised that DNA coding is very simple indeed. It is a double-binary or quadrinary coding system, which is why DNA needs to be incredibly long to store its information. In effect it is a digital tape with zeros, ones, twos and threes along its entire length. Long strands of DNA make up each gene, and many genes make up each chromosome. One turn of the DNA helices comprises 10 base-pairs and measures 3.4 nanometres in length. A nanometre is a one-thousand-millionth of a metre. An entire human genome would measure only a few metres in length if it were unravelled.

# 22 February

### Scientists announce the first adult-cell cloning of a mammal, Dolly the sheep

**1997** For many people, this is the day when the idea of the scientist as Frankenstein became a reality. This is the day when Ian

Wilmut and Keith Campbell of Edinburgh's Roslin Institute quietly announced that seven months previously they had created a
living clone of a mammal for the first time – and so finally proved
that scientists could bypass the natural union of male and female
in the creation of a baby.

Of course, there was something quite comical about it all. The
clone was not a human but a sheep, and Wilmut's team called this
sheep Dolly because the cells used to clone her were taken from an
adult sheep's mammary glands. As Dr Wilmut admitted, 'We
couldn't think of a more impressive pair of mammary glands than
Dolly Parton's'. Nevertheless, it was a landmark event.

An animal conceived naturally has a mix of genes from both
parents, and so, of course, has a mix of their characteristics. Clones
get their entire set of genes from a single animal. So they are genetically identical 'copies'. Clones had been made of mammal cells
before Dolly, but only using embryo cells. Dolly was the first not
only to be cloned from cells taken from a living adult, but the first
clone to be implanted into a surrogate mother and allowed to
develop into an infant mammal.

The news of Dolly's creation stirred up fierce controversy
among everyone, from animal rights activists to pro-life Christian
groups. If scientists could clone a sheep, surely it wouldn't be long
before they tried to clone humans? In the face of the furore, Dolly's
creator Ian Wilmut declared that human cloning was 'repugnant'
and not long after many countries, including the UK, introduced
laws banning 'human reproductive cloning' – which means
cloning to create a baby rather than just embryonic cells.

However, there were usually no such bans on 'human therapeutic cloning'. Therapeutic cloning means cloning cells for
medical purposes. This essentially means cloning to create a supply of stem cells, which are thought to have huge potential in the
treatment of a variety of ailments. In May 2005, a Newcastle
university team cloned the first human embryo and later that year
Wilmut himself was granted a licence to clone human embryos.
Even this so-called 'therapeutic' cloning, though, arouses fierce
opposition from pro-life groups who argue that all human embryos
have a right to life.

Interestingly, two years later, Wilmut put aside cloning again. Pro-life groups responded to Wilmut's decision warmly, but he insisted that it was nothing to do with ethics but simply because Japanese scientists had devised a technique for supplying stem cells directly from adult skin cells rather than from cloned embryos. Now, nearly all stem cells used for research are being taken from adults, although a new controversy has arisen over using human-animal 'hybrid' embryos, in which embryo cells are created by inserting adult human DNA into animal eggs from which all but a tiny residue of the animal's genetic material has been removed. Meanwhile, more and more one-off mammal clones are being created, from cows to dogs, as people continue to argue about the ethics.

# 23 February

### An oil tanker in Navarino Bay, Greece, has one of the all-time worst oil spillages

**1980** The *Irenes Serenade* was the name of the tanker which exploded off the coast of Pilos, Greece, and emptied 37 million gallons (100,000 tonnes) of crude oil into the Mediterranean Sea. Since that time there have been several worse oil spills, demoting it to number 13 on the list, but it was the worst Mediterranean pollution event until 1991 when the *Amoco Haven* exploded off the coast of Genoa, Italy, spilling 52 million gallons (140,000 tonnes). Needless to say, both disasters caused massive and widespread environmental damage.

Crude oil, although quite natural, has chemical and physical properties that make it extremely harmful to plants and animals. Chemically it poisons the environment, because it comprises all manner of noxious ingredients. When crude oil or petroleum is processed by fractional distillation it produces compounds such as diesel oil (diesel), petrol (car fuel), oil tar (bitumen), kerosene or paraffin (aviation fuel), petrolatum (Vaseline), grease, oil gas (naphtha) and lubrication oil.

This list is enough to demonstrate just how damaging crude oil is when unleashed into ecosystems. In addition to the chemical effects, crude oil is physically catastrophic. It forms a slick layer over water, so that air-breathing animals inevitably encounter the oil and become weighed down by it. It also blocks airways and prevents movement.

As crude oil ages, the lighter fractions evaporate making the residue more viscous and heavy. As a result, it sinks and creates a thick, sticky blanket layer over rocks and the seabed, thereby affecting marine life too.

There are three principal ways of dealing with crude oil disasters. The first is to set fire to the oil. As the fractions are flammable the oil burns off very effectively, but it produces thick noxious smoke and pollutes the environment in other ways. However, it's worth noting that the same pollutants would still be released by vehicles and so on anyway, albeit more slowly. Second, detergents can be used to attack the crude oil and effectively neutralise it. Detergents don't remove the oil, but render it soluble or break it down into microscopic smuts, so that the currents and tides eventually disperse it and the detergent chemicals disperse far and wide. Third, there is physical removal, where the crude oil is shovelled from the coastline and disposed of. In time the weather and bacteria tend to break down any remaining deposits, although the thicker tar fractions become a permanent reminder. Prevention of oil spills is clearly the preferred option.

# 24 February

*Palaeontologists unearth a fossilised dinosaur egg shown to contain a 150-million-year-old embryo*

**1989** At the time this was the oldest dinosaur embryo yet discovered. It was found amid the fossilised remains of an adult dinosaur and assumed to have been within the mother when she died. The egg, which was found in Utah, USA, was shown to contain an embryo by using a CAT (computerised axial tomography) scan. It was dated at 150 million years, which places it in the Upper Jurassic semi-period of the Mesozoic era. Up until then most other fossilised dinosaur eggs came from the Upper Cretaceous semi-period of the Mesozoic era. The Mesozoic era comprised the Triassic (245–208 million years ago), Jurassic (208–146 million years ago), Cretaceous (146–65 million years ago) and Tertiary (65–1.6 million years ago) periods.

Then in 2005 it was announced that some even older dinosaur eggs and embryos had been discovered in South Africa. They were originally excavated in 1978, but it had taken two and a half decades to complete the work necessary to expose the fossilised material from the surrounding sedimentary rock. These were dated at 190 million years ago and placed in the Lower Jurassic semi-period.

Scientists identified the embryos as those of an herbivorous dinosaur named Massospondylus. It was a long-necked species, which was bipedal (walked on two legs) and probably roamed the land in foraging herds. Intriguingly, the embryos showed that the hatchlings walked on four legs initially and gradually developed into bipedal adults. This may have offered an advantage to the young as it was a time when herbaceous plants and grasses hadn't yet evolved, so it would have been necessary for juveniles to climb trees to eat the shoots. Climbing may have afforded protection from predators too.

Massospondylus walked the Earth from the late Triassic to the early Jurassic periods. They were about 20 feet (6 metres) long and belonged to a group of dinosaurs named prosauropods. The prosauropods were initially thought to have evolved into the later sauropods, but taxonomists and cladisticians have revised this opinion. Massospondylus was one of the first dinosaurs to be named, in 1854, just five years before Darwin and Wallace offered a scientific explanation for the existence of long-extinct creatures.

# 25 February

## Corporal punishment is banned in British schools by the European Court of Human Rights

**1982** For all its pride in its liberal traditions, Britain has often lagged behind when it comes to protecting children from corporal punishment. So it was to the European Court of Human Rights that two Scottish mothers, Jane Cosans and Grace Campbell, turned for a guarantee of protection from disciplinary beatings of their sons at school.

Mrs Jane Cosans' son was suspended from his school in Fife after failing to turn up for a belting for breaking a rule. Mrs Campbell took Strathclyde education authority to court because they would not guarantee her eleven-year-old son would not be beaten with the leather strap called the 'tawse'.

After a long battle through the courts, both Mrs Cosans and Mrs Campbell won their landmark ruling. The European court ruled that beating schoolchildren against their parents' wishes was a violation of the Convention on Human Rights, because children must be taught 'in conformity with their own religious and philosophical convictions'.

Of course, this only meant that children were exempt from beatings if their parents specifically asked, creating a somewhat ambiguous situation. But as Kenneth Baker, the education secretary in Mrs Thatcher's government, said: 'After these cases, it was clear that corporal punishment could not be sustained.' A powerful 'stop smacking' campaign got under way, but even so in 1985 there were still maybe a quarter of a million officially recorded beatings in English and Welsh schools every year – one every 19 seconds, and some quite violent. So Baker decided it was time for British legislation.

The parliamentary vote on Baker's bill was won only by a hair's breadth, but it passed into law in 1987, banning corporal punishment in all UK state schools. The law not only outlawed beatings such as the cane but also slappings, rough handling and throwing of missiles. Opponents predicted that without this ulti-mate sanction, schools would descend into chaos, but even though some unruly pupils made hay with the law, saying, 'You can't hit me; I'll take you to court', teachers and pupils on the whole quickly adjusted. In 1998, the ban was extended to private schools.

Meanwhile, the UN Human Rights committee pressed for all physical punishment of children to be banned, both at school and at home. The UK relented a little and in January 2005, a law was introduced banning parents in England and Wales from smacking children hard enough to leave a mark on the skin.

There are still plenty of people in Britain who want to reintro-duce corporal punishment. In 2005, a Christian group got as far as the Court of Appeal with a bid to overturn the ban in private schools. They failed, but there are still plenty who insist British schools are suffering a major breakdown in discipline because teachers can't use corporal punishment. A 2005 survey of nearly 1,700 parents found 21 per cent would welcome the restoration of corporal punishment in schools, with 44 per cent saying they would like it to be an option. Most informed commentators, though, argue that if there are problems with school discipline, they need a far more intelligent solution than simply beatings.

# 26 February

## The printing and publishing industries enter the modern age

**1954** Prior to photoengraving, typesetting machines assembled rows of die-cast metal letters and punctuation marks, which could then be formed into printing beds. This was originally done entirely by hand, but the Linotype machine improved the speed and efficiency of the process at the turn of the 20th century. Nevertheless, typesetting was still a relatively time-consuming business and because the printing beds were flat, the process of printing itself was also slow, as the paper had to be positioned and them removed with each printing procedure.

Photoengraving changed all of this. A chemical ink, called a photoresist, is applied evenly to the surface of a metal printing bed. Ultraviolet light is then shone through a photographic negative of the image to be printed, so that the photoresist is cured in the appropriate pattern. Unwanted photoresist is then removed and an acidic etching agent is applied to the printing bed. The acid attacks the metal where it is exposed, but not where the cured photoresist has adhered to the surface. The result is an integral printing bed with a relief surface, so that printing ink only coats those parts that have been protected from the etching process.

The technique meant that duplicate printing beds could be churned out. It also meant that the printing surface could be cylindrical and fitted to a rotating drum. This revolutionised – quite literally – the printing process as the paper could now be sent through the machine in a linear fashion, while the printing bed revolved above. This made printing very much faster and cheaper. It had a particularly marked effect on the mass printing of newspapers and magazines, which could be made far more cheaply and therefore distributed to a wider readership.

The overall effect of the photoengraving process was to bring news and information to the masses in a way never seen before. As to whether that was a good thing is a matter of opinion. Initially newspapers and magazines were standardised in their contents, but eventually a differentiation developed between those aimed at the working class, the middle class and the upper class. The tabloid format of newspaper tended to reflect the ergonomic requirements and interests of those reading their news in working conditions, while the broadsheet was the preserve of those with plenty of space and worldliness.

# 27 February

## *Italian government requests help to prevent the leaning tower of Pisa from toppling*

**1964** The tower at Pisa began to shift from upright as soon as construction started in the 12th century – it was begun in 1174 and finished in 1372. It had been built on a substrate with a softer layer beneath, which began to give under the weight so that the tower's foundation subsided. The medieval solution to the problem was to add another four storeys as a counterweight. Of course all that did was to increase its overall weight and exacerbate the lean. Eight hundred years on and the tower had finally reached a point where engineering intervention was required to stop the building from razing itself to the ground. At its most extreme, the tower leaned a full 17 feet off-centre.

The first attempt to do something about the lean was at the behest of Benito Mussolini in the 1930s. He ordered that concrete be poured into the foundation to tilt the tower upright. Needless to say, this was as successful as the medieval attempt, and only added more weight. Clearly early engineers didn't appreciate the gravity of the situation, which is odd given that the tower is also famous for having been the building used by Galileo to demonstrate that objects of different sizes will fall at the same rate of acceleration (he used cannon balls). Had Galileo been assigned the task of rectifying the stoop, he would doubtless have understood the physics a bit better than most.

For a couple of decades following the request for assistance in 1964, many eminent civil engineers discussed ways of going about the job. Meanwhile the tower continued to creep further from vertical. By 1990 the tower had to be closed for reasons of safety. It was braced with steel cables and fitted with counterweights while engineers pondered their next move. Eventually it was decided to excavate substrate from the stable part of the foundation. Having removed almost 40 m$^3$ of material, the tower returned eighteen inches towards upright to a position it had been in during the early 19th century. It was thus declared open for business as usual in 2001.

Due to the unstable nature of the geology beneath the tower, it will continue to move, but engineers reckon that it will remain safe for another 300 years. The only permanent solution would be to disassemble the tower and then rebuild it on a foundation platform designed to 'float' on the substrate and distribute the load more evenly.

# 28 February

*The first man-made fibre celebrates its 50th anniversary*

**1985** The product is a 'condensation copolymer thermoplastic resin'. Its more digestible name, 'nylon', is often falsely supposed to be a contraction of 'New York' and 'London', which reflects the international importance of the fibre's invention. Prior to nylon a number of volume plastics had been invented and used, such as vulcanised rubber, Parkesine and Bakelite. The latter was the first plastic based on a man-made or synthetic polymer, although Bakelite was a hard and brittle product, used to create moulded components. Polymers are very long chain-like molecules, similar to DNA in that they can theoretically have infinite length, comprising repeated structural units, which are called monomers.

Two chemicals – diamine and dicarboxylic acid – are used in the synthesis of nylon. The chemical reaction causes the monomers to join together by forming peptide bonds between them. Filaments of nylon can be drawn off the fluid surface and wound onto spools in a similar manner to winding silk from cocoons, or indeed to the way in which caterpillars draw silk from their spinnerets in the first place.

Nylon found itself being used in the manufacture of modern garments, particularly nylon stockings, which swiftly became a must-have item for all sophisticated women. Nylon nuts, bolts and washers, for example, work very well because they are tough, hardwearing and flexible, although not as strong as their steel equivalents. Other varied uses include the fabric of tents, carpets, guitar strings, tubing and ropes.

There are, in fact, a number of types of nylon, each with slightly different properties. Engineering-nylons can be extruded, injection-moulded, pressure-moulded and tooled to make components, while fibre-nylons can be drawn into strands of varying thickness to suit different uses. Since the discovery of polymers many more plastics have been invented besides nylon. They include PVC (polyvinylchloride), polythene (polyethylene), polystyrene, epoxy resins, neoprene, acrylic, polypropylene and PTFE (polytetra-fluoroethylene).

During the Second World War nylon stockings, usually just called 'nylons', became so popular that they were used as a form of currency for purchasing rations and contraband goods. They gave women a form of sex appeal, which was tied in with the phenomenon of the wartime romance as people sought comfort from the hardships of warfare. Ever since then nylons have been a part of the modern sexual culture, because they afford a modicum of protection against the cold and show off a woman's legs to great advantage, employing the power of suggestion.

# 29 February

## Zionist terrorist bomb kills 28 British soldiers on the Cairo–Haifa train

**1948** When 28 British soldiers were killed as a mine exploded under the Cairo–Haifa train, the Zionist terrorist group Lehi, also known as the Stern Gang, claimed responsibility. According to Lehi it was in retaliation for the three car bombs that had killed 52 Jews a week earlier in Jerusalem's Ben Yehuda street. Two British deserters were involved in the Ben Yehuda street blasts and Lehi claimed British collusion.

The Cairo–Haifa bombing was just the latest – and, as it turned out, one of the last – acts of terrorism by Zionist extremists against the British who they saw as the main obstacle to the establishment of a Jewish state in Palestine. For all its justifiable anger over terrorism today, Israel itself was born on a wave of Zionist terrorism and many leading political figures in the new Israel, such as Menachem Begin and Yitzhak Shamir, played key roles in the terror campaign.

The British received the mandate to administer Palestine after the First World War when the Ottoman Empire was broken up. It proved a poisoned chalice as the British were caught between two opposing sides. On the one hand were Jews who were moving in in increasing numbers and buying up land. On the other were

Arab Palestinians who, freed from Turkish control, were keen to establish their own destiny and resented Jewish immigration.

Tensions rose throughout the 1930s as the rise of Nazism fuelled Jewish immigration, but the British somehow managed to steer a midway course – with the local administration's sympathy for the Arabs tempered by a more pro-Jewish line back in London. But the outbreak of the Second World War triggered a crisis. To keep the Arab nations on side in the war, the British agreed to halt Jewish immigration, leaving the Jews feeling betrayed.

Right-wing Zionist groups such as Irgun now saw the British as the enemy, not the Germans – and their anger was heightened when the British disastrously sank a shipload of Jewish immigrants, the *Struma*, in 1942. Inspired by the IRA, Avraham Stern formed Lehi to wage a terror campaign. Stern was killed by the British in 1942, but the Stern Gang continued to attack British targets – most notoriously murdering the British minister, Lord Moyne, in Cairo in 1944 and in 1946 blowing up the King David Hotel, the centre of British administration in Jerusalem. The blast killed 91 and was the one event which, more than anything else, persuaded the British to get out.

After the war, Jewish immigration escalated and Arab resentment rose. The United Nations agreed in 1947 on a partition of the region to create a new Jewish state west of the Jordan. The British agreed to leave on 14 May 1948, but the Stern Gang continued their terrorist campaign and the Arabs started violent protests.

With the region descending into civil war, the US called on the UN to suspend partition. The Zionist response was swift and brutal. On 9 April, Irgun and the Stern Gang massacred all 254 inhabitants of the Arab village of Dayr-yasin. Two weeks later, Zionist troops took Haifa and Jaffa. The efforts of the demoralised Arabs to prevent partition collapsed. On 14 May, the last British commissioner, Sir Alan Cunningham left Palestine and on the same day the State of Israel was declared. Arab armies immediately invaded Palestine, but were quickly routed by the Israelis. Israel was born and the one-time terrorists began to play a key role in its government.

# 1 March

## *The first spacecraft to reach the surface of another planet crash-lands*

**1966** The 1950s and 1960s were two decades of intense competition between the US and USSR. Following the end of the Second World War, the two superpowers set about trying to outdo one another in a number of respects, especially scientific and technological progress. Advances in space exploration became the conspicuous way in which each nation scored points against the other in this political game, which became dubbed the Cold War. The Soviets had done very well by 1966. They had launched the first satellite into orbit – *Sputnik 1* in 1957, and then put the first animal – *Sputnik 2* in 1957 – and human into space – *Vostok 1* in 1966.

*Venera 3* was launched on 16 November 1965 and collided with Venus on 1 March 1966. She was fitted with communications equipment, enabling the Soviet team to track her journey to Venus. However, when she reached the planet she failed to make a controlled landing and contact was lost. On 3 February 1966, *Luna 9* had made the first controlled landing on the Moon and had transmitted images and footage of the lunar surface back to the US team, so the Soviets were disappointed by the fate of *Venera 3*.

The probe hadn't been fitted with any landing equipment. Instead it simply had a robust design in the vain hope that it might survive the impact with the surface of Venus. Its successor, *Venera 4*, reached Venus on 18 October 1967 and became the first probe to return data about another planet's atmosphere, before it too was lost. It just so happened that the US probe *Mariner 5* flew by Venus the very next day and it was able to calculate that the atmospheric pressure was 75–100 times greater than that on Earth. This meant that the *Venera* probes would have been crushed during descent.

*Veneras* 5 and 6 had already been built, so they were sent to Venus by the Soviets purely as atmospheric probes. *Venera 7*, however, was built to a higher specification and became the first spacecraft to make a controlled landing on another planet and transmit data about the surface, which it achieved on 15 December 1970.

# 2 March

## *Humans send a message in a bottle*

**1972** On this day the first outer-planetary probe was launched to rendezvous with the planet Jupiter in 1973. *Pioneer X* travelled 620 million miles in 21 months, making an average speed of about 44,000 mph. It sent back the first close-up images of the largest planet in our solar system on 3 December 1973. It then continued on its way towards outer space.

A decade later, on 13 June 1983, *Pioneer X* passed Neptune, which is considered the outermost planet, now that Pluto has been relegated to a lesser planet, or planetoid. In so doing, the probe effectively left the solar system and was deemed to have completed its mission in 1997. Until 17 February 1998 *Pioneer X* was the most distant man-made object from the sun, but then *Voyager I* – launched in 1977 – overtook it and has increased its lead ever since.

*Pioneer X* remained contactable until January 2003, but subsequent attempts failed to detect a signal. After almost 31 years the probe was lost in space. It is now over 90 AU distant from the sun (AU stands for 'astronomical units'. One AU is equal to the distance between the Earth and the sun). That is 90 × 150 million km (93 million miles) or 13.5 billion km (8.4 billion miles). It has been calculated that in the year 34,600 *Pioneer X* will be just three light years away from the nearest star in the Taurus constellation. The star is 10-Tau and lies about 45 light years from Earth.

Mindful of the future travels of *Pioneer X*, the constructors of the probe fitted a plaque on its side. It features a linear diagram of our solar system and line drawings of the probe superimposed by naked male and female Caucasian humans. The man has his right palm held aloft in a gesture of greeting in anticipation that the probe will one day be encountered by other life forms.

On the question of 'what might extra-terrestrials be like?' it comes down to how specific conditions need to be in order to produce life forms. Current thinking has it that these conditions need to be the same as those on our planet and are consequently extremely rare.

It follows that evolution would have found the same optimum design solutions for similar econiches, so that organisms will be essentially the same as those on Earth. Similarly, the odds are that highly intelligent life forms will resemble humanity because they would have succeeded for the same reasons. Furthermore, they are likely to be as aggressive and warlike as humans fundamentally are. It is worth noting, though, that the chances of their existing anywhere near Earth are extremely remote. There may be just one life-supporting planet in each galaxy, as the chemistry and physics would need to replicate our own biosphere precisely.

# 3 March

## Carving is completed on Stone Mountain, Georgia

**1972** When the giant stone carving on the sheer granite face of the Atlanta suburb of Stone Mountain was unveiled on 3 March 1972, it became the world's largest bas-relief, roughly the size of a football field. Hewn out of the solid rock by thermo-jets, the carving depicts three Confederate heroes of the American Civil War, President Jefferson Davis and Generals Robert E. Lee and 'Stonewall' Jackson.

Nowadays, Stone Mountain is a major tourist attraction and people come here not simply to gape at the carving, but to take the cable car to the summit, to go hiking or take a scenic cruise on the nearby lake. In 1996, it was a venue for the Atlanta Olympics archery, tennis and cycling events. However, the story of the carving's creation is far from relaxed, tainted as it is by the darker strands of American white supremacism which remain a powerful force in this part of the world.

The idea of a carving on Stone Mountain to commemorate Confederate heroes of the Civil War was dreamed up by Mrs C. Helen Pane, a member of the United Daughters of the Confederacy, back in 1912. But it was here, three years later, that the resurgent Ku Klux Klan was born again with a group of robed and hooded men burning a cross on the mountain. As Klan activities reached their terrible climax in the 1920s, Stone Mountain became a focus of their rituals.

The same year that the Klan reformed, the UDC commissioned fervently patriotic sculptor Gutzhon Borglum, later to create the famous Mount Rushmore memorial, to carve a head of Lee on the mountain. But, as Borglum said, 'Ladies, a twenty foot head of Lee on that mountainside would look like a postage stamp on a barn door', and so he began working on a giant frieze that would include Lee, along with Jackson and Jefferson Davis at the head of an artillery troop. By 1924, Borglum had carved Lee's head, and developed strong links with the Klan, who by now were funding the project. But Borglum was a temperamental man, and eventually differences of approach led him to smash his models and resign. Another sculptor, Augustus Lukeman, took over and Borglum's work was obliterated. Within a few years, though, funds ran dry and the project was abandoned.

In 1958, the Georgia state authorities decided to resume the project and, after a competition, commissioned Walter Hancock to complete the carving. It was finally finished on 3 March 1972. Despite the state's involvement, though, Stone Mountain was still a hub for Klan activities. Eventually, however, the state managed to bar the Klan from access to the mountain, and the Klan seem to have retreated from the area.

# 4 March

## All hail Hale-Bopp

**1997** When 38 members of the Heaven's Gate group were found dead in a California mansion, after committing identical suicides by eating pudding and apple sauce laced with phenobarbital and other drugs, it was widely seen as a symptom of the modern age – and the perils of the internet. Apparently, the group's demise was a response to the appearance of Comet Hale-Bopp in the night sky and group leader Marshall Applewhite had persuaded all 38 to commit suicide so that their souls might join Jesus in the spaceship travelling in its wake.

People have long associated the appearance of comets with calamities. A comet that appeared in AD 79 was blamed for the volcanic eruption that buried the Roman city of Pompeii, while the arrival of Halley's comet in 1066 was depicted in the Bayeux tapestry as an omen for the Norman invasion of England.

Appearing suddenly in the sky, then blazing furiously and disappearing again, it is hardly surprising that comets seemed laden with meaning in the past, but we now know exactly what they are – simply lumps of ice, dust and rock. Each travels around the sun in a giant orbit that is so way off-centre that, for most of the time, it is in the outer reaches of the solar system. But when it swings in close to the sun it partly melts and throws out a vast tail of dust and gas which glistens in the light, making a brief but spectacular show in the night sky. The appearance of comets like Halley's, though sporadic, is entirely predictable.

Comet Hale-Bopp was a new discovery, first spotted in the distance in 1995 by astronomers Alan Hale and Thomas Bopp, and as it zoomed in towards the sun, it blazed brighter than any other recent comet and stayed visible to the naked eye for a record 18 months. Yet it behaved entirely as astronomers would expect.

What triggered the excitement of the Heaven's Gate group was a picture of the comet by an amateur astronomer, Chuck Shramek, which appeared to show what Shramek called a 'Saturn-like' object trailing in its wake. It seems likely that the photo was simply doctored to show the 'object', but immediately there was a buzz of speculation on the Web that this was a UFO, and no amount of denial from the scientific community could dampen the buzz.

The response of the Heaven's Gate sect was extreme, but they were by no means alone, and in the wake of the suicides there was intense speculation on what it all meant. Some suggested that it was a clear demonstration of the evils of the internet and its perils for vulnerable minds. Others argued that it was all a sign of people feeling small and alienated in the face of rapid technological and social change. In a long article on the suicides in the *New York Times*, Mark Dery wrote, 'the Heaven's Gate cult was a fun-house mirror exaggeration of ourselves as a wired society'. What would aliens make of it all?

# 5 March

*Winston Churchill gives a speech in the US, in which he coins a phrase to describe the post-war political situation in Europe*

**1946** Every now and then people come up with phrases that become absorbed into the lexicon, simply because there are no alternatives available or because they do the job better. Winston Churchill (1874–1965) was attempting to describe the way that Europe had been divided into western and eastern portions as a consequence of the standoff between the democratic and communist ideologies among the Allies following their defeat of the Axis nations. Churchill's use of the phrase 'iron curtain' perfectly captured people's imaginations. It was a metaphorical barrier, impenetrable yet flexible enough to follow the borders of the Eastern Bloc nations to form a complete shield.

Another related phrase that came to symbolise the subsequent political one-upmanship between East and West was 'Cold War'. Amazingly enough, this term had first been used in the 13th century by a Spanish writer named Don Juan Manuel, in describing the ethno-political situation in medieval Spain. At the time, the area of Granada was occupied by the Moors, who were North African Muslims in contrast with the Christians who occupied the rest of the peninsula. An American financier named Bernard Baruch gave the term its post-war meaning in 1947. He had stolen the phrase from a Herbert Swope who had independently invented the term in 1940.

A third war-related phrase was 'Catch-22', first used in the eponymous novel written by Joseph Heller (1923–99). Catch-22 was published in 1961, but the story begins in 1943 in war-torn Europe. Catch-22, which today is taken to mean an inescapable situation, is based on a form of self-contradictory circular logic. In the book, the central character, Yossarian, has Catch-22 explained to him:

> There was only one catch and that was Catch-22, which specified that a concern for one's safety in the face of dangers that were real and immediate was the process of a rational mind. Orr was crazy and could be grounded. All he had to do was ask; and as soon as he did, he would no longer be crazy and would have to fly more missions. Orr would be crazy to fly more missions and sane if he didn't, but if he was sane he had to fly them. If he flew them he was crazy and didn't have to; but if he didn't want to he was sane and had to. Yossarian was moved very deeply by the absolute simplicity of this clause of Catch-22 and let out a respectful whistle.
>
> 'That's some catch, that Catch-22,' Yossarian observed.
> 'It's the best there is,' Doc Daneeka agreed.

A fourth phrase, although still more often used in warfare situations than elsewhere, is 'blue-on-blue', meaning to be attacked, injured or killed by friendly fire. This phrase comes from the US terminology, where blue means Americans and red means Russians, in allusion to the predominant colours on their flags. Outgoing gunfire is thus described as blue-on-red, while incoming gunfire is red-on-blue regardless of who the enemy is. In the heat of battle blue-on-blue situations can arise very easily, because communication and identification errors occur. It is an unfortunate consequence of the theatre of modern warfare and, rather ironically, why soldiers used to wear conspicuous uniforms.

# 6 March

## Scientists attempt to survive in a closed system by entering Biosphere 2

**1994** The living space that exists around the globe is one very large biosphere. That is to say; it is spherical in shape and contains everything biological on planet Earth. Scientists wanted to know whether it would be possible to design and build an artificial biosphere that could self-sustain in total isolation from the natural biosphere. The motive was to explore the possibility of establishing autonomous communities on the Moon and other planets. So it was that the Biosphere Project was born.

In scientific terms it is actually impossible to have an entirely closed system, apart from the universe itself. The reason is that energy transfer will always occur in one way or another, no matter how one tries to avoid it. The best we can achieve, therefore, is a virtually closed system. Built in the Arizona desert, the Biospheres were glazed geodesic domes that sealed everything in from the outside world, except for those phenomena able to pass through the glass and framework, such as heat energy, light and other forms of electromagnetic radiation.

The idea was that the plants and animals (including humans) within the domes should find a perfect equilibrium by way of consumption and excretion of chemicals, so that the Biospheres could remain closed shut for indefinite periods. In practice finding this balance proved far more problematic than had been hoped. The natural biosphere is relatively enormous so that variables in gas levels and water availability, for example, don't cause dramatic environmental swings that might endanger the continued existence of life forms – well, not so far. In the Biospheres it was a different matter. Maintaining the right equilibrium between oxygen and carbon dioxide proved very tricky.

The scientists found that they had to install devices to remove carbon dioxide from the enclosed atmosphere and replenish the oxygen supply. They also found that solar panels were unable to generate sufficient energy for their requirements. In addition, there were psychological difficulties between the scientists. After short periods of time they argued and formed factions due to the problem of being confined together, even though Biosphere 2 had an area of 3.15 acres for seven mission crew members. It began on 6 March 1994 and was supposed to last for ten months but ended just 30 days later.

The failure of the project was largely due to problems outside of the biosphere, resulting in two people sabotaging the experiment by opening the doors. Professional rivalries and geographical isolation seem to have generated a sect-like mentality that proved disastrous to the experiment. It became apparent that aside from the artificial ecosystem itself, a special design of person might be required too, if a biosphere were ever to work in true isolation, away from the planet's surface.

# 7 March

## Britain and Iran fight over a book

**1989** This is the day that Great Britain took the drastic step of severing diplomatic relations with Iran. Tensions between the two countries had reached a head following the issuing of a fatwa by the Ayatollah Khomeini, the spiritual supreme leader of Iran, against the British author Salman Rushdie.

A fatwa is an opinion as decreed by an Islamic scholar. It is often wrongly understood to simply be a death warrant and while it can be a holy order of execution, it is not always so. However, the one given by the Ayatollah on 14 February 1989 was such a warrant. It decreed that Rushdie and his publishers were unequivocally 'sentenced to death'. A price had effectively been placed on Rushdie's head in the name of Islam.

Salman Rushdie's crime to provoke this was perhaps a curious one. In 1988, his novel *The Satanic Verses* had been published to critical acclaim. In it, he reworked a traditional Muslim story that there were suras, or verses, within the Qu'ran – the holy book of Islam – that the prophet Mohammed was tempted to deliver by the Devil, but which he later revoked. These are the satanic verses in question. Rushdie countered this, suggesting instead that Mohammed, who is called Mahound in the book, actually received these verses from the Angel Gibreel.

He had not, therefore, spoken vociferously against Islam, or attempted to desecrate any of its sacred tenets. However, by focusing upon the fallibility of the Prophet, he had produced a sacrilegious portrait of Islam's most holy figure after God. This was deemed by the Ayatollah to be an 'insult to the Islamic sanctities'.

All of this was no idle threat. Around the world, in the years that followed, others – particularly translators who worked to further the spread of *The Satanic Verses* – were attacked, injured and even killed. In heavily Muslim countries, rallies were held where copies of the book were burnt.

The United Kingdom was outraged at what it saw as deliberate murderous intent against one of its citizens, and an attack on free speech across the globe. Despite a carefully worded apology by Rushdie, the Ayatollah reiterated the death warrant against him. As a result he was forced into the protection of the British police, under whose careful watch he would have to live for the next nine years. At the same time the British government applied pressure to the Iranian authorities to try to force them to withdraw the threat hanging over the author. When they persistently refused, the British acted swiftly, immediately withdrawing diplomatic contact with the Iranian government.

This state of affairs continued until 1998, when diplomatic relations were tentatively restored amid all kinds of careful provisos from either side. However, the UK's one overriding concern that the fatwa be withdrawn could not be fulfilled – Iran declared that only the one who issued it could remove it, and Ayatollah Khomeini had died in 1989. As a result, the fatwa applies to Salman Rushdie to this day. However, the time when it could be a real threat has passed, and Rushdie has commented wryly that each Valentine's Day he receives a 'sort of Valentine's card' from Iran, reminding him of the ongoing situation.

# 8 March

*The helicopter becomes an orthodox aircraft by receiving its certificate for commercial and civilian use*

**1946** The first 'proper' helicopter was designed and built by Ukrainian–US aviation pioneer Igor Sikorsky (1889–1972). It was named the VS-300 (Vought-Sikorsky 300) and was the first rotary-wing aircraft to have the standard helicopter configuration. That is to say, it had a main horizontal rotor above the cockpit and a smaller vertical rotor at the end of its tail. Its first untethered flight was made in 1940.

During the Second World War a number of helicopters were in development, but they were very much experimental aircraft. The attraction of vertical-takeoff aircraft was their military benefits – potentially able to access difficult terrain where runways were not an option and able to alight on buildings, ships and on water. Having established the basis for a practical helicopter design, Sikorsky continued with his development. The Sikorsky S-47 of 1940 became the first production helicopter, but another aviation company – Bell Helicopter – were the first to corner the commercial and civilian market in 1946.

The Bell-47 was designed by Arthur Young, although its essential shape was stolen directly from Sikorsky, since it was the optimal form. The Bell-47 is the classic helicopter of Hollywood films. It has a bubble-shaped cockpit for good pilot visibility and an exposed tail frame. The Bell-47 proved to be such a good design that it remained in production until 1972, by which time over 5,500 had been made in more than 40 models. Even now the helicopters are flown worldwide and are considered one of the best designs for flight training.

An intrinsic problem with helicopters is, of course, that engine failure almost always results in fatalities because the aircraft have no wings with which to glide. For this reason a great deal of effort has gone into making helicopter engines reliable. The rotor blades can also be put into neutral so that they continue to spin (gyrate), thereby providing at least some lift.

Another design problem with all helicopters is that the lift rotors create counter-spin in the fuselage of the aircraft. This can be overcome with use of either a tail rotor to push against the rotational force, or else a jet of air, which has the same effect. Some helicopters, such as the Chinook, have two lift rotors. They don't require a tail rotor, as the lift rotors gyrate in opposite directions so that counter-spin is neutralised. These giant helicopters can carry enormous loads inside the fuselage, as well as suspending items underneath the body of the helicopter that would otherwise be too large to fit inside. This makes them very useful for applications such as construction and moving warfare equipment.

# 9 March

## An American GI becomes the first person to have a sex change

**1952** It just so happened that George Jorgensen made a very attractive and feminine woman. As a child growing up in the Bronx, New York, he had felt like a misfit among his male friends, shying away from violent games and always happier in his own company. As a young man he joined the army, but soon he became worried about his lack of sexual development and was overwhelmed with the urge to become a woman.

Learning about possible surgical procedures with the help of sympathetic doctors, on his own initiative he began to take female hormones and eventually decided to go to Denmark to have a full sex-change operation. This was illegal in the US at the time, as it would have excused men from doing military service. In Denmark it was legal to castrate sex offenders, and so it was the only country where the procedure was acceptable. Even so, special permission was required from the Danish minister of justice.

As Christine Jorgensen, she became a celebrity in the US following the reassignment surgery. The *New York Daily News* splashed the story under the headline, 'Ex-GI Becomes Blonde Beauty: Operations Transform Bronx Youth', and the press set up a bank of lights outside her parents' home. From then on, as 'the convertible blonde', she gained widespread fame and notoriety and went on to make a good living from the story of her gender change, selling thousands of books and interview records. Cult film director Edward D. Wood, confused about his own sexuality, was inspired by her story to produce his first feature film, *Glen or Glenda?*, in 1953.

Jorgensen is seen as an icon in the transgender community because her celebrity life was devoted to promoting the acceptance of gender change. In later life, she said that she had given the sexual revolution 'a swift kick in the pants'. Her life story, *Christine Jorgensen: A Personal Autobiography*, was published in 1967 and later made into a film, and she also developed a nightclub act based on her experiences.

Pioneering surgeries had actually been developed in the early 20th century in Germany, but Jorgensen was the first to have hormone treatment to grow breasts and reduce body hair in conjunction with the knife work. In fact, Jorgensen only had the male genitalia removed in 1952. Her vaginoplasty was conducted in the US a number of years later, when plastic surgery had advanced sufficiently. One unwelcome complication of the sex-change operation at that time was bladder infections, and this may have contributed to Jorgensen's early death in 1989 from bladder cancer.

# 10 March

*Axis Sally is sentenced to imprisonment for broadcasting Nazi propaganda during the Second World War*

**1949** During the Second World War a few people from the Allies chose to fight for the Axis nations. Mildred Gillars (1900–88) was one of those who turned traitor. She was an American who had dropped out of a drama course at Ohio University and found herself studying music in Dresden, Germany.

Before war broke out, Gillars took a job at Radio Berlin where she subsequently used her oratorical talents to broadcast propaganda. The transmissions were designed to erode the spirits of her fellow Americans fighting in Europe. She used the name 'Midge at the Mike', but the Allies gave her the nickname 'Axis Sally'.

Her most infamous broadcast came on 11 May 1944, prior to the D-Day landings on 6 June. She planted seeds of doubt about the fidelity of girlfriends and wives back home in the US and played popular American songs to make the GIs think of home. Gillars persisted in her propagandist programming until just two days before the Nazis surrendered to Russian forces on 8 May 1945. Gillars then slipped away into the chaos of post-war Europe, thinking that she wouldn't be found. However, she was tracked down and arrested in 1948, and brought back to the US to face charges of treason. The court found her guilty as charged and she duly went to prison. Her sentence lasted for twelve years from 1949 to 1961. She spent the remainder of her life as a teacher in America, where she taught music, French and German.

During the First World War, a Dutch woman named Margaretha Zelle had been executed for spying. She was an exotic dancer with the stage name Mata Hari. The Netherlands had remained neutral during the war, so she had been able to travel freely from one country to another. She wasn't beautiful, but she evidently had a certain charm and became the courtesan of various high-ranking Allied officers. Her days were numbered when a German radio message was deciphered to reveal a code name that was identified as that of Mata Hari. She was tried and found guilty of espionage, for which she was shot by firing squad in 1917. Zelle was held accountable for the deaths of thousands of Allied troops, although it was useful for the Allies to have scapegoats at a point in the war when the futility of so many deaths in the trenches was becoming a serious concern.

# 11 March

## Modern civilisation is 1 million days old

**1986** According to tradition, Rome was founded on 21 April 753 BC. The person who first documented this date was the historian Marcus Terentius Varro (116 BC – 27 BC), who stated that Romulus (c. 771 BC – 717 BC) founded the city, having killed his twin brother Remus (c. 771 BC – 753 BC). The twins are supposed to have been feral children, raised by a she-wolf. Their parents were apparently the god Mars and Rhea Silvia, princess of Alba Longa, Italy, whom he seized in the forest where the twins were subsequently born and abandoned.

It seems likely that Romulus and Remus did exist, despite the mythical tale of their origin. Romulus may or may not have killed his brother, but he is credited with establishing a society that laid the foundation stone for modern civilisations as we know them today. He established a government in Rome and structured the society so that the weak and poor would benefit from the patronage of the strong and wealthy. It was an egalitarian state, based on the notion that all people have something to offer society and should therefore be treated accordingly. Romulus also established an army and cavalry to protect Rome from other peoples living on the Italian peninsula.

In addition, Romulus developed a judiciary system, so that it became illegal to commit crimes such as murder and adultery. He saw that a civilised society needs to have a legal framework in place to ensure that things don't descend into chaos. His system remained essentially intact for 600 years before anyone dared to make any adjustments to it.

His other great achievement was to begin expanding the borders of the new city. He did so by absorbing other peoples into the fledgling Roman Empire, rather than simply annihilating them. That way there was mutual benefit to be had from bringing new territories under the jurisdiction of Rome. It turned out to be an extremely successful approach, which lasted until the Empire eventually outgrew itself and fragmented early in the first millennium AD. Nevertheless, modern civilisation is still largely based on the Roman model.

# 12 March

## *The British Empire Day becomes obsolete and is demoted to British Commonwealth Day instead*

**1958** The British Empire was founded during the great age of discovery and maritime exploration in the 15th century.

The zenith was reached in 1921 when an estimated 458 million people were members of the Empire, whether they liked it or not. That was a quarter of the world's population, occupying a quarter of the habitable landmass – a fact which brought about the worldwide spread of the English language.

It was no exaggeration to say, as many British people proudly did, that the sun never set on the British Empire. As a matter of fact, the sun had already begun to set because a number of indigenous peoples didn't like being a part of the Empire, and things began slowly to fall apart.

The real death knell came during the Second World War. Many Asian territories fell into the hands of the Japanese, who allowed the populations to govern themselves during the war years, albeit under occupation. When the Japanese capitulated in 1945 the British assumed that they could simply return to their territories and pick up where they had left off. However, the mindset of the colonies had changed forever. The British experienced a new hostility and had no choice but to return their imperial possessions by granting them their independence.

So it was that the British Empire collapsed and was replaced with the British Commonwealth instead. Now called the Commonwealth of Nations, it is an association of countries with voluntary membership, so that they might benefit from mutual trade and cultural links. There are currently 53 nations included, all of which were former components of the defunct British Empire.

Empire Day itself began after the death in 1901 of Queen Victoria, and commemorated the assistance given to Britain by its colonies during the Boer War. It was originally observed on 24 May, which had been Queen Victoria's birthday. In the early years, it was celebrated across both Britain and the Empire, but following the collapse of the Empire enthusiasm for the day understandably waned.

The name change in 1958 merely reflected the reality of the new, post-colonial relationship between the countries that had once constituted the British Empire. In 1976, the date of British Commonwealth Day was changed to the second Monday in March, a date chosen precisely because it had no pre-existing historical or political connotations.

Today Commonwealth Day is not marked in a uniform way across the Commonwealth. In the UK, however, the union flag is flown on public buildings, and the Queen delivers her Commonwealth Day message which is broadcast throughout the world. A multi-faith service is held on the day in Westminster Abbey, which is usually attended by the Queen in her capacity as Head of the Commonwealth, along with the Commonwealth Secretary-General and High Commissioners.

# 13 March

*These are many steps for three humans, one evolutionary leap forward for mankind*

**2003** It was reported that palaeoarchaeologists had stumbled across the 350,000-year-old footprints of three early humans in Italy. The tracks were formed in volcanic ash as the three individuals scrambled down the side of an active volcano. The ash was quite thick, so the impressions were deep. It is likely that rainfall then caused the ash to adhere together and chemically set firm before it was covered with subsequent layers of ash, thereby preserving the prints. In fact, there were hand prints too, as the people had made a difficult descent and needed to use their arms to steady themselves.

The tracks were discovered in a part of southern Italy called the Roccamonfina volcanic complex. The pyroclastic flow (volcanic ash, lava and pumice) is dated at 325,000–385,000 years old. This means that the people were not modern humans (*Homo sapiens*) but forebears to our species, probably *Homo heidelbergensis* or *Homo neanderthalensis*. Fossilised human footprints are very rare finds and very exciting because they offer a unique glimpse of our ancestors. Fossilised bones, tools and artefacts don't seem to make quite the same kind of connection with anthropologists.

Other examples of human footprints exist along the north-eastern coast of England. They were made perhaps only 10,000–20,000 years ago and were therefore left by modern humans. Many tracks have been found when the tide wanes, showing the movements of men, women and children. Some have even been interpreted as those of pregnant women and adults carrying infants, due to the way in which the additional weight caused their feet to impress the sand in a particular way.

The oldest footprints found so far are those known as the Laetoli footsteps in Tanzania, Africa. They are an incredible 3.75 million years old and belonged to a species named *Australopithecus afarensis*. This was an ape-like creature belonging to a genus that eventually gave rise to the *Homo* lineage. This time there were two sets of tracks, demonstrating that the creatures were bipedal and that their feet had already evolved with the hallux (big toe) and arch as seen in humans.

Today humans regularly suffer from back problems even though we have been bipedal for millions of years. Evolution has done its best to perfect our upright design because having our arms free has proven to be such an advantage, but our spine will always be subject to forces for which the blueprint was not designed to cope.

# 14 March

*The space probe* Giotto *travels so close to Halley's comet that it is able to take pictures of the nucleus itself*

**1986** *Giotto* was a probe designed by the European Space Agency and launched in 1985. In March 1986 it managed to get within 376 miles (596 km) of Halley's comet, an incredible feat given the astronomical distances involved – at its closest, the comet was still about 30 million miles (48 million km) from Earth. The comet would not pass this close to Earth again until 2061, so the timing was crucial.

The aim of the project was for *Giotto* to investigate the make-up of the comet by passing through its tail and analysing the particles it emitted. This was of course a hazardous undertaking, and indeed the probe was struck and damaged by dust particles travelling at enormous speeds. One strike sent it gyrating so that it had to correct itself to keep its antenna pointing towards Earth. A second strike destroyed its camera, but luckily this occurred after the probe had already transmitted more than 2,000 valuable images of the comet at close quarters. These included the first-ever pictures taken of a comet's nucleus.

The nucleus turned out to be relatively small (about 15 km long by 8 km wide and 8 km thick), and the comet was revealed to be an irregular mass of minerals and ice. It also possessed organic compounds, suggesting that these building blocks for life were present soon after the beginning of the universe and that they are therefore distributed throughout the cosmos. This has lent weight to the theory of *lithopanspermia*: the idea that life on Earth (and perhaps other planets) could have been started by the impact of a comet or meteorite which spewed out organic particles. Halley's comet ejected huge numbers of such particles during *Giotto's* observations.

The comet was named in honour of the astronomer Edmond Halley (1656–1742), who correctly predicted that it would return every 75 to 76 years. The probe itself was named after the Italian

Renaissance artist Giotto di Bondone (1267–1337), who observed the comet in 1301 and featured it in his painting 'Adoration of the Magi' as a great golden fireball with a long streaking tail, representing the star of Bethlehem. (It also appears in stylised form in the Bayeux tapestry of the late 11th century, commemorating its appearance in the year 1066. It was seen then as a bad omen, one that was soon fulfilled by the Battle of Hastings and the death of King Harold of England.)

After hibernating in space for several years, in 1992 *Giotto* made a fly-by of the lesser-known comet Grigg-Skjellerup. This time it got within 125 miles (200 km), making it the first probe to investigate two separate comets, though unfortunately the camera was still unable to function after the damage caused six years earlier.

# *15 March*

## *The edge of the solar system is discovered*

**2004** Solar systems extend away from their stars in all directions until objects are no longer influenced by their gravitational pull. In other words, until the gravitational pull of another star takes over. It means that the solar systems of the galaxy essentially fit together in three-dimensional space, rather like the seeds of a pomegranate. However, orbiting objects in solar systems inhabit spherical domains, which means that there are neutral spaces here and there, where the gravitation reaches equilibrium and is too weak to exert a significant influence. This is deep space, or outer space.

Sedna (90377 Sedna) is a dwarf planet that sits on the outermost perimeter of our solar system. It has a very elliptical and eccentric orbit, suggesting that it once belonged to another solar system and was caught by the gravitational pull of the sun. It is a spherical moon-like body with a diameter of about 1,500 km (800 miles). It is so distant from the sun that its temperature is incredibly cold: 33°Kelvin, which is –240°C or –400°F. Absolute zero, 0°K, is the point where there is a complete absence of energy, so that atoms and molecules come to a standstill.

The distance of Sedna from the sun is 76–975 AU, an astronomical unit being the distance from the Earth to the sun – about 150 million km (93 million miles). A Sedna year lasts for a very long time indeed. In Earth terms it lasts for 4.4 million days, or 12,059 years.

At the time of its discovery it was the farthest object in the solar system from the sun. Since then other, more distant objects have been identified. They sit in an outer boundary known as the Oort cloud, named after Dutch astronomer Jan Hendrik Oort (1900–92) who proposed an outer shell as the source for new comets in 1950.

Realising the sheer scale of the solar system alone makes one begin to grasp the size of the universe. Our galaxy – the Milky Way – contains millions of stars, each with their own solar system, and there are millions of galaxies comprising the universe, with vast spaces in between.

With this in mind, three things become apparent. First, that with so many planets out there it is very likely that other life forms exist somewhere else in the universe. Second, that those life forms are going to be an extremely long way away. So far away, in fact, that we might as well forget about ideas of close encounters. Third, even supposing that those life forms happen to have evolved into sentient beings, they will still be subject to the same constraints of physics as we are and remain trapped within their own solar systems.

To all intents and purposes our solar system *is* our universe and it seems a fair bet that humanity will never leave. Even supposing that civilisation lasts long enough for our technology to allow long-haul space missions, there would always be a big question mark over any incentive to leave, as it would be unlikely that explorers could ever return within their own lifetimes, and they would probably find nothing apart from more lifeless planets in the next solar system. Then again, perhaps living on Earth will one day become so undesirable that people consider it worth a shot.

# 16 March

*Saddam Hussein commits the atrocity that will eventually see him tried and hanged for crimes against humanity*

**1988** The plight of the Kurds is a story that goes back millennia. They were first recorded in history in c. 400 BC as a tribe of mountain-dwelling people who would fiercely defend their territory in the face of conquest. The area inhabited by the Kurds is often referred to as Kurdistan, but it has never been a politically recognised state. It straddles parts of Iran, Iraq, Syria and Turkey, none of whom wish to cede territory for the Kurds to have their own country. Consequently there is a history of the four countries having treated the Kurds as second-class citizens, tolerating their presence but otherwise marginalising them.

In truth, much of the Middle East region is populated by tribes of one creed or another. This means that governments have to either embrace this fact by having parliaments that include representatives from each population, or to control by oppression and intimidation. Saddam Hussein's Iraq was a dictatorship. This meant that members of his own people – Sunni Muslims – were in charge. The majority of the population were Shi'ite Muslims, but they had to kowtow to Sunni rule. All other minority groups, such as the Kurds and Marsh Arabs, were even lower down the pecking order.

During the Iran–Iraq War (1980–88), Saddam Hussein saw his opportunity to deal the Kurds a vicious blow in the name of war. The Kurdish town of Halabja was occupied by Iranian forces, so Hussein delivered a chemical attack from the sky. Mig and Mirage jets dropped large quantities of the lethal substances tabun, sarin, VX and mustard gas.

The chemical attack killed or lethally wounded a total of 12,000 Iranian soldiers and Kurdish civilians. It demonstrated clearly that Hussein did not regard the Kurds as fellow Iraqis. In fact he had already attacked many Kurdish villages in 1987 simply to suppress Kurdish uprisings against his rule. During his trial in 2006 the Halabja massacre was used as a key component in his prosecution for crimes against humanity.

Saddam Hussein was eventually convicted and sentenced to execution; he was hanged on 30 December 2006.

# *17 March*

## *A vaccine for chickenpox proves to be a contentious issue when it is approved by the US government*

**1995** In March 1995, the US Food and Drug Administration approved a vaccine for the prevention of chickenpox, one of the most contagious of all childhood diseases. But the approval was mired in controversy.

Vaccines are a long-proven method of preventing the spread of disease. By exposing you to dead or harmless versions of disease-causing germs, they prime your body's immune system to fight future attacks by generating antibodies. Many once-prevalent diseases such as diphtheria, polio, measles and whooping cough are now rare thanks to mass vaccination or immunisation. Small-pox, for instance, although once widespread, has been eradicated.

With diseases that are so often fatal, like smallpox, most people agree that the benefits of immunisation far outweigh any possible disadvantages. Moreover, mass immunisation programmes vastly reduce the number of host bodies that the disease can spread through, and so indirectly help protect even those who haven't been vaccinated.

The ideological problem that many people had with the vaccine against chickenpox, marketed by Mercx under the name Varivax, was that it is not a major killer disease. Before the introduction of the vaccine it was certainly widespread, affecting some 4 million in the USA every year, but only about 100 died as a result of infection. About 90 per cent of the sufferers were children under the age of 15. Yet although it causes suffering and discomfort with its itchy, disfiguring spots, its effects are mild compared with those of diseases like diphtheria and polio. Almost all victims recovered after a short illness.

Opponents of the vaccine argued that it was wrong to vaccinate against what was considered a minor childhood illness, especially since catching the disease in childhood may help reduce the chances of developing shingles later in life. In the end, though, the vaccine was introduced, and proved to be highly effective. Over the next decade, the number of cases of chickenpox in the USA dropped by 85 per cent, as did the number of fatalities. Moreover, the number of hospitalisations for the disease has dropped so dramatically that this alone more than pays for the cost of vaccination.

There are worries about how long the vaccine is effective for, and booster jabs are now being added after a couple of years to top it up and perhaps reduce the chances of getting shingles later in life. On the whole, though, the controversy over the vaccine has quietened down in the face of its clearly demonstrable effectiveness.

The subject of childhood vaccines continues to inflame debate, however, with some campaigners arguing vociferously about the problems of injecting healthy children with germs. Some people, for instance, were all too ready to leap on the now-discredited findings of Dr Andrew Wakefield that the MMR (Measles, Mumps and Rubella) vaccine can trigger autism. Wakefield is now facing charges of serious professional misconduct, but the rumours about MMR led to a significant downturn in the number of parents allowing their children to be vaccinated – a downturn which has led to a recent rise in the number of children becoming ill from measles.

# 18 March

### A cosmonaut, and not an astronaut, becomes the first person to conduct a 'space walk'

**1965** Running up to the big prize – getting a man on the Moon – the Americans and Soviets were neck and neck in the space race. Every time one party got the upper hand, the other would outdo them. On this occasion the Soviets put a first into the record books.

Alexey Leonov (b. 1934) was the cosmonaut who first set foot outside of a spacecraft while in orbit. He left the orbiter, *Voskhod 2*, for twelve minutes. He was attached to a tether to prevent him from floating off into space, but things nearly ended in disaster anyway. The vacuum of space caused his spacesuit to inflate with the pressure of the air inside it. Consequently he was rendered unable to re-enter the portal from which he had left the orbiter. Leonov had to open a valve to deflate his suit, by allowing air to escape into space. He then squeezed back inside the vehicle.

In preparation for his space walk, Leonov had made many zero-gravity flights. These were achieved by flying an aircraft along a special parabolic line so that the trajectory of the objects inside continued upwards while the aircraft fell, thereby simulating a weightless environment. As the story goes, Leonov was selected to become the first man on the Moon, but the Americans got there first, prompting the Soviets to axe their lunar plans. He was, though, to become the commander of the first Soviet crew to meet up with a US crew in space – the *Apollo–Soyuz* test project in 1975.

Today, people can pay to go on zero-gravity flights in specially fitted aircraft. They fly upwards at a steep trajectory and then dive below the parabolic curve that the aircraft would normally follow if it were left to its own devices. This means that things inside the aircraft continue to follow the natural curve while the plane plummets downwards, thereby appearing to become weightless within the aircraft. The effect can be achieved for 30 seconds or so.

The space footage of the movie *Apollo 13* was filmed by using just such an aircraft over hundreds of flights. In effect the actors were falling during each take, but at a slightly slower rate than the aircraft.

# 19 March

## Bob Dylan releases his first LP

**1962** Until Bob Dylan appeared on the music scene, chart music had followed a tried-and-tested formula. Songs were generally about falling in and out of love, or other aspects of human relationships. Dylan's songs were markedly different, because he wrote about subject matter he was personally interested in. He used the medium as a conduit for self-expression in a way that captured the imagination. Some people interpreted his songs as comments on society and the human condition, but really he was observing more than analysing. He inadvertently became an iconic voice against war and human rights abuses, as his compositions became adopted as protest songs.

More significantly, he had a direct influence of the songwriting of others, including Lennon and McCartney of The Beatles, and Jagger and Richards of the Rolling Stones. It can be said that Dylan was the catalyst for the movement of rapid experimentation that characterised the 1960s. He opened the floodgates for bands to try deal with less mainstream themes and stretch their creative abilities. If one thinks about the effect on The Beatles in particular it is remarkable, for they went from 'Please Please Me' in 1963, to 'A Day In The Life' in 1967. Four years had seen them transformed as a result of Dylan's influence.

There is always a great deal of interest when Dylan himself releases a new album of songs. This is not least because he drifts in and out of form. That isn't to say that he ever produces a bad album, but that every now and then he comes up with a particularly good one.

Of his many albums, *Blood On The Tracks* (1975) is often

regarded as his career best. As the title suggests, the songs are all about personal turmoil, yet they fit together perfectly and take the listener on a familiar journey of relationship breakdown and personal recuperation.

Dylan himself has expressed surprise at the popularity of the album, written as an expression of his pain at getting divorced. That in itself shows that he doesn't write his material with a view to cultivating commercial success, which is probably why he has been so enduring – ironically.

# 20 March

## A record-breaking blue whale is harpooned in the South Atlantic Ocean

**1947** Blue whales are the largest species of any animal that has ever lived. This specimen was the largest animal ever recorded. It weighed in at an incredible 190 metric tonnes. A metric tonne is 1,000 kg. If an average person weighs 180 lbs (82 kg), then the whale weighed as much as 2,317 people. It was also 30 metres (98.5 feet) long, but the statistics seem rather irrelevant given that the whale was slaughtered by whalers, so that it was no longer the largest living animal when it was being weighed and measured.

Whaling was an important industry throughout the 19th century. Whale products were widely used – as well as meat for human and animal consumption, the whales were processed to produce whale oils, fats and waxes, which were used for lighting, as lubricants and in chemical concoctions used as cosmetics, and so on. Even the bones were used in corsets.

However, all of these were superseded by new products derived from petroleum. The whaling industry itself was rendered obsolete, as hunting and processing were no longer economically viable.

This led to a shift in public opinion about continued whaling. As most nations didn't care much for eating whale flesh, people became more compassionate towards the animals, regarding their ongoing slaughter as an unnecessary and cruel activity. This view was reinforced by conservationists, who reported that whale populations had been depleted almost to extinction levels.

In modern times, only four populations still hunt whales. The first group are the Inuit and other indigenous Arctic tribes, who regard whale hunting as a part of their traditional way of life that goes back thousands of years. The other three are the Norwegians, the Icelanders and the Japanese. These countries also view whaling as part of their national traditions, and have markets for whale meat to satisfy.

However, while the Norwegians and Icelanders are open and honest about their motives, the Japanese insist that their whaling exercises are primarily for research and conservation purposes. Whale meat that ends up in restaurants is simply the by-product of carcasses that no longer have any scientific use. This position has drawn a great deal of criticism, particularly from environmental charities who believe that there are more constructive, non-lethal ways of studying the animals and protecting their habitats.

At the forefront of this argument are Greenpeace and the Sea Shepherd Conservation Society, who both vociferously oppose the Japanese stance. This has led to some increasingly aggressive confrontations over the years. In January 2008, Sea Shepherd members from their boat, the *MV Steve Irwin*, boarded the Japanese whaling ship *Yushin Maru No. 2*. The two men were arrested by the Japanese crew and delivered to Australian custody where, perhaps as a symbolic gesture of the opinions the rest of the world holds in regards to Japan's whaling activities, they were released without criminal charge.

# 21 March

*After only 29 years of service, the infamous island prison of Alcatraz is closed down*

**1963** Alcatraz Island actually became a prison in 1906 following the San Francisco earthquake, because the mainland prisons had been damaged. By 1912, a purpose-built jail had been constructed to hold 300 inmates. Until 1934 it was run by the military, but prohibitive running costs meant that its administration was handed over to the Department of Justice. It then cultivated a reputation as the most secure penitentiary in the US.

The only supposedly successful escape was made in 1962. Three inmates fabricated *papier mâché* mannequins of themselves to lie in their beds while they escaped via a service duct, having spent two years hewing holes in their cell walls. The official record stated that they had drowned in San Francisco Bay, as they were never heard of again. It is possible, however, that they forged new lives for themselves in South America. In 1979 the film *Escape from Alcatraz* was released, starring Clint Eastwood. It is a faithful re-enactment of the events leading up to the escape.

Apparently the escapees took two years in preparing their bid for freedom. Their secret for success was to stick to prison routine and continue with their plans only when time and opportunity came along. Patience was most definitely a virtue, as it meant that progress was slow and unnoticeable with each passing week.

As well as offering the prospect of freedom, making escape plans also provides prisoners with something to occupy themselves. It is well documented that POWs during the Second World War often formed escape committees to decide on different ways of escaping. Elaborate plans were hatched, which gave the men a sense of camaraderie and purpose during the long months of incarceration. It needs to be remembered too that they had no idea of the eventual outcome of the war, so this spurred them on time and time again even though they were often recaptured and punished for their efforts.

One of the most famous wartime prisons was that of Colditz Castle, Germany, which was used to house captured Allied officers. It was officially called Oflag IV-C and was controlled by the German defence force, the *Wehrmacht*. As most of the officers were habitual escapees, Colditz was seen as an escape challenge and all manner of methods were attempted, often successfully. There was even a glider built in the attic. The plan was to remove a section of the roof and glide away, but the war ended before the attempt could be made.

# 22 March

## The laser is invented

**1960** The important thing about lasers is that they produce coherent light. That means that the light rays are exactly parallel to one another, so that they don't diffuse when they leave the light source. It may not sound like much, but it gives laser beams certain qualities that normal light lacks. The term 'laser' is an acronym taken from 'Light Amplification by Stimulated Emission of Radiation'.

High-energy lasers can be used for drilling and cutting materials by burning or vaporising them, which is why lasers became the weapons of choice in futuristic films of the period. It was even suggested that laser guns might be used to arm satellites during the Cold War. Modern-day practical applications for high-energy lasers include their use in surgery for burning away or cutting tissue, and for lancing wounds.

Low-energy lasers are ubiquitous today as well. They are used to read CDs and DVDs, for example, as well as barcodes in shops. Hi-tech television screens and similar display devices also employ them, as do hologram production techniques and instruments for measuring distances and levels. Their inclusion in modern technology is largely due to the fact that laser devices can now be made extremely small-scale – there are diode lasers and nanolasers, able to pulse highly accurate digital information, in laser printers.

One interesting use of high-energy lasers has been as an energy source for experimental rockets. The ground-mounted laser causes air molecules to explode within a cone at the base of the rocket, thereby pushing it forwards at high speed. The only problem is that the rocket needs to stay in line with the laser beam, and the beam needs to remain uninterrupted, otherwise all forward propulsion will be lost.

The laser was developed at Bell Laboratories, USA, by Charles Hard Townes (b. 1915) who won the Nobel Prize for Physics in 1964 and Arthur Schawlow (1921–99) who won his in 1981. The term 'maser' (Microwave or Molecular Amplification by Stimulated Emission of Radiation) is used collectively in describing lasers and similar devices that produce other forms of coherent electromagnetic radiation, of which visible light is just one.

# 23 March

*Scientists claim to have achieved cold fusion, the solution to the world's energy needs that quantum mechanics denies is possible*

**1989** Cold fusion is a phenomenon that goes against established rules of physics, but some scientists are convinced that it is possible. The idea is that a controlled nuclear reaction can be conducted in 'normal' conditions. That is to say, at one atmosphere of air pressure and at room temperature.

The significance of this is that cold fusion might be used as a universal and ubiquitous energy source, rather than having to carry energy away from power stations. An experiment called the Fleischmann–Pons experiment apparently demonstrated cold fusion in action for the first time. However, since then the experiment has been discredited.

The reason for this is that no other scientists have been able to repeat the experiment with success. There is therefore no empirical proof that it works. In addition, other scientists suggest that there are a number of other factors that need to be accounted for in proving that Martin Fleischmann and Stanley Pons did indeed measure energy levels from a cold fusion reaction. The trouble is that the two scientists used such small amounts of reactive material – for reasons of safety – that the measurements were extremely small. They could therefore have arisen from associated chemical reactions, from leakage of external energy or simply from wishful thinking.

Quite apart from anything else, there were no discernible traces of radioactive fusion by-products, and the laws of quantum mechanics deny the very possibility of cold fusion. Without getting too technical, it has to do with getting the nuclei of atoms close enough together so that the attractive nuclear force is overcome by the electrostatic force. It is known as the Coulomb barrier.

This is what occurs in hot fusion, in nuclear power stations, but it is very dangerous and the reaction needs to be regulated to prevent nuclear explosions. In addition the fuel and by-products are highly radioactive. Experiments into cold fusion or 'low-energy nuclear reactions' have involved the transitional elements palladium and deuterium (heavy hydrogen).

On a philosophical level, cold fusion is an interesting cultural phenomenon. It has become something of holy grail among scientists, because it represents untold wealth and fame, as well as offering a sustainable, inexpensive, non-polluting and theoretically safe energy source for the future. No wonder then that scientists begin to convince themselves of its existence. It is similar to the pursuit of perpetual motion in centuries past, where scientists ignored the laws of thermodynamics in their obsession with designing machines that kept themselves going indefinitely, by utilising the force of gravity alone.

# 24 March

## The quadricentenary of the death of England's greatest monarch, Queen Elizabeth I

**2003** A number of factors lent themselves to the legacy of Elizabeth I (1533–1603). First and foremost was timing. She became monarch at the point in history when England was entering its High Renaissance, and she reigned for 44 years, during which period she oversaw much of the transformation of her country into a world power.

Elizabeth was also the 'virgin queen'. She did not marry or bear children, which, while perhaps unfortunate on a personal level, meant that she devoted her energies to matters of the state. She gave politicians, explorers, scientists and creative minds her undivided attention, allowing them the freedom to nurture their ambitions by way of keeping her fed with intellectual nourishment.

Finally, Elizabeth demonstrated considerable skill as a warlord. She masterminded the defeat of the Spanish Armada in 1588, which brought a time of relative peace and prosperity to her island nation. Consequently her reign is often referred to as the Elizabethan era, due to its significance in history.

English contemporaries of Elizabeth I included Francis Drake, Walter Raleigh, Francis Bacon, John Gerard and William Shakespeare, to name but a few. On the European continent there were the likes of Galileo, Paracelsus, Mercator, Fallopius and Eustachio, all pushing forwards the boundaries of knowledge about the world and how it worked. It was also a time when Europe opened its arms to embrace new materials, technologies and foods from distant lands, and when emigration to establish trade colonies was a burgeoning industry.

Although the British Empire no longer exists, it is remarkable to think that the UK is still one of the most powerful, influential and wealthy of the world's nations given its diminutive size. That is the true legacy of the achievements of Elizabeth I, because England became a liberal and progressive nation under her leadership and that general ethos remains intact four centuries later.

Elizabeth's father, Henry VIII, had separated himself and England from the Catholic Church and this lent itself to the burgeoning success of the nation. Whereas continental scientists, such as Galileo, were given a hard time by the Catholic Church for their new ways of thinking, British scientists had nothing to fear and new technologies moved on apace. Elizabeth took what her father had started and ran with it.

# 25 March

## Bicentenary of the abolition of the slave trade in Britain

**2007** The slave trade was initiated as a means of acquiring free labour in the Caribbean colonies and southern states of the USA – the New World. It began in the 15th century when explorers and adventurers first discovered new lands and established trade links. A triangular trade route was established so that ships embarking from England were always carrying a cargo of one sort or another from place to place.

The first leg of the journey was to sail around the Iberian Peninsula and down to the coast of West Africa. Once there, the crew would trade textiles, rum, ironware and other products for slaves, who had been captured by Arab slavers. The slaves would then be shipped across the Atlantic Ocean and auctioned off to plantation owners. The funds raised were used to purchase plantation commodities such as sugar, tobacco and cotton, which were duly brought back to Blighty.

The returning cargo was worth a great deal more than the outgoing, so a considerable profit margin was realised. Many people consequently grew very rich from the slave trade. In this case the love of money truly was the root of all evil, as thousands of Africans went into slavery with little or no consideration for their human rights. Their treatment and conditions of transport were like those of animals, and many died en route. The rest would never see their families again, and lived in abject poverty with the ever-present threat of severe punishment if they failed to do the work required of them.

Thankfully, as England grew civilised from its ill-gotten gains, it also produced civilised people, who began to question the moral and ethical basis for slavery. That is what eventually led to its abolition. The philanthropist William Wilberforce (1759–1833) headed a parliamentary campaign against slavery. The Slave Trade Act was passed in 1807 to make further trade in slaves illegal. Then in the year of his death came the Slavery Abolition Act, which gave slaves their manumission within the British Empire.

One city that benefited greatly from the wealth generated by slavery was Bristol, England. Being in the south-west corner of Britain, it was well placed to form a corner of the slavery triangle. Paraphernalia of slavery, such as iron shackles and chains, still exist in the cellars and basements of houses once owned by merchants who dealt in human cargoes and sometimes brought slaves back to Britain. Bristol now has a large community of African descent, many of whom originate from slave populations in the West Indies and other Caribbean islands.

# 26 March

*A vaccine is developed for polio, or poliomyelitis as it is properly known*

**1953** Poliomyelitis is also called infantile paralysis due to the devastating effect that it can have on the bodies of young children, leaving them maimed for life following the illness. It is a highly contagious viral infection and is characteristic of overcrowded and squalid conditions, where poor sanitation and malnutrition exist.

The virus is excreted from the body in faeces, and is easily transmitted inadvertently on the hands or in food et cetera. In the appropriate setting, whole populations can contract the disease, especially when conditions are warm and humid, enabling the virus to survive longer outside the body.

Thanks to the work of Dr Jonas Salk (1914–95), the poliovirus had been largely eradicated in industrialised nations by the early 1960s, but it was still rife in developing countries. However, an international effort was launched in 1988 which saw a 99 per cent fall in the number of polio cases by 2006. Of all the world's nations there are now only four where polio is considered endemic. In alphabetical order they are Afghanistan, India, Nigeria and Pakistan.

In the US the campaign against polio was synonymous with a charity named the March of Dimes during the first half of the 20th century. Polio was a greatly feared illness and the slogan helped to raise the funds, dime by dime, to pay for its eradication.

It is hoped that total elimination of polio can eventually be achieved. So far, smallpox is the only disease to have been entirely removed, although it does still exist in high-security laboratories for scientific reasons. Polio shows no symptoms in some 90 per cent of humans and it is vital that all children in a population are vaccinated, so that people don't act as carriers of the virus. The theory behind eradication is that the virus ultimately runs out of places to hide and is forced into extinction. With more than 6 billion people in the world and thousands of babies being born every day it is certainly a tall order, as it only takes one person to cause an epidemic in a population with no immunity. In Western nations the occurrence of polio has become infrequent, largely because schoolchildren are routinely vaccinated, even in places where polio might be considered something from the past.

# 27 March

### The world celebrates the centenary of the first international wireless communication

**1999** Before 1899 electronic communication, such as telephone calls and telegrams, had to be conveyed along cables. This was not such a problem nationally, or between countries bordering one another, as wires could be hung on poles or buried beneath the ground. When it came to crossing bodies of water, however, things got difficult and expensive. Submarine cables had to be laid along the seabed using special ships.

Guglielmo Marconi (1874–1937) changed international communications forever by inventing devices that could emit and receive radio signals. This meant that cables were no longer necessary as radio signals are a form of electromagnetic radiation, just like light waves, so they travel freely from one location to another.

Furthermore, they stay within the magnetic field of the globe, so that they bend around the earth's curvature.

This made possible communications between nations on opposite sides of the world. The very first radio communication was made between England and France over a distance of 32 miles (51 km), but soon messages were being sent between Europe and America or between ships out to sea.

Over the course of the 20th century, radio communication technologies advanced rapidly. The first devices were cumbersome because their components were large, but electronics gradually grew smaller and more compact. For example, the glass valve was replaced by the transistor, and the circuit board was introduced. It meant that portable devices could be designed, and over time they too diminished in size.

Today we have mobile or cell phones, palmtop computers, multimedia devices and other microelectronic radio communication devices. In addition we have a network of satellites for relaying radio signals around the world with great efficiency and reliability.

Radio waves are part of the electromagnetic radiation spectrum, which includes light waves, television signals, infrared, ultraviolet and microwaves. The different forms of electromagnetic radiation have varying frequencies or wavelengths. The same is true of different radio signals, which are often known as bands. Short-wave radio signals have waves of a few metres' length, while long-wave radio signals have waves that are thousands of metres long. Short-wave signals have limited range because their energy is exhausted quickly, so that the same bands can be used in different regional locations without interference. Long-wave signals have a much longer reach and are useful for communicating over large distances. An example of this is the BBC's World Service, which can be detected in continental Europe, while other British radio signals cannot.

# *28 March*

*A radiation leak at Three Mile Island wakes the world
up to the potential threat of nuclear power stations*

**1979** There had already been a radiation leakage at Calder Hall in England in the late 1950s when a fire broke out, but that was largely covered up by the administration at the time. Three Mile Island, in the US, was the scene of the first partial core meltdown. Things were brought under control, eventually, and no lives were lost – but the incident was a shot across the bows and came only seven years before the Chernobyl disaster in Ukraine.

Nuclear power stations are, in essence, places where controlled nuclear explosions occur. The energy produced is used to heat water, which drives steam turbines to generate electricity. Achieving a safe balance in the reactor core is not an easy operation. Too little reaction and insufficient energy is produced, too much reaction and energy is produced at a rate too high to deal with. The result is a core that overheats, so that components begin to melt and burn. The worst case scenario is a non-nuclear explosion, whereby radioactive material is sent into the air, leading to widespread contamination.

One of the most contentious issues about nuclear power is what to do with the waste products, which remain radioactive for thousands of years. Technologies have advanced to such an extent that a good deal of it can now be recycled, but there are still many tons of waste that need disposing of. The most logical thing to do is dump the waste in very deep holes in the ground, or alternatively in oceanic trenches. There is still some potential risk of environmental contamination though, as hydrology and tectonic movements may disturb the nuclear material and result in its escape.

One way of stabilising the radioactive waste has been the process of vitrification, which essentially involves embedding the waste into glass, so that it cannot escape even when fractured. The vitrified waste is then welded into steel drums and stored in subterranean vaults, where it can decay over thousands of years without causing contamination.

A far greater risk to the environment actually exists in the vast quantities of usable radioactive material which are stored in nuclear depots. Since the 1950s, many tons of fissile material have been stockpiled for use in nuclear reactors and nuclear weapons. In fact the material is being produced far more quickly than it is being used, which is why governments are pushing forward the idea of more nuclear power stations as a clean and sustainable alternative to fossil fuels. People currently use more electrical energy than solar, wind and water powered generators could ever produce, even if we all had our own domestic devices, so nuclear power may well be the most sensible way to go.

# 29 March

## Mariner 10 *reaches Mercury, the planet nearest the sun, and sends back pictures*

**1974** Most space probes travel away from the sun to explore the far reaches of the solar system, but the unmanned *Mariner 10* was sent to have a look at the two inner planets, Venus and Mercury. It was launched in November 1973 and flew by Venus on 5 February 1974.

*Mariner 10* was particularly notable for achieving a number of 'firsts' in space exploration. It was the first spacecraft to visit Mercury, to successfully observe two planets, and to use the gravitational field of one planet to reach another in a 'gravitational slingshot' manoeuvre. In addition, it was the first space probe to use radiation pressure as a means of propulsion during flight, or at least the first to do so intentionally.

Venus has a dense atmosphere comprising 95 per cent carbon dioxide, making it appear uniform and whitish in visible light. *Mariner 10* had a camera equipped with an ultraviolet filter, which revealed a more turbulent patterning of clouds from a distance of 3,584 miles (5,768 km).

*Mariner 10* went on to pass Mercury a total of three times. The first flyby was achieved by using Venus to 'slingshot' the space probe; with the help of orbital mechanics calculations carried out by the Italian scientist, mathematician and engineer Giuseppe Colombo (1920–84), the mission was able to take advantage of the gravitational pull of Venus to bring the space probe's orbit close to Mercury several times, allowing it to take the first close-up images of Mercury's surface.

The spacecraft sailed past Mercury at a distance of 437 miles (703 km) on 29 March 1974. It then orbited the sun and made a more distant traverse of Mercury on 21 September of the same year. Finally, on 16 March 1975, it came closer than ever: within 203 miles (327 km).

Needless to say, *Mariner 10* transmitted many photographic images of the planet each time it visited, and the images yielded by this innovative mission were unprecedented in the level of detail that they showed.

The mission ended on 24 March 1975 when, on its final orbit of the sun, the probe made an unprogrammed turn, which signalled to mission control that its nitrogen supply had run out. Its transmitter was turned off, and the radio signals that it had been sending to Earth ceased. It still orbits the sun today, although its onboard electronic equipment has almost certainly been damaged by the burning effect of the sun's radiation.

# *30 March*

## *Albert Einstein announces his Revised Unified Field Theory*

**1953** In the closing years of his life, Albert Einstein (1879–1955) became preoccupied with a theory that unified the Theory of Relativity with the phenomenon of electromagnetism. In other words, he wished to show that everything in the universe is related and so governed by the same laws of physics.

There are four known fundamental forces: strong nuclear force, which holds the nuclei of atoms together; electromagnetic force, which acts on electrically charged particles; weak nuclear force, which causes radioactive decay; and gravitational force, which attracts all particles with mass. Einstein had already shown that electricity and magnetism were unified as electromagnetism, due to the phenomenon of the space–time continuum. He now wanted to unify electromagnetism with the other fundamental forces.

Einstein's idea in achieving this was to propose the notion of a fourth spatial dimension, beyond the comprehension of the human senses. However, he failed in his quest to prove his ideas mathematically.

Following his death, quantum theory took precedence over unifying theory. Quantum theory involves the relationships of subatomic particles, which are known as quantum mechanics.

As yet no one has come up with a Grand Unification Theory that can merge relativity and quantum theory together, showing how the four fundamental forces can be derived from a single origin.

The interesting thing about physics is that the extent to which explanatory theories work is a matter of scale. Isaac Newton's work on gravity and light still applies in the everyday world, because it is sufficiently accurate for that purpose. Similarly, Einstein's work on relativity still applies to astronomy and cosmology, and quantum mechanics goes a long way towards explaining how things work on a subatomic scale.

One problem that scientists have encountered is that subatomic particles behave in ways that cannot be understood by conventional means. For example, scientists try to visualise models of atoms, so that they look something like miniature solar systems. In reality they are not like solar systems at all, because subatomic particles are not physical entities but bundles of energy which can behave in ways that defy logical human thought: they can be in two places at once, for example. Things get even weirder too when atoms are super-cooled. In an absence of environmental energy, subatomic particles leak their own energy and behave in very peculiar ways indeed.

# 31 March

## *The Dalai Lama finds sanctuary in India*

**1959** The Chinese made Tibet into the Tibetan Autonomous Region within the Chinese People's Republic in 1951. The Tibetans, however, wanted their own independent country, and demonstrations against the Chinese administration led to an uprising and revolt. The Chinese responded with a military crackdown, in which many Tibetans lost their lives.

On this day in 1959, after a failed uprising against the Chinese occupation, the fourteenth Dalai Lama – Tenzin Gyatso – fled for his life across the Himalayas by foot. For fifteen days he struggled across the vast mountain range, before finally finding refuge in India.

In the Indian city of Dharamsala he set up the Government of Tibet in Exile. This was followed by various additional measures, including the repatriation of around 80,000 Tibetan refugees, the establishment of a traditional Tibetan schooling system and the founding of bodies such as the Tibetan Institute of Performing Arts.

Back in Tibet, Chinese efforts to erase the memory of the Dalai Lama proved fruitless. To this day he remains the spiritual leader of the Tibetan people. At the 2003 Tibetan music awards, 'Aku Pema', a song popular in Tibet calling for his return, won the prize for best lyrics. His role was brought to the fore in the build-up to the 2008 Beijing Olympic Games. In the months preceding the games, the Chinese authorities attempted to quell the Tibetans who sought to co-opt the publicity of the games for their own cause.

Despite the intense passions that surrounded the Olympic Games, the Dalai Lama refused to be drawn into an aggressive stance against China. His adherence to his spiritual role and accompanying global message of peace and diplomacy was far stronger than any political power he might wield. Indeed, his mission to bring peace to Buddhists and others everywhere, and in particular to secure autonomy for Tibet without violence, led in 1989 to his being awarded the Nobel Peace Prize.

The Dalai Lama himself is believed to be the current incarnation of a long line of Buddhist masters who live outside the constant cycle of life and rebirth that characterises the Buddhist faith. Instead, upon their worldly passing, these masters can choose of their own free will to be reborn, intact, back into humanity in order to continue teaching enlightenment.

The title 'Dalai Lama' is a testament to the depth of wisdom and spirituality of the one holding the position. 'Dalai' is a Mongolian word for 'Ocean', and is a translation of the Tibetan name 'Gyatso'. 'Lama', on the other hand, is a Tibetan word derived from an old Sanskrit term. Common translations interpret it as 'spiritual teacher'; when combined, the Dalai Lama is the 'Ocean Teacher'.

Although the current Dalai Lama is ostensibly the spiritual head of the Tibetan people, he is seen by the Chinese authorities as a defiantly political figure. However, it was not until the time of the fifth Dalai Lama that this political edge was developed. Lozang Gyatso, with the aid of the Mongol ruler, Gushri Khan, helped to unite Tibet as a single country. Since then the Dalai Lama has been a key focus of Tibetan cultural identity.

# 1 April

*The first fixed-wing, vertical take-off aircraft goes into service. It is the Hawker Siddeley Harrier, but will be popularly known as the 'Harrier Jump Jet'*

**1969** Although helicopters had been used since the Second World War, they were not especially good for executing military raids. This was because they were too slow and were easily shot from the sky. The ideal solution was to design a jet plane with the ability to take off and land vertically. That way it could be deployed in difficult terrain or from ships, but still be effective as a strike aircraft.

The abbreviation VTOL is used in describing 'Vertical Take-Off and Landing' aircraft, such as the Harrier. However, it is also a STOVL (Short Take-Off and Vertical Landing) aircraft. The advantage of using the short take-off is that the Harrier can get airborne with more fuel and arms, thereby increasing its range and strike power.

A number of developmental VTOL aircraft existed in the early 1960s, but the Harrier was the first to have its design perfected enough to be reliable and safe. It works by redirecting the thrust from its jet engines via four swivelling nozzles. In normal flight mode the nozzles point backwards. In vertical mode they point downwards, perpendicular to the aircraft. In short take-off mode they point diagonally backwards. Each nozzle is separately controlled so that fine adjustments can be made to cope with changing circumstances. Consequently the Harrier is one of the most difficult aircraft for a pilot to master.

Harriers are not supersonic aircraft – they cannot exceed the speed of sound (Mach 1) – making them vulnerable to attack by other jet fighters. Nevertheless, they compensate for this by being highly manoeuvrable. In a chase situation they can duck and dive by vectoring their nozzles, so that they rapidly alter direction and speed. The term 'viffing' (from 'vectoring in forward flight') is used in describing a manoeuvre where the Harrier is decelerated suddenly, so that the pursuit aircraft suddenly finds itself out in front and in range of the Harrier's weapons.

The aircraft takes its name from the birds of prey called harriers. In fact, the only bird of prey capable of hovering is the kestrel, but evidently that didn't sound tough enough. The harrier bird is so called because of its habit of harrying its prey, a technique it achieves by riding on up currents and keeping low to the ground. So it seems that it is an appropriate name for the aircraft after all.

# 2 April

## You say Malvinas, we say Falklands

**1982** Understandably, Argentina has long considered the Falkland Islands to be a part of its territory. After all, they are only a few hundred miles from the South American mainland and several thousand miles away from the United Kingdom. From a habitation point of view, the Falklands are not a particularly attractive proposition. They are a bleak and flat archipelago, devoid of trees and subjected to South Atlantic weather. From a strategic point of view they also hold little value.

The reason why the Argentinians invaded the Falklands, or rather *Las Malvinas*, on this day in 1982 was twofold. It was partly a fundamental opinion that the islands should be annexed as a part of Argentina. The other reason was the possibility of obtaining wealth from oil and other mineral deposits beneath the ocean bed. Similarly, the latter reason played its part in prompting the British government to go to the effort of seizing them back.

In addition, there was the matter of being seen to be warlike on the international stage, as well as the fact that the islands were populated by English-speaking people who were reluctant to relinquish their quasi-British culture and become assimilated into a Latin American one instead. Odd perhaps, considering that so many Britons now willingly migrate to southern Spain and Portugal, but then they do take their culture with them for the Iberians to enjoy. Well, they say revenge is a dish best served cold.

One of the most interesting things about the Falklands is that they used to be home to a now extinct species of canid – halfway between a fox and a wolf. The animal was called the warrah (*Dusicyon australis*). It seems to have fed on seabirds, sea mammals and invertebrates. When settlers arrived with livestock they hunted the warrah to oblivion. As a matter of fact, Charles Darwin visited the islands during his great voyage on HMS *Beagle*. He witnessed the warrah first-hand, and wrote about the animal in his journal.

Small islands are rarely home to large native mammals, because their ecology is such that they cannot survive the variables in terms of food availability. It seems likely, therefore, that humans brought domesticated warrahs from South America during the Neolithic period, just as they brought the dingo to Australia. The islands were uninhabited when Europeans discovered them, but prehistoric evidence of human presence has been found in the form of stone tools and a preserved canoe. Those early settlers may have returned to the continent or simply died out.

# 3 April

### The Unabomber is finally arrested, having evaded detection for eighteen years

**1996** The Unabomber earned his title as an abbreviation of the FBI file on the case, which was 'University and Airport Bomber' due to his *modus operandi* of posting mail or parcel bombs to such places. His criminal career lasted from May 1978 to April 1996. By the time of his arrest he had succeeded in killing three people and maiming a further 23.

He turned out to be an antisocial academic named Theodore Kaczynski, who had an obsession with what he saw as the dangers of modern technology. By 'dangers' he didn't mean hazardous phenomena, but rather their potential to undermine world peace and stability. His feelings were so intense that he set about his terror campaign in an attempt to make society sit up and listen. Like so many disaffected individuals he lacked the wherewithal to campaign by orthodox means, so he opted for a singular approach that would take him to the top of the most wanted list in the US.

In 1995, having evaded identification and capture for over two decades, Kaczynski decided to take another approach by posting a manifesto of his political beliefs for publication as a pamphlet. The 35,000 word diatribe – *Industrial Society and Its Future* – accompanied by the promise to 'desist from terrorism' if it was published, was duly printed in the *New York Times* and *Washington Post*. There had been sixteen bombs by that point.

Kaczynski was eventually given away by his younger brother David. Having read the manifesto he was struck by its similarity to letters he had received from Theodore, both in style and content. Eventually the FBI took his claim seriously and used an expert profiler to ascertain that Theodore was very likely to be their man. On 3 April 1996, he was tracked down to a remote cabin in the mountains of Montana where he was living the survivalist lifestyle, convinced that modern civilisation was bringing about its own demise.

After his arrest, Kaczynski was put on trial on the charges of transporting, mailing and using bombs, as well as three counts of murder. The state prosecution team originally set out to achieve the death penalty, a fate which Kaczynski seemed determined to assign himself to when he refused a plea of insanity. However, David Kaczynski pleaded with the courts to apply leniency. Having turned his elder brother over to the FBI, David could not bear the thought of seeing him executed.

There was a great deal of wrangling between the courts and the defendant, but ultimately Theodore Kaczynski avoided the death penalty. On 22 January 1998 Kaczynski pleaded guilty to all the charges laid against him by the government. He later tried to withdraw this admission, claiming that it was made under duress, but his request was denied both by the trial judge and by the Court of Appeals.

Kaczynski's eventual sentence was life imprisonment without any chance of parole. Since 1998 he has been held in a maximum security prison in Colorado. David received $1 million in reward money from the FBI for his part in bringing the Unabomber to justice, but he donated this to the families of his brother's victims.

# 4 April

## The largest recorded sunspot is observed

**1947** Sunspots are dark areas on the sun's surface where the temperature is cooler – 4,500°C as opposed to 5,800°C. Although the spots themselves are cool, their perimeters can cause solar flares, or coronal mass ejections, at several millions of degrees, that radiate high levels of energy into space.

If the Earth happens to be in the path of that energy, then the electromagnetic radiation can cause geomagnetic storms. These storms are powerful enough to damage the instrumentation of satellites and affect electrical power grids. The energy is also trapped within the atmosphere, where it causes global warming.

Since 1947 further significant solar flare events have been recorded that may be contributing to the marked global warming reported by scientists in recent years. The sun has a cycle of eleven years, making the next high point due in 2013.

What happens is that the solar energy causes a very gradual and slight increase in ocean temperatures – fractions of a degree – but enough to mean that dissolved carbon dioxide gas is released from the water into the atmosphere. The carbon dioxide enhances the 'greenhouse effect' so that higher levels of ordinary solar energy become trapped too. In turn, this warms the oceans further, and the earth enters a cycle of general warming. In effect it is the opposite of an ice age – a warm age, where the globe rises in temperature until the sun enters a period of relative inactivity.

Environmentalists argue that the contribution of carbon dioxide (carbon footprint) and removal of oxygen (deforestation) from human activities to the equation may mean that the earth perpetually continues to warm up until it causes a mass extinction.

However, it is known that the oceans and other natural phenomena, such as volcanoes, still produce vastly more carbon dioxide than human industry. Also, it has recently been found that oceanic algae absorb far more carbon dioxide than terrestrial forests have ever done. So it may be that the Earth is quite capable of readjusting its atmospheric temperature relative to the sun's activity in due course.

# 5 April

## Giant panda is artificially inseminated in a campaign to save the species from its own poor record at reproduction

**2007** Increased awareness of man's impact upon the world's wildlife has meant that conservation is a key issue in modern times. Some species are able to recover quite easily, given protection and appropriate habitat. Others struggle because they have specialised lifestyles, or because they breed very slowly. In the case of the giant panda, both come into play.

Pandas feed only on bamboo, and their reproduction reflects the poor nutritional value of their food. Added to this, the giant panda has a very brief oestrus, and its fertility is low. Consequently, scientists have resorted to artificial insemination in a last-ditch attempt to save the giant panda from extinction. At present the animals are dying at a quicker rate than they reproduce, meaning inevitable extinction unless fecundity is improved. The wild population is also struggling due to habitat loss and the fact that the animals require considerable territories to find sufficient food.

The first giant panda to be produced following artificial insemination was born in 2001, at the Wolong Giant Panda Research Centre in China, and named Xiang Xiang. Unfortunately its introduction to the wild resulted in its death in 2007, because it was unable to defend itself when attacked by wild pandas over territory.

In April 2007 a giant panda at the Smithsonian National Zoo, USA, was inseminated. Mei Xiang is the panda in question. She had already given birth to a healthy cub named Tai Shan in 2005, but other attempts at reproduction have failed. If giant panda insemination can be perfected, then it should at least save the creature from extinction, even if the majority of the population continues to survive in zoos.

The giant panda is one of those species that benefits from having an appearance that humans find attractive. In fact, it is the model for the teddy bear far more than true bears, as it has a flat face and features arranged in a human-like manner. It is also covered in fluffy fur and distinctively coloured in black and white. All in all, it is regarded as cute. Had it been an ugly creature, then its story is very likely to have taken a very different turn. The Yangtze river dolphin is just such a creature: another large Chinese mammal, it has recently become extinct. Beauty clearly goes a long way in the conservation business. Have you ever met anyone who didn't like pandas?

# 6 April

## Intelsat I: Early Bird *becomes the first geosynchronous communications satellite, linking US TV, phone and fax with Europe*

**1965** When one considers that the first experimental radio communications were made in the winter of 1896–7 on Salisbury Plain in England by Guglielmo Marconi, it seems remarkable that the world had been linked up by 1965.

The advantage of having a geostationary satellite was that it remained in orbit above the same spot on the earth. This meant that the communications set-up was reliable. With a roving satellite it had only been possible to send and receive electromagnetic waves when the satellite was within a certain orbital parameter. Although *practicable*, this wasn't *practical* as it meant that there were communication blackouts for considerable periods while the satellite orbited outside its useful parameters.

Geosynchronous satellites manage to remain in fixed orbits by following the line of the equator. They are not literally stationary, of course, but in orbit at a velocity that exactly matches the spin of the globe. In fact, they do drift eastwards and westwards to a certain extent, simply because the rotation of the earth is slightly irregular.

In the modern age there are about 300 geosynchronous satellites in operation, making the equatorial line a busy place. They orbit the earth at an altitude of 22,300 miles (35,786 km). This is known as the 'magic altitude', as it enables satellites to synchronise with the earth's sidereal (daily) rotation – 23 hours and 56 minutes. It works because the gravitational and centrifugal forces exactly match. This allows them to be geosynchronous, although they may still wander if out of exact line with the equator. They become both geosynchronous and geostationary when both longitudinal and latitudinal alignments are correct.

One of the most famous early satellite links came in the shape of The Beatles performing 'All You Need Is Love' in 1967. In fact it was the first global television link to be broadcast live across the world on 25 June. John Lennon was apparently asked to compose a song especially for the occasion and the title line was designed to be understood by all nations. The song was released as a single a couple of weeks after the broadcast and reached number one in both the UK and US charts. That first satellite television picture was in fuzzy black and white, but it marked the beginning of the modern visual communications era and went a long way towards making the world a smaller place.

# 7 April

## Genetic link established between prehistoric man and living person

**2000** Britain's oldest complete human skeleton is known as Cheddar Man. His fossil remains were found in 1903 in Gough's

Cave in Cheddar Gorge, England. They have been dated to 7,150 years BC.

Remarkably, the human geneticist Bryan Sykes was able to extract mitochondrial DNA from a molar tooth to acquire a genetic profile, or fingerprint, of the 9,000-year-old Briton. Even more remarkably, a sampling of twenty residents of Cheddar village found matches for the DNA. Two schoolchildren were found to have exact matches, and an adult was found to have a near match.

While this suggests that the human population of Cheddar has remained relatively sedentary for thousands of years, it should be realised that mitochondrial DNA survives through the female lineage, and remains intact for many generations. This means that a large percentage of the entire British population might show a match or near match to the DNA too.

What it *does* definitely show is that the original population was not entirely saturated by new DNA from subsequent invasions from other parts of Europe. It suggests that native populations tended to keep to themselves, even with the influx of conquering peoples. 9,000 years equates to 450–500 generations.

Incidentally there have been around 90 generations since the time of Jesus, which makes a mockery of any notion that there is a surviving direct lineage, as some people believe. Even with only a modest increase of just 25 per cent per generation, it would mean around 100 descendants at twenty generations; 1,000 descendants at 30 generations; 10,000 descendants at 40 generations; 700,000 at 50 generations; 800 million at 60 generations; and 7.5 billion at 70 generations – more than the entire human population. Anyone descending from the Middle East gene pool is clearly related to Jesus to one extent or another – assuming he existed of course.

On the same theme, scientists use the name 'Mitochondrial Eve' in describing the single-point origin of humanity. That is to say, by testing the mitochondrial DNA of humans across the world it has been possible to ascertain that we all originate from a single female ancestor who lived in East Africa. That isn't to say that Mitochondrial Eve was the only one of her species, of course, but it demonstrates that the dawn of humanity was an unlikely event. Had Mitochondrial Eve died before reproducing then another type of humanity would have had to try its luck with another individual of her species. It may have failed or gone in a completely different evolutionary direction. In fact, evidence suggests that there were indeed other hominid species evolving parallel with our lineage until they went extinct.

# 8 April

## The lights go out for the 20th century's greatest artist, Pablo Picasso

**1973** On this day, Pablo Diego José Francisco de Paula Juan Nepomuceno María de los Remedios Cipriano de la Santísima Trinidad Martyr Patricio Clito Ruiz y Picasso died of a heart attack at his home in Mougins, on the Côte d'Azur in the south of France.

Picasso, though Spanish, had forged his reputation in Paris during the early years of the 20th century. He lived the cliché of the artist's life as a young man, sharing a single room and having to burn his work to keep warm in the winter. He would work through the night on his paintings while his room-mate slept, then sleep all day.

Picasso's initial forays into painting were dominated first by the colour blue and then pink. They weren't strictly monochromatic, but the hues reflected his state of mind – blue for depression, pink for love. Having found that he was something of a charmer, Picasso became so obsessed by sexual conquest that he found it impossible to hold down a long-term relationship. He married twice but also kept many mistresses, fathering four children by three different women.

Following his pink period and a phase of 'primitive' art influenced by African artefacts, Picasso's art matured into the phase for which he is best known when, in 1909, he began to collaborate with the French artist Georges Braque to initiate the Cubist movement. Cubism was all about interpretation rather than realistic depiction. Instead of painting an object as one visually saw it, one painted it as one knew it to be, bringing together in one image many of the different angles and perspectives that were possible. This resulted in numerous planes or surfaces colliding at different angles, giving the distinctive cube-like effect. Later, Cubism absorbed everyday objects such as pieces of wallpaper and newspaper into the artwork, using collage to achieve similar effects of juxtaposition.

The Cubist paintings and sculptures that Picasso produced came to symbolise modern art, and they were often lampooned by conservative critics and the public for their freakish appearance. Nevertheless, they freed modern art from realism and paved the way for abstraction, which is why Picasso is seen as such an important figure in the development of modern art. What is often overlooked is that he was also a superb draughtsman who received a rigorous training in classical techniques from his father, a professor of art in Málaga. Picasso's visual experiments were based on a profound understanding of form and line, and it was his life's work to try to use that knowledge to say something new about the way we see objects. As he was fond of saying: 'It took me four years to paint like Raphael, but a lifetime to paint like a child.'

It would be true to say that Picasso was also the first art celebrity. Before Picasso, no artist had been so famous during their own lifetime. To a certain extent he enjoyed the fame, but he was essentially a bohemian and socialist who had no time for the pretensions of high society.

His last words were 'Drink to me, drink to my health, you know I can't drink any more', a line later adopted by Paul McCartney as a song lyric.

# 9 April

## Cinema makes its three-dimensional debut

**1953** If you thought that 3D cinema was a recent creation that arrived around the same time as IMAX cinema screens, it's time to think again. The premiere of the very first major 3D film was held on this day well over 50 years ago, when Warner Brothers unleashed the horror flick *House of Wax* in America.

In terms of who strictly came first, *House of Wax* was actually beaten to the screens by a small-scale 1951 movie called *Bwana Devil*. Then there is a claim that Columbia Pictures' *Man in the Dark* was first shown on the 8th, the day before *House of Wax*. Despite these rival claimants, it was *House of Wax* that really set the ball rolling for 3D cinema's heyday in the 1950s.

The move from two to three dimensions itself was not, as is arguably the case with modern 3D films, simply a case of exploiting technology because it exists. In just three years between 1948 and 1951, the number of cinema-goers in the US had slumped from a high of 90 million to only just over half that figure. The Hollywood bosses were desperate to lure the public away from their new-found entertainer: television.

*House of Wax* was shot using a technique called Stereoscopic 3D. The 3D effect was then achieved in cinemas by audiences donning special glasses, like the ones still seen today in children's toys with one lens blue or green, and the other red. As a result, images that had undergone the 3D production treatment during films would appear to jump right off the screen. *House of Wax* used this to great effect with a troop of can-can girls who seemed to dance right at the audience. The earlier *Bwana Devil* had also played up to the new sensuousness of 3D technology, promising viewers 'A LION in your lap! A LOVER in your arms!'

Perhaps the greatest irony with *House of Wax* is that its director, André de Toth, was actually blind in one eye and could see nothing of the 3D effects his film was creating. Vincent Price, who played a disfigured sculptor who creates a 'Chamber of Horrors' exhibition by coating the bodies of his murder victims in wax, later remembered de Toth asking, 'Why is everybody so excited about this?', as the whole crew watched the early material with fascination.

The ultimate aim of the 3D films, which was to drag people back into cinemas, was an immediate success. But as film followed film, the public quickly tired of this novelty. After 3D cinema peaked in popularity less than three years later, production companies took to throwing more and more effects into the films. What had started out with a can-can girl here, a lion there, ended up with almost anything that could be made three-dimensional leaping off the screen in a bizarre fashion. By the end of 1955 3D cinema was a has-been craze and, despite minor revivals in the following decades, when *House of Wax* was remade in 2005 it was a resolutely two-dimensional affair.

# 10 April

## The Beatles disband

**1970** When Paul McCartney quietly announced in April 1970 that The Beatles were no more, it marked the end of an era. Fans both male and female wept, and fellow musicians lamented the passing of the greatest pop band the world had ever known.

The break-up had been on the cards for some time, with John Lennon spending more and more time with his new partner Yoko Ono, George Harrison pursuing Eastern religion and McCartney interested in his solo career. Nonetheless it seemed to bring a sudden and dramatic end to the innocent, exciting, heady exuberance of the 1960s and seemed to herald the beginning of an altogether more sober, pessimistic time.

The Beatles' origins dated back to 1958, when a group of young Liverpool lads, including Lennon, McCartney, Stu Sutcliffe and Pete Best began playing rock'n'roll together in bands called the Quarrymen and Johnny and the Moondogs. Then, as The Beatles, they spent a year or so learning their trade playing in Hamburg bars before returning to Liverpool in 1961, where they took up a residency at the soon-to-be famous Cavern club and acquired a crucial asset in manager Brian Epstein. Ringo Starr and George Harrison soon completed the foursome with Lennon and McCartney. Epstein then gave them their dapper, mop-top image and got them a recording contract with Parlophone.

In October 1962, the band's first single, 'Love Me Do' just

crept into the charts, but their next one 'Please Please Me' started the fire that quickly lead to Beatlemania as the band inspired an excited frenzy among young fans, especially girls. The sight of adolescent girls going wild in the presence of their pop idols is now very familiar, but in 1963 it was almost entirely new and caught the older generation in amazement – a symptom of the shocking, and to the youngsters exciting, revolution in behaviour that made the 1960s the decade of youth and pop culture.

With a string of hit singles including 'She Loves You', 'I Want to Hold Your Hand' and 'Can't Buy Me Love', The Beatles conquered the British charts like no other band before or since – and then proceeded to export the same chart success, along with Beatlemania, to the USA in 1964. As fan hysteria reached almost unmanageable levels, the band retired to the quiet of the recording studio and began to create the album that showed they were not simply able to turn out hit singles, but could have a huge influence in establishing pop music as a serious art form. The album *Sergeant Pepper's Lonely Hearts Club Band*, released in 1967, didn't have any singles, but was rather a self-contained album that was meant to be played from beginning to end. It is widely considered the greatest pop album ever.

After *Sergeant Pepper*, although artistically The Beatles were still to hit the heights with great songs like 'Hey Jude' and 'Let It Be', as a unit they began to crack, as each band member began to pursue his own particular agenda and the band became embroiled in financial wrangles over their media company Apple. When the split finally came, no-one was entirely surprised, though for a long while people kept on hoping they might reform until that fateful day in 1980 when John Lennon was murdered. But The Beatles' legacy lives on, and they are still the biggest-selling artists of all time.

# 11 April

## *Nazi hunters begin the long-awaited trial of Adolf Eichmann in Israel*

**1961** On this day in 1961 began the trial of Adolf Eichmann, a high-ranking Nazi SS officer responsible for the mass deportation of Jews and other ethnic groups to ghettos, concentration camps and extermination camps during the Second World War.

A member of the Nazi Party from 1932, it seems that his original motivation was simply to advance his career, and indeed he proved a very capable administrator. His boss, Reinhard Heydrich, made him the 'architect of the Holocaust', the man who was to organise the transportation of Jews and other minorities from Germany and the occupied countries.

During the 1930s, his job involved not only helping to run the newly built concentration camp at Dachau but also assessing the logistics of a possible mass exodus of German Jews to Palestine, even working with Zionist leaders to see how the process could be speeded up. When war came, though, this plan was abandoned and his efforts were directed towards extermination rather than emigration. He attended the notorious Wannsee conference of 1942, where the policy of genocide towards the Jews was officially adopted by the Nazi hierarchy. He was given the job of Transportation Administrator to the 'Final Solution'.

At the end of the war, he eluded capture and managed to escape to Argentina by using false documents. Surveillance by Nazi-hunters suggested that he was living in Buenos Aires under the assumed name of Ricardo Klement. He remained at liberty until 1960, when undercover agents from the Israeli secret service, Mossad, tracked him down and abducted him. After a brief tussle with the Argentine administration over the legality of the operation, Eichmann was taken to Israel to stand trial for crimes against humanity. In parliament, Israeli prime minister David Ben-Gurion announced his capture to a standing ovation.

The weight of evidence and emotion against Eichmann meant

that he was inevitably found guilty and sentenced to death. Central to his sentence being passed in the face of pleas for clemency was a quote taken from the Book of Samuel: 'As your sword bereaved women, so will your mother be bereaved among women.' To Christians this would equate to that oft-quoted phrase from Exodus: 'An eye for an eye, a tooth for a tooth.'

Eichmann was hanged from the neck until he was dead in the early seconds of 1 June 1962, having drunk half a bottle of wine and refused the black hood. He had played his part in the deaths of hundreds of thousands of innocent men, women and children.

His trial and death also added a chilling phrase to the language: 'the banality of evil', coined by philosopher Hannah Arendt, who covered the trial as a journalist for *The New Yorker*. This was her verdict on a man she saw as an ordinary, efficient bureaucrat, showing no rabid hatred for his victims, but who nonetheless perpetrated a huge and vile act under the excuse of simply 'obeying orders'.

# 12 April

### Yuri Gagarin becomes the first human being to leave the protective biosphere of planet Earth

**1961** The key advantage that *Homo sapiens* has over all other species is its ability to manipulate and fabricate environments to suit *it*, as opposed to having to adapt itself to different surroundings.

By the 1960s, mankind had managed to devise ways of staying alive in the most extreme locations on the planet. It was time to see whether it might be possible to survive in an environmental capsule surrounded by the hostility of space. Yuri Gagarin was the man chosen for the experiment. He duly became the first person to enter space in *Vostok 1*. His space flight lasted 1 hour and 48 minutes, the duration of one orbit.

Before re-entry into the atmosphere, Gagarin had to use retro rockets to slow the spacecraft down. Had they failed, he was equipped with ten days' rations, to allow it to decelerate of its own accord. The cosmonaut ejected from the capsule at 7 km altitude and parachuted down, as he would have risked serious injury or death had he landed inside the capsule itself, even though it had its own parachute.

This fact was kept secret by the Soviet Union as it broke the official rules set by the FAI (*Fédération Aéronautique Internationale*), that the pilot must land with his craft for a flight to be considered legitimate. Despite its illegitimacy, the flight made Gagarin the first man to enter space and to orbit the globe.

In 1968, seven years after that historic achievement, Gagarin was killed in an air crash and so never lived to see the first men on the Moon. If we take into account those rules about returning to Earth inside one's ship, then Alan Shepard is technically the first person to complete a space flight. His flight took place on 5 May 1961, although he didn't orbit the globe, but instead simply entered space and then returned. It took just over a quarter of an hour from start to finish in a capsule named *Freedom 7*.

In 1994 Shepard published a book titled *Moon Shot: the Inside Story of America's Race to the Moon*. Shepard had been the fifth person to walk on the Moon and had famously played golf there. However, the book included a faked photograph because the original images were on poor quality videotape. This was a foolish move on Shepard's part because it served to add to the conspiracy theory that the US Moon missions never happened and were elaborately concocted in a secret film studio.

# 13 April

## The CIA begins experiments with mind control

**1953** The Central Intelligence Agency used the code name MKULTRA for their research programme into mind control. It has been claimed that it stands for 'Manufacturing Killers Utilising Tradecraft Requiring Assassination'. It has also been suggested that it stood for 'Mind Kontrol Ultra', using the phonetic spelling of 'control' to avoid pronunciation problems with foreign contacts. The reality, as always, is slightly less dramatic – the prefix 'MK' merely signified that the operation was overseen by the CIA's Technical Services division and 'ULTRA' was a randomly chosen word.

The programme experimented with drugs (chemical agents), pathogens (biological agents) and physics (radiological and electrical agents), to induce mental states whereby people would be open to suggestion and willing to divulge information. In general the process was described as 'brainwashing'. It was deemed to be different from torture, as it didn't involve the element of submission under duress. Nevertheless, the drugs were often administered without either the knowledge or consent of the subject. This placed the project in direct contravention of the Nuremberg Code which was drawn up after the Second World War as a guideline for protecting humanity from live experimentation.

In 1964, MKULTRA was renamed MK-SEARCH and its main purpose was to develop an efficient truth serum for use on Soviet spies. Since the MKULTRA and MK-SEARCH trials, the use of truth drugs has been reclassified as a form of torture.

The CIA went to extraordinary lengths with their experiments because the 1950s was a decade when the Cold War between the US and the Soviet Union really heated up. Espionage was rife, so the CIA wanted to stay one step ahead of the KGB.

Despite some success with their search for a truth drug, such chemicals have ultimately been proven to be unreliable. Although they work by preventing the mind from storing secret information behind mental walls, this information cannot be targeted in any specific manner. As a result, all mental walls are broken down and the 'true' facts which emerge are freely mixed with nonsense and fantasy. Other conclusions simply point out that some truth drugs, such as sodium amobarbital, which work by increasing talking, and therefore rendering the subject unable to stop speaking the truth, actually uncover not only the truth, but also a huge range of lies alongside it. In the end, the interrogator is in no better a position to determine what is hard fact after using a truth serum than he is before doing so.

# 14 April

## The first draft of the Human Genome Project report is released

**2003** When scientists talk of genomes, they are referring to the full complements of genes that make up the DNA, or molecular codings, for different species of organism. The Human Genome Project set out to map the entire DNA sequence in our species, so that geneticists could have a better understanding of congenital and inherited diseases and defects. This would open the door to developments in human gene therapy and other related fields.

The key genes that make up the genome are those that code for the manufacture of amino acids, which link together to make proteins – the physical building blocks of organisms. It was found that humans possess remarkably few of these genes. Out of 3 billion DNA base pairs, from 24 pairs of chromosomes, there are only 25,000 genes. What is more, these genes only account for a very small percentage of the total DNA.

This discovery gave rise to the term 'junk DNA', alluding to the seeming redundancy of the vast majority of DNA present. Since 2003 it has been discovered that much of the so-called junk DNA is in fact used for controlling growth, maintenance and function in the human body. It is also used simply to provide punctuation in the genome, so that useful genes are kept discrete from one another. In this respect it might be better described as 'blank DNA', as its purpose is to have no purpose.

Evolutionary theorists have also suggested that junk DNA might exist because DNA is itself the evolutionary driver. That is to say that organisms, including humans, exist only as vehicles to ensure the continued survival of DNA itself. The concept of 'selfish DNA' is an extension of the notion of the 'selfish gene', as postulated by Richard Dawkins in his book *The Selfish Gene* (1976).

Most recently scientists have discovered that junk DNA can be switched on and off by developmental changes during the lifetime of organisms. It suggests that Lamarckian evolutionary theory may have some truth in it after all. Traditionally, scientists had concluded that it wasn't possible for individuals to develop changes during their own lifetimes and pass them on to offspring, mainly because there was no mechanism in place for affecting their genetic makeup. However, it has been realised that junk DNA is a stockpile of redundant genetic possibilities which can be switched on again according to those developmental changes. Similarly, unwanted genes may be switched off to become junk DNA in equal proportion.

# 15 April

## McDonald's burger restaurant becomes a franchise

**1955** The original McDonald's restaurant was opened for business in 1940, by brothers Richard and Maurice McDonald. By 1948 they had eight restaurants and had established the fast food ethos. In 1955 Ray Kroc set up the ninth McDonald's restaurant under franchise, and injected his ambition for global expansion. He duly purchased the brothers' equity in the company, and set about turning the McDonald's brand into a worldwide business empire.

Central to Kroc's success was maintaining the overall supply and marketing umbrella company – McDonald's Corporation. This ensured that product standards were uniform throughout the chain of restaurants. It meant that the customer would experience the exact same thing, wherever in the world they happened to be. Essentially, once inside the door, it should be impossible to tell one restaurant from another in terms of the food, the furnishings, the décor, the staff presentation, the customer service and so on.

Despite, or perhaps in spite of, the success of McDonald's, it has come under a great deal of hostile fire from those with concerns about globalisation, public health and Americanisation. In recent years the McDonald's Corporation has striven to address some of these issues, but these perceived flaws are essentially part and parcel of the reason why McDonald's has done so well. Around the world people find the brand and what it represents very attractive, because it symbolises the American Dream.

One of the unfortunate consequences of the fast food revolution initiated by Kroc is the rise in morbid obesity, especially in America. Many populations have descended into a modern cultural phenomenon where they are ignorant of the basic knowledge regarding nutritional wellbeing and exercise. Fast food is available in vast quantities at very low prices. In some US states, such as Texas, over 60 per cent of the population is obese and a good proportion is morbidly so.

When humans are in a natural environment a balance is struck between calorie expenditure and intake. This prevents people from stockpiling body fat and ensures that they remain fit and healthy. Modern society has largely removed this balance, so that populations are subject to a drop in physical activity and an increase in the amount of calories they consume. In many cases, obesity is the inevitable outcome.

Once the scales have tipped in the direction of obesity it then becomes exponentially difficult for people to escape the trap. It is a whole lot easier to gain weight than to lose it, not least because our stomachs can actually grow in response to large amounts of food, so encouraging us to eat more and more.

# 16 April

*The Nazi V-2 rocket technology is taken to the US, where it becomes the embryo for the space race against the Soviet Union*

**1946** Following the Second World War, the Allies had a great deal of V-2 rocket technology in their possession. None of the captured devices were in flying condition, but they had everything they needed to initiate a rocket development programme, including Wernher von Braun (1912–77), the German rocket scientist.

The first test launch on US soil was conducted using a V-2 rocket assembled from captured parts, at White Sands Missile Range, New Mexico. It carried a cosmic radiation experiment for the General Electric Company and achieved an altitude of 3 miles (5 km). GEC was contracted by the US Army Ordnance Department to breathe life back into the V-2.

Following that first successful launch, the V-2 became the genesis for space rocket and ballistic missile technologies that were developed in the latter half of the 20th century. The immediate descendent of the V-2 was essentially a US version of the same. It was known as the Bumper V-2 and was first flown in 1948, reaching an altitude of 80 miles (130 km).

Space rockets were considered the most advanced form of technology in the post-war years. In many respects this was because flying mechanical rockets involved an intricate marriage of onboard, launch site and control room systems. For all their enormous potential, therefore, rockets were expensive, temperamental, unreliable and dangerous pieces of kit – they still are. With so many things able to go wrong, something often does and with spectacular effect. Over the course of space flight, more rockets have failed than succeeded, because every last factor has to be perfect.

One of the major limiting factors of rockets is the enormous quantities of fuel required to generate sufficient lift to break the pull of gravity. In addition, most rocket parts are jettisoned in the process of launch and flight. For these reasons, scientists have explored other ways of getting craft into space. To date space shuttles have proven to be quite effective, as the greater part of the vessel returns to Earth unscathed and can be reused.

A radical alternative to the whole problem that is currently being tested is light propulsion. Experimental rockets have been successfully launched by propelling them on the end of a laser beam emitted from a ground-based laser. The photons comprising the laser beam strike a plate of metal propellant beneath the rocket, which emits a plasma plume and drives the rocket upwards. The advantage is that the rocket carries relatively little weight in fuel, but it only works as long as the laser can make contact with the rocket engine.

# 17 April

## The US army seizes a store of Nazi uranium

**1945** That the US developed the first atomic weapons during the Second World War is common knowledge. What is less well known is that the Nazis had an atomic weapons programme of their own. Intelligence had gleaned sufficient information to prompt the Allies into making the Manhattan Project a priority. As it turned out, the Nazis were defeated before they were able to put their nuclear technology into practice.

Before the Nazis had actually capitulated, the US army happened to be the first to reach Strassfurt in Germany, where it discovered a half-ton stockpile of uranium. It was duly seized by the branch of the Manhattan Project called Operation Alsos – 'alsos' meaning 'thicket' in Greek, an allusion to the secrecy surrounding the mission. The uranium was taken to the US and added to the nuclear material that would eventually be used in two bombs over Hiroshima and Nagasaki.

A prime concern of the US during Operation Alsos was keeping the uranium from the Soviets. Even though the USSR was effectively an ally, Stalin's communist ideology was at odds with the democratic ethos of the West, and a division of Europe was a foreseen outcome.

Of course, in the long term it made no difference, as the Soviets had established their own nuclear industry by the early 1950s, plunging the world into the Cold War, which would last for 40 years. Even now, the global community lives with the perpetual fear that nuclear technology might one day fall into the wrong hands.

Uranium is a naturally occurring element, most commonly found in an ore called pitchblende. The uranium is compounded with oxygen to form uranium dioxide and uranium trioxide.

Canada and Australia are the largest producers of uranium oxides, accounting for about 50 per cent of world production. The uranium ores are isolated to form a concentrate called yellowcake, which is then refined to extract pure uranium. Around 5 billion tonnes of good quality uranium ore are reckoned to be available. In addition there are vast deposits of poorer quality ores that may become viable in centuries to come. It may come as a surprise to learn that the world's seawater, for example, contains roughly a further 5 billion tonnes of uranium.

# 18 April

## A new European country is born in the shape of Eire

**1949** Southern Ireland became a republic and so left the British Commonwealth on this day. The legislation that set everything in motion, the Republic of Ireland Act, had been signed the previous year. It abolished the King as head of state – who had until this point been shared with the rest of the United Kingdom – and enacted a president in his place.

Great Britain as it was left standing responded in 1949 with the Ireland Act. This was a friendly piece of law, promising not to treat Irish nationals as foreigners if they came on to UK soil. The Ireland Act also set down that Northern Ireland, which had not been covered by the Republic of Ireland Act, was to formally remain a part of the United Kingdom.

The fallout of this schism in the makeup of the UK had profound effects over the following decades. Northern Ireland was to become witness to an ongoing struggle between viciously opposed factions.

On one side there are the Catholic Christians, who wanted Northern Ireland to be returned to the Republic. On the other, the Protestant Christians, who remained loyal to the United Kingdom. Various paramilitary groups – most notably the IRA (Irish Republican Army) – practised guerrilla warfare in their struggle to liberate Northern Ireland from the British. A great many shootings and bombings characterised this activity, which earned them a reputation as terrorists.

Following the attack on the World Trade Center in New York in 2001 by Islamic extremists, a sea change was seen in opinion regarding the situation in Northern Ireland. Members of the IRA and the political party Sinn Féin suddenly found themselves in a position where the label 'terrorist' was no longer representative of a proud struggle for a cause. Instead it became a deeply pejorative term, especially given that Catholics and Protestants are essentially one and the same in terms of beliefs and ideologies.

In addition, former American IRA sympathisers had an awakening about the true cost of terrorism now that it had happened on their own soil. Consequently they had a change of heart about funding the struggle. The result has been a new peace accord in Northern Ireland, where Christians have focused on their commonality as opposed to their differences.

The man who brokered the peace deal that many once thought impossible was the Reverend Ian Paisley. Famous for so long for saying 'No' to any concession or compromise that might usher peace into the region, Paisley shocked everyone when he announced that his political party, the Democratic Unionist Party, would be willing to work with their sworn enemies, Sinn Féin, in a coalition government. It was accordingly a historic day, and a case of peace at last, when on 8 May 2007, Paisley became first minister of Northern Ireland, and Sinn Féin's Martin McGuinness became his deputy first minister.

# 19 April

## *The term 'Moore's Law' enters the technological lexicon*

**1965** Gordon Moore was a co-founder of the Intel Corporation, which has been responsible for developing the semiconductors and microprocessors used in modern electronics.

In the early 1960s he realised that there was an exponential relationship between the physical scaling down of electronics technology, and the rate at which it was happening. He calculated that the number of transistors being fitted into the same physical space would double every two years, and he published his findings, which became dubbed 'Moore's Law'.

The significance of this relationship was not lost on those involved with the microelectronics industries, because it prophesied a time when continued development would reach an impasse. In other words, it would no longer be possible to keep going smaller, simply because the molecular possibilities of microelectronics would be stretched to their limit. Components would be so tiny that they would cease to function if they became any smaller. The implications are enormous, because the marketing of microelectronics relies very much on advancements in both the miniaturisation of products and in packing ever more functions into them. It is the driver of the industry, without which the world economy might easily fall into a recession.

Despite this, the end of conventional technological development and the economic ramifications of this remain a genuine concern. In order to address this inevitable outcome, microelectronics industries are looking for new solutions. Some are pursuing the idea of wholly new technologies, such as organic electronics. The notion is that it might be possible to grow electronic circuitry organically, so that it optimises use of the three-dimensional space, much like brain matter. Another avenue is simply exploring lateral developments, so that the emphasis in products is no longer placed on size reduction and compaction, but rather ergonomics and usefulness. The plan is to allow microelectronics to evolve itself out of a corner, so that Moore's Law doesn't become a self-fulfilling prophecy.

Of course, while technology companies drive ever onwards – in part to match the prediction laid down by Moore's Law, and in part to ensure that they can beat its ultimate limitations – there is still a certain element of drag on what computers can achieve. This is because Moore's Law applies to computer hardware, but not computer software. More powerful hardware can support increasingly complex software applications. Not only do these take a great deal of time to develop and perfect, but they stretch the improved hardware to its new limits. As a result, although the hardware may technically be faster, the real effect as experienced by the user is significantly less pronounced.

# 20 April

## *The first rocket-man takes to the skies*

**1961** Harold Graham was an engineer involved with the development of a device described as a 'rocket belt' by Bell Aerospace. These days they are known as 'jetpacks'. Graham became the first person to fly in this manner at Niagara Falls International Airport. The device was conceived in 1953 by Wendell Moore in response to a government directive to invent something to improve combatant mobility in difficult terrain.

The helicopter had already been invented, but it had obvious vulnerabilities. It still needed a reasonable clearing in a forest, and a flat area to land in mountainous terrain. The jetpack was seen as a perfect solution. It would enable individual soldiers to negotiate obstacles and move about rapidly within the theatre of battle.

In reality, although the jetpack worked, it was a cumbersome device to have strapped to the body. It meant that the pilot had little room for other equipment and was impeded from moving freely in combat while on the ground. In addition, the jetpack used its fuel very rapidly and the pilot could only carry the weight of a modest amount. There was therefore a real risk of finding oneself behind enemy lines without any means of escape.

Quite apart from anything else was the noise created by the jetpack. It used hydrogen peroxide to generate extremely hot steam which shot from two nozzles as the propulsive force. There would have been no chance of a surprise attack. Since the 1960s few jetpacks have been made, and they have only ever been used for the purpose of entertainment, including an appearance in the James Bond film *Thunderball*. Modern technologies have improved the prospects of the jetpack, so it might make a comeback in due course.

In recent years a Swiss aviator named Yves Rossy has perfected a jet-powered wing. In May 2008 he launched himself from a light aircraft and flew by jet engine propulsion for six minutes before descending to the ground by parachute. Perhaps unsurprisingly his invention has sparked some interest from a military point of view, as it might be very effective at deploying specialist personnel by allowing them to fly into territories rapidly and undetected. It might also be used to deploy weaponry in situations where conventional aircraft are unsuitable.

# 21 April

## The King of Rock 'n' Roll begins his reign

**1956** Elvis Presley had his first number one single in the US with 'Heartbreak Hotel'. It was released on 27 January 1956, but by 21 April it had soared to the top of the charts with over 1 million copies sold. It stayed there for eight weeks, became the bestselling single of 1956, and saw Presley catapulted into the public eye.

The song itself was written by the lyricist Thomas Durden, who had read about a suicide in a newspaper. The dead man had left a suicide note with the line 'I walk a lonely street', which became the template for the song – 'It's down at the end of lonely street, at Heartbreak Hotel'.

Presley was a revelation to the youth of America, and to the rock 'n' roll music scene he came to dominate. With 'Heartbreak Hotel' outselling all other records, he was invited to perform a new song on *The Milton Berle Show* in San Diego. To an audience of some 40 million he gyrated his way around the microphone while singing the now-famous 'Hound Dog'.

The outrage brought on by his cocky music, his unconventional style and, most of all, his thrusting hips was immense. He was lambasted as 'talentless and absurd', 'vulgar' and 'obscene'. But if conservative music critics hated him, those that loved his bold attitude cherished him even more. His gutsy reinventions of blues music – 'Hound Dog' was originally recorded by 'Big Mama'

Thornton in 1952 – struck a chord with his fans. Elvis felt it himself when he tried to explain his music and his swaying hips on television: 'If you like it, and you feel it, you can't help but move to it. That's what happens to me. I have to move around. I can't stand still. I've tried it, and I can't do it.'

'Hound Dog' itself went on to outrage even more people than 'Heartbreak Hotel'. It sold over 4 million copies on its release in July 1956 and stayed at number one in the charts for eleven straight weeks. When it was finally replaced, its successor was 'Love Me Tender', also by Elvis.

However, if Elvis' music was being bought by his fans and attacked by his critics in their numbers, it affected another group in a different way. Radio stations were the key channel by which songs could spread across America, from one coast to the other. However, rooted as his music was in blues music, white disc jockeys refused to play songs that sounded as if they were sung by a black artist, while perversely, black disc jockeys refused to play black music performed by a white man. It is a testament to Elvis' status as King of Rock 'n' Roll that he managed to overcome these racial tensions.

Having established himself upon his musical throne in 1956, that same year Elvis starred in the first of a number of films. *Love Me Tender*, a musical Western named after the title track, was panned by critics, but was nevertheless a reasonable box office hit. His acting career was never as highly regarded, even by his fans, as his singing prowess.

Elvis' later career, his descent into obesity and prescription drug abuse, and his eventual death in 1977 from a heart attack at the age of just 42, is well-documented. But it is his younger years, his musical talent and his reign as the King of Rock 'n' Roll for which he is best remembered. Nowadays there is even a real Heartbreak Hotel in Memphis, Tennessee, inspired by the song that first sent Elvis on his way to stardom.

# 22 April

## The first Earth Day is celebrated in the US

**1970** In response to increasing levels of pollution and general human abuse of the planet, Earth Day was conceived as a way of reminding people that the biosphere of Earth is the only place where we know for sure that life exists. What is more, we are the custodians of the globe and it is our duty to be mindful of the effects of human activity on the environment, for future generations and for other species of organism.

By the close of the 1960s, America was in quite a state thanks to the exhaust fumes and smoke issued from vehicles and factories. Smog blanketed cities to such an extent that it was affecting the health of inhabitants. In addition to the air pollution, rivers and estuaries were poisoned, so that life struggled to survive and people wondered about the safety of eating fish and crops. DDT had been widely used as an insecticide, and its cumulative effects on wildlife were beginning to be realised. In short, the US was in a mess.

The architect of Earth Day was Senator Gaylord Nelson, who had recently visited the scene of an oil spill in Santa Barbara. He was an environmentalist and was so shocked by what he saw, that he used his position to pass a new bill. So it was that 22 April 1970 became the first Earth Day. It was so popular that some 20 million people joined in the inaugural celebrations. Since then the event has grown to encompass 500 million people in 175 countries worldwide.

Earth Day quickly adopted the 'ecology flag' which had been devised in October 1969 by other US environmentalists. It bases itself on the pattern of the American flag, having green and white stripes. Instead of stars as its canton, it has a yellow theta, which has meanings both as the Peace Symbol, and as a sign of warning. The lower-case theta is a circle with a horizontal bisecting line, which can also be interpreted as an 'e' and 'o' superimposed and standing for 'environmental organisation'.

On the subject of pollution and carbon emissions, a major concern in recent times has been the rapid industrial growth, and consequent rise in the use of fossil fuels, in countries such as China and India, and nations of the former Soviet Union. Consequently these countries are increasing their pollution outputs as quickly as Western countries are reducing theirs. As the industrialised West was largely founded on the back of fossil fuels during the industrial revolution, however, it is difficult for it to preach on such matters with integrity. This is a conundrum that needs to be resolved if those behind Earth Day are to realise their aspirations.

# 23 April

## HIV is identified as the cause of Aids

**1984** Acquired Immune Deficiency Syndrome (Aids) is the active expression of the Human Immunodeficiency Virus (HIV). The virus can exist in the body for many years without developing into the disease, making its presence impossible to detect unless deliberate tests are made.

Aids patients don't die directly from the virus itself, but from other infections that are able to overcome the body's natural defences due to the fact that they are rendered inactive. Fungal infections such as thrush or candida are a common symptom of Aids, because the natural biotics that normally prevent spores from germinating cannot operate. The mycelia of the fungus infest the tissues with fatal consequences.

On 1 December 1981 Aids had been formally identified by the US Centers for Disease Control and Prevention. A relatively new virus at the time, as the decade wore on it became apparent that Aids was an epoch-defining illness. More and more people, initially homosexual males and drug abusers, but increasingly heterosexual individuals as well, fell victim to its onslaught. It seemed that the world was at the mercy of Aids.

Then, on this day in 1984, it seemed that the long-awaited scientific breakthrough had been achieved. Speaking in Washington, the US health secretary Margaret Heckler announced 'the triumph of science over a dreaded disease'. Aids had been linked back to a known virus, HTLV-3 (now called HIV). With its cause uncovered, Heckler confidently predicted that a vaccine for Aids would be ready for testing within two years.

However, following the formal identification of Aids back at the beginning of the 1980s, some 24 million have died as a result of the disease. The virus is now at pandemic levels and there are estimated to be some 33.2 million people living with the condition.

Since Margaret Heckler's assertion that a vaccine was forthcoming, billions of pounds have been spent on trying to develop one. However, since the turn of the millennium, only eight were ready for human testing, and just one has reached the final stages of assessment. Despite this glimmer of hope, the drug, developed by the US firm VaxGen, was ultimately proven not to work.

The hurdle that has so far proved insurmountable is the nature of the virus behind Aids, HIV. HIV is actually a retrovirus. This means that it is a form of virus containing an RNA (ribonucleic acid) genome. It uses the RNA to make DNA (deoxyribonucleic acid) copies of itself within cells. These DNA genomes become incorporated into the genome of the host cell, where they remain protected and dormant. Sooner or later the host cells have reason to duplicate themselves, depending on which cells they happen to be, so the virus progressively invades the body by stealth.

Yet in spite of everything, there have been positives in the fight against Aids. One of the earliest was the successful development of a blood test to detect for Aids. This meant that cases in which transfusion patients contracted Aids from tainted blood dramatically reduced. In addition to this, while there has been no cure, there are certain drugs which have successfully eased much of the suffering associated with Aids and significantly prolonged the lives of many victims.

# 24 April

## *A black US hero receives a posthumous medal 73 years late*

**1991** Freddie Stowers was the grandson of a slave. He was drafted into the US army in 1917 at the age of 21, and taken to Europe to participate in the First World War. The level of racial divide was still such in America that his infantry regiment was segregated for 'coloured' soldiers only.

In 1918 Stowers was involved in an assault on a German-held hill named Côte 188. It proved to be a difficult job as the enemy was dug in with machine guns. The only way to avoid being gunned down was to stay close to the ground.

Stowers was in command of a platoon, because his commanding officers had been shot dead. He evidently made the decision to advance in an attempt to take out the guns, so he began crawling toward the emplacements with bullets raking the air above his head.

The platoon made it to the first trench where they used flanking fire to silence the guns. They then readied themselves for an assault on a second trench. Stowers led the charge but was struck twice and fell. Despite his injuries he urged his comrades to battle on. They did so and managed to take the hill. Stowers died from loss of blood on the battlefield. He was buried alongside 133 of his fellow soldiers at the Meuse-Argonne Cemetery in France.

Stowers was subsequently recommended for a Medal of Honor, but the papers were never processed. The official line has it that the recommendation got mislaid. Stowers' bravery went unsung until 1990, when his recommendation resurfaced during a Department of the Army review.

It might be suspected that there was a racial element at play here in denying Stowers his medal at the time. While it would be wrong to deny that there was an institutionalised racism at play in the US military, it is also true that Stowers' recommendation was submitted at a time when the criteria for receiving the Medal of Honor were being narrowed down.

Whether a clerical oversight or racial prejudice, the matter was finally resolved on this day in 1991. During a special ceremony at the White House overseen by President Bush Snr, Freddie Stowers' surviving sisters received the award that ensures his name goes down in the record books as a soldier of outstanding bravery.

# 25 April

## The structure of DNA is revealed to the world

**1953** When James Watson and Francis Crick discovered the molecular structure of DNA, and published their findings in the journal *Nature* on this day in 1953, it was like finding the holy grail of genetics. In essence it was the formula for life itself.

Ever since Charles Darwin had published his *Theory of Evolution by Natural Selection*, scientists were searching for the mechanism by which natural selection works. Watson and Crick revealed that DNA (deoxyribonucleic acid) is a polymer. It has a linear structure comprising varying combinations of four possible units, called base pairs. As such it stores genetic code in a double-binary, or quadrinary, form. It is about as simple as it is possible for such a molecule to be. The only concession is that each DNA molecule needs to be incredibly long to store sufficient information to build an organism.

Each chromosome is a single strand of DNA, which has been coiled and recoiled to fit into the available space. Sections of the DNA store code for separate components and instructions. These are what we call genes. To keep the genes discrete from one another there are lengths of blank DNA in between. The physical form of DNA is described as a double helix. It is rather like a twisted ladder, with the coding units forming the rungs.

As these rungs are actually pairs of sub-molecules, they are able to separate, so that the ladder comes apart. This is how DNA is able to both duplicate itself and send information for cell building. An exposed length of split DNA acts as a template for the assembly of new DNA, or for a similar molecule called RNA (ribonucleic acid) which acts as a messenger, taking away information for building proteins. The DNA then zips back together.

Fundamental to progress in genetics has been genetic engineering or genetic modification. This involves the splicing of sections of DNA into chromosomes so that they are rendered able to code for new things. Similarly, gene therapy is where undesirable genetic mutations are replaced with desirable genes, thereby curing organisms of genetic diseases, syndromes or conditions.

Tampering with the genomes of organisms is a highly contentious modern-day issue. As with all technologies, it can be used for good or bad purposes, depending on one's point of view.

A central fear is that geneticists might inadvertently unleash super-organisms able to out-compete natural organisms. In reality the pressures of natural selection make it very difficult for any organism to thrive, unless it has acquired the optimum design for survival in a given environment. This means that a GM organism would be treated as a mutation and struggle to maintain a viable population.


# 26 April

### In the Ukraine a nuclear power station has a meltdown and explodes

**1986** Nuclear power stations are environmentally clean and generally safe, as long as they are well-managed, maintained and have an effective protocol to deal with potential emergencies. The power station at Chernobyl, Ukraine, was a disaster waiting to happen.

The Ukraine was part of the Soviet Union in 1986, and the infrastructure of the regime was in its demise. Consequently the power station was old and the management culture was set in its ways, complacent and lax. The USSR administration had bigger things to worry about, and it was only a matter of time before something went wrong.

The explosion was not a nuclear explosion, but a conventional explosion that sent a great deal of radioactive material into the air. It would have been termed a 'dirty bomb' had it been a deliberate act of sabotage or terrorism. As a result, the immediate effect of the explosion was not particularly damaging in a physical sense. But the reactor was left spewing nuclear material into the sky, so that a radioactive cloud began travelling in a north-westerly direction, dropping its deadly poison over the land.

Many Ukrainians risked their lives in the clean-up operation that followed. The building itself was so badly damaged that the only way of dealing with the situation was to entomb the reactor in a concrete sarcophagus. Concrete is fairly resistant to the passage of radioactivity. It can also be poured to close up any points of leakage of radioactive dust, and so eventually the reactor was hermetically sealed. To this day it remains cocooned in cement.

To give some measure of the political situation in the Ukraine at that period in history, the power station remained in use for several years afterwards, as there were three other reactors on the site. The one destroyed was reactor number 4.

Despite the lessons learnt by the Chernobyl disaster about the dangers of harnessing nuclear power, it is reckoned to be the most sensible direction for future energy production. There is a vast amount of fissile uranium available and it causes no harm to the environment as long as heightened safety measures are met and waste products are dealt with appropriately. Fossil and bio-fuels all produce combustion pollutants and are less efficient methods. Sustainable sources – solar, wind and water – are all safe but cannot produce the amount of energy required.

# 27 April

## Apartheid becomes official policy in South Africa

**1950** Just as the rest of the world, especially the US, was waking up to the idea of racial equality, South Africa descended into sanctioned racism. The word 'apartheid' is Afrikaans and translates as 'separate-hood'.

Apartheid actually came into force in 1948 with the general election that saw the National Party come to power. Two years later, on 27 April 1950, apartheid entered the law books of South Africa with the passing of the Group Areas Act. This enabled the South African administration to quite literally divide the country into separate neighbourhoods, some for whites and others for blacks and 'coloureds', as they termed people of dual heritage.

The first apartheid-era prime minister was Daniel Francois Malan. Malan was the head of the Afrikaner Party, who governed in coalition with the ruling National Party. In 1953 he passed a second act, the Separate Amenities Act, which built on the 1950 legislation. Where the Group Areas Act had defined the racial geography of the country, this new law permitted the government to reserve all types of services for the use of whites. As a result, hospitals, shops, beaches – even park benches – could be no-go areas for the indigenous black population.

The situation then proceeded to get worse for black South Africans. In 1956, under the Separate Representation of Voters Act, they suffered the ignominy of becoming largely disenfranchised. All black voters within the Cape of South Africa were removed from the electoral roll and placed on a special separate one. In all walks of life, they were treated as second-class inhabitants who worked for the whites and lived ghettoised lives of poverty.

There was dissent from within the country in the form of groups such as the African National Congress, the Black Consciousness Movement and the Pan Africanist Congress. However, struggles against apartheid, led by Nelson Mandela, were actively suppressed and activists were imprisoned for long periods of time. Some, such as Stephen Biko, even lost their lives while being held in detention.

It was not until the early 1990s, over 40 years since the Group Areas Act had been introduced, that the tide of change eventually came. The global community was a new phenomenon that pressurised nations into reconsidering their political image on the world stage. The white South African government ultimately conceded that multiracial democracy was the way forward for South Africa. Finally, in 1994, a new and freely elected government finally came to power with Nelson Mandela at its head.

Despite the democratic freedom in modern South Africa, it would be true to say that the entire population remains profoundly affected by the apartheid system. The social structure in the country is still balanced in favour of the white population. Racism is still present too, on both sides of the fence, but old habits die hard so one can only presume that the situation will improve as new generations arrive. The most remarkable thing is that the transition from apartheid to democracy was achieved without conflict, which bodes well for the future.

# 28 April

## *Anthropologist Thor Heyerdahl sets sail in the* Kon-Tiki

**1947** In the post-war years there was a new spirit of adventure. Thor Heyerdahl was a self-styled Norwegian explorer in the same vein as his fellow countryman, Roald Amundsen. He wanted to show that it was possible for the inhabitants of Polynesia to have come from South America.

In order to do so he set about building a raft, employing and basing his design on drawings made of indigenous Peruvian craft by the Spanish in the 16th century, using primitive materials and technology that would have been available several thousand years ago. He used nine balsa logs as the main components for the raft. These were lashed together with hemp ropes, and pine splashboards protected the bow. Mangrove wood was used to make the frame for the sail. The raft was then made habitable with the construction of a wooden cabin roofed with banana leaves. To aid with the steering, a mangrove oar was made, with a blade made from fir.

The raft was named *Kon-Tiki*, after an old name for the Inca sun god, Viracocha. On this day in 1947 it was launched from Callao, Peru, with a crew of six including Heyerdahl. For supplies they carried 250 litres of water stored in bamboo tubes, coconuts, sweet potatoes and other similar foods. While at sea they caught numerous fish, including sharks.

The *Kon-Tiki* made good progress westward at an average speed of 1.5 knots, and landfall was made at Raroia Atoll on 7 August 1947. They had travelled a distance of roughly 4,300 miles (8,000 km) in 101 days, and in doing so seemed to have proved Heyerdahl's hypothesis correct.

Heyerdahl subsequently became famous worldwide for his achievement and made a good living from the sale of books and a film about the voyage. He went on to further adventures in vessels named *Ra I*, *Ra II* and *Tigris*. The raft itself even achieved a certain celebrity, and the original vessel is now on display in the *Kon-Tiki* Museum in Oslo.

Despite his proving it was possible for people to have made the journey in prehistoric times, other anthropologists remained sceptical. In the 1990s, geneticists were able to show that the Polynesians were more closely related to the south-east Asians, thereby settling the argument once and for all. It seems that human groups had gradually island-hopped their way out into the Pacific Ocean. They were probably driven by the overpopulation of settled islands and the human spirit of adventure, much like Heyerdahl himself.

# 29 April

## The Los Angeles riots

**1992** On 3 March 1991, four officers from the Los Angeles Police Department, Laurence Powell, Timothy Wind, Theodore Briseno and Stacey Koon, pulled Rodney Glen King, a black motorcyclist, over for speeding. Not realising they were being filmed by a bystander, they then proceeded to beat King, holding him to the ground as they struck him with batons and kicked him.

The video, when it was shown to the media, caused outrage around the world. The policemen involved claimed that Rodney King had attempted to assault them, but nowhere in the footage – which covers the whole incident except for the first thirteen seconds – could this be seen. In Los Angeles, where the black population lived with issues such as unemployment and poverty, the accusations of police brutality pushed racial tension in the city to the fore.

The trial of the policemen was mired in controversy from the outset. After the initial charges were read out, the judge was changed, the venue moved and the jury thrown out. A new jury, comprising ten whites, one Latin American and one Asian American, was nominated in its place.

On this day in 1992, Wind, Briseno and Koon were all acquitted of the charges they were facing; only Powell was found guilty. The poor and oppressed black inhabitants of LA couldn't believe what they had seen in the courts. Even the city's mayor, Tom Bradley, declared that 'the jury's verdict will not blind us to what we saw on that videotape. The men who beat Rodney King do not deserve to wear the uniform of the LAPD.'

It didn't take long for the effects of the judge's decision to be felt. That same day saw the start of the infamous Los Angeles Riots. Immediately after the verdict, groups of people began gathering, peacefully, in the streets of the city. There was no aggression at first but tension simmered in the air. Then, at about 6.30 pm, a group of protestors converged on the LAPD headquarters. A few minutes later violence broke out elsewhere in the city.

Crowds of outraged African Americans tore through the city, urged on by LA's lawless gangs. They attacked other citizens, mainly those of white European or Latin American appearance, and looted shops, offices and vehicles.

One white truck driver, Reginald Denny, was beaten as live news cameras broadcast the event to the world. Having stopped at a red light, he was dragged from the cab of his vehicle and set upon in the street. His life was only saved when an African American resident, who had been watching the riots unfold on television, rushed to the scene and did what the police did not dare to do. He dived into the mêlée and pulled Denny to safety, driving him to hospital where he later recovered following brain surgery.

At 8.45 pm, the mayor declared a state of emergency. The state governor, Pete Wilson, sent in 2,000 National Guard troops as a result. By this stage, a central intersection between Florence and Normandie streets – where Denny had been beaten – was totally looted. The riots had also brought their first casualties and as the night progressed, the darkness was lit by the flames from burning cars and broken stores.

The rioting continued unchecked on the 30th. The city was still awaiting the arrival of all the National Guard troops and in their place, groups of citizens in armed self-defence militias fought gun battles on the streets of Los Angeles.

On 31 April, the third day of riots, the violence finally began to abate. The assignment of National Guard troops – doubled now to 4,000 – began to roll into the city in greater numbers. It would, however, be another three days until the riots finally came to an end on 4 May.

In total 53 people died during the Los Angeles Riots. There were over 10,000 people arrested and estimates to the amount of damage caused put the figure somewhere around the $1 billion mark. In light of the reaction to the original verdict, a retrial was also called for the four policemen involved in the beating of Rodney King. A federal court found Powell guilty again, and also

convicted Koon of violations against federal civil rights. Wind and
Briseno were acquitted as before.

# 30 April

## The World Wide Web comes of age

**1993** The World Wide Web was already up and running, but in
1993 the graphical user interface came into being. Before then it
had been text only and rather unappealing to the layperson. The
addition of visual information made all the difference, and the
possibilities of the Web suddenly dawned on everyone – it was
brought to life. The graphical user interface, or web browser,
responsible for this revolution was called Mosaic.

The World Wide Web is the term used to describe the network
of computers, servers and connections that cover the globe. The
internet is one of several ways in which the Web can be utilised.
Most people are only ever exposed to the Mosaic-based format,
but there are others that are used for more specialised purposes,
which have no requirement for a graphical user interface. For
example, some computer programmers work remotely by connecting with their master computers via the Web. The Mosaic
based system is the publicly accessible internet. Others are generally termed 'intranets', because access is restricted to those with
permissions. Some intranets are geographically contained within
buildings or campuses, while others employ the Web.

Since 1993, the internet has grown in accessibility and popularity to become a ubiquitous form of communication and source of
information. In essence, it is a vast electronic library and highway
combined. The concept of the Web itself is such that there should
always be a route for electronic signals from one computer to
another, even if a section of the Web 'goes down' for whatever
reason. This concept was dreamt up in 1989 by Tim Berners-Lee
and Robert Cailliau in response to the scenario of potential damage caused by nuclear conflict.

One of the most significant changes made to the world as a result of the World Wide Web is people's ability to telecommute. In other words, they can work remotely, as long as they have a computer connected to the Web. This phenomenon has transformed the concept of what work is or should be. The industrial revolution established the notion of people performing specific tasks and working for set numbers of hours and days per week. Transportation then introduced the idea that people could physically commute to and from their place of work. What the Web does is enable people to effectively commute with their minds, so that their physical presence is no longer required in many industries.

# 1 May

## *A radio broadcast reveals that Adolf Hitler is dead*

**1945** Adolf Hitler took his own life on 30 April 1945. He finally conceded that all was lost, and decided to take the coward's way out. As a military tactician, Hitler had made some fatal errors of judgement that had seen the impetus of the Second World War go the way of the Allies. This was in part because Hitler had the notion that he was fated to win the conflict whatever move he made. He saw himself as something of a Teutonic messiah, sent to save the Germanic people and lead them to glory. In reality he was in the right place at the right time, and managed to climb the political ladder through a combination of beguilement and thuggery.

As with all dictators, his immediate entourage were a bunch of sycophantic cronies who relished the power that Hitler bestowed upon them. Consequently most didn't think to question Hitler's military strategy, and those who did faced his wrath. Hitler didn't take criticism very well at all, even if it was intended as professional advice. He would fly into a seething rage, like a reprimanded child, and those on the receiving end considered themselves lucky if they got away without further punishment. Military failure, surrender and retreat were entirely unacceptable in Hitler's mind. Consequently he lost some of his most effective officers, when he could have deployed them elsewhere for military benefit.

Ultimately the delusion of invincibility got the better of Hitler. Rather than face his people and take the lead in their hour of need, as Winston Churchill had done after Dunkirk, Hitler retreated both mentally and physically. He spent the final weeks of his life confined to a bunker beneath the Reichstag in Berlin, while the Soviets pounded the city to ruins.

In the end he only cared about himself, and opted to commit suicide rather than face the indignity of capture and the revelation of his mortality to the German people. When, for example, one considers how insignificant and emasculated Saddam Hussein became when captured, it seems remarkable that Adolf Hitler garnered so much power. Such is the potency of myth building, and Hitler didn't want to destroy that myth.

# 2 May

## *The modern age of jet travel arrives*

**1952** The *De Havilland Comet* was the first commercial jet airliner. The inaugural flight was between London, England and Johannesburg, South Africa. Thirty-six passengers were taken on the journey, which took just short of 24 hours to complete – about as long as it now takes to travel from the UK to Australia.

The journey was not non-stop but in six stages, so that the aircraft could be refuelled – at Rome (Italy), Beirut (Lebanon), Khartoum (Sudan), Entebbe (Uganda) and Livingstone (Zambia). New crews also took to the controls at Beirut and Khartoum. The cost of the flights was £175 for a single ticket and £315 for a return, which was quite a lot of money. The average weekly wage was £7 11s in Britain and $64 in the US. Needless to say, only the wealthy could afford international air travel in those days.

Two years after this inaugural flight, things started to go wrong for the *Comet*. There were two crashes in 1954, which resulted in its design being called into question. The first crash happened on the island of Elba, Italy. BOAC Flight G-ALYP fell to earth with the loss of all crew and passengers. Ironically it was the very same aeroplane that had made the historic journey in 1952 that also became involved in the world's first modern air disaster.

The second was South African Airways flight G-ALYY, which crashed near Naples, Italy. Investigations showed that fatigue of aluminium components was to blame. Stresses and strains from pressurisation and vibration had caused parts to fail. Fatigue cracks around window rivets were of particular concern, because they had led to catastrophic fractures of the airframe. The solution was to redesign the windows to avoid the use of rivets and change their shape from rectangular to oval, thereby removing corners which were the points of focus for fatigue.

Stress fractures at the corners of openings is a common problem when designing transport. That is why the doorways of ship, trains, aircraft and even cars have curved corners. This allows the forces of stress to be spread out and dissipated. Ships have been known to split in two from fractures originating from doorways. Unlike wood, metals lack a grain to resist the travel of cracks, so once they get started there is no stopping them. The emphasis is therefore on preventing them from occurring in the first place. It is surprising that such a fundamental error should have been made with the *Comet*.

# 3 May

## *An aeroplane lands at the geographical North Pole*

**1952** Today, explorers know what to expect when they embark upon expeditions to the Arctic. They have sophisticated communications equipment, state-of-the-art survival paraphernalia, and a good chance of rescue if they get themselves into difficulties. However, there was once a time when exploration of the polar regions was a genuinely unknown risk.

On this day in 1952, things were very different from what they are today. Firsts were still being set in terms of polar exploration, and the hazards involved with each visit were exponentially greater than they are now. When a Skytrain aircraft successfully landed on the ice cap at the North Pole, it was an incredible achievement. On board were US Air Force officers Joseph Fletcher and William Benedict, accompanied by US scientist Albert Crary.

The first officially recognised successful trip by land to the North Pole region had been accomplished by an American, Robert Peary, in 1909. Later analysis of his journey, however, showed that while he had travelled deep into the Arctic wastes, he had fallen some 30 miles short of reaching the exact geographical pole itself. Peary's expedition was most likely disorientated by the strange effect the magnetic North Pole has on compasses. The closer to the North Pole the compass is, the less reliable it is. In other words, Peary may have thought he had reached the North Pole ... but he hadn't.

As the modified C-47 Skytrain touched its skis down onto the hard ice, therefore, it was arriving at a place no one had reached before. Benedict had piloted the flight, but it was Fletcher who took the initial steps outside the plane. As he crunched down into the frozen snow, he became the first person to set foot on the exact location of the geographical North Pole.

In 1952, Fletcher, Benedict and Crary may have been making history, but they were hardly amateurs when it came to the extreme conditions and challenges of the Arctic. Earlier that same year, on 19 March, Fletcher had landed the Skytrain on an iceberg and established a weather station there. The station was known by the nicely dramatic name 'Fletcher's Ice Island' until the iceberg broke up some 22 years later. Crary also had a significant career in polar exploration. In 1961, just five years after being part of the first party to reach the North Pole, he successfully led a team to the Antarctic. In doing so, he became the first man to have stood on both poles.

However, all of this may be rather inaccurate, if a Russian claim dating from 1948 is to be believed. As the Cold War tightened its grip on global relations, a number of operations were kept secret from the opposing side. The details of the supposed USSR mission are sketchy, even to this day. However, they assert that on 23 April 1948 Aleksandr Kuznetsov and 23 others successfully landed a Soviet plane at the North Pole, and that it was Kuznetsov, not Fletcher, who first walked on top of the world.

# 4 May

## The UK gets its first female premier

**1979** When Margaret Thatcher became Britain's first female prime minister in 1979, it seemed at first as if the feminist fervour of the women's rights movements of the 1970s had achieved a major victory. It was an extraordinary achievement that inspired many women to reach for the top in their careers in the following decade.

Yet nearly three decades later, women make up a tiny minority of MPs in the British parliament, there are very few women in senior cabinet positions and the prospect of another female prime minister seems as remote as ever. Less than 20 per cent of British MPs are women, and in Gordon Brown's first cabinet of 22 in 2007, there were just five women – even though almost a third of Labour MPs are female.

Despite her own personal success, Mrs Thatcher herself was not a supporter of further advances in the status of women, saying in 1982: 'The struggle for women's rights has largely been won. The days when they were demanded and discussed in strident tones should be gone forever. I hate those strident tones we hear from some Women's Libbers.' Indeed, she went even further, lamenting the feminist assault on the 'man's role as bread-winner'. She herself did little to help women in politics, appointing only one woman to her cabinet in over a decade in power.

Some argue that Mrs Thatcher's personal manner was actually a setback for women, showing, apparently, that women have to behave in an aggressive, masculine way to get to the top. That wasn't a problem for some feminists, though. Towards the end of the 1990s, Natasha Walter wrote in *The New Feminism* that Thatcher was 'the great unsung heroine of British feminism'. It was Thatcher, says Walter, who 'allowed British women to celebrate their ability not just to be nurturing or caring or life-affirming but also to be deeply unpleasant, to be cruel, to be death-dealing, to be egotistic'. There is no doubt that many people were positively shocked by the apparent sudden rash of dynamic, aggressive women in business in the 1980s, replete with large ambitions and even larger shoulder pads.

On the whole, though, life seems to have become tougher for British women during the Thatcher era. In real terms, the gap between women's wages and those of men increased rather than decreased, and women at the lower end of the social scale found life harder as social support was cut and traditional industries went into decline. Despite her championing of family values, Thatcher may have done more in her market policies to contribute to the breakdown of the traditional family than any other post-war prime minister. Ironically, though, some sociologists argue that the very problems that the Thatcher era caused enabled women to advance their status. Many women were forced, by poverty or simply being left as unsupported single mothers, to work and provide their own incomes – thereby gaining a new kind of independence from men.

There is no doubt that Mrs Thatcher made a dramatic mark on British politics and society. But it was probably through her ardent advocacy of market values that she made her lasting impact, not her status as first female prime minister.

# 5 May

## The US sentences the Rosenbergs to death for espionage

**1951** Julius and Ethel Rosenberg became the only Americans to be executed for treason during the Cold War. During the Second World War, the US had decided to keep the Manhattan Project a secret from the Soviets. Even though they were allies during the war years, there was no love lost between them as the Americans were deeply suspicious of Stalin and his communist principles. It made perfect sense, therefore, to prevent the Soviets from being able to develop their own nuclear weapons.

Despite its best efforts, the US administration was unable to prevent communist sympathisers from leaking vital information, both during and after the war. It meant that the USSR was able to conduct its first nuclear test by 1949. Consequently the search was on for the traitors who had undermined US national security.

A number of people were eventually arrested. They included Klaus Fuchs, who had worked on the Manhattan Project, and Harry Gold who had acted as the conduit between Fuchs and the Soviets. A third man, David Greenglass, had been an engineer on the Project and had also given Gold secret information. During interrogation he revealed that the Rosenbergs had also been involved. Ethel was his sister and Julius his brother-in-law.

The Rosenbergs' trial began in March 1951. They were charged with conspiracy to commit espionage, alongside Morton Sobell, another conspirator. Sobell was sentenced to 30 years imprisonment, but the Rosenbergs were sentenced to death. It seems that their being husband and wife was somehow seen as a symbolic betrayal of the American way, more so than the other spies. To make an example of them in the public consciousness they were executed by electric chair. Fuchs received only a fourteen-year sentence, while Gold also got 30 years.

Greenglass was sentenced to fifteen years. His wife was also involved, but Greenglass agreed to testify against his sister and brother-in-law in exchange for his wife's immunity. As a result the Rosenbergs' two sons were orphaned by their execution, while Greenglass' children remained with their mother. So much for brotherly love.

The most famous American traitor is Benedict Arnold. He was an important military officer on the side of the Americans during the War of Independence against the British, before subsequently switching sides. Exiled from America, he died in London in 1801. Just as the expressions 'quisling' and 'Judas' are used to describe a treacherous person in Britain, so 'Benedict Arnold' is used in the US.

# 6 May

## The four-minute mile is achieved

**1954** The world record for the mile run in 1954 stood at 4 minutes 1.03 seconds. Set by the Swedish runner, Gunder Hägg, in 1945, it had stood for nearly nine years when Roger Bannister took his place in the starting line at Oxford University's Iffley Road track. Partly due to the sheer longevity of this record, and partly also because of the psychological barrier that four minutes represented, there were some who thought the magical mark could never be reached.

Bannister was a 25-year-old medical student at the time of the race. Still heavily involved in his studies – he would go on to become a practising neurologist – Bannister would train during his lunch breaks at university. In fact on this day in 1954 the odds were stacked against any sort of world record being set, let alone one of such magnitude. With overcast skies, uncertain weather and winds reaching up to 25 mph, racing conditions were far from ideal.

In the months building up to the race, however, a number of runners had been closing in on the four-minute mile. Bannister's main rival for the record was an Australian athlete, John Landy. Three times already in that year Landy had run just over 4 minutes 2 seconds. Roger Bannister knew that sooner or later the record would fall; he just had to make sure he got his run in before Landy could.

Less than half an hour before the Oxford race was due to start, Bannister was still uncertain as to whether he should run. Part of him wanted to hold back and conserve his energies for another occasion when the weather was more favourable. Another part of him knew that Landy's next race was in Finland the following month, and he did not dare let his opponent have a fourth attempt at the record. When the gusts of wind finally dropped just twenty minutes before the start, only then did Bannister decide that he would run.

The race itself was incredibly tight to the required time at each stage. Over 3,000 spectators were crowded around the track, waiting to see if this was the race in which someone would finally achieve the impossible. When the stadium announcer read out the time at 3 minutes 59.4 seconds they went wild with excitement at what they had just witnessed.

Roger Bannister had finally proved that the four-minute mark could be surpassed. He had set the new world record, and in doing so had taken middle-distance running into the modern competitive period. He was also subsequently proved right in his decision to run that day in Oxford; just 46 days later, John Landy ran 3 minutes 57.9 seconds in Turku, Finland.

Since Roger Bannister's historical run, four minutes has become something of a benchmark time that serious runners expect to pass. In the 50 years that followed, times continued to fall, and the current world record, held by Hicham El Guerrouj from Morocco, stands some seventeen seconds faster than Bannister's time at 3 minutes 43.13 seconds.

# 7 May

## Germany capitulates to bring victory in Europe

**1945** The Führer of the German Third Reich, Adolf Hitler, had been dead for a week. Karl Dönitz had succeeded him as head of state on 30 April, but he and the remaining Nazi officers realised the game was up, and opted to surrender themselves to the Allies.

On 7 May, Alfred Jodl signed an unconditional surrender in Reims, France, so that hostilities would cease at one minute past 11 pm on the evening of 8 May. The British were on double summer time, which meant that it was recorded as one minute into 9 May in London. Celebrations duly followed across Europe when dawn broke on 9 May, but VE Day (Victory in Europe) is officially 8 May in continental Europe. VJ Day (Victory in Japan), was not to come until 15 August 1945, marking the closure of the Second World War. Estimates have it that around 50 million people lost their lives in the war.

In the end, both the Germans and the Japanese failed in their ambitions of conquest. On one level it meant that many lives had been lost in vain, but on another it meant that the world was able to enter a new order by demonstrating that oppressive regimes would be confronted and defeated at all costs. We only need to imagine what the world would now be like if there were a Nazi Europe and Imperial Japanese Far East, in order to appreciate the debt we owe those who laid down their lives for a free world. The adage goes that one doesn't appreciate what one has until it is taken away. They had their lives taken away.

There is a novel titled *Fatherland*, by Robert Harris, an English writer and journalist. The plot supposes that Hitler won the war in Europe and therefore becomes a parallel or alternative history. The premise of the storyline is that the Third Reich has reached a point in the mid-1960s where its infrastructure is fragile. Information is leaked about the Holocaust, which has until then been hidden from the US. This ultimately leads to the decline of Hitler's empire. Japan, meanwhile, has become a possession of the USA following the war and the political map of the world is somewhat different from the way things have actually turned out.

Although the war was so terribly costly in terms of human lives and damage done to towns and cities, it was a significant driver of technology. The need for technological supremacy meant that all manner of programmes were prioritised to ensure victory. In fact, had the war not happened at all then the world would probably be about twenty years behind its current state of progress.

# 8 May

## David Attenborough becomes an octogenarian

**2006** David Attenborough was fortunate enough to enter the world of documentary television and film making in its infancy, and played an active role in developing the medium. He had cultivated a passion for the natural world since childhood, and used the burgeoning industry to explore ways of making programmes that focused on this area of interest.

In the 1950s he went on a series of expeditions to locations such as Guyana, Madagascar, Papua New Guinea and Australia, where he investigated both the wildlife and the native peoples. During these projects Attenborough refined his presenting and narrating techniques, which were to become famous worldwide in the decades to follow.

Attenborough had spells in management at the BBC, but ultimately opted to concentrate on the area that he found most fulfilling. In 1979 his groundbreaking project *Life on Earth* was broadcast. It was the first time a series of programmes had been made to encompass the natural world in its entirety. After that a number of other *Life* series were produced, such as *The Life of Birds*, *The Life of Mammals* and *Life in the Undergrowth*. He has thus made it his aim to expand on all of the themes set down in the original series, so that his legacy is a comprehensive document of the natural history of our planet.

One of the biggest challenges encountered by Attenborough and his camera crew was how to record the hugely varied pace of life in a manner suitable for television viewing. As well as adopting a huge range of existing tricks from motion-triggered cameras to state-of-the-art night-vision lenses, the filming team honed a number of innovative shooting practises.

Using an exceptionally precise stop-motion setup, whereby an image is captured repeatedly over a long period of time, Attenborough's documentaries were capable of dramatically speeding up the slowest of events. In *The Secret Life of Plants*, woods full of bluebells explode with colour in a matter of seconds rather than days, and a bramble can be seen deliberately moving its shoots across the woodland floor.

At the other end of the scale, the crew became masters of slowing down footage that in reality took place in the blink of an eye. Perhaps the most famous example is a shot of a great white shark surging out of the water to grab a leaping seal in its jaws. A sequence that in the living room lasts for around 40 seconds was over for the shark in less than two. David Attenborough himself has paid tribute to the skill of his film crew: 'People assume I do all the work. I keep having to tell them: "It was the cameraman, not me. Usually I wasn't even there."'

# 9 May

## Richard Nixon faces impeachment

**1974** As president of the United States of America, Richard Nixon achieved an incredible amount. During his first term in office he spoke live to Neil Armstrong and Buzz Aldrin as millions watched them step onto the Moon. He also oversaw the integration of racially segregated schools in the southern states and brought an end to the Vietnam War. Then in 1972 he won a landslide election that saw him ushered back into the White House with over 60 per cent of the vote.

The good times were not to last, however, and the events of his second term have ensured that he is remembered for one thing, and for one thing only: the Watergate scandal. On 17 June 1972, five men with links to Nixon's Republican administration were discovered in the act of breaking into the Democratic Party headquarters at the Watergate Hotel in Washington. When arrested and questioned by the police, they confessed to a further Watergate burglary that had taken place the previous month, on 28 May. Despite Nixon's attempts to cover up the story, it was broken to the disbelieving nation by Bob Woodward and Carl Bernstein, two investigative reporters with the *Washington Post*.

With the information out in the open, and with suspicions that there might be further underhand goings-on to uncover, the authorities set to work investigating the Nixon White House and all those associated with it. The detective work was initially conducted by the FBI – whose acting chief at the time, L. Patrick Gray, was later forced to resign over allegations of destruction of evidence – before being taken over by the Senate Watergate Committee and the House Judiciary Committee. In addition to the events at the Watergate Hotel, they discovered evidence of wire-tapping, campaign fraud, and a secret stash of laundered money in Mexico used to fund these illegal activities and buy the silence of those involved in the crimes.

Despite the wealth of incriminating material pointing its finger directly at the Oval Office, Nixon steadfastly refused to admit to any wrongdoing and doggedly continued to hold on to power. By late 1973, it had become clear that the president's position was untenable, and then on this day in 1974, formal impeachment proceedings were opened against him.

As the trial progressed with the release of damning tapes, Nixon realised that the outcome was inevitable. To avoid the disgrace of being impeached, he became the first and only US president to resign from office on 9 August 1974. Whether you liked the man or not, or even agreed with his politics, it is undeniable that what had started as a presidency full of glittering promise had ended in the most ignoble of ways.

# 10 May

## The Rolling Stones gather some moss

**1963** Having seen them playing live, George Harrison tipped Decca Records that the Rolling Stones were an act worth signing up. Initially the Stones performed cover versions of rhythm and blues standards. The Beatles then wrote some songs for them so that they could break into the mainstream.

Eventually they tried their hand at writing some of their own songs. It turned out that Mick Jagger and Keith Richards worked well as a songwriting partnership, and the Rolling Stones evolved into a world-class band. In fact they were second only to The Beatles in popularity, and eventually took ownership of the throne when The Beatles split in 1970.

Between 1968 and 1974 the Rolling Stones enjoyed a period of creative excellence, producing a series of albums that are still regarded as some of the best ever recorded. Since that time they have garnered a reputation for supremacy in live performance, and still continue to tour at a time when many people opt for retirement. Their inspiration comes from the old blues legends who saw their music as a lifelong career, rather than the preserve of the young. They argued that with maturity comes a certain artistic gravitas, in a similar way to a fine wine improving with age. There is every reason to feel that they will continue entertaining audiences until they can no longer perform.

Keith Richards and Ronnie Wood use the term *simpatico* in describing the way their guitars interweave when performing live, so that it is difficult to tell whom is playing what part. It is Spanish for 'agreeable' or 'sympathetic'. They see this as an important development in the sound of the Rolling Stones because it is indicative of a mutual resonance. In technical terms it provides a backbone of consistency in their performance, so that each show is as good as the last. In addition Charlie Watts has a passion for jazz, which has honed his drumming to such an extent that Keith Richards describes it as the 'roll' in rock 'n' roll. Also, Mick Jagger is still surprisingly energetic and full-voiced for someone with a free bus pass. In many respects the Rolling Stones are the blueprint by which other bands measure their own prowess as songwriters and performers. They are the original rock 'n' roll band.

# 11 May

## *The first successful heart–lung transplant is performed*

**1981** Mary Gohlke was the recipient of the organs for this historic procedure, and Bruce Reitz and Norman Shumway of Stanford University were the pioneering surgeons. Although it sounds alarmingly complex, it is in fact a fairly basic process. This is because the lungs are connected to the heart via the pulmonary artery and vein. It means that the transplant surgery only involves the disconnection of the old heart and connection of the new heart, via the aorta (aortic artery) and the inferior and superior venae cavae (cavae veins).

Nevertheless, dealing with such a major organ had proved difficult for surgical teams in the past. Prior to Mary Gohlke's operation, three other such procedures had been attempted. Unfortunately, in each case the patient had died as a direct result of complications during the surgery. The last of these had been in

1971, after which a moratorium had been declared until medical technology could catch up with medical theory.

The history behind Gohlke's operation, which took place on this day in 1981, was not, therefore, especially promising. As well as the problems associated with successfully attaching the primary blood vessels securely enough in order to effectively plumb the new system in, there were the continuing issues regarding the body's acceptance of new organs.

The surgery, however, was a resounding success. Prior to the operation, Gohlke, a 45-year-old advertising executive, had been suffering from severe hypertension and had been given just weeks to live by her doctors. Afterwards her quality of life was transformed. She was sitting up just a day after the procedure, and although she lived for only another five years, she did so with the knowledge that every day was thanks to her historic operation.

Since this surgery at the beginning of the 1980s, medical practice for heart-lung transplants has remained essentially the same. During the procedure the patient is kept alive with a heart–lung machine. Once the donor organs are sewn in place, the new heart is electrically stimulated to begin beating and the chest cavity is closed. Once closed, the vacuum is restored in the thorax so that the diaphragm and rib cage can expand and contract the lungs once more.

When patients suffer from heart problems, they often have defective lungs as part of the equation, so it can be very useful to transplant both simultaneously. However, it is fairly unusual for donors to have both heart and lungs undamaged and in healthy working order. Consequently, relatively few heart–lung transplantation procedures are performed, compared with separate heart or lung transplants. Gohlke was, in fact, the first person to receive a lung transplant of any kind. Since then surgeons have perfected techniques for transplanting lung lobes, single lungs and double lungs.

# 12 May

## Soviets lift their blockade of Berlin

**1949** On 24 June 1948 the Soviet Union put a land and air blockade in place around Berlin. Europe was still in the process of being politically restructured following the Second World War, and Stalin wanted to annexe sizeable portions of Eastern Europe as part of the Eastern Bloc. Germany itself had been divided into four zones occupied by Britain, the US, France and the USSR, but Berlin remained a subject of disagreement. It lay within the USSR-held zone, so the Soviets decided to blockade the city.

The result was the Berlin Airlift, where thousands of Western aircraft dropped parcels of supplies for those beleaguered behind the blockade. Eventually a diplomatic solution was found by bisecting the city into Western and Eastern areas. Ultimately relations between the Soviets and the West got so bad that in 1961 the Berlin Wall was constructed to physically and culturally separate the two halves of the city.

As Berlin was inside East Germany, it meant that the wall had to run the entire perimeter of West Berlin, effectively making it into an island. Initially it was no more than a wire fence erected in a swathe of cleared ground, but eventually a concrete barrier was put in place, which remained until 1989. German reunification came in October 1990.

As propaganda the Berlin Airlift served the Soviets very well. It demonstrated in no uncertain terms that Stalin meant business following the Second World War. It came as something of a psychological blow to the West to find that defeating the Axis nations had only led to a new adversary. At the heart of the perceived threat was a realisation that the Soviets were a defensive enemy, rather than offensive, as Germany and Japan had been. The Soviets had no territorial ambitions, rather they simply wanted to lock the West out. That made them mysterious and alien to Western populations and somehow more frightening because it seemed that they might overreact and initiate a nuclear exchange. The thing to remember is that the Berlin Wall and the Iron Curtain were put in place and patrolled by the Soviets, while the West saw no need for such measures. Ironically, too, they only served to keep disaffected Soviets from escaping rather than to prevent Westerners from going in.

# 13 May

## Assassination attempt on Pope John Paul II

**1981** On this day in 1981, Mehmet Ali Agca and Oral Celik sat writing postcards in St Peter's Square in the Vatican City. Three days earlier, on the 10th, Agca had caught a train from Milan to Rome. This was the final stage on a long winding journey that had started in Sofia, Bulgaria in August 1980. Unassuming in the Italian sun, they were awaiting the arrival of Pope John Paul II. Agca was there as the gunman in an audacious attempt to assassinate the head of the Catholic Church. Celik, his backup gunman, was to detonate a small bomb after the shooting, allowing them both to escape amid a mass of confusion.

As the Pope entered the square, Agca leapt up from his seat and fired several shots at him. The Pope was struck four times: two bullets stuck in his gut, one hit his right arm and the other his left hand. Before the two assassins could complete the task, however, or make their getaway, Agca was jumped on and wrestled to the floor. Panicked, Celik bolted to safety without exploding the bomb.

On his arrest, Agca's motivation seemed clear. He was a Turkish Muslim and a member of the fierce nationalist movement, the Grey Wolves. Assassinating the Pope, it appeared, was a way of drawing attention to the Grey Wolves' cause, as well as removing the head of a major world religion.

Agca's trial was swift and decisive. In July 1981 he was sentenced by an Italian court to life imprisonment.

After he was locked away, controversy began to arise as to whether he really was just a nationalist seeking to bolster his movement's profile. Attention focused on the tortuous trip he made to

Rome, winding his way through several different European countries, presumably in an attempt to hide his origins. Why he should have done so was unclear, and what muddied the waters even further – once his route had been unravelled – was why a Turkish nationalist should be hatching a plan in Bulgaria.

If the authorities who questioned Agca hoped to discover the truth from the man himself, they were sorely disappointed. Agca was not reticent in giving information; in fact he gave so much information, and so much of it conflicting with other parts of his testimony, that police were unable to determine how to uncover the true perpetrators of the plot.

One thing that was certain was that the Bulgaria connection implied some form of definite Eastern European involvement. Indeed, this overlapped with part of Agca's own story implicating the USSR in some form or another. If Agca was just a pawn, then there was also a definite motivation for the Russians: Pope John Paul II was Polish, and Poland, under Lech Wałęsa, was suing for separation from the Soviet-controlled Eastern Bloc.

It remains though, a big 'if' and the Bulgarians always denied any involvement in the assassination attempt, instead claiming that Agca was a plant by the Italians and Americans as part of an attempt to destabilise communism in Eastern Europe.

While conspiracy theorists concerned themselves with the masterminds of the failed assassination, Pope John Paul II asked people to 'pray for my brother, whom I have sincerely forgiven'. After making a full recovery from his injuries, the Pope visited Agca in prison in 1983. In June 2000, after serving just nineteen years of his life sentence, he was pardoned by the Italian president, Carlo Ciampi, and released from jail upon the request of the Pope.

# 14 May

### The first Jewish state in 2,000 years comes into being

**1948** Historically, people of the Jewish faith have had rather a rough ride of it. They were expelled from their homelands in

Biblical times, and managed to maintain their identity by living in Jewish quarters in cities around the world. This survival instinct led to resentment from the populations of the countries they inhabited, because their autonomy meant that they prospered while other economies fluctuated. They were therefore persecuted for seeming selfish and greedy, when all they were doing was keeping themselves to themselves and adhering to their cultural and religious traditions.

Jewish persecution found its ultimate expression in the form of the Nazi Holocaust, when they were blamed for the economic collapse of Germany following the First World War. It suited the Nazis to blame others, rather than accept that Germany had brought hardship upon itself. Millions of European Jews were consequently rounded up and transported to camps, where they were systematically exterminated.

Three years after VE Day, the Jews had their own country in the form of Israel; on this day, the Israeli Declaration of Independence was made as the British Mandate expired. Of course, the very formation of Israel wasn't without its problems. In order to free up the territory, it meant that other peoples had to be removed from lands that they and their ancestors had called home for many centuries. Unfortunately the inevitable hostilities between the Palestinians and the Israelis has now developed into one of the world's ugliest ongoing conflicts.

Racial tensions in the Holy Land have now reached a sorry state of affairs. The Israelis have become a sedentary nation and any humility they had has been largely lost due to perpetual and ongoing hostilities. The Palestinians persist in lobbing rockets onto Israeli soil and the Israelis persist in punishing the Palestinians by ghettoising them and bulldozing their homes. Inevitably, Israelis and Palestinians alike are indiscriminately killed every week and the slaughter seems set to continue. These peoples are racially, religiously and culturally disparate, so it seems impossible that any lasting peace will be won unless there is a rethink about territories and the creation of a Palestine as a bedfellow for Israel. Even then it would only be a peace of sorts. They might stop waging war but resentments would still fester for generations to come.

# 15 May

## A toad is kissed goodbye

**1989** On the island of Costa Rica there used to live a golden toad (*Bufo periglenes*). Actually, only the male was golden, and even then he was more of a Day-Glo orange, while the female was dark green with red spots. So striking was the male's colouring that he was often used on posters advertising Costa Rica as a destination for wildlife tourists.

Jay Savage, the scientist who discovered the toad in 1966, said that the male looked like he had been dipped in enamel paint. Another biologist, Martha Crump, called them 'dazzling jewels on the forest floor'. The livid colouring may have been a warning to potential predators, or simply a way of attracting mates.

The toad lived in an area of tropical cloud forest above the town of Monteverde, and its habitat comprised a territory of only 24 km². Despite being in a heavily protected area, it seems that the population was already in steep decline, and on this day in 1989 the last specimen was seen, a solitary male. A number of organised searches in following years were arranged in the hope of finding a surviving population, as the toads were known to live for long periods underground, but to no avail. In 2004 the International Union for Conservation of Nature listed *Bufo periglenes* as officially extinct.

It seems that a number of agents may have been involved with the demise of the golden toad. Loss of habitat, global warming, disease, specialised lifestyle and having a single population probably all conspired against the survival prospects of the species.

Observation of the breeding habits of the toad showed that climatic changes affected the duration of seasonal pools in which they laid their eggs. If the pools dried up too quickly, the tadpoles were unable to develop into toadlets. Martha Crump noted one occasion in particular when weather systems associated with the El Niño effect dried up the breeding pools, with a significant loss of toad eggs.

Amphibians across much of the Americas are also threatened by a fungal disease, chytridiomycosis, which thrives in cool, damp areas such as the Monteverde cloud forest. Because they have soft, permeable skins, frogs and toads are particularly vulnerable to such diseases, as well as to polluting toxins in the environment.

Historically the toad probably inhabited other parts of the forest where water was always available, so that new generations would have survived during times of drought and supplemented dwindling sub-populations elsewhere. The phenomenon of having several sub-populations in slightly different habitats is seen as a vital evolutionary mechanism, but it was powerless to stop the extinction of this particular forest jewel.

# 16 May

## The Cultural Revolution begins in China

**1966** On 16 May 1966, China's Mao Zedong launched a programme that was to prove one of the most shocking and profound social upheavals of the 20th century: the Great Proletarian Cultural Revolution.

Mao's avowed aim in the Cultural Revolution was to rid the country of bourgeois ideas and recapture the early zeal of communism by mobilising the country's youth. Yet it was clear he also wanted to get rid of his opponents in the ruling party. Eight years earlier, Mao had launched his Great Leap Forward, the economic programme meant to turn China into an industrial powerhouse. The Leap was a disaster, completely wrecking China's rural economy and starting a famine that claimed the lives of more than 30 million inhabitants. Mao accepted the blame for this catastrophe and resigned as chairman of the Chinese Communist Party, but the Cultural Revolution was his comeback, designed to wipe out his opponents, including Deng Xiaoping and Mao's successor as chairman, Liu Shaoqi.

Urged on by Mao, students at Beijing University began to agitate against 'bourgeois' university and government officials.

When Liu Shaoqi tried to damp down the agitation, Mao immediately launched a stinging public attack on him and guided the students to form their own political militia, the Red Guard. At the same time, Mao's supporters encouraged the growth of a personality cult around Mao by distributing copies of his sayings in his *Little Red Book*.

The Red Guard swelled dramatically and schools and universities across China closed down as young Red Guards took to the streets to target the Four Olds – old ideas, old culture, old customs and old habits. Academics were assaulted, books were burned, temples and monuments were attacked, shops selling anything remotely Western were burned to the ground and the gardens of the bourgeoisie were ripped to shreds. Government officials right up to the top, including Liu Shaoqi and Deng Xiaoping, were driven from office. Tens of thousands of people were beaten up, abused, killed or driven to suicide as the campaign rolled on.

As fighting broke out among Red Guard factions and the country was beginning to descend into lawlessness, Mao finally yielded to pressure. He sent in the military who took control, rounding up millions of young Red Guards and sending them off to the country to preach the communist message to the rural community. Today, many millions of these exiles are now in middle age and bitterly rue the way they were separated from their families and deprived of their chance of education when, as teenagers, they were sent away from the cities. Many never went home.

In 1969, Mao was re-elected as chairman of the Republic amid great fanfare, and the Cultural Revolution rolled on until his death in 1976. Estimates of the Revolution's death toll are varied, but it could easily have been at least 750,000. Tens of millions more were persecuted and had their lives ruined. The effect was particularly devastating for minorities, such as the Tibetans. And besides the terrible human suffering, much of China's rich and ancient historical heritage was utterly destroyed in just a few years by the zealous modernisers.

Even the Chinese Communist Party now admits that the Cultural Revolution was a disaster for China. But there is some disagreement about just what went wrong and who was to blame.

The official line is that there is a problem when a personality cult develops, although interestingly, it is the Gang of Four – Mao's four principal allies (including his wife) – who are criticised more heavily than Mao himself.

# 17 May

## Aircraft carrier becomes an artificial reef

**2006** The USS *Oriskany* was scuttled with high explosives in the Gulf of Mexico so that it would sit on the seabed to be colonised by oceanic plants and animals. In the past, a warship of this size would usually have been cut up for scrap and recycled, so there is a clear sense of the US administration having given with one hand and taken away with the other. The sunken ship may provide habitats for sea life, but the additional energy required to build a new warship from iron ore, as opposed to scrap iron, will be enormous and therefore add significantly to unseen environmental pollution.

It is one of those gestures that works well as a public relations exercise, but actually achieves little or nothing when the greater picture is considered. The whole point about recycling metals is that they require far less energy to turn into usable material than metals sourced from raw materials. Some 40 per cent additional energy is required to reduce iron ore to pig iron in a blast furnace as compared with melting down scrap iron. In addition, about 60 per cent of the heat produced by the fuels in the furnace is lost due to thermodynamics.

Then again, one can't deny the benefit that will come to marine life as the ship becomes colonised over the coming decades. In preparation for scuttling the ship, a team had to carefully remove anything potentially toxic to the marine environment, including lead-based paints that had been used as protection from saltwater corrosion. Only when the ship had been cleansed entirely could it be sunk.

Another objective of the sinking was to make the vessel rest upright on the ocean floor. This was to ensure that the conning tower was only a matter of metres from the surface, so that it could be used as a dive site for tourists and to attract species that prefer shallower waters. After all, there would be little human benefit from the exercise if it were not possible for divers to appreciate the plants and animals.

To achieve the upright immersion it was necessary to use carefully positioned packets of explosives beneath the hull. Aircraft carriers are designed to be 'unsinkable' and have extremely thick armour plating and double-skinned hulls as a result. The explosives had to breach the hull evenly so that the vessel took on water in a uniform manner and descended into her watery grave on an even keel.

# 18 May

## India goes nuclear

**1974** On this day, India became the sixth nation to possess nuclear weapons by successfully exploding a fission bomb similar to that used on Hiroshima during the Second World War.

At 8.00 am on the morning of the 18th, a group of scientists led by Dr Raja Ramanna from the Bhabha Atomic Research Centre (BARC) gathered at Pokhran army test range in the Great Indian Desert, Rajasthan. Buried 107 metres below the desert sands, in a specially constructed shaft, was a device codenamed the 'Smiling Buddha'.

The Smiling Buddha, formally called the 'Peaceful Nuclear Explosive', was a twelve-kiloton nuclear bomb. Development of the weapon had begun in 1967, and actual manufacture some two years earlier when, on 7 September 1972, Prime Minister Indira Gandhi gave the go-ahead to Dr Ramanna and his team to enter the final stages of production. With this project, India was bidding to become the first country outside of the five permanent members of the United Nations Security Council to generate a nuclear capability.

The research and construction of the Smiling Buddha was carried out in the utmost secrecy. During the seven years it took to acquire a nuclear bomb, fewer than 80 scientists and engineers were involved with the project. Other than the prime minister, in the government only the national security advisor and the Indira Gandhi's private secretary knew of its development.

Dr Ramanna could not have been certain of what to expect. The Indian bomb was closely based on the American devices, but the end result was like a pared-down version – much simpler and less sophisticated. As the seconds ticked down to detonation, tensions would have been running high. Then, at 8.05 am, the bomb was exploded.

The test was a success. The bomb went off exactly as planned. Indira Gandhi had stayed well away from Pokhran, not wanting to attract attention to the place. Dr Ramanna could not wait to tell her the good news. Upon finding that the blast had ruined the pre-installed hotline, he ran to a nearby village and telephoned from an ordinary landline, telling her: 'Madam, Buddha has finally smiled'.

Those behind the development of the Smiling Buddha were feted when the announcement was made public. Dr Ramanna received the Padma Vibhushan – India's second highest civilian award. Perhaps to assuage global concern, the Indian government announced they would not be building any more nuclear weapons, and would instead be harnessing their nuclear potential for energy purposes. This was a position they seemed to adhere to until May 1998 when they conducted five further tests as a part of Operation Shakti.

Nowadays India is one of the world's foremost nuclear powers. It has a nuclear arsenal estimated at 200 nuclear warheads. Worryingly for some, India has refused to join the Nuclear Non-Proliferation Treaty. This is a binding agreement under which treaty members agree not to assist non-nuclear countries to develop nuclear capabilities. The Indian administration does, however, pursue a rigorous policy of 'no first use' when it comes to nuclear weapons, and since the detonations in 1998, they have declared a moratorium on all future testing.

# 19 May

## Mount St Helens creates the largest volcanic eruption in US history

**1980** The force of the eruption was estimated to have been equivalent to about 500 atomic bombs. Fewer than ten people died, because the eruption had been predicted and the area evacuated of its 2,000 residents. The plume of smoke and ash reached a height of 15 miles in as many minutes and was followed by an immense pyroclastic flow, which is a stream of superheated gases, ash and lava cascading down a volcano's slopes. The pyroclastic flow kills everything in its path by instantly incinerating it. Consequently most of the plants and animals living on the slopes and foothills of the volcano were destroyed before being blanketed by lava, ash and pumice.

In effect, the result was to create virgin landscape devoid of life forms. In this respect the eruption has been used for scientific study to examine the processes involved in recolonisation. Over time, pockets of soil build up comprising ash, mineral dust and organic matter. This provides a foothold for pioneer plants, which provide rudimentary habitats for pioneer animals. Gradually the soil builds up, so that the habitat can support more species of plant and animal, until it resembles the habitat that was destroyed in the first place.

Volcanoes are a consequence of seismic movement. In areas where tectonic plates are being forced together, one plate will slip beneath the other and this causes an immense build-up of pressure. The extreme pressure causes energy to collect and melt the subterranean rock, so that bubbles of magma form below the Earth's crust. Eventually the magma finds its way to the surface, where it erupts. Over time, cones of solidified larva are formed, which are the bodies of volcanoes.

Volcanic eruptions are largely random, as there are many variables involved. The best that scientists – volcanologists – can do is calculate that a particular volcano has erupted once every ten years,

50 years, 100 years and so on. It gives some idea of when an eruption is due, but warning signs are a more reliable means of escaping harm. Unlike earthquakes, which suddenly happen, volcanoes tend to give some indication of an imminent eruption. There is usually some activity by way of smoke escaping from the crater and scientists now have the necessary technology to detect ground swelling as the magma pushes upwards. This kind of activity can continue for days and weeks before an eruption actually occurs, giving people plenty of time to evacuate.

# 20 May

## *The journal* Science *publishes the first information about HIV*

**1983** Two scientists claimed to have discovered the cause of Aids (acquired immune deficiency syndrome) at the same time. They were American Robert Gallo and Frenchman Luc Montagnier. It turned out that they had indeed both discovered it, although they had given it different names: HTV-III (human T lymphotropic virus type III) and LAV (lymphadenopathy-associated virus) respectively. A row ensued but things were brought to a close in 1986, when the US and French presidents met. From that point onwards the agent became known as HIV (human immunodeficiency virus).

In fact it is a retrovirus, because it has an RNA genome as opposed to one of DNA. This is regarded as a more primitive biological entity. It reproduces by splicing itself into the DNA of a cell nucleus. This means that it corrupts the DNA coding of the cell, but cannot be dealt with by the body's immune system. Once inside the DNA it becomes a provirus and is reproduced whenever mitosis (cell division) occurs. It therefore invades the body progressively, so that the host organism eventually loses its functional integrity. The retrovirus can also target new types of cell, enabling it to implant itself as a provirus in new types of tissue.

Initially it was thought that there may be no effective ways of dealing with HIV infection. Since the 1980s drug therapies have come a long way, so that it is possible to slow the advance of HIV invasion considerably. This means that patients are no longer faced with certain death in the short term, but can survive for decades with the infection. One key problem with the drugs is that the retrovirus develops immune strains within the body, so that options eventually run out. This has the knock-on effect of introducing drug-resistant strains into newly infected patients.

Most major diseases have been present in human populations for centuries if not millennia, and scientists are not generally interested in their points of origin. With Aids it is different, as it clearly arose in the 1980s, seemingly out of nowhere. This has prompted investigation into where it came from. Unscientific theories range from its being a divine punishment for homosexuality to people catching it by having sex with baboons, while scientific theories tend to agree that it originated from Africa. Recent work suggests that the virus reached Haiti from Africa in the mid-1960s, before arriving in the US in 1969. It then took a decade for enough people to be infected in America for it to be noticed and identified as a distinct disease. In Africa it may have been present in a small population for a long period of time but never noticed due to already short life expectancies and the prevalence of many other fatal diseases.

# 21 May

## *The birth of a Notorious rapper*

**1972** This the birth date of Christopher George Latore Wallace, better known as the late rapper The Notorious B.I.G. Also using the names Biggie Smalls, Big Poppa and Frank White, Notorious was born into a world where poverty and crack cocaine were ways of life.

Raised by a single mother in Brooklyn, New York, Wallace started selling crack on the streets at the age of just twelve. At around this time he acquired the nickname 'Big', after his physical stature. Despite excelling at school, he dropped out at seventeen to pursue a life of crime. Shortly afterwards he was dragged in front of the courts on weapons charges and sentenced to five years' probation. When he was arrested in 1991 for dealing crack cocaine, he was sent to remand prison for nine months.

There were few prospects in the poor black ghettos of Brooklyn, especially for one who seemed so intent on living as a career criminal. Wallace's saving grace was his talent as a rapper. For many this was the way out of the ghetto life, or at least the means by which money, possessions and notoriety may be achieved.

In 1992, after hearing a demo tape made by Wallace under the name Biggie Smalls, Sean 'P Diddy' Combs, the rapper and record producer, signed him to his new record label, Bad Boy Records. Later that same year, Wallace featured on a remix of Mary J. Blige's 'Real Love' as The Notorious B.I.G.

After two years of reasonable success rapping on various singles, Notorious released his debut solo album, *Ready to Die*, on 14 September 1994. It was an instant hit, selling over 4 million copies.

The success of *Ready to Die* served to propel Notorious to the heights of stardom, but also to his demise. In 1995, Notorious lifted his protégé band, Junior M.A.F.I.A., into the limelight. Combined with his solo recordings and collaborations with other hip hop and R&B performers, at the end of the year Notorious was the biggest-selling male solo artist in the US.

This rapid rise by the rapper from Brooklyn came at a time when West Coast music was very much the dominant force on the American hip hop scene. Almost overnight, in Notorious and figures around him such as Combs, the Junior M.A.F.I.A. and fellow New York artist, Tupac Shakur, the East Coast had emerged as a serious rival.

Tensions between East and West Coast rappers began to run high. There were quarrels, unrest and even incidents involving firearms. Then, in April 1995, following a shooting the previous year, Tupac accused Notorious and Combs of having a part in it. In October 1995, Tupac quit the East Coast grouping to sign for the Los Angeles-based Death Row Records.

In 1996, the spats from the previous year broke out into outright violence. On 13 September, Tupac Shakur died as a result of gunshot wounds received in a drive-by shooting.

In the March of the following year, Notorious travelled to California to promote his forthcoming second album, *Life After Death*. However, in the early hours of 9 March, on his way home from an awards party, Notorious was shot through the window of the vehicle he was travelling in. He died just hours later at the Cedars-Sinai Medical Center, a violent end for the talented rapper who could never escape the violence of his youth.

# 22 May

## *Most powerful earthquake on record rocks Chile*

**1960** The earthquake that rocked Chile in May 1960 was the most powerful ever recorded. Only the Indian Ocean quake of Boxing Day 2004 came anywhere near. Seismometers reported that it reached a phenomenal 9.5 on the moment magnitude scale, the refinement of the famous Richter scale that scientists use to measure really big quakes. By comparison, the quake which devastated Sichuan in China in May 2008 reached 7.4.

There were actually several quakes. A moderately sized quake of 7.5 magnitude rocked Chile on the morning of 21 May. Then, just as the emergency services were getting the situation under control the next afternoon, another struck ... and this one was a monster. The focus of the earthquake was about 160 km offshore, but it was so powerful that it rattled all of Chile, causing devastation in the town of Valdivia.

But the quake wasn't the end of it. It originated under the Pacific Ocean, shifting a slab of the seabed a massive twenty metres along a 1,000 km rupture. This huge shift in the seabed propelled gigantic waves of water bowling out through the ocean in all directions at the speed of a jet plane. In just an hour and a half, tsunamis reached the Chilean coast and as they rolled up the shore, they rose up to form a series of waves up to ten metres high which swamped coastal villages.

As if this wasn't enough, the Chilean authorities soon faced another, even greater danger, as landslides triggered by the quake blocked the San Pedro River. Lake Rinihue very quickly filled up and threatened to burst its dam. If it had done, the many towns and villages below the dam – home to over 100,000 – would have been utterly obliterated. Soldiers and engineers went into action with anything they could get their hands on, from bulldozers to hand shovels, to dig relief channels to let some of the water out before the dam burst. After a heroic effort, they succeeded the following afternoon.

Meanwhile, the tsunami had been rolling westwards out across the Pacific, as well as eastwards towards Chile. Fifteen hours after the quake, the tsunami hit Hawaii, where a wave nine metres high swept away 61 people who had ignored the tsunami warning. Lives were also lost in Japan and the Philippines, and damage was record as far away as New Zealand.

It is always hard to pin down precisely what damage earthquakes do, but it seems likely that fewer than 6,000 people lost their lives in this quake. Despite its massive power, the Chilean quake caused only a tiny fraction of the fatalities of the Indian Ocean quake of 2004 and the much smaller Sichuan quake of 2008. What matters with a quake is not how powerful it is, but where it strikes. The Chilean quake was relatively mild in its effects because it struck far from major centres of population. In other words, we were relatively lucky this time. If a quake this size were to occur near one of the world's major cities, the devastation would be unimaginable.

# 23 May

## *Hitler's successor ends his administration*

**1945** Following Adolf Hitler's suicide, Karl Dönitz became Reichspräsident (President of the Third Reich), but his government didn't last very long. From 30 April until 23 May in fact. His administration was known as the Flensburg government, as that is the name of the place where they hung on to power until they were captured by the Allies.

The Flensburg government presented the Allies with a small headache. Although the German armed forces had surrendered unconditionally, Dönitz had not conceded a similar civilian settlement. By taking up station in Flensburg, it seemed that he wanted to maintain a low-key civilian government, and keep Germany under German control.

This was something the Allies were very much against. A similar state of affairs had existed at the end of the First World War and Hitler had used the surrounding conditions to claim a betrayal by the Allies under the conditions of the 1918 surrender. This then became the platform from which he built his vicious brand of nationalism.

On this day in 1945, determined not to let the same thing happen again, the Allies declared that they would not recognise the legitimacy of Dönitz's administration, and forced him to dissolve the Flensburg government.

Dönitz himself was an unlikely choice for Hitler to make as his successor, as he could have chosen Hermann Göring, Heinrich Himmler or Joseph Goebbels, who were all fanatical followers. It seems that he chose someone who was more likely to run things on an even keel. It made little difference when all was said and done, but perhaps Hitler had a notion that his last decision should be a sound one. Indeed, Dönitz was the only one brave enough to face the music after the war instead of committing suicide. In fact he served just ten years in prison and lived a free man until his death in December 1980, at the age of 89.

Following the war and his spell in prison, Dönitz retired to a village in West Germany and wrote his memoirs. He was not regarded as a war criminal, because naval operations had little or nothing to do with any of the atrocities that were committed by the German army and to a lesser extent by the German air force. He made it clear that he was merely a sea commander going about his job as efficiently as he could, largely removed from the mindset of Hitler's regime.

Albert Speer, who had been Hitler's architect and minister for armaments, was another who sought to distance himself from the Third Reich after the war. He was repentant for his role in the regime and became known as the 'Nazi who said sorry'. Speer had been privy to information about the death camps and felt guilty about turning a blind eye. He died a year after Dönitz in London, England.

# 24 May

## *Russians try to get to the centre of the Earth – and fail*

**1970** The Kola Peninsula in Russia was where the deepest-ever hole was bored by man. It was begun in 1970 and drilling continued until 1989. By then the hole reached 12.3 km (7.6 miles) down into the crust of the planet. It was and still is the deepest hole ever dug. The temperatures at that depth proved to be so high that the equipment began to malfunction. It was hoped that 15 km might be reached, but scientists calculated that the technology simply wouldn't cope with the heat.

Because of the depth of the 'Superdeep Borehole' the Russians invented a new drilling technology. They realised that a rotating shaft would become progressively stressed as it grew longer, until it could no longer remain intact. So, the solution was to design a system whereby only the drilling head rotated. They achieved this by using hydraulic principles. A lubricant fluid, or engineering mud, was pumped down the shaft and the pressure drove the drill bit. The mud also lubricated and cooled the drill bit, as well as cleaning it and carrying debris back to the surface as it travelled upwards around the outside of the shaft. The mud could then be filtered and recirculated.

This is the principle by which all modern deep boring, for the purpose of extracting crude oil and natural gas, is done. The cutting head itself is driven by an impeller, and is equipped with diamond teeth so that it lasts as long as possible before needing to be replaced or refurbished.

Jules Verne wrote a classic novel titled *Journey to the Centre of the Earth*, published in 1864. In an age when scientists knew little of the composition of the planet, Verne gave himself licence to imagine a subterranean world where explorers encounter extinct prehistoric creatures, including a primitive ancestor of humanity. The 19th century was a time of scientific enlightenment when fossils of dinosaurs, human ancestors and other ancient creatures were being identified, so Verne brought these elements to life in his dystopian vision. In 1870 he published a companion novel about marine adventurers, *Twenty Thousand Leagues Under the Sea*. While it is true that the world's oceans do indeed harbour exotic creatures, alas the Earth itself is nothing more than a ball of molten rock and iron.

# 25 May

## A New Hope *for science fiction films*

**1977** In 1971 Universal Studios offered George Lucas a deal to finance two of his films. These were to be *American Graffiti* and *Star Wars*. Two years later, in 1973, *American Graffiti* was released; *Star Wars*, however, had been rejected at an earlier concept stage.

It was not until 1976, with the script having undergone four drafts and under the guidance of a new studio, 20th Century Fox, that the filming of *Star Wars* finally began. Over a year later, on this day in 1977, the first film in the *Star Wars* franchise eventually made its debut in US cinemas.

Originally scheduled for release in Christmas 1976, shooting and production were fraught with difficulty and delay: location filming in Tunisia – where traditional underground houses were used as the set for Luke Skywalker's childhood home on Tatooine – was hampered by an unseasonal deluge; the special effects were both untried and over budget; and the crew and actors were occasionally bemused by Lucas' somewhat chaotic directing style.

When an early cut was shown to some of Lucas' fellow directors, Steven Spielberg among them, only Spielberg professed a liking for the film.

Fortunately for Lucas, *Star Wars* and the film's many fans, the production studio kept faith in the unwieldy beast that the movie was turning into. They accepted the delayed finish and the budget that spiralled from $8 million to $11 million. They stuck with Lucas as the mammoth production struggled under its own weight. And then, when cinemas were reluctant to subscribe to the completed film, 20th Century Fox threatened to withhold another highly anticipated film due for release later that summer unless they first screened the new sci-fi movie.

Their belief in the project was handsomely rewarded. Undergoing four further cinema releases, in 1979, 1981 (upon which it acquired its now-famous subtitle, *Episode IV: A New Hope*), 1982 and 1997, it earned over $300 million in the US, and $797 million worldwide. In doing so it shattered all previous records, becoming the first film to pass $300 million and, until the release of *Titanic* in 1997, it stood as the highest grossing film of all time.

Since 1978, *Star Wars*' principal characters have gone on to appear in a further five films: *Episode V: The Empire Strikes Back* (1980), *Episode VI: The Return of the Jedi* (1983), *Episode I: The Phantom Menace* (1999), *Episode II: Attack of the Clones* (2002) and *Episode III: Revenge of the Sith* (2005). The apparently disjointed nature of the production is a reflection of Lucas' original concept of nine titles, comprising three largely independent trilogies. It remains uncertain, however, if the remaining *Episodes VII–IX* will ever be made as films.

Today *Star Wars* boasts an influence around the globe. As well as the films, there have been hugely successful lines of merchandise, including original books and video games, as well as clothes, toys and spin-off films and television shows. The symbols of the films have been adopted into all aspects of 20th-century history, from Ronald Reagan's 1983 'Star Wars' missile defence programme – which involved shooting lasers from space – to the more tongue-in-cheek responses to the 2001 England and Wales census in which some 0.7 per cent of the population declared themselves to be followers of the 'Jedi religion' – exceeding the number of Sikhs, Jews and Buddhists. In total, a world audience of well over a billion people have sat down and felt the force.

# 26 May

## Mars Odyssey *detects water on Mars*

**2002** The planetary orbiter *Mars Odyssey* used its gamma ray spectrometer to detect the presence of hydrogen atoms beneath the surface of Mars. This has been interpreted as the presence of water, in the form of permafrost under the poles. This isn't seen as a sign that life may be present, but rather as a supply of water, hydrogen and oxygen for when astronauts eventually visit Mars. It is significant because it means that the payload of a spacecraft need not include additional water tanks and gas bottles.

As Mars is a considerable distance from Earth, the plan is to set up a biosphere of some kind, similar to the life support modules that are used in Antarctica. That way people can come and go without needing to take everything with them. Moreover, it should be possible to grow fresh food.

On 25 May 2008, a new robotic spacecraft named *Phoenix* became the first to land at a Martian pole. It made a soft landing exactly where intended. Its primary mission is to analyse water samples in the soil of the landing site to determine whether they might ever have been a suitable habitat for simple life forms. This is seen as an important investigation on a number of levels. First, if life or the evidence of life is found then that would suggest that life is more common in the universe than is currently thought likely. Second, it might point to the possibility of Earth's having been 'seeded' with life rather than being the point of genesis.

*Mars Odyssey* now acts as a communications link between the Earth and *Phoenix*, as well as two planetary rovers, *Spirit* and *Opportunity*, that patrol the Martian surface, sending back all sorts of detailed information about its geology.

From what scientists know about creating amino acids – the

building blocks of organisms – the conditions required to kick-start life were present on Earth about 4.8 billion years ago. A concoction of water, chemicals and electrical storms seem to have spontaneously created the first nucleic acid molecules, which then found a way of building cell walls around themselves to become single-celled organisms. It seems unlikely that similar conditions ever existed on Mars, but the *Phoenix* mission may help us understand our planetary neighbour better all the same.

# 27 May

## *The greatest Russian literary mind returns from exile*

**1994** Alexander Solzhenitsyn was exiled from Soviet Russia for revealing too much about the atrocities committed in the name of communism. He had already won the Nobel Prize for Literature, and his profile was too high for the regime to have dealt with him in the way they would normally have done, by sending him to a labour camp in Siberia. Ironically, it was Solzhenitsyn's portrayal of life in the gulag that had caused such consternation in the first place. He had previously experienced life in labour camps for criticising Stalin, which was why he felt compelled to tell the world of their horrors.

Solzhenitsyn was awarded the Nobel Prize in 1970. In 1973 his masterpiece *The Gulag Archipelago* was published in the West and began to circulate in Russia in an underground form. This led to his being exiled in 1974, when the Soviet administration could tolerate criticism no more. Ultimately the collapse of the USSR in 1991 meant a new beginning for Russia. Solzhenitsyn was duly pardoned and he returned to his homeland from the US in 1994. Afterwards, he became the voice of the people in many respects and openly commented on the post-Soviet government with impunity.

For all his notable achievements, Solzhenitsyn does still have his critics, both back home in Russia and in Western critical circles. He may have decried the communist system, but some still argue that while he may not have supported the Soviet political system, he nevertheless believed in Russian supremacy over other nations. One of their major arguments is a perceived anti-Semitism that runs through his work, where he portrayed the Jews as blocking the national interests of the true Russians.

However, to his supporters, right up until his death in August 2008 he retained a forthright view, unafraid of highlighting the grim reality of political and social life in the USSR. Unfavourable depictions that come to light in his work are creations of the Soviet-era system, not of Solzhenitsyn himself.

Whichever side of the debate one falls on it is undeniable that Solzhenitsyn was one of Russia's greatest writers. The first truly significant Russian novelist in this vein was Leo Tolstoy, who did eight years before the birth of Solzhenitsyn. With *War and Peace* and *Anna Karenina*, Tolstoy established the genre of realistic fiction which seemed to suit the Russian mindset so well. With so much tragedy and drama happening in real life, novels were employed as a tool for expressing such events. Tolstoy wrote about pre-communist Russia, but his stories were no less engaging as they focused on the Napoleonic wars and their effects on Russian families. It was this blueprint that Solzhenitsyn transferred to communist Russia and the hardships suffered by the population under Stalinist rule.

# 28 May

## Chichester completes his solo circumnavigation

**1967** Francis Chichester was the first person to sail around the world in splendid isolation. He set off from Plymouth, England, on 27 August 1966 and took 226 days to complete his voyage. The rules of circumnavigation are rather peculiar, as they do not require the sailor to follow a route as close to the equator as one might think. From England the journey involves sailing down the Atlantic Ocean, going round Antarctica and then retracing the route back up the Atlantic. This is known as the 'clipper route'. In other words, it is valid as long as a pole has been encircled. Presumably it won't be long before the North Pole is used instead, which will mean slashing the time taken considerably. To solve the problem it might be better to simply set a course that covers an exact distance of 40,075.2 km (24,901.5 miles), which is the circumference of the Earth at the equator.

In 1968 the *Sunday Times* newspaper set up a round-the-world race called the *Sunday Times* Golden Globe Race, which ran between 14 June 1968 and 22 April 1969. Robin Knox-Johnston became the first person to circumnavigate without stopping. Rather sadly, another competitor, Donald Crowhurst, decided to fake his journey when he realised that he stood no chance of winning the race. He eventually took his own life when he realised that his plan wouldn't work. Knox-Johnston donated his winnings to Crowhurst's bereaved family. A third sailor, Nigel Tetley, lost his boat because he mistakenly thought Crowhurst was closing in on him, and sailed it so hard that it disintegrated. When the truth of Crowhurst's deception was discovered, Tetley was given a consolation prize. Tetley also committed suicide, in 1972, having failed to raise enough money to make another attempt at the round-the-world record.

On 20 January 2008, French sailor Francis Joyon set a new world record for solo circumnavigation of the globe at 57 days, 13 hours, 34 minutes and 6 seconds. It beat the previous record held by Ellen McArthur by a margin of fifteen days and seems set to stand for some time to come. Although technology has transformed yachting since the 1960s, there is still a strong element of chance as to whether weather conditions and winds are favourable. Joyon was extremely lucky to find himself on a perfect run, thereby enabling him to take a huge chunk out of the previous record time. It is not impossible, but it is certainly unlikely, that anyone will beat 57 days anytime soon.

# 29 May

## *Mount Everest is conquered*

**1953** At 11:30 am on 29 May, New Zealander Edmund Hillary and his climbing partner Tenzing Norgay made the last final shimmy up an ice crack and hauled themselves up the snow with their ice axes to stand clear on the summit of the world's highest mountain. 'To my great delight, I realised that we were stood on top of Mount Everest and that the whole world spread out below us,' was how Hillary remembered the momentous occasion.

The pair stayed on the summit for just fifteen minutes, while Hillary took photos, and then they began the descent. A little way down they met George Low, one of the huge support team, and Hillary succinctly reported: 'We knocked the bastard off.' News quickly spread around the world, making Hillary instantly famous.

Although Hillary was a New Zealander and Tenzing a Tibetan Sherpa, this was essentially a British expedition. When the news of the ascent reached London four days later, it was the eve of the young Queen Elizabeth's coronation and it was widely seen as the perfect start to the new reign. Elizabeth's first act as queen was to knight Hillary. Some stories suggest she wanted to knight Tenzing too, but the offer was apparently declined by the Indian Prime Minister, Nehru. For decades, debate raged over whether it was Tenzing who reached the summit first or Hillary. Before Tenzing's death in 1986, Hillary always refused to confirm that he got there first, but he finally revealed the truth in his 1999 book, *View from the Summit*. 'I continued cutting a line of steps upwards. Next moment I had moved onto a flattish area of exposed snow with nothing but space in every direction. Tenzing quickly joined me and we looked around in wonder.'

Since Hillary's famous ascent, over 4,000 climbers have made the attempt on Everest, now known more often by its Chinese name, Qomolangma. About 660 have succeeded, and 142 have died in the attempt. On 8 May 2008, a Chinese team lead by a

Tibetan woman carried the Olympic flame to the summit as part of the build-up to the Beijing Games.

In fact, climbing Everest has become big business. An attempt on the peak is rarely just a few hardy climbers going it alone. Even Hillary had a support team of over 400. There are literally queues of people waiting to give it a go in the climbing season, leading Hillary, an ardent conservationist, to protest vociferously at the vast piles of rubbish left behind. In April 2008, the Chinese completed a tarmac road all the way to the Everest base camp to make it easier for followers of the Olympic flame. Tourists are expected to begin travelling this route after the Olympics.

# 30 May

## Evel Knievel clears sixteen cars in California

**1967** Evel Knievel is one of those odd characters in modern history who achieved notoriety through his failings rather than his successes. He was a motorcycle daredevil who forged a career for himself by performing ever more dangerous feats. His early successes at jumping rows of vehicles established his reputation, but it was his spectacular crashes that earned him worldwide fame and financial reward. He wasn't known so much for his jumping records as for the number of bones he had broken. The facts gave way to rumour and myth, so that people came to know him as the man who had 'broken every bone on his body'. In fact it was about 40, which was still quite something.

He was dashingly handsome and a natural showman, both of which go a long way to explaining the phenomenon that built up around Evel Knievel. Merchandise items sold in their tens of millions and his cartoon persona spread his image around the world. In reality he wasn't a particularly good role model. He was temperamental and given to moments of aggression.

Nevertheless, Knievel's legend continued until his death in 2007, and will undoubtedly live on even though other stunt riders have achieved far greater feats. It only goes to show that there is no such thing as bad publicity, and that people identified with his have-a-go spirit combined with his image as a kind of mortal superhero.

One of Knievel's more amusing feats was a failed attempt to jump the Snake River Canyon in 1974. He used a steam-propelled machine called a skycycle, which was launched like a rocket. Unfortunately for Knievel a safety parachute deployed itself during the flight, which would have been successful had it not. The machine hung pendulously from the parachute and drifted down into the canyon, where it came to rest on the nearside bank of the river. Knievel was lucky not to have drowned, as he was strapped in and required assistance to escape the vehicle.

In England a motorcycle daredevil named Eddie Kidd made a name for himself in the 1980s. After in excess of 3,000 successful jumps Kidd made a bad landing in 1996 and suffered severe injuries. They left him physically and mentally handicapped and put an end to his glittering career.

# 31 May

## The Trans-Alaska oil pipeline is completed

**1977** Begun on 27 March 1974, it took only three years to construct a single 48-inch (1,220-mm) pipeline all the way across Alaska, north coast to south coast – a distance of about 800 miles (1,286 km). Engineers elected to build the pipeline above ground for a number of good reasons. It made the project far easier and cheaper not having to dig trenches through varying types of substrate. This also meant less disruption to the environment, even though the pipeline is visible. Having the pipeline held aloft allows wildlife to migrate beneath the pipeline, and it also allows maintenance crews to identify and repair defects and leaks with relative ease. The project employed over 20,000 people, of whom 31 were killed due to accidents along the way.

The purpose of the pipeline is to transport crude oil from the north of Alaska to a sea port on the south coast. It means that tankers don't need to navigate their way around Alaska and through the Bering Strait to pick up their cargo. From the seaport at Valdez, tankers carry the oil to the US mainland where it is refined. The pipeline has survived a number of natural and man-made events, including earthquakes, explosions, forest fires and gunshots. A number of major leaks have resulted, and clean-up involves the removal of affected soil to ensure that pollution is kept to a minimum. Corrosion and general weathering are also inspected for on a regular and frequent basis.

Although crude oil reserves are finite and will eventually run out or become too expensive to tap, there are still enormous oil fields to keep the world going for another few decades at least. Crude oil isn't just used to produce fuels, as its 'fractions' (constituent chemicals) come with a range of chemical properties that can be used in different areas of industry. They are separated by a process called 'fractional distillation', which involves heating the crude oil so that the fractions boil off at different temperatures. These component parts of crude oil include petrol (gasoline), diesel oil, kerosene (paraffin oil), petroleum spirit (aviation fuel), petrolatum (Vaseline), liquid petroleum gas (LPG), lubrication oils, greases, naphtha, benzene, asphalt and other heavy fractions which are 'cracked' (broken down) to produce chemicals for making plastics, drugs, rubbers and synthetics.

# 1 June

## Two war criminals are executed

**1946** and **1962** In 1946 Ion Antonescu, leader of Romania during the Second World War, was executed by firing squad. Antonescu had collaborated with the Nazis during the war and been instrumental in the deaths of hundreds of thousands of Jews and Romany gypsies during the conflict. Following the defeat of Germany, Antonescu was put on trial in Romania charged with betraying the Romanian people for the benefit of the Third Reich, as well as the aforementioned atrocities. He sought to 'purify' the Romanian race just as Adolf Hitler had done with the Teutonic peoples. In Antonescu's case, his own stepmother and first wife had both been Jewish, so it may have been that his motivation was coloured to some extent by ingrained personal prejudices.

Adolf Eichmann was an SS officer responsible for managing the deportation of European 'undesirables' to ghettos, concentration camps and extermination camps. Following the war he fled to Argentina, where he assumed a false identity and lived without detection for a number of years. He was discovered in 1957, although it took some time for Mossad (the Israeli intelligence agency) to verify his identity and formulate a plan to capture and arrest him. In May 1960, Eichmann was abducted and flown to Israel without the knowledge of the Argentinian government. It took several months of negotiation and diplomacy before Israel could try Eichmann once his capture had been made known to Argentina. He was indicted for crimes against humanity, among other charges, and duly found guilty. He went to the gallows in 1962. Eichmann is often regarded as the architect of the Holocaust. However, it seems that he wasn't in possession of a particularly vindictive or cruel personality, but simply wanted to do his job in an efficient and exemplary manner to please Adolf Hitler.

Romania has had its own fair share of despotic rulers. In 1967 Nicolae Ceauşescu, a former shoemaker, became president, having become leader of the Romanian Communist Party two years earlier. He and his wife Elena initiated 'reforms' which involved their effectively being elevated to royalty and gathering immense wealth by stealing it from the nation. They built a vast palace in Bucharest, which involved obscene amounts of public money and the demolition of thousands of homes. In 1989 their crimes caught up with them and they were executed by firing squad. Since then, Romania has been governed as a democracy.

# 2 June

## Beagle 2 *becomes the first European planetary probe to be launched*

**2003** *Beagle 1* was in fact HMS *Beagle*, the ship that carried Charles Darwin around the globe on the expedition which inspired his theory of evolution by natural selection. It was hoped that *Beagle 2* would prove to be the vehicle that revealed information about the possibility of life on Mars. Alas, it was not to be. Carried to its destination by *Mars Express*, the probe broke contact with mission control six days before it was due to descend to the planet's surface and begin transmitting data.

Since then no further signals have ever been received from *Beagle 2*, and on 6 February 2004 the probe was declared officially lost by the European Space Agency. Scientists are uncertain as to why *Beagle 2* went missing. It may be that it didn't penetrate the planet's atmosphere and so failed to reach Mars' surface. Other theories suggest that it was badly damaged in a crash landing, or that it simply developed a minor technical fault and is currently roving over Mars, unable to transmit any of its data.

On 31 December 2003, photographs taken of the proposed landing site revealed a large crater at the centre. It was initially thought that the probe had ended up trapped inside the crater and that its signals were being restrained by the high walls. On a closer inspection, however, this proved not to be the case.

*Beagle 2* was equipped with various apparatus to sample and test the environment chemically for signs of life currently on Mars or once having been there. Life forms would only be very simple organisms, if they exist at all. As yet, Earth is the only planet known to provide the necessary conditions for DNA to exist and organisms to evolve. If signs of rudimentary life are eventually found on Mars, then it would at least mean that biological entities are considered likely to be more common in the universe than current scientific opinion says.

The funding for *Beagle 2* was extensive. Half of the £44 million budget was supplied by the British government, with the remainder being raised from the private sector. However, not only is the outlay for Martian missions considerable, the chances of seeing any return on that investment is very slim indeed. Since 2006, 37 missions have set off on their way to the red planet. Of these, only eighteen – less than half – have successfully reached their destination.

# 3 June

## *The force of nature kills 43 scientists and journalists*

**1991** Mount Unzen, Japan, had been quiet for nearly 200 years when it erupted in 1991. The eruption began properly on 20 May when lava began flowing from the newly awakened crater. With such dramatic photo opportunities available, news teams had moved into the area alongside volcanologists who were studying the volcanic activity.

Although lava flows are dangerous they are nothing compared with pyroclastic flows, which suddenly roll down the sides of volcanoes at high speed. Pyroclastic flows are streams of tephra, or superheated gases and particles of rock. Animals and plants that happen to be in the way are instantly incinerated, and that is what happened to the unsuspecting onlookers that day. Without any prior warning, a pyroclastic flow raced down the side of the volcano to a distance of 4.5 km (3 miles) from the crater, erasing all life in its path. Three eminent volcanologists lost their lives: Harry Glicken, and husband-and-wife team Katia and Maurice Krafft.

Mount Unzen is one of sixteen volcanoes worldwide that are listed as potentially dangerous to human populations and therefore continually monitored. They are termed 'decade volcanoes', not because they have a tendency to erupt every ten years, but because the list was assembled as a part of a project, initiated from the UN, to reduce deaths by natural disasters. Thus the 1990s were pronounced the International Decade for Natural Disaster Reduction.

The trouble with events such as eruptions, earthquakes and tsunamis is that they occur when tectonic stresses cause sudden movements in the Earth's crust. Scientific methods have so far failed to predict such events with much accuracy. Consequently more emphasis is placed on alerting and evacuating the population as quickly as possible during seismic activity, in the hope that lives will be saved. Volcanoes aren't quite as dangerous as earthquakes in this regard as crater activity tends to give some warning, such as a plume of smoke.

Geological evidence shows that volcanic eruptions were far more commonplace millions of years ago. Volcanic activity created a good deal of the land that is present today and played an important role in shaping the evolution of plants and animals. Some archipelagos, for instance, owe their existence to past volcanic activity. The Galapagos Islands are a good example. They were all made by the same volcanic vent, and each island is a dead volcano sitting on the ocean floor.

# 4 June

## Cash comes out of the wall

**1973** The very first cash machine was a mechanical contraption installed by the Citi Bank of New York in 1939. Designed by

Luther George Simjian, it failed to catch on with the public and was dismantled after just six months.

The idea hadn't died though, and with the advent of more complex and more manageable computer systems in the 1960s, inventors got back to work. On 27 June 1967, De La Rue unveiled the first electronic cash machine at a branch of Barclays Bank in Enfield, London. Single-use cards with magnetic strips allowed customers access to pre-packaged envelopes with £10 inside.

It would take a few more years for the first recognisably modern cash machines to establish their dominance. In 1968 Don Wetzel, an employee of the baggage handler Docutel, led a development team that put together a truly modern machine. Unlike previous variations, this cash machine was networked and worked by accepting a bank card with a PIN stored on the magnetic bar. Now, rather than just picking up convenient cash, bank customers could actually withdraw funds from their bank accounts at any time of the day or night.

After perfecting the design, Wetzel submitted his plans for patent approval and on this day in 1973, the first patent for a modern cash machine was awarded to Wetzel and his colleagues, Tom Barnes and George Chastain. That same year, a similar electronic machine commissioned by Lloyds Bank made its way into the British banking system. On both sides of the Atlantic, regular customers suddenly had significantly greater access to and control over their money.

Cash machines these days are spread all over the world. They are commonly known as ATMs (Automated Teller Machines) in the US, cashpoints and holes-in-the-wall in England, Wales and Northern Ireland, and cashlines in Scotland. It is estimated that there are currently well over 1.5 million of them operating globally, located everywhere from cruise ships to the McMurdo Station in Antarctica.

Of course, the ubiquity of cash machines has led to them becoming regular targets for gangs who are eager to get at the money inside. For the most part this is kept securely inside a reinforced vault, but since the late 1990s organised criminals in Japan have taken to acquiring heavy construction equipment and uprooting machines from their foundations in order to force them open elsewhere. There are more subtle ways of stealing from cash machines as well, most of which focus upon card fraud. This is a growing problem worldwide, and increasingly companies are required to protect and monitor their machines to try to ensure that criminals can't use them illegally.

# 5 June

## News of Tiananmen Square reaches the world

**1989** On 4 June the Chinese administration decided to crack down on pro-democracy student protesters assembled in Tiananmen Square, Beijing. At that time the communist government saw Western ideology as its nemesis and overreacted by opening fire on the students.

On this day in 1989 news of the atrocity reached the world at large, and one image in particular came to symbolise the determination of the students to stand up for what they believed in. That image was of an unidentified man standing in front of a line of tanks, refusing to let them advance at the risk of being mown down. There had been reports of tanks ploughing through crowds of protesters the day before, and this knowledge only added to the tension of the footage.

It is not known for certain how many died in Tiananmen Square, but it was certainly hundreds and maybe thousands. At the time it seemed like a futile gesture against the communist regime. Since then, however, the administration has relaxed its grip on the nation, realising that the only way forward for communism is to adapt it to a market economy.

These days those who fought for democracy are seen as martyrs who gave their lives for the sake of a greater good. Interestingly the population of China still operates in communes, but those communes are allowed to establish industries and set up trade links with other nations. So far it is proving to be a very effective and lucrative way of operating and it satisfies the fundamental tenet of communist philosophy that the individuals comprising a society should all benefit equally.

China is now a leading producer of consumer goods because the country has a ready supply of relatively cheap labour. As a result, a great deal of wealth is now flowing into China and it is evolving from a developing to a developed nation very rapidly.

For the time being this suits the West because it provides its populations with affordable goods and prevents inflation from getting out of hand. Inevitably the dynamic will change in years to come, because the Chinese themselves will become accustomed to a higher standard of living. Then economies will shift so that it becomes more viable to manufacture goods in other parts of the world.

As for the man who stood in front of the line of tanks, little is known for certain about him these days. Often referred to enigmatically as 'The Unknown Rebel', he was quickly subsumed into the crowd after his iconic demonstration. From there the story runs out fairly rapidly; he may well have been arrested by Chinese police, and indeed Bruce Herschensohn, part of Richard Nixon's White House staff, believes that he was executed by the authorities shortly afterwards. Other theories, however, claim that he is still alive and that he could be anyone from a man named Wang Weilin, who was a nineteen-year-old student at the time, to an unnamed man who, as of 2006, is known to be residing happily in Taiwan.

# 6 June

## A certain reminder of the uncertainty of continued existence

**2002** Near-Earth asteroids are celestial bodies orbiting the sun in close proximity to Earth. Their orbital paths are either just inside or just outside our own. Asteroids tend not to have circular orbits but elliptical ones and this means that they cross the orbital path of our planet, creating the potential for a collision. This is precisely what happened on this day in 2002. An asteroid measuring ten metres (30 feet) entered the atmosphere and exploded over the Mediterranean Sea, south of Greece. The explosion had the force of a small atomic bomb, but the energy was dissipated and debris fell into the water.

At this period in astronomical history the Earth is not hit by significant asteroids very often, as most have been mopped up since the formation of the solar system. The dynamic systems of the Earth mean that little sign of their impacts remains, but the surface of the moon is peppered with craters that have been preserved as a prehistoric record.

The asteroid was undetected on its approach, which makes something of a mockery of the notion that it might be possible to detect, intercept and deflect asteroids and meteors. They travel at extremely high velocity and provide relatively small 'footprints' when approaching directly. It is rather like attempting to alter the course of an approaching bullet. In 1908 a large meteor exploded over Tunguska in Siberia. On that occasion the force of the explosion burned and flattened forest over an area of hundreds of square kilometres. As it occurred in a remote region relatively few people were killed or injured, but it would have been a very different story had it fallen over a town or city.

Cosmologists use a number of terms in describing different astronomical bodies. Asteroids are sometimes termed minor planets or planetoids, as they can range from objects the size of our Moon down to tens of metres in diameter. They differ from comets as they lack atmospheres (comas) and do not produce tails when near the sun. Meteoroids are those fragments smaller than asteroids, right down to objects just a millimetre across. The term 'meteor' is used to describe the streak of light in the sky when a meteoroid enters our atmosphere, and a 'meteorite' is a piece of a meteoroid that has landed on the ground.

# 7 June

## Israel makes a 'pre-emptive' air raid on an Iraqi nuclear power plant

**1981** Looking back at Israel's extraordinary 'out-of-the-blue' bombing raid on Saddam Hussein's nuclear bomb plant at Osirak prompts the question: 'what if … ?' At the time, Iraq was on course to have its first operational bomb by 1985. If it hadn't been stopped in its tracks by the Israeli raid, would Saddam have used nuclear bombs on Iranian cities in the Iran–Iraq war? It is a horrifying possibility. Saddam was not slow to use terrible chemical weapons and bomb Iranian civilians. Would he have stopped short of using nuclear weapons if he had had them?

The Israelis, of course, were worried not about the Iranians' but rather their own safety in the face of Iraq's developing nuclear potential. Ironically, the plan for an Iraqi bomb was inspired by a PLO report on Israel's own nuclear weapons, entitled *The Israeli Bomb*. Like the Israelis, Iraq turned to the French for help building their bomb, and the French, desperate for Iraqi oil in the wake of the energy crisis, were willing to give it.

Israel's intelligence forces learned of the Iraqi bomb in 1977, the same year that Menachem Begin, a former terrorist, was elected as prime minister and the country adopted a more aggressive stance. Immediately, agents of Mossad (Israel's secret service) began destroying bomb parts in French warehouses, provoking international outrage but doing little to stop the programme. By June 1981, Mossad estimated, the Osirak plant would go 'hot', making it impossible to bomb it without causing a nuclear explosion. So Begin decided he had to act fast.

The only planes Israel had for the raid, codenamed Operation Opera, were American F-16s. The F-16s had been supplied on condition they would only ever be used defensively. The Israelis decided to use them anyway. On the afternoon of 7 June 1981, eight F-16s took off to fly the 1,600 km from the Israeli airbases in Sinai to Osirak. Flying low all the way to avoid radar detection, they reached the plant while the Iraqi anti-aircraft unit personnel were having dinner. They dropped their bombs, destroyed the plant and returned home so swiftly that for a day or so it wasn't clear that the raid had actually happened.

However, it had, and as soon as the news leaked out there was a storm of international outrage at the unprovoked Israeli attack on a neighbour in peacetime. The UN, the Soviet Union and the Arab League all furiously condemned the Israelis. The US was particularly embarrassed since American planes had been used. Yet it was not so very long before President Reagan was saying: 'What a terrific piece of bombing!', and Bob Dylan wrote a song praising the 'neighbourhood bully' who destroyed a bomb factory.

Initially, the French agreed to help Iraq restart the programme, but then quietly withdrew in 1985. It seems likely that without their help Saddam could make no progress – although many feared that he had, which is why the intelligence reports about Iraqi weapons of mass destruction prior to the second Gulf War seemed so credible. Although Israel's 'pre-emptive' raid gave the country a hostile, belligerent image, the protest gradually ebbed away. As Israeli prime minister Yitzhak Shamir later said, many people criticised the raid, but very few, in the long term, regretted that it happened.

# 8 June

## George Orwell nods to the future with
Nineteen Eighty-four

**1949** The dystopian novel is a genre spawned from the rapid technological advancement that occurred over the 19th and 20th centuries, which, when combined with the world wars, highlighted the differences between the views of the world's populations.

The first person to have a go at imagining a future world was H.G. Wells, who published *The Time Machine* in 1895. He envisaged that the human race would evolve into two species – the dominant and aggressive Morlocks, and the submissive and passive Eloi. It was a comment on the apparent divisions in the human condition. That is to say, that we can all behave humanely or inhumanely depending on the circumstances.

In 1932, between the world wars, Aldous Huxley published *Brave New World*, in which he created a world anticipating the control of humanity by technology. Orwell's dystopia was based on the notion of a society in which people's movements and thoughts are controlled by a regime, so that the idea of freedom is severely compromised in all respects. Ray Bradbury's *Fahrenheit 451*, of 1953, was influenced by the onset of the Cold War and similarly presented a future scenario in which people were brainwashed and indoctrinated by ideologies.

By the late 1950s authors were imagining post-apocalyptic scenarios, where surviving populations are dealing with the consequences of human actions. John Christopher (aka Samuel Youd) published *The Death of Grass* in 1956. In it, a virus kills off all species of grass, so that crops such as wheat, barley, corn and rice are lost and livestock have nothing to graze upon. The following year, Nevil Shute unleashed *On the Beach*, which imagined a post-Third World War world, with people scraping a living in a radioactively contaminated wasteland. J.G. Ballard released the books *The Drowned World* (1962) and *The Drought* (1965), in which he explored the ideas of a world with, respectively, too much water and too little as the result of environmental abuse.

The latter years of the 20th century and early 21st have seen no let-up in the dystopian vision, but the earlier works stand out as seminal books for having established the genre. Since then there have been so many authors jumping on the bandwagon that the modern stories are nothing more than attempts at finding different angles on a long-established theme.

In reality, of course, the world has never been a utopia or a dystopia but rather a 'mesotopia', comprising elements of both good and bad, depending on the individual's perspective and circumstance.

# 9 June

## Thomas Sutherland is taken hostage in Lebanon

**1985** The Lebanese Civil War (1975–90) was born of a complex political situation, which was largely triggered by the formation of Israel in 1948. Many Palestinian refugees poured into Lebanon, which already had ethnic tensions between Christian and Muslim native populations. The country had reached critical mass by the 1970s, and civil war was the unfortunate outcome.

Israel, Syria and the West all played their parts in supposedly intervening, but all they really succeeded in doing was pouring fuel on the fire of ethnic discord. In 1982 the capital city, Beirut, fell under siege. Those on the inside were Muslims, while those on the outside were Christians and Jews. It was this stalemate situation that led to hostage-taking as the beleaguered Muslims tried to find ways to struggle out of the situation.

The hostage takers operated across a broad, largely undefined area and high-profile Western figures were considered prime targets. Those who had cause to be in Beirut – news reporters and others who worked in the city – constantly found themselves in dangerous situations with a high risk of capture. Thomas Sutherland was the dean of the American University. Other Westerners taken hostage included Terry Waite, who was envoy to the Archbishop of Canterbury, Mike McCarthy, a British journalist, Brian Keenan, a teacher at the American University and Terry Anderson, a news correspondent. All were held by Shiite Hezbollah militants who were attempting to force US troops out of Lebanon. They were all released in 1991, having spent about five years in captivity, sometimes together, sometimes in isolation.

To this day those who were held hostage are mentally scarred by their ordeal. Five years of uncertain incarceration is a terrible form of psychological stress. There are phases that captives go through during their imprisonment, which vary according to conditions and personality. Initially, there is always fear, frustration and anger. This has a caustic effect on the mind and can prompt it to eventually turn in on itself into an imaginary world. It is a form of subconscious protection that can inadvertently lead to insanity and despair if the sufferer is afforded no respite.

When hostages are released the process of adjustment and reintegration into society can also be a difficult road. It is similar to the phenomenon of institutionalisation in prison inmates, who become so used to the routine of prison that, upon their release, it becomes a sanctuary, where they would rather be. Recidivism – a relapse into criminal ways – is high in such former convicts, because they simply cannot cope with the outside world.

# 10 June

## The Six-Day War comes to an end

**1967** Israel, having by then been established for almost two decades, found itself in conflict with a collective Arab force, comprising Algeria, Egypt, Iraq, Jordan, Kuwait, Saudi Arabia and Syria. The war only lasted from 5–10 June, but the outcome was a reshuffling of territory in the Middle East, with Israel having gained the Gaza Strip, eastern Jerusalem, the Sinai Peninsula and the West Bank.

The end finally came on this day in 1967 when the Arab nations realised that they could not contain Israel's tactic of precise strategic strikes. After Israel had seized the Golan Heights from Syria earlier in the day, a ceasefire was signed in which the combined forces ceded all the newly occupied territories to Israel.

Although the difference in troop numbers was huge, this had little effect on the course of the battle. The Israelis had a well-equipped and well-trained army that was able to overcome the massed Arab forces. Many Jews in the US had Israeli connections, and they provided the financial backing to create an extremely effective defensive army. The Arabs, on the other hand, suffered from a chronic lack of cohesive strategy, due in part to the logistics of managing their larger numbers.

The lasting effect of the Six-Day War was to demonstrate to the

Arab nations that the Israelis meant business and that they were there to stay. Until then they had regarded Israel as something of a tumour waiting to be removed when they got round to it. Afterwards it was a matter of realising that the Jews would not easily relinquish their hard-won homeland.

There was also an important religious result regarding Jerusalem. Contained within the city is the Western Wall, Judaism's holiest site. Prior to the war, Jews were barred from entering the part of the city where the Western Wall was located. Following the ceasefire, access was opened up and this proved to be a significant victory for Jewish identity – the very thing that their opponents had been trying to crush.

Since the 1960s it has become ever more apparent that those responsible for administering the creation of Israel did so in a desperately short-sighted manner. In their haste to remedy the wrongdoings of the Nazis, things were pushed along without due consideration for the Palestinians who had occupied the region for many centuries. Palestine, which had a largely agricultural economy, was deemed to be occupied by ignorant farmers and any need for any diplomacy was more or less dismissed. Israel was created and the Jews poured in from around the world.

It was a mistake for which the Israelis continue to pay the price. Had a separate nation been created with clear-cut territorial boundaries to accommodate the Palestinians, then tit-for-tat disputes might have been settled by now. As it is, resentments continue unabated. Perhaps it is time, after 60 years or so, for everyone to sit down and work out a solution.

# 11 June

*The world's first hovercraft goes into service ferrying passengers across the Solent, between Southampton and the Isle of Wight*

**1959** Just as Alexander Graham Bell prototyped the telephone by assembling various inventions devised by others, so Christopher

Cockerell developed the hovercraft. The first machine he built had a rigid rim. This meant that it hovered only a few inches from the surface of land or water and was unable to negotiate obstacles that made the surface anything less than flat. Nevertheless, he was able to demonstrate the potential usefulness of having a vehicle that hovered on a cushion of air. As a sea-going vehicle it meant that it didn't matter where the tideline was, as it could ride straight over beaches, mudflats and marshland, between water and land.

Cockerell's work began in 1952, but it wasn't until 1962 that the hovercraft had its stability problems solved with the rubber skirt, the invention of Denys Bliss. The skirt effectively contained the air cushion, so that the vehicle was held several feet above the surface. This meant that it could ride over waves and rocks without physical damage. It also meant that the air pressure was kept uniform because the skirt moulded itself to uneven surfaces.

The hovercraft has been used as a passenger vehicle in many parts of the world since the 1960s. The largest civil hovercraft is the BHC SRN Mark III. It is 185 feet (56.4 metres) in length and can accommodate 418 passengers and 60 cars. Most hovercrafts are somewhat smaller than that, as the energy output required for motion becomes exponentially greater with size. There are many hobbyists who build their own mini hovercrafts for the purpose of racing and leisure. A few hovercrafts have also been developed for military applications, as they have obvious potential as landing craft in sea invasions and as amphibious transporters in swamps and marshes, where conventional boats would get into difficulties. They are very noisy, however, so the element of surprise would certainly be lost.

An alternative to the hovercraft is the ground-effect aircraft or ekranoplan. It is an aeroplane that doesn't fly, but instead sits on a cushion of compressed air that lies between the wing and the water surface. Although ekranoplans are primarily sea-based vehicles, they can also travel over land or ice. Land-based travel, though, is exceptionally dangerous as the surface has to be totally flat for the ekranoplan to operate. The Russians developed them as troop and cargo transporters for the Caspian and Black seas. Smaller versions have been manufactured in other countries and are seen as potentially important, as they have a greater fuel efficiency than both boats and aeroplanes.

# 12 June

## *The first man-powered flight across the English Channel, or* La Manche *in French*

**1979** The trouble with human-powered flight is that we have a poor power-to-weight ratio. Animals adapted for flight have all evolved to be as light as possible. Those that achieve flight by constantly flapping their wings, such as hummingbirds, have to be very small as their volume increases eight-fold while their dimensions increase twofold. Others that glide, such as albatrosses, have very long and narrow wings so that lift is achieved over a large surface area. The latter principle was the one opted for by the team who built the channel hopper. It was named the *Gossamer Albatross* in allusion to its inspiration. The overall shape of the aircraft was indeed albatross-like, but it was also amazingly lightweight – hence the reference to gossamer, which is used by young spiders to transport themselves after hatching.

The subframe of the aeroplane was made from carbon fibre, while the wing ribs were made from expanded polystyrene. All the surfaces were made from a lightweight plastic film. The whole machine could be lifted by the pilot alone.

The cockpit was slung beneath the centre of the wing and was essentially a bicycle, so that the pilot powered a propeller via a chain and rode along the ground on two wheels until take-off was achieved. The aircraft was so fragile and light that it required very calm conditions to fly reliably. Minimal turbulence was enough to blow the plane off-course and cause it to crash-land. Nevertheless, Bryan Allen managed to cross the English Channel in 2 hours and 49 minutes and put himself into the record books. The distance covered was 22 miles and 453 yards (35.82 km), which equated to an average speed of about 8 mph (13 kph).

The constructor of the aircraft was Paul MacCready, who has

gone on to develop some remarkable solar-powered planes. As yet none of these machines have any real practical application because they can carry very little payload, but the work is valuable in extending scientific knowledge and may one day prove very useful indeed.

Human-powered helicopters have also been built, although only to show that it is possible. Such machines have to be extremely lightweight with huge dimensions in order to find the necessary lift. As a result, they can only be flown within hangars where wind conditions are very still. So far it has only been possible for such an aircraft to reach an altitude of a few centimetres for just a few seconds. There is a prize of $20,000 waiting for the first team to build a vehicle capable of reaching three metres (ten feet) in altitude and sustaining it for one minute.

# 13 June

## *The first V-1 falls on London, heralding a new type of warfare*

**1944** The V-1 flying bomb was affectionately known as the 'doodlebug' or 'buzz-bomb' by Londoners, because its propulsion unit made a distinctive buzzing noise rather like a giant insect. The German name for the weapon was the *Fieseler Fi 103*. Its method of propulsion was a simple jet engine called a pulsejet. Fuel and air were ignited in a combustion chamber and the exhaust gases shot through a valve at the rear, which then slammed shut again, ready for the next cycle. It was this open–close system that produced the buzzing noise, which was audible from some distance away.

The V-1 was the first guided missile, as it had a guidance system onboard to ensure that it remained on target. Altitude, direction and speed were all regulated by mechanisms that effectively worked together as an autopilot. Range was determined by the amount of fuel. In other words, the bomb was given a measured quantity of fuel, so that it simply fell to Earth when the fuel ran out. It was this sudden silence that Londoners feared, as they knew that a bomb was about to find a target. The precise location of detonation was entirely random, but that gave the weapon a terrorising quality, as it was indiscriminate in the death and destruction it caused.

Some 8,025 V-1 bombs were sent to London, from various locations in continental Europe. On average, nearly three people were killed by each one and they caused untold damage to buildings and roads. The advantage to the Germans was immediately clear, for they lost no personnel during the V-1 operations as the weapons were unmanned. Counter-measures were devised by the British, but with limited success. Apart from simply shooting the bombs in flight, it was discovered that Spitfires were capable of intercepting the bombs and tipping them off course. The Spitfire's wing was raised beneath that of the bomb until the air streams were pushed together. This caused the bomb to yaw to the other side. It would then crash before it had time to rectify itself.

Before the end of the Second World War, the Germans had developed the V-2 flying bomb, which was even more deadly than the V-1. The V-2 was a proper rocket and flew supersonically. This meant that it made no sound on its approach, so that strikes were entirely unanticipated. Only after the explosion did the noise of the rocket engine catch up. The V-2 could not be shot down or intercepted either, because it travelled at high velocity and at very high altitude. A total of 1,358 were targeted at London. Some 2,754 people lost their lives to the V-2 in London, giving an average of about two deaths per bomb.

# 14 June

## John Logie Baird – 'The Father of Television' – comes to the end of transmission

**1946** Following the development of the radio – for sending and receiving audio information – by Guglielmo Marconi as the 19th century became the 20th, inventors were wondering whether it might be possible to do something similar with visual information, specifically moving images. John Logie Baird became the first to succeed in developing a machine for achieving this aim with any reliability. His first successful experiments were conducted in 1924, which is now often regarded as the year that television began. As with so many groundbreaking inventions there were many others pursuing the same goal and some had succeeded in transmitting still images long before Baird dreamt up his system.

Baird's television system was a combination of electromechanical and analogue engineering – in other words, it had moving parts as well as electrical components. Modern systems, by way of contrast, are entirely electrical and digital. The key to Baird's invention was a large disc punched with spiralling holes, called a Nipkow disc. As the disc rotated, the holes allowed light to pass through in a sequence of adjoining curved bands. Seen together, these bands comprised the television image, and the human eye interpreted the changing bands as a continuous moving image because they moved too quickly for the brain to notice the gaps between them.

By 1925 Baird was performing public demonstrations with his machine, which he called the 'televisor'. By 1929 the BBC had begun broadcasting the first television programmes and his system had the monopoly until 1935, when a new electronic system was introduced by EMI. This sounded the death knell for Baird's system, which became obsolete in 1937.

The Second World War then suspended further developments in television, as the BBC had more important duties to attend to with its radio service. Baird did continue with his work on television systems during the war years, but died the same year that television was reborn.

The human eye is able to interpret television images as one continuous picture because that, in essence, is its everyday job. The retina comprises thousands of photoreceptive cells, and the optic nerve therefore carries thousands of individual messages to the brain. In effect this means that the brain receives many individual dots of light, which it then interprets as a whole image. Combining lots of pictures from a television screen into a moving sequence is therefore a doddle.

# 15 June

## *The Mega* Borg *supertanker initiates the first experiment with bioremediation*

**1990** The orthodox way of dealing with spillages of crude oil is to physically recover as much as possible and then use detergents to chemically break down the rest. Sometimes fire is also used to burn the oil off. Needless to say, these methods still leave the environment polluted in one way or another. Bioremediation is the application of oil-eating microbes or bacteria that decompose the crude oil in a natural way. The component chemicals are converted into other compounds by the microbes and then dispersed harmlessly into the environment without causing any lasting damage.

Liquid cultures of the bacteria are sprayed onto the oil, along with nutrients called biocatalysts, to encourage the bacteria to multiply and begin their work. The first culture of this kind was called *Alpha biosea* and was developed by Franz Hiebert. The first test following the Mega *Borg* spill off the coast of Galveston was inconclusive, but subsequent tests following the first Gulf War showed that the microbes were very effective at cleaning up oil residues contaminating the Saudi Arabian coastline.

The oil-eating microbes naturally feed on hydrocarbons (which are the constituent chemicals of crude oil) and reduce them to carbon dioxide and water in the digestion process. Quite where these helpful microbes originally came from is somewhat uncertain. There are, however, some parts of the world where oils and tars exist in exposed deposits and they may well have evolved here. Alternatively hydrocarbons can be found in different states in other sources, as they are a natural product of biological composition. One such bacterium that supports this latter contention is *Alcanivorax borkumensis*, which is known as a proteobacterium (sea bacterium). It is especially fond of compounds in the alkane or paraffin group, which include methane, ethane and propane. Its genus name, *Alcanivorax*, translates as 'alkane-eater'. In the absence of crude oil it feeds on the products of marine decomposition.

In recent years scientists have discovered that simple life forms have evolved for survival in the most unlikely of environments. They are microbes generally grouped under the name 'extremophiles', and they actually require extreme conditions which would kill other organisms. Oil-eating microbes are relatively tame by comparison, as some extremophiles inhabit places that are both exceptionally hot and poisonous, while others live in environments that are incredibly cold and almost entirely devoid of accessible energy.

In geological terms the environments chosen by these intrepid microbes would have been more commonplace in the past, while the planet was evolving to its present state. Microbes have the ability to multiply very rapidly. This would have made them perfect early life forms as they would have been able to adapt very quickly in order to find ways of exploiting the harsh conditions on the planet in its infancy.

# 16 June

## Life itself becomes a patentable product

**1980** The purpose of a patent is to provide protection for an inventor of an idea, so that no one else can exploit that idea without permission from or financial benefit to the inventor – the principle of intellectual property rights. In 1980 a bacterium became the subject of a patent application and was duly licensed. The bacterium in question was a genetically engineered microbe and was therefore the unique invention of its creator. The patent had in fact originally been applied for in 1972 but turned down at that time. By 1980 the importance of the new bacterium had increased significantly because it was designed as a crude oil digester, and clean-up operations were becoming more of an issue in the public consciousness. There was therefore big money to be made in the field of bioremediation, which became a burgeoning industry from that year onwards.

The inventor of the new bacterium was a scientist at General Electric named Ananda Mohan Chakrabarty. The microbe itself was derived from the *Pseudomonas* genus and the patent application was for: 'Micro-organisms having multiple compatible degradative energy-generating plasmids and the generation thereof.'

After Chakrabarty's 1972 application had been refused, it was overturned by the United States Court of Customs and Patent Appeals. This second decision, however, was in turn opposed by Sidney Diamond, the US Commissioner of Patents and Trademarks. He applied to the Supreme Court to try and get the patent repealed. On this day in 1980, the Supreme Court cast its verdict, rejecting Diamond's contention and finding in favour of Chakrabarty. They upheld the argument made by the earlier appeals court that had stated that 'the fact that micro-organisms are alive is without legal significance for the purposes of the patent law'.

This set a significant precedent by making genetically modified (GM) organisms and their manufacture patentable. Since then it has become commonplace to patent GM organisms and selectively bred organisms too, be they animal, plant, fungus or microbe. The 1980 ruling was based on the notion that 'relevant distinction is not between animate and inanimate things but whether living products could be seen as human-made inventions'. In other words, if an organism would not result from natural selection then it was to be considered a human invention and could therefore be patented.

This area of patent law is now described as 'bioprospecting', although those opposed to it use the term 'biopiracy'. They argue that the basic building blocks of any organism are common to all life forms (which is indubitably true), so therefore no organism should be patentable regardless of whether a human assembled those building blocks in a certain order. The undercurrent to this point of view is that GM organisms should always be designed for the good of humanity and that if they are, then they should be freely available to all of us, like air and water. Faced with environmental catastrophes, people shouldn't have to pay for the means to remedy the situation.

# 17 June

## The first kidney transplant proves a success

**1950** Ruth Tucker became the first person to get a new kidney in Chicago, USA. At that time no drugs had been developed to guard against the possibility of her body rejecting this new organ, but she was lucky and her immune system accepted the donated kidney. In fact, she lived for another five years before succumbing to an unrelated illness.

Following this landmark operation surgeons gradually developed their techniques and things really took off when immunosuppressive drugs became available. Nevertheless, it has always been standard practice to find donors who are as compatible as possible to reduce the risk of rejection. Blood relatives are always a good option, especially identical twins, as they are an exact match.

For many patients without viable relatives, or for conditions which require organs of which we only have one, such as a heart or liver, donor organs can be very difficult indeed to acquire. Because of this, scientists are now looking to cloning and stem cell technologies with the intention of growing new organs for patients from their own tissue.

Should this dream become a reality it would spark a revolution in the medical world. It might one day be a matter of routine to order a new organ in advance of an operation, with the safe knowledge that compatibility is 100 per cent guaranteed. Even in the case of organ loss through cancer, it should be possible to keep people alive indefinitely by removing cancerous tissues and replacing them with spare parts grown in laboratory conditions.

However, before the vast amount of ground between dream and reality can be covered, we must live with the fact that, unfortunately, the human body is far better at rejecting organs than it is accepting them. This is because the body naturally treats any

231

foreign tissue with suspicion. It reacts as if the tissue is an invading organism and so the immune system goes on the defensive just as it would with unwelcome bacteria or viruses. This is consequently described as the immune defence mechanism. Immunosuppressive drugs, which prevent the mechanism from working, are used to overcome this in the hope that donor organs will be treated as part of the body. Not only is success not guaranteed, but the drugs must also be taken continuously as the body will revert to its immune reaction as soon as the drugs wear off.

The body actually produces its own immunosuppressive hormones, so that it doesn't reject parts of itself – a phenomenon known as autoimmunity. If one thinks about it a person comprises the genetic material of two parents, so the body needs to be able to recognise and cope with this. Moreover, the genetic material of the parents has four points of origin and so on. We are all assemblages in this respect, so the immune system has to be finely tuned to understand what is a part of the body, and what is not.

# 18 June

### 'Killer bees' cement their reputation by killing a dog in Arizona

**1993** Killer bees are the result of accidental hybridisation. They are a cross between domestic honey bees and a strain of wild African bees, which were introduced into Brazil for experiments to improve honey productivity in tropical climates. Little did the scientists realise that they had inadvertently brought together a genetic combination that would result in an extremely hostile and aggressive new bee. The domestic honey bee is *Apis mellifera*, while the killer bee or Africanised honey bee is *Apis mellifera scutellata* – a subspecies. As it turned out, their honey productivity is superior to that of the domestic honey bee in the tropics, but they are tricky to manage due to their aggression and have spread throughout the Americas.

The first Africanised bees had been brought to Brazil in the

1950s. While the scientists were conducting their experiments, however, a number of bees were released before all their aggressive instincts had been eliminated through selective breeding. Once in the wild, the bees proved impossible to manage. Their spread, while not rapid, was relentless. It was not long before they had established themselves in their new environment.

Their arrival in America took place at some point in the early 1990s, first in Texas and then Arizona. It was on this day in 1993 that the reports broke that a couple of weeks earlier the bees had claimed their first victim, a small dog in Tucson who is thought to have wandered too close to a nest in the roof of a house. When the colony was examined by experts, it was estimated that it had been there for between four and eight months.

This fact quickly spread alarm through the people of Arizona. If the bees had been there for that long, then it was quite possible that other colonies also existed nearby. By mid-1995, these fears had been confirmed and 95 colonies had been discovered throughout Arizona.

Shortly after this figure had been confirmed, the bees claimed their first human casualty. On 6 October 1995, an 88-year-old woman living near Phoenix was stung over 1,000 times. Less than two weeks later, a 66-year-old man from the same area also died after receiving nearly 150 separate stings.

The fundamental problem is that their behaviour is designed to ward off African predators such as honey badgers, so they attack en masse. This is the cause of death in unsuspecting victims, as they receive so many stings that their bodies cannot deal with the level of toxins introduced to their bodies. Added to this, there is the problem of anaphylactic shock, whereby an extreme allergic reaction ensues. This can lead to death because the airways become blocked by swollen tissue, especially if stings are received in the mouth and throat. Even if victims don't die they certainly have a very unpleasant experience, as the bees are behaviourally programmed to defend their nests at all costs, committing suicide in the process of delivering their stings.

# 19 June

## Valentina Tereshkova becomes the first woman to complete a space mission

**1963** In the fierce rivalry between the USSR and the USA that fuelled the race into space in the mid-20th century, it was the Soviets that had the clear edge for a long while. Getting the first woman, Valentina Tereshkova, into space was just one of a whole string of firsts for the Russian space programme.

Back in 1956, the USA, which greatly benefited from Nazi wartime V-2 rocket technology, had triumphantly announced that it intended to launch an artificial satellite. It was something of a shock, therefore, when two days later, the Russians announced that they would do exactly the same. In fact, they got their satellite, *Sputnik 1*, up first on 4 October 1957, and followed that up less than a month later with the first animal in space, a dog called Laika. Then on 12 April 1961, the Russians put the first man in space, Yuri Gagarin, who afterwards trained Tereshkova for her flight.

The Russians owed their edge in the space race partly to their study of V-2 technology and partly to the genius of their chief designer Sergey Korolyov, only recently acknowledged even in Russia because of the secrecy surrounding the Soviet space venture. Russia had long been a pioneer of rocket propulsion, and Korolyov had headed their GIRD rocket programme in the 1930s. But it was in the 1950s that Korolyov really made his mark.

Of course, it was Cold War rivalry that spurred the Russians on, and although Korolyov proposed a rocket, the R-7, that would put a satellite and a dog in space as early as 1953, he was at first directed to work on missile technology. So the R-7 was, in fact, developed as the world's first Intercontinental Ballistic Missile in spring 1957. But suddenly the prestige of being first in space began to seem an even more powerful weapon in the Cold War than a missile, and Korolyov's team were instructed to redirect their efforts towards this goal. Since Korolyov had originally conceived the R-7 for space, in less than a month he and his team were able to create *Sputnik 1*, which was little more than a missile with a sphere containing a transmitter and measuring instruments.

The success of *Sputnik 1* so excited Khruschev that Korolyov was given the green light to progress further, and just four weeks later the Russians launched *Sputnik 2*, six times the size of the original and able to carry the dog Laika into space (but not, sadly, back again). With the bit between its teeth, the Soviet space programme now worked feverishly to achieve as many space firsts as it could. In 1959 *Luna 2* became the first spacecraft to reach the Moon, and *Luna 3* took the first pictures of the far side of the Moon. In 1960, the dogs Belka and Strelka were the first animals brought safely back from space, and *Marsnik 1* was the first space probe launched to Mars. And in 1961, Gagarin made his historic flight.

The Soviet Union had long allowed women a status in the armed forces that was far beyond what they had in the USA, but it was maybe to achieve another first, rather than out of any desire for sex equality, that impelled the Russians to send Tereshkova up to become the first woman in space. Of course, the Americans achieved the most glittering space first five years later, by putting men on the Moon, but for ten years the Russian space programme, led by the brilliant Korolyov, who died in 1965, had set the pace in the most astonishing technological achievements of the 20th century.

# 20 June

## *Insectivorous bats are shown to live far longer than expected*

**2005** It has long been accepted that very small mammals, especially insectivores, have short lifespans. Shrews, for example, live only a year or two and famously have to eat their own bodyweight in invertebrates every day just to stay alive.

The rate of the heartbeat, which is proportional to the size of the animal, was taken as a rule of thumb with regard to longevity in mammals. Elephants and whales, which live for a very long period, have correspondingly very slow heartbeats. Short-lived rodents and insectivores, on the other hand, have fast heartbeats. Humans fall somewhere between the two. The rough theory is that the hearts of all mammals beat approximately the same number of times throughout their lives: the faster the heartbeat, the quicker it reaches this limit and the shorter the lifespan.

That idea has been somewhat overturned by the discovery that insectivorous bats can live for remarkably long periods of time. In 2005 a Brandt's bat was found to be 41 years old. It had been ringed in 1964 in Siberia and then rerecorded in the same colony over four decades later.

Bats tend to be particularly long-lived creatures for their size, and many species regularly reach twenty years or so. Nevertheless, 41 years is an incredible length of time for any bat to live and how the bat achieved this has so far baffled many academics.

Scientists have tried to explain this anomaly by suggesting that their long periods of hibernation effectively extend their lifespans due to the fact that their metabolisms and heartbeats slow down almost to a halt. Based on that theory it might seem reasonable to assume that bats might live perhaps twice as long as other small mammals, but clearly 41 years is way past the mark.

Bats in general, and the elderly Brandt's bat especially, have been recommended as areas of study for researchers interested in the mechanisms surrounding slow ageing. Quite how bodies age no one is quite sure, but the benefits of evolved longevity in certain organisms have been well-documented, suggesting that ageing is a biological function much like any other (alternative theories point to biological accidents, such as increased genetic mutations during tissue replenishment, or environmental contributors).

# 21 June

## *The vinyl 33⅓ rpm LP record kicks off the record industry*

**1948** Vinyl plastics were revolutionary at the time of their invention in the 1940s. Previous plastics had been hard and brittle materials, otherwise known as thermosetting plastics, that became permanently cured when heat was applied. Vinyls, on the other hand, are thermoplastics, which means that they soften when heat is applied. When set, they are flexible and pliable.

The first gramophone records were made from the early unyielding resins and had to be made quite thick and weighty to give them sufficient strength. The nature of the material also meant that fidelity was lost quite quickly due to wear. The grooves had to be made so far apart and the records revolved so quickly – at 78 rpm – that they could only fit four minutes of recording on each side of a 12″ disc.

On this day in 1948, Columbia Records unleashed the first vinyl records. The introduction of vinyl discs reinvented the record industry virtually overnight. The disc themselves were lightweight and tough and the material allowed for closer grooves and slower rotation – 33⅓ rpm. It was suddenly possible to put 23 minutes of recording on each side, which meant a collection of recordings, and so the album was born. It soon became known as the LP, an abbreviation for 'long player', to distinguish it from the 7″ disc, which was known as the 'single' or '45' as it was played at 45 rpm. There were also EPs (extended players) which usually fitted two songs on each side of a 7″, 45 rpm disc.

The vinyl record reigned supreme until the introduction of magnetic tapes in the 1960s and then the CD in the 1980s. The modern age has made all of these formats obsolete as people have switched to electronic storage on silicon chips, which are fitted into computers, memory sticks, MP3 players and so on.

While all this modern technology has revolutionised the way in which we store music, the manner in which we now listen to it is surprisingly similar to habits that existed before the introduction of vinyl. In the days when records were very limited in the recording space they offered, most artists sold their songs as single products. Following the invention of the LP, singles became secondary to albums, but now that customers can buy any song from an album as an individual MP3 file, the format is enjoying a resurgence.

Vinyl, however, is unlikely to ever die out. Not only do some music aficionados prefer its more gutsy sound quality, but it is an integral tool for many nightclub DJs. The physical nature of vinyl playback – the needle that can be placed with precision by the DJ and the ability to introduce effects such as 'scratching' – are traits that can be partially replicated only by extremely expensive computer hardware and software. As a result, much electronic dance music such as drum and bass or techno is still released almost exclusively upon vinyl discs.

# 22 June

## *The first successful experiment in cybernetics*

**1999** It has long been the dream of scientists to develop bionic limbs and other body parts. That aim came a step closer in 1999 when a team of researchers managed to get a rodent to control a water dispenser by thought alone. The 'guinea pig' was a rat with its brain wired up so that minute electrical signals that would normally control its paws were redirected to the electronics of the machine. The rat was therefore fooled into thinking it was activating the water supply with its real paw, when in fact it was a virtual paw. It became a primitive cyborg – a combination of artificial and natural systems. The ramifications of this breakthrough were enormous, as it essentially opened the door to the development of human prosthetics that can be controlled by the mind.

One of the first people to benefit from these animal experiments was Jesse Sullivan. In 2001 he suffered a horrific electrical accident which caused him to have both of his arms amputated at the shoulder. Doctors originally attached mechanical arms to the muscle stumps that remained from his arms. Termed myoelectric prosthetic limbs, they are controlled by sensors that sense the voltage changes generated by the muscles when they flex and relax. These are translated into electrical instructions for the motors within the new limb.

Early use, however, proved to be extremely painful for Sullivan, who had developed hypersensitivity in the areas where his arms had been removed. As a result, doctors ingeniously adjusted the surviving nerve endings so that they ran to his chest, rather than his shoulder. They then attached electrodes to them that could be wired up to advanced prosthetic arms. The nerves now transmit electrical signals when Sullivan thinks of moving his hand, which causes the artificial hand to respond.

In essence this is no different from the way in which we control our real body parts, but the difficulty was developing an interface between the biological and the non-biological – not least in terms of scale, as real neurons are extremely small, so constructing a non-biological nerve enters into the realm of nanotechnology.

There is still much perfecting to be done and this is one reason why scientists have been searching for a biological method of growing microelectronics. To do so would mean neurological compatibility. Added to this it might be possible, one day, to grow new body parts from stem cells. If so, then a new limb would actually be a biologically compatible replacement rather than a prosthetic.

There has also been progress in developing bionic eyes, which 'plug' into the optic nerve and actually enable the brain to see, albeit very crudely so far. Needless to say, this is a very exciting area of scientific endeavour.

# 23 June

## The microelectronic integrated circuit board is invented

**1964** This marked the beginning of the Electronic Revolution that we are currently enjoying. Up until then, electronic circuitry had been macroelectronics, now it was microelectronics. It meant that electronics could be fitted into far smaller spaces and it consequently paved the way for all of the modern microelectronically controlled devices that now define our material culture.

The first integrated circuit board (IC) had been invented in the mid-1950s, but it still used relatively large components soldered onto the board. The new invention utilised a new material called a semiconductor. These days it is known as a 'chip' and made from silicon. The first semiconductor material used was the element germanium (Ge), which has similar characteristics. By embedding the circuitry into the semiconductor material it made the entire thing stable and meant that it was possible to keep reducing the circuitry in size. That is exactly what happened, so that today it is possible to fit vast amounts of circuitry into very small spaces.

It also meant that data, or electronic information, could be stored in ever- tinier spaces. This led to the publication of Moore's Law just a year later, which predicted a doubling of electronic storage in a given space every two years. So far that has proven to be a fairly reliable prophecy, but the point of the law was to warn the industry that there will come a time when physics does not allow the compression of data to continue.

Given that microelectronics started in 1964, Moore's Law states that in 2004 data storage would have increased by a factor of $2^{20}$, which is a 2.1 million-fold increase. This would then rise to a 4.2 million-fold increase in 2006, an 8.4 million-fold increase in 2008, a 16.8 million-fold increase in 2010, and so on. This has significant economic ramifications, as the marketing of new microelectronic products is largely driven by the ability of designers to fit increasing amounts of memory and functionality into devices. When that ability is curtailed, it is bound to have a profound effect on the world economy as both manufacturers and consumers inhabit the global village. In effect, it will mark the end of the Electronic Revolution.

# 24 June

## Tennis enters the Open era

**1968** There was a time when a British tennis player dominated the tennis at the Wimbledon Championships. The competition having begun in 1877, between 1880 and 1889 Willie Renshaw won an incredible fourteen titles at the All England Club (seven singles and seven doubles). In contrast to today's highly paid stars, Renshaw was an amateur who didn't receive a penny in prize money for any of his victories. Indeed, for the 91 years from its inception until 1968, Wimbledon and the other Major championships – the French Open, the US Open and the Australian Open – were open only to amateur players.

The advent of the professional era came on this day in 1968 when, for the first time, Wimbledon admitted both amateur and professional tennis players. The dramatic shift was a response to a piling up of commercial pressures; from the fans who wanted to see a higher standard of tennis, from potential investors in the sport who wanted to be able to make a return on their capital, and from the players themselves who felt that they should be fairly rewarded for the entertainment they provided. So it was that Wimbledon, along with the other three Majors, entered the Open era in 1968.

Turning professional, however, didn't solve all the problems with the game of tennis. Although the men's and ladies' tournaments were run side-by-side during the fortnight of competition, the new prize money was significantly greater for the men than for the women. As some of the biggest sporting stars of the 20th century – Martina Navratilova, Steffi Graf and Billie Jean King (who played both pre- and post-1968) – came and went, the gap between male and female pay persisted. Ultimately it wasn't until 2007 that the women finally reached parity with the men at Wimbledon when both prizes were set at £750,000.

Since 1968, the game of tennis has advanced immeasurably,

both in the standard of the players and the quality of the equipment they use. Racquets, which were once wooden affairs, are now constructed from super-lightweight man-made materials, and the balls are engineered to produce just the right amount of speed and bounce off the surface.

The pantheon of tennis greats has expanded too, although none of the now-familiar modern names are British. Indeed, the last Briton to win the men's Championship was Fred Perry in 1936, and only Virginia Wade in 1977 has won a professional Wimbledon title for the UK. Instead, the legendary names include Pete Sampras from the USA, who equalled Renshaw's record by winning the men's singles seven times between 1993 and 2000; Björn Borg and Roger Federer, both of whom won six Wimbledon singles titles in a row; and on the women's side there is Navratilova, who achieved an incredible twenty crowns in the 27 years between 1976 and 2003 (nine singles, seven doubles and four mixed doubles). However, one record of Renshaw's remains unbeaten to this day – his seven titles came in consecutive years. The closest anyone has come to matching this was Federer who, having won every year from 2001 to 2007, could manage only the runner-up position in 2008, losing to Rafael Nadal in the longest men's singles final ever – an exhausting 4 hours and 48 minutes.

# 25 June

## Confirmation of a new antelope species in Vietnam

**1994** It isn't often that a new species of large mammal turns up. The natural habitat of the saola (*Pseudoryx nghetinhensis*) is the Vietnamese jungle, where until 1994 it had managed to remain hidden from view and unknown to science. It was, in fact, well known to the indigenous people of the forest who hunted it for meat. Science 'discovered' it only when a number of skulls were noticed in a village by zoologists in 1992. Then, two years later, a live specimen was caught. Since then only a dozen individuals have been recorded, suggesting that the saola is quite a rare animal.

The saola is not actually a true antelope. Nor is it a deer or a goat or a buffalo or a species of cattle. Cladistically it was found to be unique, although it was definitely a member of the bovine group. It was therefore assigned its own genus, *Pseudoryx*, which translates as 'fake' or 'pretend oryx'.

The real oryx is an antelope of Africa and the Middle East and the overall form of the saolo is indeed oryx-like, being antelope-shaped with long spiralling horns. In colouring it is reminiscent of a tapir and it is evidently camouflaged for life in the sunlight-dappled clearings of the tropical forest, where it forages and grazes on the leaves and shoots. Its muzzle is rather pointed as one might expect of an animal that needs to run through undergrowth at speed to escape predators, and its horns are swept back to provide a streamlined profile. It seems likely that the horns are a defence against tigers, which favour attacks from the rear. Having long, sharp backward-pointing horns would be quite effective at preventing a tiger from grasping at the neck and also afford the saola a chance at slipping away unharmed while the tiger recovers from being pronged.

The discovery of the saola does raise questions about the possibility of other large species waiting to be discovered. This is especially true for those who persist in ideas of the yetis and sasquatches who supposedly inhabit remote and mountainous regions in Asia and America respectively. However, while the saola lives in dense forest where a viable population was able to exist without detection, it seems highly unlikely that large humanoid creatures could do the same in open terrain. It is interesting to note, however, that a third human-like creature called the orang pendek is thought by some to exist in forested areas of south-east Asia.

# 26 June

## *The barcode transforms the way we shop*

**1974** Today we are so used to doing our food shopping at high speed that we get extremely frustrated if we find ourselves stuck in a queue, or if the checkout is a bit too slow for our liking. Imagine what it would be like if the barcode system were scrapped and things went back to how they used to be. Doing a supermarket shop would take up half a day.

The barcode was an invention of IBM and had been shown to be reliable in 1973. The very first item to have its barcode scanned and read was a packet of chewing gum in a supermarket in Troy, Ohio, on this day in 1974. Since then it has become such a familiar thing that we simply take it for granted, and get very annoyed when the checkout assistant has difficulty scanning an item and has to punch in the digits manually.

A barcode is simply a row of black stripes of varying width and spacing that provide a twelve-number code in binary form, known as a UPC (universal product code). The barcode is scanned with a laser beam, either from a handheld scanner or through a window built into the checkout. The information is then relayed to a computerised database, where it is processed. Barcodes are most effectively scanned on flat surfaces and when intact. Damage to a barcode or an uneven surface can make it difficult for the laser to interpret the code stripes, but generally speaking it is a tried and trusted system. These days very few items are sold without a barcode.

There are various types of barcode readers which use a number of ways to detect the difference in light measured from the bars and the gaps in between. Laser scanners emit beams which reflect from the barcode and are then scanned. CCD (charge-coupled device) scanners don't emit anything but detect reflected ambient light from barcodes. Imaging scanners actually 'see' the barcode as an eye would and read it that way.

This new technology is known generically as MV (machine

vision). It isn't as sophisticated as a real human eye, as it cannot interpret unfamiliar objects as we can, but machine vision is finding a number of uses in industry. For example, machine eyes can be used in factories to count objects on conveyor belts and their processing ability is considerably better than that of humans in this respect.

# 27 June

## Nuclear-sourced electricity becomes a reality

**1954** Like many new technologies, nuclear fission had the dual potential to harm humanity and to benefit humanity; it was a matter of application. The two atomic bombs dropped on Japan in 1945 were a more-than-adequate demonstration of the destructive power of nuclear energy. In the post-war environment it occurred to scientists that it should be possible to harness that energy and convert it into electricity, and so the first nuclear power station began operating nine years later in Obninsk, Russia.

Nuclear power stations are not dissimilar to nuclear bombs, except that the fission reaction of the radioactive fuel is controlled, so that the energy is released progressively, in a manageable and safe way. The energy is emitted in the form of heat, which is used to boil water into steam. The steam is then used to drive steam turbines attached to dynamos which, in turn, generate electricity. Despite the inherent dangers associated with using radioactive materials, nuclear power is environmentally clean and an incredible amount of energy can be derived from a very small amount of fuel.

In the case of the Obninsk power station, it was also used to heat the town's water supply directly, so that the community was centrally heated. Due to the laws of energy conversion there is always some energy that cannot be converted from heat into electricity, so using it to heat the water supply was a cunning move, as the energy would otherwise have been lost to the surrounding environment. As a matter of fact, the power plant continued to heat the community's water until 2002, even though it had stopped generating electricity in 1968.

With increasing concern about the release of carbon compound gases into the atmosphere, there has been renewed interest in the development of new nuclear power stations. For one thing, many countries have enormous stockpiles of fissile material amassed during the Cold War, so it makes sense to put it to good use. Secondly, modern technologies should mean that it is possible to build new-generation power stations that are failsafe, so that communities have nothing to fear in terms of nuclear accidents or terrorist attacks on power stations.

# 28 June

## *Primate-to-primate transplantation*

**1992** In 1992 a patient with a liver ravaged by hepatitis B was given a new liver from a donor. What was remarkable in this case was that the organ came from another species of primate, a baboon.

Cross-species transplantation is known as xenotransplantation – the prefix *xeno* meaning 'foreign' in Greek. The patient, a 35-year-old man, lived for a further 71 days before succumbing to a brain haemorrhage. The sex and age of the donor remain undisclosed.

At the time it was hailed as a significant step forwards in medicine, but fears of zoonotic, or cross-species, disease transmission have led to a hiatus in progress in recent years. One might think that monkeys and apes would be the only species with suitable organs for xenotransplantation, but pigs have also been experimented with. For example, a number of patients have been plumbed into pig livers outside of their bodies while waiting for human livers to become available.

Aside from disease concerns there is, understandably, a huge amount of controversy over what some see as the harvesting of animals for their body parts. Those in favour of the practice point to the untold advantages of having a readily available supply of organs for human use.

This desire to manage organ production also drives other areas of medical research. One potentially viable field, and one that is also running into ethical difficulties, is the growing of spare organs using stem cells taken from the patient. This has the added bonus that the cultivated organs would be an exact genetic match for the patient, making immunosuppressant drugs unnecessary.

There has even been speculation that it may be possible to combine these two branches of research by using other species as places to grow those organs, so that monkeys or pigs provide appropriate environments within their bodies to cultivate human replacement organs. If possible, it would certainly be easier than trying to grow them in laboratory conditions.

The history of xenotransplantation is not confined to what we might like to consider our more mechanical organs. In 1994 a female stroke victim had the damaged part of her brain replaced with 30 million cells from the brain of a pig. Since then her thought processes and speech have improved, suggesting that the new neural cells have been successfully incorporated. This is difficult to prove conclusively though, as many patients partially recover from stroke without treatment by developing new neural pathways and employing previously redundant areas of the brain.

# 29 June

## *The pygmy mammoth steps out of prehistory*

**1994** When Charles Darwin published his theory of evolution by natural selection, a significant part of the evidence he used to support the theory was the adaptation of species on islands. They are isolated habitats, where animals are confronted with very specific ecological problems to deal with and populations are also cut off from the gene pool of their species. The result is that island populations begin to evolve in subtly different directions; a phenomenon known as speciation.

Twenty thousand years ago, sea levels were quite a bit lower than they are now, which meant that landmasses had larger areas and the oceans were smaller. When sea levels began to rise, the oceans encroached on the land, submerging the low-lying areas and surrounding high-lying areas to form islands. In this way, many populations found themselves separated from the mainland by stretches of water and subsequently took their own evolutionary paths. This is what happened to the mammoths on the islands of the California Channel, namely Santa Cruz, San Miguel and Santa Rosa.

Many fossilised bones had been found over the 20th century to suggest that small mammoth species had evolved on the islands, while those on mainland America had remained, well, mammoth-sized. Then, in 1994, an almost complete fossilised skeleton was found on Santa Rosa, confirming that there were indeed pygmy mammoths. It was given the name *Mammathus exilis*, which translates as 'exiled mammoth' alluding to its plight. The fossils were dated to almost 13,000 years old and the adult stood at a height of 5.5 feet (1.65 metres), which is tiny when one considers that the imperial mammoth (*Mammathis imperator*) of California was sixteen feet (five metres) tall.

Stranded on islands, the mammoths found themselves compromised. They had a finite amount of food, so the number of individuals that could survive was dictated by food supply. The answer was to evolve to pygmy size. That way the food could support larger numbers of the mammoths and fluctuations in food supply would still support viable breeding populations. Natural selection favoured those individuals that were naturally smaller to start with, so they were the ones to pass on their genes, while the larger specimens died of malnutrition. In addition, there were no large predators to deal with, so getting smaller was not a disadvantage in that respect. Interestingly, a similar thing happened in the Mediterranean Sea, between Europe and Africa. Fossil remains of pygmy or dwarf mammoths (*Mammathus* species) and elephants (*Elephas* species) have been unearthed on many of the Mediterranean islands, which were also once part of a greater landmass.

# *30 June*

## *Concorde chases the shadow of the Moon*

**1973** During a solar eclipse the Moon stands between the sun and the Earth, so that the Moon's shadow is cast on the planet. To those on the ground, the sky suddenly goes dark and then abruptly returns to daylight again some time later. In fact, the shadow is travelling across the Earth's surface at several thousand miles per hour, so an eclipse lasts as long as the shadow is covering a particular point of observation.

In 1973 astronomers predicted that an eclipse crossing the Atlantic Ocean and diagonally down across North Africa would be travelling more slowly than usual, at only 3,000 mph (5,000 kph). It meant that anyone observing the eclipse along the central line, where the Moon's shadow is widest, would be in darkness for 64 minutes. At that time it just so happened that Concorde was being developed, so it was put to use chasing the eclipse. Scientists from the US, the UK and France pursued the Moon's shadow at supersonic speed and managed to extend the duration of the eclipse to 74 minutes. During a solar eclipse it is possible to observe the corona of the sun because the light level has been reduced.

Lunar eclipses also occur from time to time. This is when the shadow of the Earth falls on the Moon, so that it looks as if a circular chunk of the Moon has been taken away. Incomplete eclipses of both the sun and Moon occur too, so that only a portion is covered at any one time.

Lesser known eclipses are called transits. As the planets Venus and Mercury are nearer to the sun than the Earth is, they occasionally stand in the path of the sun. They are too distant, however, to cast shadows on our planet and appear only as small dots on the sun. It follows too, that it is possible to observe the transit of Earth from Mars and other planets farther away from the sun. Interestingly, scientists have calculated that the next transit of

Earth from Mars will occur in 2084 and so it has been given as an incentive to establish a manned base there. In the case of the Earth's transit, it is sometimes possible to see the Moon too, although it has only been achieved in computer-generated images so far.

# 1 July

## A revolutionary architect dies

**1983** If humans are ever to establish research stations either on the moon or on Mars, they'll need to build suitable structures in which to live and go about their duties. Just as they do in space, the best way to do this is with transport modules, which can then be joined together to make a warren of living spaces. However, long-term habitation will undoubtedly require 'astrosettlers' to grow their own foods in order to remain healthy. This is where the geodesic dome comes into the equation.

The inventor of the geodesic dome was Richard Buckminster Fuller, an American architect who wished to push forward the boundaries of material use. The term 'geodesic' is derived from 'geode', which is a cavity found in rock formations and lined with crystals. It therefore alludes to the uniform and geometric appearance of the dome from within.

The geodesic dome itself is a spherical structure comprising triangular or polygonal cells that fit together, rather like a three-dimensional jigsaw puzzle. The construction principle has a very high strength to weight ratio, and the unique quality of increasing in strength the larger it becomes.

Another advantage of the dome is that the component cells can be flat-packed to take up relatively little room – which would be an obvious advantage when it comes to shipping them across the interplanetary highway.

An odd phenomenon that exists both on the Moon and Mars, although to different extents, is the lack of atmosphere, or more specifically atmospheric pressure. For geodesic domes to be useful, they will need to be filled with gases that simulate the atmosphere on Earth. This means that the domes will need to cope with pressure from within.

On Earth there is usually a pressure equilibrium, so that the domes only have to cope with the force of gravity pushing them downwards, in which case they are immensely strong. While the

Earth has a pressure of one atmosphere, Mars has less than 1 per cent of this and the Moon has virtually no atmosphere at all. In addition the Moon has only about a sixth of our gravity and Mars has about a third. With little outside pressure or gravity to counter the internal forces, the seams of a geodesic dome would therefore need to be airtight and have high tensile strength to avoid leakage or tearing apart.

In 1985, two years after Buckminster Fuller's death on this day in 1983, scientists discovered a new form of carbon, called $C_{60}$. It turned out to have a geodesic structure, comprising hexagonal and pentagonal spaces between the 60 carbon atoms that made the molecule. In fact, it resembled a soccer ball. Soon afterwards, it was discovered that there was a whole family of similar carbon molecules that all had geodesic structures. Consequently they were named fullerenes in honour of Buckminster Fuller.

# 2 July

## Bipolar disorder leads to an author's suicide

**1961** In the 1960s people with bipolar disorder were known as manic depressives, an allusion to their tendency to jump from mania to depression and vice versa. For a long time bipolar disorder has been associated with individuals of high intelligence and creativity. It manifests itself as a fluctuation in mental state from baleful depression to hyperactivity, with little in between.

Ernest Hemingway was a writing colossus and manic depressive. His earlier novels had utilised the theme of warfare, as he had started life as a journalist and lived through the two world wars as well as the Spanish Civil War. In 1954 he achieved the ultimate accolade by becoming a Nobel laureate in literature. The previous year he had written the short story 'The Old Man and the Sea', for which he won the Pulitzer Prize. While on the surface it was a deceptively simple tale of an old man determined to get the better of a marlin fish, it was steeped in symbolism and allegory, and seen as a comment on the human condition.

However, Hemingway's joy at receiving the type of recognition he had longed for was short-lived. Before he could travel to Stockholm, Sweden to collect his prize, he suffered two successive aeroplane crashes while on safari. As a result of these he suffered all kinds of serious injuries, including a crushed vertebra, ruptured liver, kidney and spleen and temporary blindness. Then, just one month later, he was caught in a bushfire that left him with second-degree burns from his legs up to his face. By the end of 1954, not only was Hemingway in a great deal of pain, but he was unable to attend the Nobel prize-giving ceremony and receive his award.

From there he entered a long downward spiral, battling against his twin demons of depression and alcohol. By the end of the 1950s he was suffering from increasingly extreme bouts of depression for which he received ECT (electro-convulsive therapy). The treatment involves the induction of seizures in the brain by the use of an electrical stimulus. The idea is that the brain somehow realigns its neural pathways with subtle changes in personality, so that susceptibility to depression is removed.

Although it does seem to work in some cases, in Hemingway's it did not. His heavy drinking was not enough to drown his sorrows, and in the end he shot himself in the head to escape the pain.

# 3 July

## *The oldest form of flight becomes the last to circumnavigate the globe*

**2002** The thing about ballooning is that it is easy to get airborne, but difficult to steer and adjust altitude as there is no form of propulsion. Pilots are essentially at the mercy of the air currents. Consequently, while ballooning became the first way in which people experienced flight, it has never been put to any use that is both practical and reliable.

To be scientifically accurate, ballooning is not flying anyway, as flying requires the phenomenon of sustained lift, which is achieved by an aerofoil propelled through the air. Even gliding isn't techni-cally flying, so ballooning would be better described as 'random air-based travel'.

No wonder, then, that it became the last form of flight to achieve a circumnavigation of the globe. Put simply, it is unpre-dictable and dangerous to attempt such a journey in a balloon. The first success came in 1999, when a two-man crew flew the *Breitling Orbiter 3* around the globe in the northern hemisphere. In 2002 came the first successful solo flight in *Spirit of Freedom*, which completed the journey in the southern hemisphere.

The reason why they couldn't follow the equatorial line is that the balloons needed to use phenomena called jet streams. These are high-altitude and high-speed currents of air that encircle the Earth, both north and south. By using the jet streams, it was a relatively simple process of entering the airflow and then being dragged round the world before dropping out again at the right time. The jet streams themselves weren't discovered until the 1940s. During the Second World War the Japanese used the northern jet stream to send balloon bombs across the Pacific Ocean to the US.

The *Spirit of Freedom* was piloted by the adventurer Steve Fossett, who went missing while flying a private plane over the Nevada desert in 2007. It used a combination of hot air and helium to stay afloat and adjust altitude. The balloon took to the skies in Australia and landed back on terra firma thirteen days later. It was Fossett's seventh attempt, as he had made two others in the southern hemisphere and four in the northern hemisphere.

When the search began for the wreckage of Steve Fossett's light aircraft in the US, satellite images were scrutinised unsuccessfully. However, a significant number of previously unknown plane wrecks were discovered in the process.

# 4 July

## *The USA celebrates its bicentenary*

**1976** While the American Revolutionary War lasted until 1781, independence from British rule was actually declared in 1776. American forces eventually defeated the British army with the help of the French, which led to the US coming close to adopting French as its national language. At the time the Americans were a mix of immigrants from many nations, so English wasn't the natural choice for a common language – or *lingua franca*, as it is put in Italian. One can only imagine how the adoption of French might have changed contemporary world culture, especially in the UK and France. Presumably the UK would not feel the same allegiance to the US that it does now, and conversely France would not be as anti-American.

It's instinctive for the British to identify with America, even though there are large differences between the two. Having a shared language has bridged those gaps for so long now that a certain degree of cultural assimilation – acculturation – has occurred. This is particularly true in terms of popular culture, and trends in areas such as fashion, music, art, films, food and literature often move between the two countries.

The evolutionary biologist Richard Dawkins coined the term 'memes' for these cultural elements, as he saw that a Darwinian process of selection was in operation. So the 'meme' is the cultural equivalent of the gene, and there is thus a 'memepool' just as there is a genepool. In the same way that genes are selected or discarded by nature, so humans choose or reject memes. Some memes consequently die out in favour of others that flourish.

The flow of memes is not restricted to countries that share a common language, but it certainly makes a significant difference. This is simply because it is easier for the separate populations to familiarise themselves with, and choose between, cultural differences. Generally speaking, if a certain meme makes life more enjoyable then it will inevitably find itself absorbed into a cultural framework and establish itself for as long as it takes for something else to oust it.

On the subject of the English language, it would be fair to say that there is a meme flow there too. American English is certainly quite different from British English, and the two languages are constantly in flux with one another, so that linguistic and literary memes travel back and forth across the Atlantic Ocean. There are those in the UK who try their hardest to prevent what they see as the corruption of English in this way, forgetting that the English language has always been evolving. Somehow the invention of the dictionary led to a perception that English had been set in stone. This was never the intention, which was rather to document the diversity of the language and the origins of the words that comprise it.

# 5 July

## The bikini makes its debut

**1946** A few months earlier in 1946, French fashion designer Jacques Heim introduced a new swimsuit, the 'atome', so called because it was the smallest bathing attire yet invented. Soon after, on this day, Heim and his new collaborator, the engineer Louis Réard, unveiled a revised version at a fashion show at the Piscine Molitor in Paris. The new outfit was dubbed the bikini, after the Bikini Atoll where a nuclear weapons test had taken place on 1 July. The designers explained that they expected the explosion of excitement caused by their swimsuit to be similar in scale to the blast produced by an atomic bomb.

Whether it got hearts racing in the way they intended or not, the bikini certainly provoked a strong reaction. With its skimpy top and revealing bottom half (this first bikini had a g-string back), Heim and Réard couldn't find any conventional models willing to don it for the exhibition. In the end they employed Micheline Bernardini, a nude dancer at a Parisian club, to pose in the swimwear.

At the time of its release, strongly Catholic countries such as Spain and Italy banned the bikini from their beaches. In America, where the bikini is now a much-loved piece of clothing, one earlier commentator criticised it as revealing 'everything about a girl except for her mother's maiden name'. Indeed, in 1951 the bikini was banned from Miss World competitions after one worn by Miss Sweden prompted several other contestants to withdraw in indignation. Even today the bikini still excites opposition in various corners of the globe where it is seen as offensive to moral and religious sensibilities.

However, if the bikini had a bit of a rocky start with some traditionalists, it was swiftly embraced by the trendsetting influence of popular culture. In 1960, Brian Hyland released the novelty pop song, 'Itsy Bitsy Teenie Weenie Yellow Polka Dot Bikini', and then in 1962, Ursula Andress turned the bikini into an icon of the 20th century when she emerged from the waters in the James Bond film *Dr No* wearing a flattering white version. By this time, and with the bikini firmly established as a European favourite, the US was beginning to come around to the idea. From the mid-1960s onwards, a specialised genre of Hollywood films known as 'beach party' films and featuring tides of bikinis enjoyed a boom in popularity across America.

Still, if mid-20th century attitudes were a little sensitive to the original bikinis, it is hard to imagine how they would have reacted to some of its modern variations and uses. As well as being worn for swimming and sunbathing, there are also bikini contests in which girls dressed in bikinis take part in a beauty pageant. Outside of the competitive arena women can be seen lounging around on deckchairs in string bikinis and microkinis – the latter of which covers only the bare minimum, and then sometimes not even that.

Perhaps, though, we've actually had longer than we think to get used to the idea of revealing bikinis. Although the first true modern template was certainly displayed on this day in 1946, there is archaeological evidence to suggest that female athletes wore similar two-piece garments in Ancient Greece – some 1,400 years ago.

# 6 July

## *The first man-made vehicle to traverse the surface of another planet*

**1997** This is perhaps the most remarkable achievement of mankind so far, not just because of the feat itself, but also in terms of the collaborative effort involved. We're talking about thousands of people, a rocket launch, a spacecraft travelling from Earth to Mars, the deployment of a probe to land safely on the planet's surface and then the activation of a remotely controlled vehicle, capable of sending back images of another world. Beat that!

The Martian rover was called *Sojourner* and made its journey within the space probe *Mars Pathfinder*. It landed on 4 July and made its first movements two days later. *Sojourner* was solar-powered and had six metal wheels with which to negotiate its way over the Martian soil and between rocks strewn on the surface.

Since the success of *Sojourner*, NASA has begun a mission programme named MER (Mars Exploration Rover). In 2003 and 2004 two more rovers were successfully deposited and activated on the planet – *Spirit* on one side of Mars and *Opportunity* on the other. Both vehicles have performed their jobs very effectively and have remained serviceable for far longer than anticipated.

The term 'sol' (short for 'solar day') is used in describing the length of a Martian day, which is almost 40 minutes longer than an Earth day. The rovers were expected to last for 90 sols, but have lasted for over a Martian year – which is 668.6 sols long!

Of course, the next milestone will be to land humans on Mars, although it is certainly worth asking why we should do this when robots can do this perfectly well. Indeeed, technology is reaching a point now where humans would probably be less reliable on a mission to Mars or elsewhere. A robot can remain dormant for long periods of time and then be switched on when it arrives. It can even be controlled to maintain itself, or back-up robots could remain dormant until replacements are needed. Humans, on the other hand, present all sorts of problems. They need to be fed and watered, they need to be kept healthy in body and mind and they can't simply be abandoned when they reach the end of their usefulness. In short, living organisms are wholly unsuited to space exploration while electromechanical machines are perfect for the job.

# 7 July

## Solar power goes airborne and crosses the English Channel

**1981** *Solar Challenger* was the name of the world's first solar-powered aircraft able to carry a human pilot. Solar power is the conversion of solar radiation into electrical energy through the use of photovoltaic cells. The cells work on the basis of photons striking a layer of semiconductor. Energy is absorbed and this frees electrons which cause a potential difference between the semiconductor and another layer. The electrons then flow across the interface to generate an electric current. The more intense the sunlight, the more photons there are and the stronger the current will be. Increasing the number of photovoltaic cells also allows for more electricity to be generated.

To provide *Solar Challenger* with sufficient power it was fitted with enough photovoltaic cells to cover its four wings – over 16,000 individual cells. They were able to provide 2,600 watts in full sunlight, enough to power 43 standard light bulbs.

The original prototype was named the *Gossamer Penguin*. It wasn't airworthy enough to attempt any proper flights, but it paved the way for *Solar Challenger*, which managed a journey from northern France to southern England. The aircraft was capable of reaching an altitude of 12,000 feet (4,850 metres). At that height it was above the clouds and therefore had no shortage of sunlight.

The main problem with solar-powered aircraft is their poor power-to-weight ratio. Payloads have to be kept to the bare minimum, which renders them impracticable as vehicles for humans or cargo. What they can do is tasks such as monitoring the weather and surveillance, where the equipment necessary is relatively light-weight. In this respect they might prove themselves very useful as they should be able to remain airborne indefinitely.

Most solar-powered aircraft that are currently built are largely research and design projects, rather than commercial enterprises. Just managing to develop such aircraft teaches designers a lot about the use of appropriate materials. Such technologies might then be applied to conventional aircraft for the sake of improving efficiency. If a conventional airliner can generate its own electricity for lighting and heating, for example, then it will use less fuel and leave a smaller carbon footprint.

# 8 July

## The Roswell Incident

**1947** On this day in 1947 the *Roswell Daily Record* carried a front-page headline that read 'RAAF Captures Flying Saucer On Ranch in Roswell Region'. Little green men, it appeared, had finally come to Earth ... and they had crash-landed in New Mexico, USA.

Later on that same day, the Roswell Army Air Field issued a statement confirming that an object had indeed been recovered from a crash site on the previous day. For a while there was close media interest until a clarification from the army personnel involved reported that the flying saucer had, in fact, been a weather balloon.

Perhaps there were no aliens in Roswell after all. The story then lay dormant for some 30 years until 1978 when Major Jesse Marcel, who had been part of the clean-up operation, claimed in an interview that the debris found at the site had actually come from an alien spacecraft.

Suddenly there was renewed interest in the whole affair. Reporters began to delve back into the archives from the 1940s. Over the next few years articles were written, books were published and even a film was made. Throughout the 1980s concerned 'ufologists' interviewed Jesse Marcel again and again, drawing out new information, building uncertain facts together to create the myth of the alien landing.

Marcel was a willing interviewee during the time. He described how he had found a material like tin foil, but that it wouldn't burn and couldn't be creased. Other metallic substances found there were so hard it was impossible to dent them. Journalists added these loaded statements to earlier accounts of farm workers like William Brazel whose nondescript account of a peculiar shiny object in 1947 now seemed to be irrefutable proof that it was a spaceship that had been recovered, not a weather balloon.

Around this time, the first concrete claims that not just a UFO, but also the dead bodies of the aliens within it, had been found. The controversy and excitement was so powerful to the popular imagination that a poll conducted in 1997 showed that a majority of the US citizens asked believed that aliens had indeed come to Earth some 50 years previously.

While we might be rather hard-pushed to join in the conviction that the Roswell Incident of 1947 did indeed involve a UFO, it is certainly probable that something peculiar came down that day. All eyewitness accounts point to something with a shiny silver appearance, and the RAAF was a likely venue for secret military testing that was going on at the time.

With the Cold War ongoing, both the US and the USSR conducted hundreds of top-secret experiments with new and potential technologies. Of course military testing itself is open to all sorts of fanciful scenarios, but perhaps one of the most serious is the implication of the Roswell Incident in an army operation dubbed Project Mogul. This was clandestine research that explored whether sensors attached to high-altitude balloons could detect incoming Soviet missiles.

That the events surrounding Roswell should have morphed into a story about aliens, especially after such a long lull, is not wholly surprising. The public consciousness was familiar in a peripheral sort of way with the secretive activities of the military during the Cold War. After the fall of the Soviet Union, and without such an obvious contemporary reference point, the manoeuvres of the past began to seem all very suspicious. It only took a bit of media stirring for the public to attach a new explanation to the events and convince themselves that the Roswell Incident was a big government cover-up of alien visitations.

# *9 July*

## *The Big Bang theory is saved from imploding*

**2001** The substance that makes up everything we are and see around us is known collectively as matter. Matter comprises atoms of many different types, but they all have positively charged nuclei that are orbited by negatively charged electrons. Imagine the surprise when, in 1928, a British physicist named Paul Dirac postulated that there might be such a thing as antimatter.

At the time it seemed a preposterous idea, but scientists have since been able to create antimatter by using a particle accelerator. Antimatter is the exact opposite of matter, so its atoms have negatively charged nuclei and positively charged electrons, called positrons. Consequently, it can exist only very briefly in our world because matter atoms and antimatter atoms cancel one another out.

However, in the vacuum of space there are places where only antimatter exists. It follows that there should be equal amounts of matter and antimatter in the universe, as the Big Bang theory works on the basis that both originated from the same source, and exploded apart at the beginning of time.

This reasoning presented a conundrum to cosmologists, as calculations suggested that the universe should have cancelled itself out by this point in time. In 2001 physicists discovered that antimatter atoms decay at a different rate to matter atoms, indicating that there should now be more matter than antimatter in the universe, which is why it all still exists.

As a sideline to this field of physics, scientists have not yet managed to observe gravity in antimatter, which may be turn out to be relevant. According to the law of conservation of energy, antimatter should attract both itself and matter, but no one is certain of this. The trouble is that antimatter atoms cannot be generated in sufficient numbers and for long enough periods of time to measure their gravity.

Some scientists speculate that antimatter might be shown to actually repel matter gravitationally, despite the fact that the two cancel each other out on contact. It might therefore be the driving force for the current expansion of the universe, although ultimately this cancellation will bring it to an end.

# 10 July

## Car safety enters the US public consciousness with the seat belt

**1962** Until 1959 safety belts in cars were either nonexistent or based on those used in aircraft – a simple strap across the waist with a central buckle. They were found to cause internal injuries as sudden deceleration focused all of the momentum energy into that region.

This consequently gave rise to people generally feeling that it was safer to drive without a belt as that way there was a fair chance of escaping injury altogether. Many people would tell of accidents where one person had been thrown clear and survived, while another had been strapped in and died horribly at the scene. In reality it was tantamount to people saying that it was safer to walk in the middle of the road because they had once heard of someone being mown down on the pavement, but such is the logic of the layman.

The person who invented the familiar three-point seat belt was a Swedish engineer named Nils Bohlen. He worked for the Swedish car manufacturer Volvo, which introduced his design in August 1959. The new belt made a significant difference to the outcome of road traffic accidents and went a long way to boosting Volvo's car sales.

Rather than financially exploiting their patent, the company made the design freely available to other car manufacturers in the interests of general road safety. By having a strap across both the chest and waist, the force of deceleration was distributed more evenly across the torso, and the ribcage was far more able to absorb the energy without causing internal injuries.

The US patent was issued in 1962, but it took another couple of decades before road users began to accept that seat belts were an advantage and not a hazard. In Britain it is against the law not to wear a seat belt while driving. It may seem ludicrous that a law is needed to persuade people that they should help themselves from avoiding injury, but such is the logic of the layman, again.

It is also compulsory for children to be provided with adequate safety harnessing in vehicles. These can be seats with integral harnesses, that use the car seat belt as an anchor, or they may be booster seats that raise the child to an appropriate height for the car seat belt to be employed safely. Parents and guardians need to be mindful of safety airbags in cars with regard to children. Although they are designed to cushion the chest and face of adults during a collision, they can suffocate smaller passengers.

# 11 July

## China reveals the terracotta army to the world's press

**1975** In 1974 a Chinese farmer took it upon himself to begin digging a well. While breaking the soil he unearthed a statue made from fired terracotta, then another, and another. He informed the authorities who began an archaeological dig.

By 1975 the Chinese government was ready to announce that they had discovered a vast army of terracotta foot soldiers and cavalry, along with their horses. In fact, there were 8,099 figures altogether, and they were evidently made to accompany the first emperor of the Qin Dynasty, Qin Shi Huang, who died in 210 BC, for they were found near to his mausoleum.

The figures are all slightly larger than life-size and made with incredible detail, and it may be that each face was actually modelled on a particular person. They are constructed from components, rather like china dolls, so that they have individual heads, torsos and limbs. Each body part was made from hollow terracotta clay and assembly took place before firing.

Unfortunately the necropolis housing the army was raided and razed to the ground in 205 BC, leaving the figures damaged. All but one has some degree of imperfection, but for the most part they are intact. Following the fire, the figures became buried over time and the surrounding substrate preserved them from further decay. Now that they are exposed to the air they are being eroded by oxidation and the growth of moulds.

There are also erosive pollutants in the environment due to the vast quantities of coal burnt in Chinese power stations. The figures are consequently breaking down in the same manner as old flower pots, so it will be necessary to apply stabilising chemicals to halt this process.

Qin Shi Huang was also responsible for building one of the Great Walls of China. The main wall, familiar in photographs, was built over 1,000 years later and farther south. Most of the Qin Dynasty wall has now eroded, but it was built by using local materials along its length. Consequently there are ruins built in stone in some places and compressed earth in others. The Great Wall is famously 'the only man-made structure visible to the naked eye from space' although that is not actually true anymore, as there are plenty of large structures that are visible, such as canals and dams, not to mention cities.

# 12 July

## Bill Shankly resigns as Liverpool manager

**1974** So extraordinary was the loyalty inspired by Liverpool football manager Bill Shankly, that when he suddenly resigned in 1974 distraught Liverpool fans besieged the club's switchboard with phone calls pleading for him to stay, and local factory workers threatened to strike unless he was reinstated.

There were rumours of boardroom politics in play, and certainly Shankly seemed to regret his decision, later turning up at training sessions, unable quite to let go, until new manager Bob Paisley had to insist on being left alone to do his job. Probably, though, it was just that Shankly simply lived and breathed football. Famously, Shankly once said: 'Some people believe football is a matter of life and death. I'm very disappointed with that attitude. I can assure you it is much, much more important than that.'

When he resigned in 1974, Shankly had been managing Liverpool for fifteen years, and it had been an extraordinary time. When he had taken over in 1959, Liverpool had been a small club languishing in the lower reaches of the second division. By the time he left, it was the league's biggest club, on a par with Manchester United. He had set the foundations for future achievements under Paisley's stewardship, during which Liverpool won the league title six times and the European Cup three times in just nine years.

Under Shankly himself, Liverpool won the league title three times, the FA cup twice and the UEFA cup. There were said to be two great Shankly teams. The first one, in the mid-1960s, contained such talented players as Roger Hunt, Ian St John, Ron Yeats, Gordon Milne and Peter Thompson. The second, in the early 1970s, was built around players such as Kevin Keegan, Steve Heighway, Emlyn Hughes and goalkeeper Ray Clemence.

Yet it was not just his football success that inspired such loyalty amongst Liverpool fans. It was his down-to-earth personality and his acerbic Scottish wit. Shankly was an ardent socialist, and believed very much that the club's first duty was to its fans and to the city, once saying, 'I wanted to bring back happiness to the people of Liverpool'. And his socialist ethic extended even to the way his team played. If a player was having a bad game Shankly expected a teammate to cover for him and bail him out, just as they would a fellow miner down the pit.

There are still websites devoted to anecdotes about Shankly and his biting sense of humour. At the funeral of the legendary Dixie Dean, who played for Liverpool's great adversaries, Everton, he mused: 'I know this is a sad occasion, but I think Dixie would be amazed to know that even in death he could draw a bigger crowd than Everton can on a Saturday afternoon.' When rival manager Tommy Docherty bragged of one of his players, 'A hundred thousand [pounds] wouldn't buy him', Shankly shot back, 'Yeah, and I'm one of the hundred thousand'.

Shankly died of a heart attack in 1981, just seven years after resigning, but he remains one of the best-loved football managers of all time, and over three decades on Liverpool remains at the top of football's tree.

# 13 July

## The Great New York Blackout

**1977** Every now and then events occur that reveal something about the state of society. That is exactly what happened in New York in 1977. At about 9 pm on the evening of 13 July, lightning struck the high-voltage transmission lines causing a total blackout that plunged millions of unprepared citizens into darkness.

New York, at that time, was a city afflicted by high unemployment and the disaffected masses saw the blackout as an opportunity to take what they could from shops under the cover of darkness. Throughout the night the police had their work cut out, trying in vain to stop thousands of people from looting and plundering. What probably began as a search for candles turned into a mass free-for-all.

It took the cops until 10 pm the following evening, more than 24 hours later, to bring things under control. By that time they had arrested 4,500 for looting and wanton vandalism, and 1,616 shops had been badly damaged. Total estimates for the cost of the destruction ranged anywhere from $60 million right up to $300 million.

It wasn't just the police that had things to deal with; as a result of the looting fires broke out all over the place. The New York fire department responded to 1,037 fires burning throughout the city, 50 of which were serious blazes.

Life for the citizens of New York had temporarily been brought to a standstill. Not only was violence raging virtually unchecked in the streets, but many of those who were outside their homes when the blackout struck found themselves stranded. Both of the city's airports were out of action, road tunnels had to be shut and up to 4,000 passengers were hurriedly rushed up from the subway system as ventilators stopped circulating air.

The 1977 blackout is now seen as 'a defining moment in the city's history'. It revealed the endemic anger that was coursing through New York and America in general at the time. When a similar power cut had occurred in 1965, there had been no trouble on that occasion. In the twelve intervening years, American society had undergone a metamorphosis due to the cultural shifts of the late 1960s and early 1970s, and the disillusionment spread by factors such as the Vietnam War.

# 14 July

## An assassination attempt on a president

**2002** Bastille Day, or 14 July, is a national holiday in France that commemorates the storming of the Bastille in 1789. The Bastille was an infamous prison in the heart of Paris and its capture is seen as a symbol of the French Revolution and therefore of the emergence of the modern French Republic.

On this particular day, during the annual celebrations, the presidential cavalcade was proceeding down the Champs Élysées. President Jacques Chirac was sitting in an open-topped jeep, inspecting the troops that had assembled as part of the traditional parade. Standing at the other end of the famous boulevard is the famous Arc de Triomphe, built to commemorate all of those who fought for France during the Napoleonic Wars.

From a position near the Arc de Triomphe, 25-year-old Maxime Brunerie had carried an unassuming guitar case past the eyes of the security guards who were patrolling the crowd. Suddenly there was a cry from the members of the public standing close by. As the president continued to roll down the road, exposed in his vehicle, Brunerie had pulled a hunting rifle from the case and taken aim at the jeep.

Civilians and the police were quick to act. Before Brunerie could fire an accurate shot, they had leapt on him and wrestled the gun from his hands. The single bullet that he did fire thankfully went wildly astray and no one was injured.

As news of the assassination attempt spread, its intended target, Chirac, was informed of the incident. In a remarkably calm response, his interior minister, Nicolas Sarkozy, reported that he simply shrugged and said 'Oh, really', before continuing with the Bastille Day celebrations as planned.

The shooting brought back memories of the failed assassination attempts on the previous French president, Charles de Gaulle, in the 1960s, as well as a similar attack on Bastille Day in 1922 against Alexandre Millerand, then leader of the country. However, while there had been political motivations behind these, the evidence at Brunerie's trial pointed to something quite different. Although Maxime Brunerie had links to extreme-right political groups, including the Unité Radicale, which was dismantled following the incident, his actions were not deemed to be fuelled by politics. Instead, he was described in court as an alienated individual who sought a high-profile victim in order to propel himself to notoriety. It had never been his intention to survive the assassination; rather he had planned either to die by being shot by the police or by committing suicide live on television. At his trial he was found to be of diminished mental responsibility and in 2004 he was sentenced to ten years' imprisonment.

As for Jacques Chirac, having completing the day's schedule, he went on to govern France for another five years before stepping down on 16 May 2007, after exactly twelve years at the helm.

# 15 July

## *A possible case of wrongful execution sways opinion on the death penalty in Britain*

**1953** Timothy Evans had been hanged in 1950 for murder. The bodies of his wife, with unborn child, and two-year-old daughter had been found hidden in a small washroom in his house at 10 Rillington Place, Notting Hill, London. Evans had confessed to the crimes and duly been convicted, although he had also implicated another tenant, John Christie, who he claimed had agreed to perform an abortion on his wife. But Christie had been a key witness for the prosecution, impressing the judge with his plausible manner and respectable ways. Three years later, the bodies of six women were found in the same building, hidden behind panels, underneath floorboards and in the garden. One of them was John Christie's wife. Christie was tried for her murder and subsequently hanged on this day in 1953.

As it was necessary only to try people on one count of murder, Evans had been found guilty only of murdering his daughter and Christie of murdering his own wife. This meant that the murders of Evans's wife and the five other women were not contested in court. Circumstantial evidence suggested strongly that Christie had, in fact, been a serial killer and had murdered all eight, even though Evans had made a confession. It's possible that this confession was made under duress, and in any case Evans was often in a confused state and had an IQ of only 70. It also seems unlikely that two murderers were living in the same house at the same time and both strangled their victims.

Inevitably the case caused great concern about the possibility of wrongful execution. A parliamentary inquiry ensued, and a book sympathetic to Evans written by the broadcaster Ludovic Kennedy, *Ten Rillington Place*, was published in 1961, followed by a film of the same name in 1971 starring Richard Attenborough as Christie and John Hurt as Evans. However, it has never been conclusively proved that Christie was the sole murderer. Whatever the truth, the case caused such a shift in public opinion on the death penalty that capital punishment was finally abandoned in Britain in 1964.

In the modern era of forensics and DNA fingerprinting, proof of guilt would become far more definitive. It was a French police officer named Edmond Locard who famously stated that 'every contact leaves a trace'; a principle that is still followed by forensics teams some 40 years after his death. With sophisticated new techniques for detecting chemicals, it has become possible for the police to prove guilt in cases that would once have relied on circumstantial evidence alone. Many old cases have in fact been reopened and investigated successfully. Luckily, police officers in earlier times often had the foresight to store items of evidence in anticipation that science would one day provide a new way forward.

Rillington Place was later demolished during the construction of Westway Road, but not before its Victorian terraced houses had been used as a location in the 1971 film of the Evans case.

# 16 July

## The first atomic bomb is detonated, in America

**1945** The atomic bombs dropped on Hiroshima and Nagasaki are so well known that people often forget that the first detonation of an atomic weapon took place on American soil. It was known as the Trinity Test. The bomb was an imploding plutonium bomb, the same as the one dropped on Nagasaki. The moment of detonation marked the beginning of the Atomic or Nuclear Age.

What was rather frightening about the Trinity Test is that the scientists didn't know for sure what was going to happen. One theory was that it might cause a chain reaction in nature and destroy the entire world. On the other hand, since no one had ever tried it before, some simply thought that it wouldn't work at all. Two observation bunkers were constructed at distances of ten miles (sixteen km) and seventeen miles (27 km) from ground zero, which was located in the desert of New Mexico.

When the explosion came it was both a relief and a horror. The scientists were relieved that the Manhattan Project hadn't been in vain, but they were also very aware of the technology they had just unleashed on the world. Robert Oppenheimer, the project director, paraphrased a Hindu scripture when he said, 'I am become death, the destroyer of worlds'. In the years following the Second World War he did all he could to voice his concerns for the future of humanity.

The classic image of the nuclear bomb is the mushroom cloud. When the bomb first detonates it actually explodes in a ball shape and spreads out like a vast doughnut of energy. When the explosive force is spent the heat begins to rise in a huge convection current, which forms the stalk of the mushroom and a cloud of debris and water vapour plumes out at the top to form the head. Anything on the ground first experiences a shockwave of energy and heat moving away from the epicentre of the explosion. It is then subjected to a reverse nuclear wind as the convection current draws upwards. Non-nuclear bombs do the same thing, in fact, but not on such an impressive scale.

The Trinity Test bomb was positioned atop a pylon, while the Japan bombs were detonated some distance from the ground to maximise the effect on their targets. If a nuclear bomb is exploded at ground level then a good deal of the energy is wasted because it is dissipated through the substrate. Uneven terrain can also impede the effectiveness of the weapon and certain areas can remain relatively unaffected.

# 17 July

## Disneyland becomes the 51st state of America

**1955** This was the day that the 'happiest place on Earth' first opened its gates. Inside there were to be parades, celebrations, revelry – and, of course, a theme park the likes of which no one had seen before.

Unfortunately for Walt Disney, when the day came for his brand new venture in Anaheim, California to welcome a select group of specially invited guests and journalists, things went rather wrong. In the sweltering summer heat, the asphalt softened, causing high heels to sink down into the paths. Elsewhere, a plumbers' strike meant that people clamouring for refreshment were confronted with drinking fountains that didn't work. Disney had had to choose between flushing toilets and flowing fountains, and had opted for the former. On top of this, there were huge problems with overcrowding as the original tickets had been copied many times over, enabling thousands of extra visitors to pour into the park.

This was not the start that Disney had wanted for his $17 million attraction. However, he kept to his original schedule and opened the park to the general public the following day – exactly one year after construction had begun. During its early years, Disneyland alternated its off-peak opening hours with those of the nearby Knott's Berry Farm so as to reduce operating costs for both companies. It also charged guests to use each individual attraction, much like a traditional funfair.

As time went by, Disneyland put its inauspicious opening behind it and began to grow at an impressive rate. In 1982, Disney decided that the administration costs of charging hundreds of thousands of visitors for each individual ride were too high. As a result, Disneyland did away with this system and introduced a single entrance fee to the park which then allowed the visitor to ride any attraction they wanted to. Starting out at a relatively modest $12 in 1982, current full-price guests are charged around $70 a time.

The park underwent changes as well. In the 1990s it was expanded to become a full-blown resort, with hotels, shops, restaurants and car parks. All the while, visitor numbers continued to rise and regular thrill-seekers were joined by royalty and presidents from around the world. It hadn't always been so easy for heads of state to enjoy the rollercoasters though; in 1959 the Russian premier, Nikita Krushchev, had been denied entry to the park on the grounds of Cold War fears.

For Disneyland's 50th birthday in 2005, a huge eighteen-month celebration was held that ran from May of that year all the way through to September 2006. Not one to undersell itself, Disneyland proudly named the mammoth party the 'Happiest Homecoming on Earth'. The first visitors to pass through the entrance on 17 July 2005, the birthday itself, had been queuing since midway through the previous afternoon.

Nowadays, Disneyland is the most popular theme park of its kind in the world. In 2007, a record-breaking 14.8 million guests flocked to its attractions and since its opening on this day in 1955, well over half a billion people have visited Anaheim to experience the rides within.

# 18 July

## The first heart implantation is performed

**1963** The first heart transplantation took place in 1964, when a patient received the heart of a monkey, but the first heart implantation was performed in 1963. An implant is a man-made device, designed to do the same job as the original organ. In this instance it was a 'left ventricular assist device' or left-VAD.

VADs do not replace the failing heart, but rather help it to do its job properly. Normally the blood flows through two valves and two ventricles in the heart. The basic idea of the implant is that the blood bypasses the defective ventricle and is instead sent rushing into the artery via the VAD, which contains a mechanical pump. This isn't to be confused with a heart bypass operation, which is surgery to allow the blood to miss out sections of artery with restricted blood flow due to atherosclerosis or fatty deposits.

VADs are used when the heart is impaired but not so diseased that it requires removal. Patients are often fitted with them while waiting for the opportunity of a transplant from a human donor. In cases where the heart is badly diseased it may be removed and replaced by a 'totally artificial heart' or TAH. In essence this is a robotic organ, entirely man-made and plumbed into the main veins and arteries. The main risk with VADs and TAHs is mechanical failure. In healthy people the heart is very good at regulating itself and maintaining itself in good working order. Machines are not so reliable, even though they happen to be better than the defective hearts that they are replacing.

Of course, the reliability of implant hearts has a good deal to do with the technology employed. With modern materials and microelectronics such devices will undoubtedly become far more trustworthy. The problems really lie, however, with knowing when to replace worn parts, as a patient has very little chance of survival if a machine heart ceases to function. In fact, this is tantamount to a heart attack, albeit an artificial one. Regular inspection, maintenance and telemetry are therefore the solution, so that medics know when something is about to go wrong.

By far the most common implants are replacement joints – especially hips. Humans are not especially well designed, as we put a great deal of force on our hips by walking upright. Inevitably this leads to wear and tear of the ball and socket joints so that they eventually become diseased and painful. The first replacement hips were fitted to patients in England in 1960. They typically comprise a metal ball that fits into a plastic socket, thereby mimicking the design and function of the real joint.

# 19 July

## A newly discovered dinosaur is aquatic 'T-Rex'

**1983** The term 'piscivorous' is used to describe animals that eat fish. Baryonyx (*Baryonyx walkeri*) is one of the few dinosaurs that was adapted to catching and eating fish. Its name is taken from the Greek *barus*, meaning 'heavy' and *onyx*, meaning 'claw' in a reference to its talons which were perfectly designed for skewering fish.

It was a terrestrial species, but would have frequented places where it had easy access to water – rivers, lakes, marshes, lagoons. The most telling physical adaptations are seen in its forelimbs and snout. It was a bipedal species, leaving its front limbs free to secure prey, which it did with foot- (30 cm-) long claws, rather like the feet of fishing eagles and ospreys. Its mouth was fitted with many fine and serrated teeth, so that it could seize fish and then swallow them whole.

Baryonyx walked the Earth around 125 million years ago, some 60 million years before the dinosaurs finally died out. When alive, Baryonyx would have been about 30 feet (nine metres) long, and weighed up to two tons (1,800 kg). This huge size, while considerably shorter than the king of the dinosaurs who could measure up to 42 feet (thirteen metres) long, nevertheless earned it the nickname 'the aquatic T-Rex'.

On this day in 1983, the first Baryonyx fossils were found in Smokejacks Pit, a clay pit located in Surrey, southern England by William Walker, after whom the species is named.

When it was excavated by a team from the Natural History Museum, it was discovered to be nearly 70 per cent complete. Such a level of detail allowed the scientists to build up quite a level of interpretation when they published their findings three years later.

This first Baryonyx, now housed within the Natural History Museum, remains the best specimen to be found so far. Since 1983 other fossils have turned up, notably a skull in Spain and claws in both West Africa and the Isle of Wight, indicating that the dinosaur had quite a considerable range.

For a number of years Baryonyx was in fact the only known piscivorous dinosaur. Then, in 1998 a related dinosaur – Suchomimus – was discovered in West Africa. At up to 40 feet (twelve metres) long, Suchomimus was much larger than his smaller cousin. The name, literally translated from the Latin, is 'crocodile mimic', and in terms of their diet and the general shape of their snouts, it is perhaps best to think of both Baryonyx and Suchomimus in these terms.

# 20 July

## Ceylon gets the world's first female prime minister

**1960** The world's first female prime minister, Sirimavo Bandaranaike, was not from some enlightened, progressive Scandinavian country, but from Sri Lanka, then known as Ceylon. It was over twenty years before Scandinavia got its first female premier in Norway's Gro Harlem Brundtland.

Interestingly, while the election of a woman to high office would be a major progressive step for the status of women in Europe, in southern Asia it required no such shift of attitudes. It is no coincidence that the world's second female prime minister, Indira Gandhi, elected in 1996, was Indian. In southern Asia politics was, at least at this time, very much a family affair, and just as it was natural for a woman to become head of the family after the death of her husband or father, so it was quite easy for a woman to become head of the country in the same way.

Mrs Gandhi took the reins in India shortly after the death of her father Jawaharlal Nehru, and her daughter-in-law Sonia Gandhi took a leading role in Indian politics after the death of her husband Rajiv, Indira's son. Mrs Bandaranaike came to prominence after the death of her husband, Solomon Bandaranaike, the Ceylonese prime minister, who was assassinated in 1959. Indeed, for a long time Mrs Bandaranaike was known as 'the weeping widow' by her opponents for her tendency to break down in tears at crucial (and fortuitous) moments and insist that she was simply carrying on her late husband's socialist policies.

When she first came to power in 1960, Mrs Bandaranaike proved her socialist credentials by nationalising key sectors, such as banking and insurance. But her state takeover of industries such as oil antagonised foreign businesses, provoking the Americans and British to impose an aid embargo in 1962. Her decision to switch from English as the official language to Sinhala proved even more of an irritant. The country's Tamil population regarded the change as targeting them, since they did not speak Sinhala, and so began a campaign of civil disobedience which forced Mrs Bandaranaike to impose a state of emergency.

Mrs Bandanaike was roundly defeated in the 1964 elections, but she bounced back in 1970 to become prime minister for a second time. This time, the changes she made were even more radical, as she turned Ceylon into the Republic of Sri Lanka in 1972. After outfacing a youth rebellion with the aid of Indian troops, she became increasingly intolerant of opposition. As the oil crisis pushed the Sri Lankan economy into real trouble, her party altered the constitution to extend her premiership by a further two years, before she was eventually brought down in 1977, and stripped of her civic rights in the same year.

She made a third comeback as prime minister in 1996, but the real power now lay in the hands of the president, who just happened to be her ambitious daughter, Chandrika, still keeping Sri Lankan politics a family affair. In 2000, she left office, and then died on election day on 10 October, just after casting her vote.

# 21 July

## Humanity sets foot on the Moon

**1969** At 2:56 UTC on 21 July 1969, Neil Armstrong became the first human to set foot on the Moon, stepping down from the 'Eagle', the *Apollo* space mission's Moon landing craft, and uttering the famous words, 'One small step for (a) man, one giant leap for mankind'. People didn't hear him say 'a' man, but apparently he said it, and the 'a' simply got lost in transmission. Either way it was a transcendent moment in human exploration, and 35 years on Stephen Dick, head historian at NASA, asserted that in 1,000 years' time, the Moon landing will probably be considered the greatest achievement of the 20th century.

It was the culmination of a dream set in motion by President John F. Kennedy eight years earlier, when he said in a speech in 1961: 'I believe that this nation should commit itself to achieving the goal, before this decade is out, of landing a man on the Moon and returning him safely to the Earth.' After one of the most intensive technological development programmes ever undertaken, the *Apollo* spacecraft, with its three-man crew of Neil Armstrong, Buzz Aldrin and Michael Collins, took off from the Kennedy Space Centre in Florida at 13:32 UTC on 16 July, powered into the upper atmosphere by the giant Saturn V rocket. After about half an hour, the Saturn V dropped away, leaving the *Apollo* craft to head on towards the Moon.

Seventy-six hours later, the *Apollo* reached the Moon and went into orbit. After 30 orbits, the lunar module 'Eagle', with Armstrong and Aldrin aboard, separated from the command module *Columbia* and descended to the lunar surface. The spot chosen for the landing was the flat area known as the Sea of Tranquility. As the module touched down safely at 20:17 UTC on 20 July, Armstrong radioed back the now-famous words, 'The "Eagle" has landed'. Back home on Earth, millions of people all round the world were watching on TV transfixed. Six hours later, Armstrong took his historic step, followed shortly onto the Moon's surface by Aldrin.

For two-and-a-half hours, the astronauts moved around on the lunar dust gathering rock samples, doing tests, setting up scientific equipment and taking photos. They also placed an American flag, a plaque, drawings of the Earth and their autographs and that of President Nixon, before climbing back into the 'Eagle'. After seven hours' rest, they took off and rejoined the *Columbia* for the return journey to Earth. They splashed down safely near Johnston Atoll in the North Pacific on 24 July.

A further series of *Apollo* missions put twelve more men on the Moon between 1969 and 1972. But then the idea of flying people to the Moon disappeared almost as suddenly as it had begun. For more than three decades after the last *Apollo* landing, there were just a handful of unmanned missions, and nothing more. Finally, though, NASA are planning to return to the Moon. There is now a programme afoot to establish a permanent lunar base by 2020 and in 2014, astronauts will finally set foot on the Moon again – nearly half a century after that momentous first landing.

# 22 July

## A comet is photographed striking Jupiter

**1994** There is plenty of evidence to suggest that celestial bodies collide with one another from time to time. The Moon is covered in craters where meteors have struck its surface – the Earth has a number of such pock marks too. In 1994, astronomers had their first chance to actually witness a significant collision when a comet, named Shoemaker-Levy 9 (SL9) was discovered to be on a collision course with the planet Jupiter.

As the comet was drawn towards the planet by the enormous gravitational pull it began to break up and ended up as a procession of 23 fragments, which were listed alphabetically A to W. They were as big as two miles (3 km) across. The spacecraft *Galileo* was used to collect photographic images of the event as it unfolded. It was 148 million miles (238 million km) away at the time, but the scale of the planet and the comet fragments was so large that it was able to record some reasonable pictures. The Hubble Space Telescope was also used to collect data from its orbit around the Earth.

Over a period of about six days the comet pieces plunged into the atmosphere of Jupiter, one by one, leaving a clearly visible scar that lasted for some time after the event. The comet was travelling at a speed of 133,000 mph (216,000 kph) and each fragment caused a bright flash of light called a bolide, due to friction with the atmospheric gases. Shooting stars are bolides caused by small meteors entering the atmosphere of the Earth.

Comets, unlike asteroids and meteors, have a kind of atmosphere called a coma. Solar radiation causes the surface to sublimate (change from solid to vapour) so that the comet has a fuzzy appearance. The vapour often creates a tail. It isn't in the wake of the comet as one might expect, but instead always points towards the sun. It may come as some surprise to learn that more than 3,000 comets are currently on record and more are added to the list every year. Very few are visible to the naked eye, however, and even

Halley's comet wasn't especially prominent in the sky when it last visited in 1986.

# 23 July

## *The world's most beautiful bridge is resurrected and reopened*

**2004** Once in a while people come up with designs that possess an innate aesthetic and proportional beauty. The Stari Most, which translates literally as 'Old Bridge', is one of those designs. It has an elegance and economy of form that makes it look almost like a work of nature.

It was a desperate shame, then, when in 1993 it was destroyed by artillery shellfire during the Bosnian War. The bridge had existed since 1566 and spanned a gorge between two parts of the city of Mostar.

Following the war it was decided that the bridge should be rebuilt using as much of the original stone as possible, most of which lay in the Neretva River below. UNESCO orchestrated the project, which cost about €12 million. Reconnecting the two halves of the city was seen as a symbol of peace and renewed ethnic harmony.

The builders of the replica bridge were mystified by how the original builders, who took nine years to finish construction, had managed the job in the absence of modern technology. The bridge comprised a huge single-span arch constructed with perfect symmetry, although some deformation had occurred over the 400 years. Nevertheless, it would have required an absolute mastery of material and method. There is a legend that the architect prepared for his own funeral before the bridge was opened, as the penalty for structural failure would have been death. It turned out that he had nothing to worry about.

The arch is one of those simple ideas that set humanity on the path to modern civilisation. The greater the compressive force on an arch, the stronger it becomes. This property enabled architects to erect vast buildings, such as temples and cathedrals, and to construct gargantuan bridges, viaducts and aqueducts. Arches, when laid on their side, are also very useful for building dams. The only points of weakness are where the ends of the arch are supported. When used in buildings such as cathedrals, flying buttresses are required to prevent the footings of arches from separating and causing structural failure.

In the case of the Stari Most this was not a problem, because the arch was anchored into solid rock on either side of the gorge. Instead of ungainly supports, at either end of the bridge stand two beautiful guards, the Helebija tower on the northeast and the Tara tower to the southwest. Together they are known as 'the bridgekeepers'.

# 24 July

## Quarantine for astronauts returning to Earth

**1969** An interesting aspect of the *Apollo XI* mission is that the American administration seriously considered the possibility of there being alien pathogens present on the Moon. When the three astronauts splashed down in the Pacific Ocean, they were wearing special suits in order to biologically isolate them from the team sent to retrieve their landing capsule. They were then taken on board USS *Hornet* and kept in quarantine for a period of three weeks to determine whether any alien bacteria or viruses were likely to incubate themselves and develop into diseases.

We now know that the Moon is utterly barren, but the idea that there may be dormant micro-organisms waiting for a host organism to arrive was a genuine concern at the time. Scientists knew that the anthrax bacterium, for example, had the ability to survive in the form of spores for indefinite periods, so they reasoned that a deadly disease might have been waiting for aeons. Indeed, there was a theory at the time – *lithopanspermia* – that life on Earth might have originated from spores disseminated through space.

Buzz Aldrin, Neil Armstrong and Michael Collins, however, spent three weeks in quarantine. Much of this was in the Lunar Receiving Laboratory at the Manned Space Center, where they were visited by President Nixon while still inside their confinement capsule.

Eventually the team of doctors and scientists assigned to them decided that they hadn't picked up any space flu and they were given the all-clear. On 13 August 1969, the astronauts walked out of quarantine and into the arms of the American public. After a state banquet at which they each received the Presidential Medal of Freedom – the highest civilian award – parades were held in their honour in cities across the United States.

If one thinks about it, the spore idea doesn't stand up to close scrutiny. It would still mean that the spores had originated on another planet somewhere, so how would they have found themselves in space? As far as we know, the only organisms to have escaped the biosphere of the Earth are humans, dogs and chimps (admittedly with a little human help), plus the odd experimental plant and animal. While it is true that all of the above will have been accompanied by bacteria and viruses, there is no way that they could have hitched a ride on interstellar objects and spread to other parts of the universe.

# 25 July

## The first 'test-tube baby' is born

**1978** Nowadays IVF babies are relatively commonplace, but the birth of Louise Brown on this day in 1978 was hailed as a major step in scientific progress. The technology resulted in efforts to treat women who had blocked Fallopian tubes (the ducts via which eggs travel from the ovaries to the womb). Such blockages were bypassed by taking eggs from the ovaries, fertilising them in a lab and then reinserting them into the uterus. *In vitro* fertilisation – 'in glass fertilisation' – as it was dubbed was snappily characterised by the press as 'test-tube babies'.

Louise's parents, John and Lesley Brown, had been trying for a baby for months to no avail. IVF had previously been tried as a method of conception with other childless couples, but at the time no case had been a success. The theory was established and understood by medical practitioners, but they just couldn't get it to work.

Lesley Brown's IVF treatment took place under the guidance of doctors Patrick Steptoe and Robert Edwards. On 10 November 1977 fertilised eggs were implanted into her womb. Just under nine months later, at 11.47 pm on 25 July 1978, baby Louise was born at Oldham General Hospital.

As a child, Louise Brown grew up with a great deal of media attention, but she soon learnt to deal with the constant stream of questions that would come her way over the years. Lesley and John Brown subsequently had another IVF pregnancy, also facilitated by Steptoe and Edwards, and Lesley successfully gave birth to Louise's younger sister, Natalie, as a result. Patrick Steptoe, who died in 1988, and Robert Edwards went on to establish the Bourn Hall Clinic in Cambridgeshire as a pioneering centre for IVF treatment in Britain.

At the time of the procedure, Steptoe and Edwards attracted a great deal of criticism for their work. Although IVF is now widely accepted and welcomed, there are still those who oppose it on moral and religious grounds. At the forefront of these is the Catholic Church, which argues that infertility is God's sign that he wishes the couple to adopt an unwanted child. They also take issue with the fact that the creation of a fertilised egg requires the attempted fertilisation of many eggs. As not all are subsequently needed for implantation, potentially viable embryos are destroyed and this is seen as a violation of these embryos' human rights.

Despite certain objections of this type, Louise Brown, now in her thirties and with a child of her own, is testament to the ability of science to grant life in cases where nature fails. These days a number of different fertility treatments are employed. They are known collectively as ART (assisted reproductive technology). IVF itself now envelops a number of different techniques which are used in specific situations, depending on the nature of the infertility.

ART includes IVF as well as methods such as artificial insemination and surgical sperm retrieval.

# 26 July

## Britain drops Churchill for Attlee and his Labour party

**1945** When the votes for the British general election came in and revealed that the Labour party had won, and won handsomely, it was a terrible shock for Winston Churchill. There were no opinion polls in those days, and all the pundits had said Churchill was a shoo-in after his heroic wartime leadership. How could the man who had led Britain doggedly through those dark times lose now that the victory had been won? But that's exactly what happened and Churchill felt bitterly betrayed, waking up, he said, with 'a sharp stab of almost physical pain' that day.

But Churchill had forgotten what the British people had been fighting for. They had been fighting for peace, and fighting for a better world – and they wanted to put the terrible days of the war entirely behind them. They wanted a fresh start and a better home for all those weary heroes to come home to. The war had been a great leveller, and people no longer wanted to live in a nation divided along lines of privilege. In their own mild, very British way, they wanted to build a New Jerusalem in the wake of the horrors of war. Roy Jenkins, later Labour chancellor and Liberal Democrat leader, summed it up beautifully when he described how on the campaign trail, he saw 'a sea of tired faces looking up in hope'. Churchill got the mood badly wrong when he suggested in an election speech that Labour's socialist ideals would need the Gestapo to make them work.

The extraordinary thing about the new Labour government is just how effectively they delivered that hope, leading some to argue that it was the best British government of all time. The problems they faced were huge. Britain's economy was in a catastrophic state after the war effort. The country might have won the war but the economy was just as badly wrecked as if it had lost. When the

Americans abruptly halted their wartime funding, the economist J.M. Keynes was forced to go to Washington to beg for money – and got a loan so small and on such bad terms that it was not until 2006 that the UK finally managed to pay it back. So the years under the Labour government were years of unimaginable economic crisis, culminating in 1947 with the rationing of bread and potatoes, along with so much else – tolerable in wartime, but hateful in peace. A 1946 exhibition at the Victoria and Albert Museum intended to show off Britain's consumer design skills entitled 'Britain Can Make It' was quickly dubbed 'Britain Can't Have It'. No wonder then, that Churchill got back into power in 1951.

Yet despite these problems, Attlee's government managed to begin the peaceful wind-down of Britain's empire days, with, notably, the granting of independence to India – although this was not done without tragic immediate consequences. More unambiguously at home, they nationalised key industries such as the railways and coal, built a huge number of homes for the less well-off, extended the education system wider than ever and, most lastingly, established the National Health Service.

When the Labour minister Nye Bevan's new NHS opened on 5 July 1948, there was an immediate flood of people to surgeries, hospitals and chemists – and the flood has continued ever since. The NHS is now such an enshrined part of the British way of life that even the Tory party hopes to be elected on how well it will look after the NHS.

# 27 July

### The world's first jet airliner takes to the air on the birthday of its creator

**1949** Geoffrey de Havilland was flying his own self-built aeroplane in 1909, just six years after the Wright brothers had shown that it was possible to achieve mechanical flight. He built the aircraft by trial and error until it was airworthy and then taught himself how to master the controls. He went on to pioneer aviation in Britain and played a significant role in the war effort by making the Mosquito fighter-bomber, which was extremely fast and manoeuvrable, thanks to its plywood frame beneath a canvas skin.

When the jet engine was developed during the Second World War, he immediately saw the potential in using it to propel airliners rather than just the jet fighters that it had been initially designed for. Only four years after the war the Comet made its maiden flight and in doing so became the world's first jet-propelled airliner. Until this point airliners had been propeller-driven. Not only did this make long-haul flights very time-consuming, but the aircraft had to remain at relatively low altitudes so that the air was thick enough for the propellers to work. This meant staying below cloud level and coping with varying weather conditions. The jet engine meant shorter flights above the clouds and totally transformed the nature of global travel. On the day of the Comet's inaugural flight, De Havilland was also celebrating his 67th birthday.

One interesting aspect of flight is that scientists don't fully understand how it is possible. The phenomenon of 'lift' is one of those things that just exists, much like gravity. What essentially happens is that the upper surface of a wing is curved, so that it has a larger area than the lower surface. Air molecules are divided by the leading edge of the wing, and some travel over the top while others make their way under the wing. Those travelling over the wing have slightly further to travel in the same time, so they need to spread out more than those travelling underneath. This creates a pressure difference between the two surfaces of the wing and it, plus anything attached to it, such as the fuselage and passengers, is lifted into the air.

The mystery arises when we consider the mighty air molecules holding the plane in the sky. As well as pushing the wing up, they also need to push down on the air below. This has by far the less resistance of the two, and so it should mean that the movement of the air molecules in this direction is greater than the upward one, leading the aeroplane to fall to the ground. Fortunately, in normal flight, this doesn't happen. It is proposed that because planes travel so fast, the wings have moved forward before this air has had time to collapse under the weight of the aircraft.

# 28 July

## The discovery of prehistoric Kennewick Man

**1996** The most interesting thing about Kennewick Man is that his skull is not typical of other native North American specimens. In fact his facial bone structure is much more reminiscent of the native South Americans – and it is quite possible that successive migrations pushed existing ancestral populations northwards in order to find new territory.

However, this may also turn out to be a false match. One study by the anthropologist James Chatters, who examined the skeleton, found that the only partial link to modern-day populations was with the Ainu people of south-east Asia. Furthermore, when the criteria against which the skeleton was judged were narrowed down, Chatters discovered no discernable link with any modern group at all. In short, no one quite knows exactly who Kennewick Man is an ancestor of.

This uncertainty has presented a certain amount of trouble and bad feeling over the treatment of his remains. Five Native American tribes have laid claim to the bones, asserting that they are ancestral remains. Under the Native American Graves Protection and Repatriation Act, all cultural artefacts must be returned to the tribe from which they originated. In the case of Kennewick Man, each tribe wanted to give him a traditional burial.

The scientists involved in the find, however, were strongly opposed to relinquishing the bones. They wanted to analyse the bones and duly filed a plea with the American courts that as the skeleton was not related to any of the tribes concerned in any identifiable way, it should not be released. The Native Americans were consequently extremely displeased when the judge considering the evidence found in favour of the research team.

As for Kennewick Man himself, his skeleton was found on this day in the bank of the Columbia River, Washington. It has been dated to around 7,500 BC, making it roughly 9,500 years old. Analysis of his DNA, which was partially recovered, is inconclusive although the presence of certain amino acids suggests that his diet was rich in fish.

The skeleton, which was all but complete, showed signs of injuries which he probably sustained as a result of warfare, or possibly hunting accidents. These included several broken ribs, which may well have been linked to the cause of his death.

The first true American ancestral evidence was found near Clovis, New Mexico, in 1932. Many stone tools, now known as Clovis points, were unearthed in association with fossilised mammoth bones. They have been dated to 9–9,500 years BC. Further sites on the American east coast have yielded stone tools that some experts claim bear similarity to those made in France around the same time. To explain this, they have advanced the hypothesis that some prehistoric people crossed the Atlantic from France when the ocean was frozen over during the last ice age.

Another American site, named the Meadowcroft Rockshelter, in Pennsylvania, has yielded evidence that humans have been present in North America for almost 20,000 years.

# 29 July

## *A man dies who may have beaten the Wright brothers into second place*

**1953** For every great invention in history, there are always those who some ardently claim 'got there first'. Some of these claims are justified. Englishman Joseph Swan almost certainly did invent the electric light bulb long before American Thomas Edison, and it was proven in court. The ancient Greek Hero of Alexander, on the other hand, did not invent the steam engine far ahead of his time.

In 1953, a New Zealander called Richard Pearse died at the age of 76, and in recent years, people have begun to claim that he actually beat the Wright brothers to make the first powered flight on his remote farm at Waitohi on New Zealand's South Island. Advocates claim that his flying machine was in the air in 1902, and indeed eyewitnesses confirmed that they saw it flying at least as early as 10 July 1903, several months before the Wright brothers' historic flight at Kittyhawk.

Pearse himself, though, never claimed to have beaten the Wright brothers, and the assertion that he did so is wrong on two counts. First of all, Pearse's flying machine was not the first powered craft to get off the ground. Secondly, nor was the Wright brothers'! There is good evidence that a small model of William Henson's steam carriage, a remarkable plane powered by a lightweight steam engine, flew inside a hangar as early as 1848 – more than half a century before Pearse. And some time around 1877, a French naval officer with the wonderful name Félix du Temple de la Croix made a short flight in a monoplane powered by a petrol engine. Then in the early 1890s, another Frenchman, Clement Ader, made a whole series of powered flights – all of which ended with a crash-landing, and it is here that the Wright brothers' achievement comes in.

The Wright brothers did not make the first powered flight as people so often, mistakenly, say. Their great achievement was to make the first powered *sustained, controlled* flight. All those earlier pioneers of powered flight may have got their machines off the ground, but once in the air they had no control, so the flight was inevitably short, and often ended in a crash. With their clever wing-warping, the Wrights were able to maintain a stable flight for some distance, and bring the machine safely back to the ground in a controlled fashion.

Pearse may also have achieved some degree of control in flight, using wing flaps as all modern planes do rather than the Wright brothers' wing-warping, which proved to be a dead end. But Pearse probably made his first genuinely controlled flight in 1904, a little while after the Wrights. Nevertheless, his achievements were remarkable. Unlike the Wrights, he was working in one of the remotest parts of the world, with no access to any engineers. That means that he had to build every single part of his flying machine himself – including the engine. And his monoplane design was in many ways more sophisticated than the Wrights' biplane. So although Pearse did not 'beat' the Wright brothers, or anyone else, he deserves to be recognised as a true pioneer of flight.

# *30 July*

### *England wins the World Cup Final on home turf*

**1966** 'Some people are on the pitch. They think it's all over. It is now.' So BBC TV commentator Kenneth Wolstenholme famously said as Geoff Hurst completed his hat-trick in the last ten seconds to seal England's astonishing World Cup victory in 1966.

For English football fans, this was the greatest day in history. It was not just the first and only time England have won the World Cup – but the victory was that much sweeter because they did it on home turf at Wembley, in front of their own fans.

The road to victory began in 1960, when after an epic battle with the Germans at the FIFA Congress in Rome, England won the right to stage the 1966 World Cup. However, things began to look decidedly shaky when, just four months before the Cup was due to begin, the trophy was stolen from Central Hall, Westminster where it was being exhibited. Fortunately, the thief was apprehended and the trophy was recovered shortly afterwards when a dog called Pickles found it in a south London garden.

England's World Cup campaign started slowly with a mundane 0–0 draw against Uruguay. Then in the second match, against France, England's star player Jimmy Greaves was injured, and West Ham's Geoff Hurst had to be drafted in to replace him. Nevertheless England played solidly and progressed steadily to the semi-finals. Here, in a classic match against Portugal, they won through as Bobby Charlton really found his form. In the other half of the draw, meanwhile, West Germany were powering their way past all opposition to arrive in the final as favourites.

Greaves was fit for the final, but England manager Alf Ramsey, a quiet, almost dull but unusually respected figure, decided to stick with Geoff Hurst, much to Greaves' distress. Hurst proved Ramsey right in abundance, with the only-ever hat-trick in a World Cup Final.

The game, watched by 400 million people around the world, started badly for England as Germany's Haller nipped in to score after just thirteen minutes. Six minutes later, though, England were back on level terms with Hurst's first goal. With captain Bobby Moore in commanding form and midfielder Martin Peters playing a blinder, the game began to go England's way, and when Peters scored with just twelve minutes left, it looked as if the trophy was theirs. Then, with just seconds to go, Germany's Weber scrambled in a goal to force the game into extra time. Ramsey urged his tired players on, barking, 'Look at them; they're finished!'

Ten minutes into extra time, Hurst hammered the ball on to the underside of the cross-bar. It bounced down and its spin took it out of the goal. The goal was given but ever since, controversy has raged over whether or not the ball crossed the line as it bounced down. Fortunately, though, victory was put beyond dispute in the dying seconds as Bobby Moore fed a great long ball out to Hurst on the left, and Hurst galloped forward on his own, leaving the exhausted Germans behind, and fired the ball into the roof of the net to complete England's victory.

# 31 July

## The summit of K2, the most dangerous mountain of them all, is reached

**1954** Although K2 is only the second highest mountain in the world above sea level behind Everest, it is the higher of the two above ground level. This means that the foothills are lower in relation to the summit than those of Everest. K2 also has atrociously unpredictable weather and its famously difficult climb arguably makes it more of a challenge than Everest.

The name of the mountain derives from the fact that it is part of a range of five peaks called the Karakoram, which are listed in order from K1–5. It is one of just fourteen mountains worldwide higher than 8,000 metres. The name 'Karakoram' is Turkic for 'black-gravel', so chosen because there are glaciers flowing between the mountains that are littered with black scree.

On this day back in 1954, the mountain was finally scaled by two Italians, Lino Lacedelli and Achille Compagnoni. It brought an end to 52 years of failed climbs, which had begun in 1909 when Oscar Eckenstein and Aleister Crowley attempted the ascent. As it was, Lacedelli and Compagnoni very nearly didn't make it themselves.

Starting out in a party of four, along with Walter Bonatti and Muhammad Ata-ullah, they began to make their way up the formidable mountain. Of the 70 days Lacedelli and Compagnoni would spend at base camp, 40 of them were in bad weather. K2 was in no mood to be conquered.

The climb went better than perhaps could be expected. A combination of extreme fitness and strong team spirit saw the four men all reach the base of a 200-metre cliff that led to the summit. However, at the same moment, they discovered that disaster had struck. Some 8,150 metres above sea level, the oxygen supplies had run out. To be at such an altitude, in such unpredictable weather, without oxygen was bad enough; to try and scale a sheer rock face – even if it was the final one – seemed foolhardy in the extreme.

Bonatti and Ata-ullah selected really the only sensible course of action. Having come further up the mountain than anyone before them, they turned around and headed back down while it was still safe to do so. Lacedelli and Compagnoni, staring danger in the face, pressed on.

That they successfully made the summit, before having to descend quickly as the bad weather closed in, was as much down to luck as mountaineering skill. As they headed back to camp, one of them slipped and only stopped himself plummeting thousands of feet by digging his axe into the mountainside and clinging on. Together, they carefully helped each other down to safety and into the record books.

Since Lacedelli and Compagnoni, only 145 people have managed to make it to the top of K2 and then back again. When compared to the figure for Everest, which stands at over 2,000 (despite Everest only being conquered the year before K2, in 1953), it is a reflection of just how difficult and dangerous K2 is. For those that have successfully attempted the climb, a further 53 have died while trying. This puts K2's fatality rate at 26.8 per cent – and makes it nearly three times as dangerous as Everest.

# 1 August

## The first lone-gunman massacre in the US

**1966** Until Seung-Hui Cho killed 32 students and teachers in a rampage at Virginia Tech in 2007, the worst and first of a whole series of massacres of students at American colleges was the Austin campus massacre on 1 August 1966.

That morning 25-year-old Charles Whitman, a one-time engineering student at the University of Texas, began his killing spree. After stabbing his wife to death, he went to his mother's house and killed her too. After writing a suicide note, he went to hire a gun, saying it was to hunt hogs. Then, just before midday, he climbed to the observation deck at the top of the University's 307-foot-tall main tower. From there, Whitman opened fire on the mall far below and went on shooting at anyone who moved for the next 96 minutes. Fourteen people were killed in the shooting spree that followed and 31 were seriously injured. One of the injured finally died in 2001 from complications created by his gunshot injury, bringing the final death toll for the day to seventeen. Eventually, the shooting stopped when an Austin policeman shot and killed Whitman.

After the massacre, there was huge speculation about what had driven Whitman to this terrible crime. Some speculated that family issues were to blame. Others said it was depression. The campus psychiatrist, whom Whitman visited for help with this depression, described him as 'oozing with hostility'. Whitman, who was treated first with Valium and later Dexedrine, described in his suicide note his visits to the psychiatrist as to 'no avail'. A post-mortem revealed a small brain tumour. Some experts speculated that the pressure of this tumour on Whitman's amygdala turned him aggressive.

Whatever the reason for Whitman's outburst that day, it sadly proved not to be an isolated event. Since then a whole series of tragic shootings has shocked and stunned US schools and college campuses. There have been more than 40 so far, the worst of which were the California Fullerton library killing in which seven students died; the Columbine High School massacre in 1999 in which twelve students and a teacher died at the hands of two students, Eric Harris and Dylan Kiebold; the Red Lake High School massacre in 1999 in which sixteen-year-old Jeffrey Weise killed five students, a teacher and a security guard, as well as his grandfather and his partner; the Amish school shooting in 2006 in which a milk truck driver killed five little Amish girls; and worst of all the Virginia Tech massacre in 2007.

The Virginia Tech massacre in particular drew a barrage of criticism from around the world of US gun laws and culture, as well as the treatment of the mentally unbalanced. Prompted by the killings, the US government passed one of its toughest gun control laws, designed to halt the purchase of guns by criminals and those declared mentally ill. But most outside commentators think this will make little difference in a country where guns are widely and easily available and the right to own a gun is enshrined in law. Many commentators also think the problem goes much deeper, and point to a fundamental malaise at the heart of American culture as young people are alienated by the pressures of the country's ambitious, individualistic, celebrity-based consumer culture. Other people point the finger at violent computer games and films. The truth is no one knows, and the school killings are still going on, with five more young students killed at North Illinois University on 14 February 2008.

# 2 August

## Iraq invades and annexes Kuwait

**1990** Just before dawn on 2 August 1990, an army of some 100,000 Iraqi troops along with hundreds of tanks swept over the border into Kuwait. There was scattered resistance from the Kuwaiti Army, but they had little chance against the vast invasion force. Within less than five hours all of Kuwait was in Iraqi hands and the Kuwaiti royal family had fled, with the emir speeding across the border just minutes before the Iraqis stormed his palace, killing his younger brother as he tried to defend it.

The Iraqis immediately proclaimed their takeover of the little oil-rich state as the 'Revolution of August 2'. As far as they were concerned, they were reclaiming territory that was rightfully theirs, since it had been part of Iraq before the Ottoman Empire broke up in 1899. They also had other grievances against Kuwait. Kuwait, the Iraqis felt, was boosting oil production dramatically in a bid to destabilise Iraq by undercutting oil prices. And they insisted that the Kuwaitis were extracting Iraqi oil by slant drilling to get at oil which was actually under Iraq.

It is hard to get at the truth of what really happened since there are many conflicting versions of the events leading up to the invasion. Some argue that the Iraqis, who had US backing in their long war against Iran which had just finished, may have thought that the US had given them the green light for their invasion. The *New York Times* later reported a meeting between Saddam Hussein and US Ambassador April Glaspie in July 1990, in which Glaspie apparently said, 'We have no opinion on the Arab–Arab conflicts, like your border disagreement with Kuwait'.

Whatever the truth, after the invasion the USA, along with most of the rest of the world, was quick to condemn the Iraqis, seeing it as an unprovoked act of aggression by a large state against a smaller neighbour. The world community demanded Iraq's immediate withdrawal and began to impose economic sanctions. Far from being cowed, Baghdad announced its formal annexation of Kuwait and cracked down hard on any opposition in Kuwait, arresting and torturing thousands.

US President George Bush Snr had no problem building a coalition to expel the Iraqis by force, and on 17 January 1991, he announced the start of Operation Desert Storm on television, saying, 'Just two hours ago, allied air forces began attacking military targets in Iraq and Kuwait. These attacks continue as I speak. Ground forces are not engaged. This conflict started 2 August when the dictator of Iraq invaded a small and helpless neighbor. Kuwait, a member of the Arab League and a member of the United

Nations, was crushed, its people brutalized. Five months ago, Saddam Hussein started this cruel war against Kuwait. Tonight, the battle has been joined.'

The Iraqis were quickly driven back, first with the longest bombing campaign since the Second World War, which reduced parts of Baghdad to rubble, and then with a dynamic ground invasion by the sixteen-nation coalition. The coalition troops drove the disintegrating Iraqi forces back to within 150 miles of Baghdad before finally calling a halt and withdrawing. Just 100 hours after the ground invasion began, President Bush declared a ceasefire. Kuwait had been liberated, but if anyone thought the troubles with Iraq were over, they were very much mistaken.

# 3 August

## Mathias Rust is released from prison

**1988** On 3 August 1988, after serving a 432-day sentence, 21-year-old German Mathias Rust was released from jail in the Soviet Union. His astonishing crime had been to fly a Cessna light aircraft without permission all the way from Finland and through Soviet airspace to land right in the middle of Moscow, just metres from Red Square and the Kremlin.

Young Mathias was, it emerged, deeply concerned about the continuing Cold War confrontation between the USA and the Soviet Union. In particular, he was especially upset by the way the talks on a nuclear wind-down between Reagan and Gorbachev at Reykjavik in 1986, which had seemed so hopeful, had ended in failure. The then-teenager was determined to do something about it and hit on the outrageous plan of flying to Moscow, afterwards saying, if he could 'pass through the Iron Curtain without being intercepted, it would show that Gorbachev was serious about new relations with the West ... How could Reagan continue to say [Russia] was the empire of evil if me, in a small aircraft, can go straight there unharmed'.

It was a dangerous idea, since the last plane to stray into Soviet airspace, Korean Airlines flight KAL007, had been shot down in 1983, killing all 269 passengers on board. Yet young Rust was convinced that the Russians wouldn't do it again. He flew first over the Atlantic to Reykjavik to practice his still-quite-rudimentary flying skills, then turned east and flew to Helsinki via Iceland and Norway, reaching the city on 25 May 1987.

Early on the morning of 28 May, he took off from Helsinki, apparently bound for Stockholm, but a short way into his flight he turned right round and started heading east into the Soviet Union. Two Soviet fighters were sent to intercept and decided that Rust's Cessna was a harmless Soviet Yak sports plane. Further on, another fighter flew right up to Rust, but the Soviet pilot's report that the plane was West German was apparently disbelieved or simply ignored. In fact, though, the Soviets had little option. After the Korean airline tragedy, pilots were under strict orders not to take action against civilian planes. And so Rust flew on to Moscow and, with remarkable luck, managed to make a safe landing right next to St Basil's Cathedral on the corner of Red Square.

As he got out of his plane, he was surrounded by intrigued and generally welcoming Russians until the KGB came along and carted him off to Lefortovo prison. He was sentenced to three years in prison but released on parole after 432 days.

Opinion is divided over what Rust's exploit achieved. Some are convinced it genuinely helped Gorbachev by giving him an excuse to sack a number of hard-line military bosses, as well as more than 2,000 other soldiers. That's what Rust thinks anyway, but some people believe he is simply unbalanced. That seemed to be proven when shortly after his release from jail, he stabbed a student nurse – who either refused to kiss him or mocked his exploit. Rust says it was a moment of extreme stress after his time in Soviet prison.

Rust is now a Hindu and still campaigning for world peace, but with none of the celebrity of old. Whether his flight to Moscow really did help achieve the breakthroughs that ended the Cold War no one knows, but there is no doubt it was one of the most sensational stunts of the 20th century.

# 4 August

*Prince's* Purple Rain *enters the Billboard 200 at number one and stays there for 24 weeks*

**1984** The year 1984 was a remarkable one for the diminutive Minneapolis musician Prince. For a while that year, his record *Purple Rain* was the number one album, a single from the album, 'When Doves Cry', was number one song, and the movie inspired by the album, also called *Purple Rain*, was number one film. To cap it all, Prince won an Oscar for the music for the film.

*Purple Rain* was an extraordinary album. It sold in huge numbers, entering the Billboard charts in the USA at number one and staying there for 24 weeks, then alternating with Bruce Springsteen's classic *Born in the USA* in the top spot for almost two years. Altogether some 13 million copies of the album were sold.

Many critics regard *Purple Rain* as the definitive album of the 1980s, just as The Beatles' *Sergeant Pepper* was the album of the 1960s. It ranks 72nd in the '*Rolling Stone* Greatest Albums of all Time', while in 1993, *Time* magazine nominated it as the fifteenth greatest album ever. In 1997, *Vanity Fair* described it as the best film soundtrack of all time.

There's no doubt that the album, and especially the stand-out single 'When Doves Cry', hit a chord with young people in the mid-1980s. Although of mixed black and white parentage, Prince Rogers Nelson, to give him his full name, began his music career with black music – soul, R&B and funk. In *Purple Rain*, though, the R&B and funk was blended with rock and pop to create a highly original sound that had an incredibly wide appeal.

But it wasn't just the music that made Prince something of an icon. His outrageous stage image tuned in well with the flavour of the times – and a taste for decadent, tongue-in-cheek sexuality that was somewhat removed from the everyday world resonated with young people at a time when an increasingly fast-moving consumer society seemed to leave many out on the edge. The film *Purple Rain*, in which Prince played himself as a struggling

Minneapolis musician with a difficult home life and a doomed, sexually charged relationship, chimed in well with many of the decade's disaffected youth.

Prince had always shocked with his stage persona, and wearing high-heeled shoes and tight, shiny clothes gave him a transgender look that made some question his sexuality. In 1981, when supporting the Rolling Stones, he was booed off stage for wearing just bikini briefs, high-heeled boots, leg warmers and a trench-coat. But by the time of *Purple Rain* that was part of the appeal.

He still had the power to shock though. When Tipper Gore (wife of the future Vice-President Al Gore) heard her twelve-year-old daughter Karenna listening to 'Darling Nikki', a sexually explicit song from *Purple Rain* in which he describes Nikki masturbating with a magazine, she was driven to push for the law that makes the Parental Advisory: Explicit Lyrics warnings mandatory.

Since the heady days of the 1980s, Prince has fallen out of the headlines, and for a while people knew him best for changing his name during a dispute with his label Warner to just two symbols, known as the Love Symbols, so that he became known as The Artist (Formerly Known as Prince). But those who have seen him live in recent years confirm that he remains both a brilliant musician and an extraordinarily charismatic stage performer.

# 5 August

## Marilyn Monroe is found dead

**1962** When Norma Jeane Mortenson was born on 1 June 1926, the girl who would go on to become Hollywood's first major sex symbol had arrived.

After starting a career as a model under her married name, Norma Jeane Dougherty, she underwent screen tests in 1946 and starred in her first films the following year. At the same time she adopted the distinctly more alluring name, Marilyn Monroe (after the actress Marilyn Miller and her mother's maiden name).

For the next few years she acted in a number of movies and began developing her iconic image. Her naturally brown hair had turned blonde during her modelling years, and now she added to that a little plastic surgery on her nose and chin.

Then in 1953 she really exploded into the public awareness by appearing in the first issue of *Playboy* magazine. Suddenly she went from supporting actress to main star and quickly became an A-list celebrity. Hollywood couldn't get enough of Marilyn Monroe and she appeared in a succession of hit films, including *Gentlemen Prefer Blondes* (1953), *How to Marry a Millionaire* (1953) and *The Seven Year Itch* (1955). During publicity filming for the latter she famously stood on an air vent in New York as gusts of air sent her skirt billowing upwards. Such roles cast her as a dizzy blonde, however, an image that she struggled to get away from. In an interview with the *New York Times*, she lamented: 'I want to grow and develop and play serious dramatic parts ... but so far nobody's interested.'

Marriage followed to the baseball player Joe DiMaggio, which lasted for less than a year in 1954. DiMaggio would later comment after she died that 'if it hadn't been for her friends, she might still be alive'. Two years later, in June 1956, Monroe wedded the playwright Arthur Miller, a union that would last until January 1961.

By this time, Marilyn was involved with the Kennedy family and on the way to her untimely end. Speculation still lingers to this day as to whether the president or his brother had a role in the death of Hollywood's golden icon. Her last significant public appearance was to come on 19 May 1962, singing 'Happy Birthday Mr President' to John F. Kennedy at Madison Square Gardens.

Less than three months later, on this day in 1962, her body was found by her housekeeper, Eunice Murray. The post-mortem results delivered a verdict of 'acute barbiturate poisoning' and her death at the age of just 36 was recorded as 'probable suicide'. The lack of evidence either way made it impossible to conclude that it was suicide or homicide, but this also meant that neither cause could be ruled out.

Marilyn Monroe remains to this day one of the most instantly recognisable actresses of all time. Apparently capable of being both petulant and passionate, she summed herself up – human failings, glorious celebrity and all – when she said: 'I'm selfish, impatient and a little insecure. I make mistakes. I am out of control at times and hard to handle. But if you can't handle me at my worst, you sure as hell don't deserve me at my best.'

# 6 August

## 'Little Boy' is dropped on Hiroshima and nuclear war becomes a reality

**1945** At 8:15 on the morning of 6 August 1945, the American B-29 Superfortress *Enola Gay*, piloted by Paul Tibbets, released its single bomb, codenamed 'Little Boy', from high over the city of Hiroshima in Japan. 'Little Boy' dropped rapidly for 57 seconds as *Enola Gay* sped on and then when it was just 600 metres (1,900 feet) above the city, it exploded with the biggest, most devastating blast ever unleashed in war – but for the even bigger one detonated over Nagasaki three days later. The age of atomic bombs had begun.

The effects of the explosion on the unsuspecting people of Hiroshima are unimaginable. A blindingly brilliant flash was followed by a searing hot fireball that instantly incinerated everything within a few hundred metres, leaving one unknown victim as a black shadow on the stone steps of a bank. A fraction of a second later, a blast wave sped out at the speed of sound like a monumental clap of thunder, instantly flattening virtually every building within a mile (1.6 km) of the bomb. As electricity cables split and gas pipes cracked, fires broke out and quickly merged into a devastating firestorm that cremated anyone who had survived within the blast area. And for those who survived the blast and the fire, there were the slower and equally terrible effects of radiation from the explosion, which claimed its victims slowly, one by one, not just hours afterwards but for decades to come.

Some 70,000 people were killed instantly by the Hiroshima bomb, and perhaps a further 70,000 died over the next few years as a direct result. Many who survived longer had their lives blighted by sickness and cancer, or simply trauma, and came to be known as the *Hibakusha* (blast victims).

Three days after Hiroshima, a second, even bigger, bomb, codenamed 'Fat Man', was exploded over Nagasaki with equally devastating effects, and just as many casualties – some of whom included survivors who had fled from Hiroshima.

Ever since, the debate has raged over the rights and wrongs of these two ter- rible bombs. At the time, very few people within the American military opposed them. Japan had an ardently military culture which seemed to make it impossible for it to surrender. Prior to the atomic bombs, an American campaign of 'conventional' firebombing had devastated dozens of Japanese cities and had killed 100,000 in Tokyo alone, yet failed to bring the Japanese to the negotiating table. Every month, some quarter of a million Chinese and southern Asians may have been dying as a result of the Japanese occupation. And countless lives could have been lost on both sides if the US had invaded Japan. If the bombs were designed to shock the Japanese into surrender, they had the desired effect. Five days after Nagasaki, Emperor Hirohito broadcast the news of Japan's surrender to the nation.

Yet the effects of the bombs were so terrible that some argue that no end justifies such means. Albert Einstein, whose theories had paved the way for the development of the bomb, pointed out that if the Germans had dropped such bombs on American cities, this would rightly have been regarded as a war crime. Others argue also that it was only the entry of the Soviet Union into the war that prompted the Americans to go ahead with the bombing. But whatever the verdict, the world was changed forever that day at Hiroshima, and the effects were so shocking that although enough nuclear weapons have since been built to destroy every city and village on Earth, no one has yet dared to repeat it.

# 7 August

## *The first person swims the Bering Strait*

**1987** The section of ocean between Alaska and Siberia is known as the Bering Strait. During the winter, conditions get so cold that the water freezes over, making it possible to walk across. To swim in these kinds of waters, therefore, is to expose oneself to the very limits of what the body can withstand.

As it happens the first person known to have swum the Bering Strait was an American woman named Lynne Cox. The distance is only 2.7 miles, but she had to contend with strong currents and a water temperature of just 5°C, which is as warm as it gets even in August. Water is very good at removing heat energy from anything immersed in it, so Cox had to put on a good deal of body fat as insulation from the cold. At the time of the swim she weighed an impressive thirteen stone (82.5 kg).

The cooperation that took place between Russian and American parties during preparations for the swim was also seen as a step towards thawing Cold War tensions between the two countries, and both Ronald Reagan and Mikhail Gorbachev were warm in their praise for her.

If swimming the Bering Strait was a chilly task for Cox, however, her next challenge pushed her body even further. In the sub-zero waters of Antarctica, where most people would succumb to hypothermia inside five minutes, she somehow managed to swim for an incredible 25 minutes, covering a distance of more than a mile.

The Bering Strait itself is named after Vitus Bering, a Danish-born Russian navigator. He died of scurvy and was buried on Bering Island in 1741 during an expedition to explore the North Pacific. He was responsible for mapping much of the coastline of Siberia.

In 2006, Briton Karl Bushby and French-American Dimitri Kieffer became the first people to walk across the Bering Strait. They took fifteen days to traverse 56 miles (82 km) of frozen ocean. Bushby is on a sixteen-year journey from the tip of South America to England using no other form of locomotion than walking, with unbroken steps. He plans to end his travels in the town of Hull in 2014. In doing so, he will have crossed three entire continents: South America, North America and Eurasia.

# 8 August

## The Great Train Robbery occurs in England

**1963** Few crimes have captured the public imagination like the Great Train Robbery of 1963. First of all, there was the sheer scale of the robbery – the thieves got away with £2.6 million in used notes, more than any crime in British history until the 2006 Securitas robbery. Then there was the audaciousness of the way in which the thieves stopped the train that seemed almost like something from *Butch Cassidy and the Sundance Kid*, or the legendary American Hole in the Wall Gang.

The gang of fifteen, masterminded by Bruce Reynolds, had a tip-off that the *Up Special*, the Post Office train from Glasgow to London, had a carriage that night that was carrying a huge number of used notes on their way to be pulped. Using a six-volt battery, they illuminated the red stop light on a signal on a remote stretch of the line near Cheddington in Buckinghamshire, covering the green light with a glove. Seeing the red light, the driver brought the *Up Special* to a halt.

As the co-driver climbed out to call the signalmen, the robbers threw him down the bank, decoupled all but the front two coaches of the train (one of which contained the mail bags of money), and forced the train driver to move the train on to a bridge further up the line. While 75 postal workers in the stranded carriages carried on sorting oblivious to what was going on, up the line on the bridge, the gang broke into the 'high-value' coach, overpowered the four postal workers inside and quickly loaded 120 mail bags full of money into Land Rovers parked on the lane below.

The following morning, police investigating the crime said,

'This was obviously a brilliantly planned operation', and so began the myth-making about the crime that kept the public and the media fascinated for years. Yet it was never the non-violent crime it was often thought to be. Although the thieves hadn't used guns, they had used iron bars to intimidate train staff and had coshed the driver, Jack Mills, so badly over the head that he never fully recovered.

Nor was it quite so brilliantly planned. Just five days after the robbery, a tip-off led police to a nearby farm, where they found a Monopoly board game, which the thieves had played using real banknotes, covered in their fingerprints. Thereafter, the police investigation, led by Detective Jack Slipper (dubbed 'Slipper of the Yard'), moved swiftly and within six months most of the fifteen-strong gang had been caught. Mastermind Bruce Reynolds eluded police for a further five years, but it was hardly a successful crime.

The story was kept alive in the public imagination when gang members Charlie Wilson and Ronnie Biggs escaped from prison. Wilson was tracked down four years later in Canada, but Biggs became something of a folk hero as he evaded capture first in Australia, then in Rio de Janeiro, where he was subsequently able to live openly, free of the fear of extradition because he had fathered a Brazilian child. Eventually, Biggs became ill and returned to the UK voluntarily in 2001 for treatment, knowing that he would be jailed. Another gang member, Buster Edwards, also gave himself up after briefly going on the run in Mexico. The myth-making continued when in 1988 his story was dramatised in the film *Buster* starring Phil Collins.

# 9 August

## 'Fat Man' delivers the decisive blow

**1945** If 'Little Boy' was the alarm call to Japan, then 'Fat Man' was the signal that time was up. Two entire cities destroyed by nuclear bombs were enough to make the Japanese administration realise that the US had them in checkmate. The Japanese capitulated a few days later and the Second World War came to an end.

On this day in 1945, Major Charles Sweeney flew a US Air Force B-29 bomber, the *Bockscar*, into the skies over Nagasaki, the capital city of the Nagasaki Prefecture that bordered the East China Sea. On board was 'Fat Man', the second of America's two nuclear bombs to be dropped on Japan. With a blast yield of 21 kilotons, 'Fat Man' was nearly half as destructive again as its compatriot, 'Little Boy', which had been exploded over Hiroshima just three days earlier.

Shortly after 11 o'clock in the morning, bombardier Kermit Beahan sighted the target. 'Fat Man' plummeted towards the ground for 43 seconds before unleashing its blast over the city. The immediate blast killed around 50,000 inhabitants, and up to a further 30,000 died from their injuries in the following days. The explosion also caught a number of refugees who, having survived the Hiroshima bombing, had fled to Nagasaki for safety. Sixty per cent of Nagasaki was reported to have been destroyed, and the Japanese press reporting on the bombing described the wasted remains as 'like a graveyard with not a tombstone standing'.

It remains unclear how many more lives would have been lost had the war continued by conventional means and whether wreaking mass destruction on Japan was a way of militating against future, greater casualties. There are those who now argue that uncertain outcomes can never justify certain means, and that the deployment of nuclear weapons by the Americans should be treated as a war crime. It is certainly true that a vast number were lost in Hiroshima and Nagasaki at the time.

Since 1945, some additional 777 individuals from Nagasaki have succumbed to radiation-related cancers, tumours and heart attacks. Foetuses whose mothers were survivors of the blasts have been further victims, and 30 babies born in the months following Hiroshima and Nagasaki went on to develop mental difficulties. However, despite these figures, the lasting effects of 'Fat Man' have been less severe than feared, especially when compared to 'Little Boy', and there have been no subsequent related defects in children conceived after the explosions.

It is a little known fact that the city of Kokura was the primary target for 'Fat Man'. When the *Bockscar* arrived at its destination though, there was cloud cover, making the drop difficult to judge. Without visibility the crew decided to detonate the bomb over Nagasaki instead.

# 10 August

## Magellan *reaches Venus on the same day that the real Magellan set off to circumnavigate the world in 1519*

**1990** Ferdinand Magellan is known as the first person to circumnavigate the globe. In fact he only very nearly did. He died in the Philippines in 1521, leaving the rest of his expeditionary team to complete the journey back to Spain.

Intriguingly Magellan had not intended to circumnavigate the globe, but rather to find a new commercial route to the Spice Islands. One of his ship's masters, Juan Sebastian Elcano, was left in charge following Magellan's death at the hands of hostile islanders. He decided to press on westwards, feeling that it might be an easier passage. When he reached Spain in 1522 he had seventeen crewmen left aboard a single ship, the *Victoria*. About 230 had lost their lives along the way and four ships had been lost.

The *Magellan* planetary orbiter was the first planetary spacecraft to be launched from a shuttle orbiting the Earth. Having reached Venus, it spent four years scanning the planet's surface and collecting data about its gravitational force and atmospheric pressure. In 1994 it was instructed to leave its orbit and head towards the planet itself. It disintegrated when it struck the atmosphere, littering the planet with debris.

Venus is a hostile place, wholly unsuited to human visitation and life in general. The planet has an extremely dense atmosphere of carbon dioxide which, at surface level, is equivalent to more than 90 times our atmospheric pressure at sea level. Furthermore, its clouds are made of sulphur dioxide and temperatures reach 460°C (860°F). All in all, not a particularly pleasant place to be.

Mars, on the other hand, also has a carbon dioxide atmosphere, but it is extremely thin at about one per cent of the Earth's atmospheric pressure. It is also cold enough for dry ice (frozen carbon dioxide) to form at its poles. Even though this sounds hostile, it would be possible for humans to survive a visit, given the right equipment. To all intents and purposes it would be rather like visiting Antarctica, only colder and with no air to breathe. It might not be anything to write home about, but it wouldn't be life-threatening with climate- controlled suits. The suits used for the lunar landings had to perform similar functions.

# 11 August

### The action painter Jackson Pollock is killed in a car crash

**1956** Expressionism is the term used to describe creativity that comes from the emotions of the artist. Vincent Van Gogh was the first true expressionist and his vivid use of colours sought to express his heightened moods. By the time Jackson Pollock became an artist, expressionism had evolved into its abstract form. It no longer presented the viewer with identifiable images or any form of visual realism. Instead the art used fundamental elements abstracted from reality to produce a condensed imagery.

Pollock began as an abstract expressionist, but soon realised that the abstraction of any real imagery was irrelevant to him. He wanted the very action of applying the paint to be an extension of the expressiveness. He abandoned orthodox conventions entirely until he would simply throw, splash or dribble the paint onto the canvas in an almost random way. He had control over the choice of colours and the overall distribution of the paint, but the rest was left to chance.

For all his wild inventiveness, Jackson Pollock often struggled to keep his own life moving forwards with the same strength. A lifelong battle with alcoholism finally proved to be his undoing on this day in 1956. While driving his car, a convertible Oldsmobile, he crashed in an alcohol-related accident close to his home in Springs, New York. A passenger in the car, Edith Metzger, also died, but Pollock's girlfriend Ruth Kligman survived.

Pollock was just 44 when he died. His legacy was preserved over the following decades in the face of a rapidly changing art scene by his wife and fellow artist, Lee Krasner. When Krasner died in 1984 at the age of 75 she was buried alongside her husband in the Green River Cemetery at Springs. Both graves are marked with a simple rough-hewn boulder.

In a way, Pollock's 'action expressionism' took painting to its very limit. There was nowhere else to go with the medium and his early death brought things to a natural conclusion. Ever since Pollock, there are some who believe that painting has struggled to find itself again in terms of progression in art. Increasingly bizarre art forms are explored in the hope of finding another all-defining mode of creativity.

To this day, as artists continue to define new approaches to art, Pollock's work remains a beacon of its time. This didn't stop Teri Horton, a 73-year-old former truck driver from California, being ignorant of his existence. When she bought a large messy painting in a charity shop for $5, she was shocked to discover she had landed an original Jackson Pollock worth millions of dollars.

# 12 August

## The Russians up the stakes by exploding a hydrogen bomb

**1953** When American airborne sampling planes detected radio-active fallout – an unmistakable sign of a nuclear explosion – near Soviet territory in 1949 it was a real shock. The Americans had not expected the Soviet Union to develop an atomic bomb for years, and it forced them to change their way of thinking.

The problem was that the atomic bomb was not the worst that could happen. The atomic bomb worked by splitting large atoms, but American scientists knew it was possible to build a hugely more powerful 'super bomb' by fusing small hydrogen atoms. If the Soviets could build an atomic bomb, they surely could build a hydrogen bomb. In fact, unbeknown to the Americans, they had already been working on one for three years.

The idea of the Soviets having such a superbomb, while they did not, unnerved the Americans so much that they immediately embarked on an arms race that had no logic in conventional military thinking. They would be building a weapon so powerful that using it would destroy the defenders as much as the enemy. It would involve a strange kind of bluff. They had to build a weapon they could never imagine actually using – yet they had to convince the Soviets that they would, for otherwise it would be pointless. President Truman said in 1950, '[We] had got to do it – make the bomb – though no one wants to use it. But ... we have got to have it if only for bargaining purposes with the Russians.'

The Americans built their superbomb first. On 1 November 1952, in what was called Operation Ivy, the Americans detonated a hydrogen bomb called 'Mike' on the Pacific atoll of Enewetak, completely obliterating an island in the process, scattering radioactive debris over an area at least 100 km across and creating a mushroom cloud 161 km across and 37 km high. The Soviets, though, were not far behind. Just nine months later, on 12 August 1953, they exploded their hydrogen bomb in a Central Asian desert.

Awed by the terrifying scale of what they had done, both American and Russian scientists described the tests in similar terms. In the absence of human victims, they observed in quiet horror birds that were blinded and incinerated in the air, and one Russian scientist noted that it 'transcended some kind of psychological barrier'.

Seven months after the Soviet test, in March 1954, the Americans detonated an even bigger superbomb in the Pacific, a thermonuclear bomb 750 times as powerful as the Hiroshima bomb, in a test called, ironically, BRAVO. But the BRAVO test got out of control and killed Japanese fishermen in a boat hundreds of miles away with its radioactive fallout. The event shocked the world. Twelve days later, Kremlin leader Georgiy

Malenkov warned that a war fought with modern weapons would now mean 'the end of civilisation', while Churchill told the British Parliament that the Americans and Russians had now achieved 'equality in annihilation'.

It was clear to Malenkov and Churchill that a nuclear war would now cause such universal destruction that it could never be fought. Yet that was not how Eisenhower, who was by now the American president, saw it. And Malenkov was soon ousted by Khruschev, who also saw it differently. And so the Americans and Russians embarked on an arms race to build up a stockpile of weapons so powerful that they could destroy life on Earth many times over – a race that was to develop into the strategy chillingly dubbed MAD – Mutually Assured Destruction – which relied on the dubious assumption that if no one could be sure of surviving a nuclear war, no one would start one. The jury is still out.

# 13 August

## The last executions in Britain

**1964** On 13 August 1964 at 9 am Peter Anthony Allen, at Walton Prison in Liverpool, and Gwynne Owen Evans, at Strangeways Prison in Manchester, were each executed for the murder of John Alan West on 7 April earlier that year. These were the last executions in the United Kingdom. The following year, the Murder (Abolition of the Death Penalty) Act 1965 suspended the death penalty in the UK for five years, and just over four years later, in December 1969, it was abolished for good.

It had taken a long time to get to this point. Enthusiasm for capital punishment reached its height in the 18th century when the new middle class wanted protection for their property and a stricter degree of civil order. At one time, over 200 different crimes could be punished by death, including 'being in the company of gypsies'. With public executions nearly every week, some of little children who were hanged for stealing a loaf of bread, many began to sicken of this brutal regime and call for reform.

Gradually, over the next 150 years, the number of crimes for which death was the penalty was reduced, until by 1957 only five crimes warranted the punishment: murder in the course of furtherance; murder while resisting arrest or during an escape; murder of a police officer; murder of a prison officer by a prisoner; and the second of two murders committed on different occasions (if both done in Great Britain). At the same time, the process of execution moved from prolonged public hangings to quick hangings in the secrecy of a prison.

Finally in 1965, complete abolition arrived. Capital punishment is now banned throughout the European Union, and the elimination of the death penalty is a condition of entry to the Union. Around the world, around 2,000 people are executed each year, with China, Iran and the United States at the top of the killing tree. In the USA, there is at least a moratorium on the death penalty in an increasing number of states, and in 2007, the state of New Jersey abolished it altogether.

The move, then, in most of the world is away from capital punishment. Yet there are still many people in the UK who believe it should be brought back for at least certain crimes. Every now and then the House of Commons debates the issue, and most MPs invariably follow their conscience and vote against bringing back the death penalty – apparently in a clear rejection of the will of the majority of the people who, according to opinion polls, favour its return.

Those against the return of the death penalty argue that it is simply an unacceptable violation of the right to life. Or that it is cruel and inhumane, and has no place in a civilised society. It brutalises and desensitises society, and creates secondary victims – the family and friends of the condemned. It may also rob the condemned of the chance for remorse and retribution – or worse still rob an innocent person of another chance to prove their innocence. Those who support the death penalty argue that it is just retribution for the violation of the victim's right to life. Moreover, they argue that only the death penalty is a severe enough deterrent for the worst crimes.

# 14 August

## *A new country, Pakistan, is born*

**1947** Following the Second World War the British found that the mood in India had changed to such an extent that offering independence was the only workable solution. As independence approached, ethnic resentments which had been suppressed during the course of colonial occupation began to surface. Hindus, Muslims and Sikhs who had lived alongside one another under British rule since 1858 now wanted their own territories.

The British administration recognised a need to divide India, but no one anticipated the level of violence that would erupt as Mountbatten and his staff tried to put their plan into action. The trouble was that they had to mark out a border between the areas that were to become Pakistan and the new India, and then get Muslims to migrate one way and Hindus and Sikhs the other. In their efforts to maintain control the British held back from revealing exactly where the border would lie until it was time to return independence, but this turned out to be the worst thing they could have done.

The populations in the border region began making their own minds up about where exactly the line would be drawn. What would now be described as ethnic cleansing took place on both sides of the line and hundreds of thousands, if not millions, lost their lives. The British, whose responsibility it was to smooth the transition as far as possible, resolutely failed to install any kind of effective policing system. The escalation of ethnic violence became a sorry chapter in the history of India and Pakistan, one which reverberates to this day.

When the new state was declared on 14 August 1947, it turned out that the territory as marked out by the British was wholly unworkable. Rather than annexing a single swathe of land, the British split the fledgling country into East Pakistan and West Pakistan, where the government was based. Between them lay hundreds upon hundreds of miles of India.

As a result, Pakistan struggled to retain stability throughout its early years. For the first nine years of its existence, Pakistan retained close ties to its former colonial ruler as a dominion within the British Commonwealth. In 1956 it declared itself a republic, but civilian rule came to an abrupt end in 1958 when General Ayub Khan seized power in a military *coup d'état.*

Ayub Khan ruled for eleven years until 1969 when he was succeeded by Yahya Khan. However, in 1970, Yahya Khan had to deal with a cyclone that caused half a million deaths in East Pakistan. A poor response from the central government partly precipitated the civil war that broke out in 1971 and which then escalated to become the Indo–Pakistani War.

This proved to be the final straw for Pakistan's two wings. In December 1971, after Indian troops had defeated the Pakistani forces, East Pakistan declared its independence. West Pakistan regrouped itself under a new Pakistani constitution in 1973, and the former East Pakistan went on to autonomous rule as Bangladesh.

# *15 August*

## *VJ Day ushers in the New World Order*

**1945** When Japan agreed to capitulate to the Americans, the Second World War came to an end and the dust of conflict began to settle on a human world altered profoundly by the experience. Old colonial empires found themselves in their death throes because colonies in Asia had experienced relative freedom under occupation by enemy forces, and they were in no mood to return to pre-war circumstances. The British Empire began decolonisation in 1945 and became a commonwealth in 1949. The smaller French Empire was no more by 1960.

Europe underwent major reshuffling of territory in the post-war environment. The borders of several countries were redrawn on the map and the establishment of the Soviet Union divided the continent into the ideologically opposed Western and Eastern Europe.

Interestingly the two countries chiefly responsible for initiating the Second World War, Germany and Japan, both went through a post-war metamorphosis and began to emerge as leading nations on the world stage of economic success. It seems that humiliation at losing the war had somehow revitalised their peoples when other nations were exhausted by the effort of victory.

The precise terms of the surrender were not officially determined until 2 September, but on 15 August (14 August in the USA and elsewhere) the first announcements of Japan's unilateral submission were broadcast. This followed a message sent from Emperor Hirohito to the American government on the 13th. The recording of the emperor's speech on Radio Tokyo at noon (Japanese standard time) on 15 August is known as the *Gyokuon-hoso*, 'Jewel Voice Broadcast', and was the first time that the emperor had officially spoken to his people.

Following the formal surrender just over two weeks later, Japan gave itself over to occupation by the Allies. The victorious nations, led by the Americans, remained in place until 1952, during which time a revised constitution placed Hirohito as a largely symbolic head of state.

VJ Day is now commemorated around the world as the final act of the Second World War. In the state of Rhode Island, in America, it is a public holiday celebrated on the second Monday of August. In Japan, VJ Day is officially called the 'day of mourning of war dead and praying for peace', although its commonly used name, *Shuusen-kinenbi*, translates simply as the 'memorial day for the end of the war'. It is observed each year on 15 August.

# 16 August

## The King of Rock 'n' Roll is dead

**1977** On 16 August 1977, Elvis Presley, the so-called King of Rock 'n' Roll was found dead in the bathroom of his multimillion-dollar Graceland Mansion in Memphis, Tennessee. He was just 42, and an autopsy indicated that Presley had died of a heart attack. Distraught fans around the world could not quite believe it, and for decades afterwards many refused to believe he was dead, leading to a whole wave of 'sightings' of the deceased star and a raft of conspiracy theories.

With his dynamic, raunchy singing style, his rebel image and his dark good looks, Elvis had revolutionised popular music and become a hero to rock 'n' roll fans around the world. Elvis had sold more than 500 million records, made 33 films and become a millionaire many times over. But more than that, he had made the kind of impact on youth around the world that no other performer ever had. And it wasn't just in America; Elvis was a hero even behind the Iron Curtain. In 1958, Soviet politicians blamed him for a riot in East Berlin as youths threatened to kill a border guard.

When Elvis's unique sound first hit the airwaves in 1956, it seemed to strike a special chord with young people who were trying to move away from their parents' values. Presley, with his sexually charged, essentially black music, his hip-thrusting, and his cocky, sullen manner, was everything parents feared their teenage children would become – and everything those teenagers wanted to be. When Elvis appeared on the Ed Sullivan TV show in 1956, millions of teenagers went wild at the sight of this brash, leather-clad, sharp-shoed, devil-may-care young man with an attitude, while a Catholic priest condemned Sullivan for 'moral injury' for bringing Presley on the show.

It was above all the music, however, that made Elvis so exciting. In those days of segregation, most white teenagers had never heard anything like the black blues music that inspired Presley when he sneaked off as a teenager to the places where it was played. But Presley created an entirely new sound by mixing the black blues with the white country music he had been brought up with. When at the age of just eighteen in 1953 he recorded the blues song 'That's All Right' with his unique white holler, backed by the country song 'Blue Moon of Kentucky', the impact was instant – and the disc sold 20,000 copies, which was remarkable for an unknown teenager on the small Sun record label.

RCA snapped him up and his next record 'Heartbreak Hotel', released early in 1956, became an overnight sensation right across America. Later that year came the appearances on the Ed Sullivan show which made him a huge star among the young, and a figure of fear and distrust among the older generation. From America, Elvis and the new style of music rippled rapidly out around the world, making him an icon for a new generation of young people who celebrated their rebellious youth in a way that none had ever done before.

# 17 August

### Peter Fechter is shot trying to escape from East Berlin

**1962** Construction on the Berlin Wall had been begun a year earlier on 13 August 1961. On this day in 1962, Peter Fechter and his friend Helmut Kulbeik decided to try their luck at escaping to the West.

Their plan was to hide near the wall where they could watch the border guards going up and down their patrols. When an opportunity presented itself, they would make a mad dash to scramble over the two-metre-high wall, which was topped with barbed wire, and fall into the Kreuzberg district of West Berlin.

Luck was on the side of Kulbeik who leaped to sanctuary in the nick of time. Fechter was struck in the pelvis with a bullet from a border guard. He fell from the wall into a no-man's-land called the 'death strip' where he lay dying in full view of onlookers. Those in West Berlin dared not try to rescue him, despite his desperate calls, for fear of being shot themselves. The border guards dared not come to his aid for fear of being attacked by the angry mob. In this horrifying stalemate Fechter steadily bled to death after about an hour. He was the first person to die trying to cross the wall, and was just eighteen years of age at the time. Hundreds of people staged protests in response and angrily accused the guards of murder.

In 1997, following the collapse of the Eastern Bloc, the two guards involved were tried in court and found guilty of manslaughter. They were sentenced to a year's imprisonment for their actions 35 years earlier.

The last person to die at the wall was Chris Gueffroy, on 6 February 1989. He was riddled with ten bullets in the chest as he clung onto the fence. In total, at least 133 people died while trying to cross from East to West Berlin, although this number could well be above 200. Many, however, did manage the journey, with up to 5,000 refugees successfully entering West Berlin during the course of the Cold War.

Soon after Fechter's death a cross was placed in his memory on the western side of the Berlin Wall. When the wall came down, construction began on a memorial on the eastern side in the Zimmerstrasse – on the exact spot where he was shot and killed. After German reunification in 1990, the Peter-Fechte-Stelle was opened as a lasting commemoration of his tragic death.

# 18 August

## The US is introduced to 'the pill'

**1960** It can surely be no coincidence that the beginning of the Sexual Revolution occurred at the same time as the introduction of the world's first contraceptive pill in 1960. The two are inextricably linked, because 'the pill' meant that sex could be viewed as solely a leisure activity for the first time in human history. By removing the risk of impregnation, the youth of the 1960s were effectively given licence to become as promiscuous as they wished. Tied in with the decline in conservative views, it meant that the new generation had carte blanche to experiment with sexual freedom.

It wasn't actually until the following decade, however, that sexual liberation really took off. When the pill was first marketed in the 1960s in the US, its use was limited to married women.

Single girls didn't get a look-in on the action until the 1970s when the age of majority was lowered from 21 to eighteen.

The contraceptive pill works by regulating a complex balance of hormones that can either stimulate or impede egg development. In the normal course of things, egg growth occurs through the menstrual cycle. When the pill is in use the menstrual cycle still takes place, although the ovaries do not release any eggs. As a result, pregnancy cannot occur.

Ironically, perhaps, the introduction of the pill actually led to an increase in unwanted pregnancies during the 1960s. Although legally the pill was only accessible to married couples, a large number of unwed women were able to secure supplies as well. As a consequence, far more people were having sex before marriage, but not all were fastidious with their use of contraceptives. The term 'baby boom' is often used in describing the mid-1960s because general optimism in the post-war environment meant that people were reproducing in greater numbers. However, a good many of those babies went for adoption and are now viewed as victims of the Sexual Revolution.

By the 1980s the West had lived through a recession and people were beginning to feel that the restoration of conservative values might not be all that bad an idea. In the US the Republicans came into power and in the UK it was the time of the Tories. This coincided with the rise of HIV and Aids which served to re-establish the taboos surrounding promiscuity. From then on the official view on sexual freedom would change.

Despite this initial consequence, the pill – and contraceptives in general – have in general been seen as a primary benefit to humanity. Nevertheless, it touches upon certain ethical issues and there are schools of thought that oppose the pill on these grounds. The Catholic Church, for example, is vigorously against any type of contraception as they believe it is sacrilegious to engage in sex without the intention of producing God-given life. The pill did at first lead to some uncertainty in Catholic circles as to whether it was acceptable because, unlike the earlier condom, it did not represent a physical barrier to sperm. In 1968, however, the Pope published a pamphlet entitled *Humanae Vitae* which reiterated the traditional Catholic view that all artificial contraception was wrong in the mind of God.

# 19 August

## US pilot Gary Powers is sentenced

**1960** In the late 1950s, the Cold War nuclear arms race was at its most intense, and it seemed that the Russians were winning. The apparent 'missile gap' unnerved Americans, making President Eisenhower seem weak, while at the same time strengthening Khrushchev's negotiating hand. But the Russian bluff was about to be called, for on 4 July 1956 an amazing new American spy-plane, the Lockheed U-2, began flying over the USSR taking excellent photos of Soviet military installations.

The Russians knew these flights were going on, but could do nothing about them because the U-2 flew at 70,000 feet, well above the operating range of any Soviet fighter. Eisenhower may have been concerned about the morality of these intrusions into Soviet territory, knowing that a similar intrusion over America would prompt a declaration of war, but he could always deny their purpose if ever a U-2 was downed since it would be bound to be destroyed, crashing from so high. Yet although they had no fighters able to reach the U-2, by 1959 the Russians had developed SA-2 surface-to-air missiles that could.

After twenty U-2 flights, the Americans knew the Russians' long-range bomber force was fairly weak, but it had taken longer to confirm that their missile capability was pretty limited, too, and that it was actually the Americans, not the Russians, who were way ahead. On 1 May 1960, CIA pilot Francis Gary Powers took off from Peshawar in Pakistan in a U-2 on a flight that would take him across the USSR to Norway, photographing Russian missile bases en route. Powers was tracked by Soviet radar as he flew over Afghanistan, but the Russians could not get their SA-2s launched fast enough to catch him. By the time he reached Sverdlovsk

(Yekaterinburg), though, they were ready, and after several misses, one of the SA-2s exploded near enough to Powers' U-2 to make it begin to disintegrate. Powers bailed out.

When the Russians announced that they had the wreckage of the U-2, the Americans issued their preplanned lie: that the U-2 was simply a weather plane that had strayed off course. What they didn't know was that the wreckage was intact enough for the Russians to have recovered the camera complete with the film of Russian missile bases – and more embarrassing still, they had picked up Powers alive and well, complete with his suicide pills. To Khrushchev's glee, Eisenhower was forced to admit the lie. Few incidents have ever done quite as much to dent the American claim to the moral high ground. Later, Eisenhower wrote, 'I didn't realize how high a price we were going to pay for that lie'.

Khrushchev must have known that the U-2's photos exposed the missile gap as a myth, but he turned the situation to his advantage, cancelling the next USA–USSR summit due to take place in Paris a fortnight later and demanding an apology. Eisenhower refused to apologise, but promised to fly no more U-2 missions over the USSR. It was an easy promise to make because on this day in 1960, the day Powers was sentenced to ten years in prison in Moscow, the first American Corona satellite flew over the USSR, rendering the U-2s redundant and allowing the Americans to photograph anything they liked without fear of political incident.

Powers served less than two years of his sentence. In what would be the first of many such exchanges in the Cold War, he was swapped for Soviet spy Rudolf Abel on Berlin's Glienicke Bridge on 10 February 1962. By that time, Kennedy had ousted Eisenhower from the presidency, with a campaign partly based on the assertion that Eisenhower had allowed the Russians to open up the missile gap – an assertion he discovered was false even before he took office. Just eight weeks after the Powers–Abel exchange, the Soviet Union was sending nuclear missiles to Cuba – perhaps, some historians have said, because of Khrushchev's embarrassment at the exposure of the missile gap as a sham – and the USA and USSR were on the way to a confrontation that brought them the closest they have ever been to a nuclear war.

# 20 August

## Warsaw Pact troops enter Czechoslovakia to end the Prague Spring

**1968** On the night of 20 August 1968, somewhere between 200,000 and 600,000 Warsaw Pact troops marched into Czechoslovakia. The next morning, tanks were rolling through the streets of Prague. They met with little violent opposition, but over 70 people were killed and hundreds injured as troops sought out 'antisocialist' elements with batons and guns.

At first many Czech people tried to talk to the troops to persuade them to leave, but then they realised that the Soviet media was using the images of these conversations as evidence that the people welcomed the troops. A few riots broke out and walls were daubed with anti-Soviet graffiti. Dissidents and artists were arrested, and protest went underground. As censorship of the press returned with a vengeance, it became clear that the country's brief flirtation with reform, soon known as the Prague Spring, was over.

On 5 January that year, Alexander Dubcek had become leader of the Communist Party in Czechoslovakia. People have argued since about whether he was a genuine reformer or just a Party member angling for position. Whatever the truth, that spring he lifted censorship of the press, freed political prisoners and initiated an Action Programme to give factories and farms independence and move the country towards multi-party democracy. He also split the country into two separate nations, Czech and Slovak – the one change that survived the invasion.

Thirty years on, Czech President Vaclav Havel, who in 1968 was a young playwright and in 1989 led the Velvet Revolution that finally ousted the communists, said the Prague Spring was 'a beautiful time because after twenty years it was possible to breathe and speak freely'. Yet he also said it was not a libertarian revolution but simply a conflict between two groups of communists that 'revealed the totalitarian nature of that system'. In the 1990s, the

Russians revealed a letter of invitation from members of the Czech Communist Party who were planning a coup, inviting them to intervene against the 'antisocialist' elements threatening Czechoslovakia's stability.

There was no doubt that the Soviets were rattled by what was going on in Czechoslovakia. Outsiders saw the invasion as a demonstration of Russian brutality and confidence, at a time when they had achieved parity of nuclear weapons with the USA. Yet in reality it was a sign of Russian weakness, unnerved by the fear that the Czech reforms would spread to other Warsaw Pact countries. Later that year, Russian politician Leonid Brezhnev claimed for Russia in the Brezhnev Doctrine the right to violate the sovereignty of any country trying to replace communism with capitalism. But the Doctrine was just a bold front in a time of vulnerability. Within twenty years, the Soviets had lost control of Eastern Europe without it ever being applied.

# 21 August

## A strange natural disaster in Africa

**1986** When one thinks of natural disasters the list includes earthquakes, tsunamis, volcanic eruptions, forest fires, landslides, floods, hurricanes, tornados and so on. Mass hypoxia is unlikely to feature, but that is what happened in Cameroon in 1986.

Lake Nyos sits in a geological feature called a maar. It is a low-relief crater in the Earth's crust caused by an explosion of steam when ground water hits magma beneath the surface. Underneath the bed of the lake there is still a zone of seismic activity, which generates carbon dioxide gas. Every once in a while a surge of gas escapes from the water and cascades down the slopes surrounding the maar.

This is exactly what happened on the night of the disaster. About 2,000 people went to bed and failed to wake up the next morning. Being heavier than air, the $CO_2$ filled the crater and spilled down the slopes like an invisible blanket a few feet thick.

The people and their livestock were starved of oxygen and asphyxiated where they slept.

The Cameroon government has since banned people from living near the lake, which still releases carbon dioxide frequently if not regularly. It tends to sit in depressions in the ground where unsuspecting animals wander and simply drop down dead from suffocation, not realising that higher ground is their sanctuary.

Gaseous exchange occurs in the lungs of animals in a spontaneous manner by diffusion. Carbon dioxide in the blood wants to escape, while oxygen in the air wants to be absorbed. An absence of oxygen disrupts this process immediately so that animals have only a few seconds to escape before they lose consciousness. That is why so many people and animals died. The carbon dioxide could have been avoided by simply standing up, but it affected the victims too quickly and it is unlikely that anyone would have understood the phenomenon anyway.

Carbon dioxide is effectively a poison to humans and other animals. Air naturally contains about 0.04 per cent $CO_2$, while our exhaled breath contains about 4.5 per cent. The gas is considered to be toxic when breathed in at 5 per cent or above, although prolonged inhalation at just 0.5 per cent is undesirable. Interestingly it is the toxic effect of carbon dioxide that stimulates breathing, as opposed to a requirement for oxygen. In low-pressure air, such as at high altitude, the body is unaware of low oxygen levels because there is no rise in carbon dioxide to stimulate a sense of suffocation. Consequently pilots and climbers can fall unconscious and die from oxygen starvation.

# 22 August

*A version of Munch's* The Scream *and his* Madonna *are stolen at gunpoint*

**2004** At 11.10 on the morning of 22 August 2004, two gunmen, their heads covered in black ski masks, walked into the crowded

Munch Museum in Oslo. While one held security staff and visitors at gunpoint, the other snipped the wire holding the iconic Edvard Munch painting *The Scream* and another Munch painting, *Madonna*, to the wall. Witnesses described the thieves as clumsy, even dropping the paintings once. But within minutes they were out of the museum with the paintings under their arms before speeding off in a black Audi estate car.

The theft and the apparent lack of security were hugely embarrassing for Norway, for this was not the first time that thieves had stolen *The Scream*. There are actually four versions of the famous painting, which shows a haunted-looking stick of a man holding his head and howling in anguish. Munch, who lived from 1863 to 1944, said the inspiration for the picture came from a walk just after sunset. 'I felt a tinge of melancholy ... Suddenly the sky became a bloody red ... I stood there, trembling with fright. And I felt a loud, unending scream piercing nature.' One version of the painting was the one stolen from the Munch Museum. Another was in Norway's National Gallery, and the two galleries had always argued over which was better. There are also two other sketchier versions, one in storage at the Munch and another with an unidentified private collector.

What made the theft from the Munch Museum so embarrassing was that, just ten years earlier, the National Gallery's version of *The Scream* had also been stolen, when thieves broke in on the opening day of the Winter Olympics in Lillehammer in 1994. Remarkably, the stolen National Gallery version was recovered just three weeks later during a brilliant sting operation in which British Scotland Yard detectives posed as representatives of the John Paul Getty Museum in Los Angeles offering to pay a huge ransom. But for Norway's most famous painting to be stolen again was too much. After the theft, the lead detective on the case, Leif A. Leir, said, 'Hasn't the city of Oslo learned anything about security in ten years? ... I am shocked that once again it was so easy.' Gallery bosses were quick to point out that it was the safety of the visitors that was paramount with gunmen in the gallery. As the museum's Director Gunar Sorensen said, 'If you have a pistol or a revolver pointed at your head, there is not much you can do'.

Two hours after the theft, police found the smashed wooden frames and glass of the stolen paintings – leading to fears the paintings had been irreparably damaged – but no sign of the paintings themselves. Although the paintings would fetch an absolute fortune if publicly auctioned, they were far too famous for the thieves to sell, although they may not have realised this. But police expected they would ask for a ransom as the previous thieves had done. No ransom demand came, apparently, but eighteen months later the police caught the driver of the getaway car, the man who supplied it and the man who planned the heist. They also, amazingly, recovered the paintings in September 2006, surprisingly little damaged. The police would not say how or where, and denied paying any ransom. In May 2008, after a little restoration, the painting went back on display – but not before the Museum had been closed for ten months for a $6 million security revamp. The gunmen, though, were still on the loose.

# 23 August

## The psychological condition 'Stockholm syndrome' is defined

**1973** In 1973 a bungled robbery in Stockholm, Sweden resulted in the villains holding a number of people hostage for a period of five days. By the end of the episode the beleaguered hostages displayed an intriguing mental condition; they had sided with their captors and pleaded leniency for them in their sentencing. Following this event a new psychological term was born in the shape of Stockholm syndrome, which described the way in which humans have the ability to empathise with other people's points of view and how they begin to adopt these in the absence of alternatives. In effect it is a form of indoctrination brought on by stress and a desire to survive. It can also be amplified by a previous lack of awareness or ignorance of alternative views, so that hostages feel enlightened and educated by their captors.

There have been many cases of Stockholm syndrome documented since 1973 and others that predate the Stockholm siege. It would be true to say that most people held hostage eventually begin to empathise with their keepers after a while. There is a spectrum of degrees by which the syndrome takes hold, depending on the strength of opinion held by the hostage and the development of their mind. Children are generally easier to indoctrinate because their minds are susceptible to suggestion, while adults tend to have formulated their views. Self esteem also plays a large part in the process.

In 2006 a case in Austria made front-page news. A girl named Natascha Kampusch had been held against her will for eight years since the age of ten. She had had opportunities to escape, but publicly admitted afterwards that she feared for the safety of her captor as she had grown fond of him.

An interesting twist on the syndrome is seen in the American pop star Britney Spears. Some US psychologists have noted similarities between Stockholm syndrome and the behaviour displayed by celebrities pursued by paparazzi photographers. Eventually, it has been suggested, Spears spent such a long time in the company of the paparazzi, who besieged her home, that she began developing relationships with the very people who held her captive. A similar arrangement exists when people find themselves in abusive relationships. They allow themselves to be psychologically and physically abused, yet they jump to the defence of their abuser whenever the authorities attempt to come to the rescue.

# 24 August

## An interesting new chemical compound is revealed

**2000** The chemical element argon (Ar) is well known as an inert gas (one that doesn't react with other elements to form compounds). Until 2000 it was thought that argon could exist only in its pure or native state. Then scientists in Finland experimented with the gas at very cold temperatures. They discovered that argon could form a compound with hydrogen and fluorine – argon fluorohydride (HArF) – at a temperature of –265°C. However, the chemical bonds were so weak that the compounds decomposed when warmed to –265°C.

The discovery that took place on this day is credited to a group of Finnish scientists led by Markku Räsänen. The team cooled caesium iodide to a chilly –265°C, and then combined argon and hydrogen fluoride onto it. The resultant mixture was exposed to ultraviolet radiation, which acted as a catalyst for the reaction.

Argon itself, while it is perhaps unfamiliar to many due to its notable absence from many day-to-day items, is actually around us all the time. Its name is derived from the Greek for 'inactive', and this placid gas makes up 0.93 per cent of the Earth's atmosphere. At this concentration it is the most abundant natural gas on the planet.

Although it may seem odd that chemists are able to pursue hitherto non-existent chemicals and compounds in such a precise manner, this is actually a helpful property of the periodic table. Created by Dmitri Mendeleev, it catalogued known elements in such a way that it was able to predict properties of ones yet to be discovered.

Argon is not the only chemical that behaves in unusual ways at super-cooled temperatures. Absolute zero is –273°C, but it has never been achieved because it is impossible to remove all of the energy from matter. Scientists have come very close, however, and discovered that atoms metamorphose at such low temperatures, taking physics into a different realm. The atoms become 'Bose–Einstein condensates' at close to absolute zero, which means that they condense and begin to behave like fluids due to their absence of energy.

This is an area of intense study because it is uncharted territory. Amazingly, an Indian physicist named Satyendranath Bose predicted condensates in 1925, but only Albert Einstein was prepared to support his theory. The first condensates were created in a lab in 1995, by Eric Cornell and Carl Wieman.

# 25 August

### Voyager 2 *reaches Saturn and then Neptune eight years later to the day*

**1981** and **1989** The arrival of the *Voyager 2* space probe at Neptune, the most distant planet of the solar system, on 25 August 1989, marked the culmination of what mission design manager Charles Kohlhase would later describe as 'the greatest mission of discovery in the history of mankind'. Whether it was the greatest in terms of achievement remains open to debate but it was by far the greatest in terms of distance, except for its companion *Voyager 1*.

When the two *Voyager* probes were launched on 20 August and 5 September 1977, these little robot crafts, each smaller than a mini-car, were only meant to go as far as Jupiter and Saturn, wrapping up their mission in just four years. But after *Voyager 1* passed Jupiter in 1980, mission controllers decided to swing it upwards out of the plane in which the planets orbit the Sun and towards interstellar space. *Voyager 2*, meanwhile, after passing Jupiter in 1979, then Saturn on 25 August 1981, was directed on past first Uranus and then Neptune.

*Voyager 2* is the only probe to have reached either Uranus and Neptune, and the images it sent back of those two blue planets are stunning and invaluable to scientists. In fact, by visiting these two planets, along with Jupiter and Saturn, *Voyager 2* has visited more planets than any other space probe. Between them, the *Voyager* crafts also visited and studied 48 moons.

Yet, remarkably, their journey is still not over. After passing Neptune, *Voyager 2* was sent out towards interstellar space like its twin. Today, the two little craft are cruising at tens of thousands of kilometres an hour out from the Sun, and they are still beaming back information. They are so distant that it takes almost a day for radio signals to reach or come back from *Voyager 2* and even longer to and from *Voyager 1*. They get enough power to study their surroundings and beam back signals from the heat of decaying plutonium, which generates about 310 watts of electricity.

331

Scientists reckon that *Voyager 2* will finally lose the power to steer in about 2015, almost 40 years into the mission, and it will send its last radio broadcast back after almost half a century, in about 2025.

Both probes have now passed the helioshock, the very furthest point reached by the solar wind, which is the stream of radioactive particles thrown out by the Sun, and are now travelling through the heliosheath, the very edge of the solar system. They will soon be out into the nothingness of interstellar space. *Voyager 1* is the most distant human-made object, nearly 16 billion kilometres away in June 2008. *Voyager 2* is not that far behind, over 13 billion kilometres away. But they are not headed for any particular star. They will soon be entirely alone in deep space, and *Voyager 2* will pass by the star Sirius over four light years away – in 296,000 years' time!

# 26 August

## *The Mini car is launched by Austin Morris*

**1959** Occasionally products develop 'cult popularity' because they are designed in such a way that people view them as possessing aesthetic and functional perfection. Alec Issigonis achieved this with the car that would become known simply as the Mini. Just as the Vespa motor scooter became the iconic two-wheeled urban vehicle, so the Mini became its four-wheeled counterpart, especially during the 1960s. Being so small and perfectly formed it encapsulated a certain ideal of economy and became the 'cool' car to drive in the eyes of the public and celebrities alike. It was also cheap to buy, cheap to run and cheap to maintain, which made it immediately popular amongst the youth of the UK and other countries where it was manufactured and sold.

From the point of view of automotive designers the Mini set a standard that has been emulated ever since in small cars. Most importantly it had front wheel drive, which meant that the floor of the car didn't need to accommodate a drive shaft. This turned the cab into a self-contained unit for the driver and passengers and enabled Issigonis to compact the overall shape of the vehicle. As a runabout for towns and cities it was revolutionary, because it could zip about down narrow streets and be parked in the smallest of spaces.

Production of the Mini continued until 2000 with very few changes to the fundamental external design. The modern way of keeping cars fashionable is to regularly launch new models with subtly different body shaping so that the car evolves. In the case of the Mini it was superseded by the New Mini, which attempted to evolve the shape in one fell swoop. Purists hated it because, they claimed, its considerably larger size meant that it wasn't really a Mini at all.

Another classic design is that of the Vespa scooter by Piaggio. It originated in 1946 post-war Italy and reached its zenith in the 1960s. The design is regarded as perfect both in terms of ergonomics and styling, which is why modern versions are virtually identical. In Britain the Vespa became the vehicle of choice for Mods whose sharp, simple style was in marked contrast to the oily motorbikes and greasy leathers of the Rockers. The Vespa allowed the rider to wear smart clothes without dirtying them. Before the compulsory introduction of the safety helmet Vespa riders looked pretty cool too, sporting shades and letting their hair ride the breeze.

# 27 August

## *The world's largest battery is switched on*

**2003** As a rule, power stations generate electricity only as and when it is needed. They try to regulate their production levels according to peaks and troughs of consumption because it is not easy to store electricity. Capacitors or condensers can be used in small electrical devices to store electric charges, but to do so on a large scale would be impracticable.

Electrical cells, collections of which are commonly known as batteries, don't store electricity as such. They convert electrical energy into chemical energy and vice versa. In rechargeable batteries this two-way process is repeatable until the chemicals eventually degrade and have to be replaced.

Using batteries to generate electricity in this way is fine for cars and other vehicles, because they can recharge their own batteries once they are running. Batteries are also useful for powering relatively small devices with low energy consumption – but they are not a good option for powering entire households simply because of the amount of electricity required to light, heat and run a home. Nevertheless, that is precisely what the world's largest battery is for.

Fairbanks, in Alaska, has to cope with severe winter weather conditions that frequently cause electrical blackouts. When blackouts do occur there is a race to start emergency diesel generators before the population begins to suffer from the cold, as temperatures can fall lower than $-50°C$. For this reason an enormous battery of 13,760 nickel-cadmium electric cells was built, which can keep 12,000 people in comfort for a seven-minute period while the generators are started. As well as providing the city folk with electricity, the generators also recharge the battery ready for the next time it is needed.

The company behind the battery – commissioned by the Golden Valley Electrical Association – was the Swiss firm AAB. The record-breaking battery they constructed is huge. Put together, its thousands of cells weigh in at over 1,300 tonnes and cover an area of some 2,000 $m^2$ – making the battery larger than a football pitch. Each individual cell, which is over half a metre in length, weighs twelve stone. The entire structure, built not only to withstand the subarctic climate of Fairbanks, but also any other challenges that the environment may throw its way, is earthquake-proof.

# 28 August

## The world's longest pontoon bridge is opened

**1963** There are various ways to bridge a stretch of water. Arch bridges, box bridges, suspension bridges, beam bridges: all attempt to do so with little or no contact with the water itself. Pontoon bridges actually use the water as their means of support – they float. The construction of floating bridges introduces different problems to engineers. The bridges have to cope with potential changes in water level, water flow and wave action. They also have to allow vessels to pass through or beneath them. Changes in temperature also affect the buoyancy of pontoon bridges.

The longest pontoon bridge is the Evergreen Point Floating Bridge, which spans a stretch of water between Seattle and Bellevue, in the US. It is 7,578 feet (2,310 metres) in length. At each end it has under-passing points for small boats. In the middle it has a retractable drawbridge to allow the passage of larger boats and ships. The bridge crosses a lagoon and is not subjected to water flow or strong currents, but it is still anchored in position by steel cables to prevent winds and waves from moving it. Even a slight sideways bend in the bridge would cause its ends to dislocate from their foundations.

In structure the bridge comprises 33 pontoon sections made from pre-stressed concrete. They measure 360 feet (109 metres) in length and 60 feet (eighteen metres) in width. Depth varies between fourteen and nine feet. In effect they are concrete barges joined end to end. The middle sections retract within the bridge in a similar way to cupboard drawers, making them a 'drawer' bridge, as opposed to a drawbridge. The bridge is nearing the end of its useful life due to wear and tear. A number of vessels have crashed into it and it has also been damaged by storms and tremors. It will make better sense to replace it rather than maintain it, especially as it only carries four traffic lanes when six are needed to meet demand.

Pontoon bridges were famously used during the D-Day landings in 1944. As the landings occurred on beaches there were no harbours in which to moor cargo ships. Floating bridges were used instead to convey weapons, arms, vehicles and general supplies from the ships to two structures called Mulberry harbours, which were floated across the channel and sunk in position. The pontoon bridges were badly damaged by storms but they proved invaluable in getting Allied equipment onshore rapidly enough to force the Germans to retreat.

# 29 August

## Hurricane Katrina wreaks havoc in New Orleans

**2005** Hurricane Katrina was one of the deadliest and most costly natural disasters ever to hit the United States. More than 1,800 people died, and estimates place the cost of the damage at more than $110 billion. New Orleans, which was right in the hurricane's path, may never fully recover. Yet it was not simply the scale of the damage that made Katrina such a distressing event, but also the authorities' patchy response – which seemed to some to be slowest in relation to the poor, the elderly and the black communities.

Before the hurricane struck, New Orleans was a thriving city of 455,000 people. During and after the hurricane, it was almost entirely evacuated as four-fifths of the city was affected. A year later, less than 200,000 had returned and the city remained a ghost town. By 2008, the population had climbed back up to 300,000 in the city, and many districts, like the famous French quarter, were as vibrant as ever. But there are still vast blighted areas, and many people believe it has reached the limits of its recovery.

Katrina was one of only four Category 5 hurricanes ever known in the USA – that is, a storm with winds greater than 249 kph (155 mph). The massive surge of water piled up by the storm was between five and nine metres (sixteen–30 feet) high – the highest ever recorded in the US – and it was this, rather than winds, that did the damage in New Orleans. Such big storms seem to have become more frequent in recent years, prompting many people to point to Katrina as a consequence of global warming, but there is not yet hard evidence that this is so.

As Katrina approached on 28 August, it became clear that it was headed for Mississippi and Louisiana. Warnings went out and people all along the coast began to prepare. Roads out of New Orleans were jammed as those with cars fled the city. Many poor people, especially among the black population of New Orleans, could not afford to go – leading to much criticism later of how little help they received.

On 29 August, the storm lashed America's Gulf Coast, wreaking havoc, but the worst was yet to come on the 30th, when the storm surge hit New Orleans. The city's levees – the banks designed to protect the city from floods – were breached and water poured into the city from Lake Pontchartrain which rose rapidly as the storm's deluge was hemmed in by the rising sea. Although the worst of the storm was soon over, the flooding ensured that the devastation went on much longer. Conditions in the city deteriorated rapidly, and the sports Superdome, the best available refuge, became a hellhole after water and power failed and desperation drove some to looting. Aid was slow in coming, and President George W. Bush was widely criticised for the inadequate response. Eventually the levees were repaired and the water pumped out. Slowly some people returned to pick up the pieces while others gave up hope of ever recovering what they had lost.

Over the years since the disaster, the federal government, stung by post-Katrina criticism, has poured over $100 billion into the rebuilding of New Orleans, but the city is still beset by problems such as homelessness, poverty and inadequate facilities. When Barack Obama was campaigning as the Democratic nominee for President, he pledged special treatment to help the city get back on its feet. 'When I am President,' he said, 'if there is a job that can be done by a New Orleans resident, the contract will go to a resident of New Orleans. And we'll provide tax incentives to businesses that choose to set up shop in the hardest hit areas.' But, despite these tentative hopes, the city's future is still far from assured.

# 30 August

## 'Hot Line' opened between US and USSR

**1963** With the Cold War at its height there was genuine concern about the possibility of a nuclear war. With the onset of the threat of what became known, rather appropriately, as MAD (Mutually Assured Destruction), the American and Soviet administrations decided that it would be a good idea to have a direct communications link between Washington and Moscow, so that any problems could be addressed immediately to prevent the deployment of nuclear weapons.

This first 'Hot Line' was a duplex (two-way) cable, routed halfway around the globe. It wasn't a telephone link, but a telegraph link, so that written messages could be conveyed in both directions. East and West apparently agreed quite readily to the idea of the communication line, because they knew that simple misinformation, misinterpretation, miscalculation *etcetera* might easily lead to one side initiating hostilities and passing the point of no return. Events like the Cuban missile crisis in 1962 had demonstrated that things could very easily get out of hand.

The idea of having contact with the enemy was alien to conventional warfare, but nuclear technology changed the rules entirely. The Cold War ultimately made it very apparent that it was no longer appropriate for nations to go about their business in secrecy, as the very future of humanity was at stake. Before the disintegration of the Soviet Union, the Cold War was played out rather like a game of chess where both sides could see exactly what the other was doing. And, just like the endgame in chess, the communists found themselves in checkmate and capitulated without the Americans needing to actually take their king.

Word has it that the 'Hot Line' was partly inspired by the 'bat line', a telephone connection used by the mayor of Gotham City to contact Batman in the comic strip of the same name. There is something psychologically reassuring about having a line of communication that can be used to solve problems. *Batman* first appeared in 1939 and became very popular between 1950 and 1963. In a way, Batman's struggle with the forces of evil became a metaphor for the perceived ideological contrast between the US and USSR. Of course, the conflict was originally representative of the Allies versus the Axis powers, but that changed in the post-war years. In the 1980s Ronald Reagan alluded to another element of science fiction by using the name 'star wars' in describing a project to develop laser-armed satellites for the purpose of nuclear defence.

# 31 August

## *A death shocks a nation*

**1997** Princess Diana's death in a road traffic accident in Paris, France, caused the most remarkable reaction in the UK. It must have been the familiarity of seeing her face in the media, day in day out since the early 1980s, that made so many react as if they had lost a sister. She had grown up in the spotlight having been chosen by Prince Charles as his bride. The nation had seen her come out of herself and develop a personality – they had fallen in love with her.

Inevitably the vagaries of the events surrounding the car crash led to conspiracy theories left, right and centre. The fact that Diana had died with an Egyptian Arab – Dodi al Fayed – convinced some people, particularly Dodi's father Mohamed al Fayed, that she had been assassinated as part of a plot initiated by the Duke of Edinburgh. Quite apart from anything else, if it had been an assassination then this would have been a highly unreliable way of going about it.

Indeed, despite these concerns, in 2008 a lengthy official report into Diana and Dodi's deaths ruled out any possibility of such a scenario. Costing upwards of £12.5 million, the extensive inquiry headed by Lord Justice Scott Baker declared on 31 March that there was 'not a shred of evidence' that any of the royal family had had any role at all in her tragic death. If anywhere, the report concluded, the blame lay with the pursuing paparazzi and the negligence of the chauffeur, Henri Paul. Lord Justice Scott Baker passed a verdict of unlawful killing, although it has proved impossible to identify the accused photographers for prosecution.

When all was said and done it was clearly an unfortunate collision brought about by a high-speed chase at night and with Diana's driver tired and having had too much to drink. Careering through a tunnel lined with concrete pillars at over 100 mph with paparazzi flashing their cameras in the driver's eyes is inherently dangerous. If Paul had taken the car off the road anywhere else then the chances are that they would all have survived, but crashing within the tunnel itself left the occupants of the vehicle with little or no chance.

Three million mourners attended her funeral in London a few days after her death, on 6 September. In 2007, on what would have been her 46th birthday, a huge charity concert was held in her name. There are also numerous memorial constructions, including a fountain in Hyde Park and a playground in Kensington Gardens. Diana has gone, but her memory lives on in the hearts of the nation.

# 1 September

## The US beats the USSR at chess

**1972** Just as diplomats were playing their metaphorical game of Cold War chess between East and West, so Bobby Fischer beat Boris Spassky to become America's first World Chess Champion. Chess was very much an Old World game by tradition and the Soviets had dominated the international field since the first modern championship in 1948. There had been three Russian, one Latvian and one Armenian champion in that time. Spassky, a Russian, had been champion since 1969 when Fischer made his challenge in 1972.

Fischer beat Spassky in Reykjavik, Iceland to become the first and only US champion. When he arrived back in the US after his victory, New York greeted him with a full civic reception. To some extent, Fischer was unhappy with the level of recognition he received and complained that President Nixon had not extended the offer of an invitation to the White House.

When he refused to defend his title in 1975, it was removed by the controlling body FIDE. Fischer was a complex personality and became somewhat reclusive. His behaviour also became rather eccentric and he turned his back on America, choosing to live instead in various other countries.

In 1992, some 20 years after the match in Reykjavik, a Fischer versus Spassky rematch was finally declared. By this time, Spassky was no longer living in his home country either, having left Russia to take up residency in France.

The match itself appeared to be something of an oddity. Spassky was ranked 99th in the world, and Fischer had relinquished serious involvement in chess shortly after the original encounter. Indeed, Fischer seemed to take the game as an opportunity to make his political feelings clear. At the opening press conference, he pulled out a letter from the US government threatening imprisonment and a fine if he played – and then spat on it in front of the watching television cameras.

If the build-up to the match was rather incongruous, the competition between the two men was intense. There was a $3.3 million prize for the winner, with the loser taking home $1.6 million. After 30 games of tight play, of which fifteen ended in draws, Fischer triumphed over Spassky for a second time with a 10–5 scoreline.

In January 2008, at the age of 64, Bobby Fischer died in Iceland, the place where his extraordinary mind had made him champion.

# 2 September

## Capitulation in writing

**1945** Two weeks after the unconditional surrender of Japan to America, the Japanese High Command signed the document of surrender in Tokyo Bay. Following the official surrender aboard the battleship *Missouri*, the US landed 13,000 troops to occupy Japan in the aftermath of the war. The Supreme Allied Commander, US General Douglas MacArthur addressed the dignitaries with a speech, which contained these words:

> It is my earnest hope and, indeed, the hope of all mankind, that from this solemn occasion a better world shall emerge out of the blood and carnage of the past; a world founded upon faith and understanding, a world dedicated to the dignity of man and the fulfilment of his most cherished wish, for freedom, tolerance and justice.

The Second World War had lasted for six long years, although the Americans hadn't become directly involved until the Japanese attacked Pearl Harbor in December 1941.

Japan had formed an alliance with Germany and Italy in 1940, called the Tripartite Pact. The three nations became known as the main Axis Powers, a name selected because Germany and Italy had originally demarked a geographical swathe through Europe, from north to south, seen as the axis point about which the political situation revolved. A number of other nations joined and departed from the Axis during the course of the war, either voluntarily or through coercion. They included countries all over the world from such varied continents as Europe, Asia, Africa and South America.

There are those who now argue that the Second World War really began in 1937 as opposed to 1939. Although Germany invaded Poland in 1939, to initiate the war in Europe, Japan had already begun hostilities with China two years beforehand. Some war historians refer to the China–Japan conflict as the Second Sino–Japanese War, but its transition into the Second World War was seamless when the US became involved in 1941. Germany and Japan both had designs on building empires, so the war was like a fire burning the world map from opposite directions. Fortunately those fires never connected, and the flames were beaten back in two quite separate campaigns.

# 3 September

## School siege ends in over 300 deaths

**2004** Chechnya is a small republic, currently a federal subject of Russia. For political reasons Russia failed to allow the Chechen people their independence following the disintegration of the Soviet Union in 1991. Perhaps not surprisingly there has been a struggle for sovereignty ever since.

Having realised that an orthodox political effort for independence wasn't going to succeed, many Chechens decided that terrorism was the only way to make the Russian administration take them seriously. This has led to a great deal of conflict and bloodshed. In September 2004, in an attempt to force an end to the Second Chechen War and gain recognition for Chechnya as a sovereign state, a group of armed Chechen rebels took drastic action.

School Number One is in a town called Beslan in North Ossetia, Russia. On 1 September 2004, a number of Chechen terrorists, armed with guns and bombs, took more than 1,100 children and teachers hostage in the school hall.

Perhaps learning from the experiences of a Moscow hostage crisis in 2002, the first thing they did was smash the windows of the hall in order to prevent a sleeping-gas attack by the Russian army. Then they set rudimentary mines and tripwires around the entire site to prevent the Russian authorities from launching a rescue raid. Finally, in an attempt to warn off the army and police further still, they threatened to kill 50 hostages for each one of their members who died.

The Russians seemed to take the message to heart. They immediately requested a special meeting of the United Nations Security Council, and for the first two days all negotiations seemed to be directed towards a peaceful resolution.

During the second day, however, discussions between the Russians and the rebels started to break down. The hostage-takers had been depriving their captives of food and water, but despite repeated requests to desist, they refused to do so. For their part, the Russian authorities angered the terrorists by attempting to downplay the numbers involved, to suppress the demands for a formal recognition of Chechnya's independence, and in general to impede the rebels in their aims.

On the third day of the siege, this day in 2004, violence broke out between the Chechen group and the Russian authorities. Shortly after 1 pm, as the Chechens waited for a hostage negotiator to arrive, two explosions were set off, one of which caused the roof of the hall to collapse onto the hostages below. Over 100 hostages are suspected to have died as a result. Precisely what caused the detonations is uncertain; while official reports claim that two of the rebels' own devices exploded accidentally, there is no conclusive proof for this.

Amid the confusion that followed, several hostages made a burst for freedom. The Chechens responded by opening fire on all the hostages, and the Russian forces stormed the school as a result. In the resulting gun battle, rebels, soldiers and hostages all lost their lives.

The sole hospital in Beslan was overwhelmed with the strain

placed upon it. Small and under-equipped, many of those brought in injured could not be effectively treated by the doctors. In total at least 334 hostages died, 186 of whom were children; hundreds more were reported injured or missing.

# 4 September

## Mark Spitz wins his legendary seven Olympic gold medals

**1972** When Mark Spitz led the US swimming team to a stunning victory in the 400-metre medley at the Munich Olympics, it capped one of the most extraordinary athletic performances in history. That victory bought Spitz his seventh gold medal in the Munich Games – and, even more extraordinarily, his seventh world record.

Spitz that year was quite simply unbeatable. No one before him had won Olympic golds in seven separate events at a single games. His astonishing haul of seven gold medals was finally beaten by fellow American swimmer Michael Phelps, who won eight gold medals in the 2008 Beijing Olympics. But even Phelps did not match Spitz's astonishing triumph of breaking the world record in every event he competed in – he set world records in seven of those winning finals.

It was as if Spitz was supercharged at Munich. He certainly had a lot to prove. A precocious swimmer, he had made his mark at a young age and arrived at the Mexico City Olympics in 1968 at the age of seventeen with ten world records already under his Speedos. Feeling naturally confident, he brashly predicted that he would win six golds in Mexico. The outcome for Spitz was humiliating. His only golds were in the team events, and in his star 200-metre butterfly, in which he was the world record-holder, he actually came last in the final.

Naturally, the pressure was on Spitz to redeem himself at Munich and the first event was that 200-metre butterfly. Right from the start, though, there was no doubt about the outcome.

Spitz leaped straight into the lead like a flailing torpedo and kept going further and further in front throughout the race. With that psychological barrier down, there was simply no stopping Spitz and he went on to win convincingly in every single event.

This is the sequence:

> Gold 1: 200 m butterfly (2 min 0.70 sec)
> Gold 2: 400 m freestyle relay (3 min 36.42 sec)
> Gold 3: 200 m freestyle (1 min 52.78 sec)
> Gold 4: 100 m butterfly (54.27 sec)
> Gold 5: 800 m freestyle relay team
> Gold 6: 100 m freestyle (51:22 sec)
> Gold 7: 400 m medley relay.

With this series of swims, Mark Spitz has a good claim to be the greatest swimmer of all time. Yet his celebrations were cut spectacularly and tragically short when just hours after his seventh win, in the medley relay, five Palestinian terrorists burst in on the Israeli quarters in the Olympic village. The terrorists killed two and took nine hostages. Spitz, who is Jewish, was immediately bundled out of Munich under tight security, while the hostage crisis, which ended in the death of all the terrorists, unfolded.

Knowing that he could never hope to top his Olympic triumph, Spitz, still only 22, retired from swimming after Munich to try, unsuccessfully, to establish an acting career. At the age of 41 he attempted to make a comeback to compete in the 1992 Barcelona Olympics, with a $1 million reward offered as an incentive, but he failed to qualify. In some ways it seems better like this, with his 1972 triumph an unalloyed pinnacle.

# 5 September

## Mother Teresa's number is called

**1997** By the time she died in 1997, the Blessed Mother Teresa was already halfway to the beatification that was bestowed on her in record time in October 2002. No figure in modern times has achieved such worldwide celebrity and genuine reverence simply for helping the poor. Even back in 1975, *Time* magazine featured her on its front cover as a 'Living Saint' and by 1999, the magazine listed her in the *Time* '100 Most Important People of the 20th Century'.

Mother Teresa certainly had her critics. After being called as a witness for her beatification, Christopher Hitchens wrote a stinging article in which he accused her of being a fanatic, a fundamentalist and a fraud, and criticised the Catholic Church for surrendering 'to the forces of showbiz, superstition and populism'. In particular, Hitchens and others attacked her stand against abortion, and her willingness to fraternise with dictators such as Haiti's Jean-Claude Duvalier. Interestingly, in letters revealed after her death, Mother Teresa questioned her own faith. 'What do I labour for?' she asked in one letter. 'If there be no God, there can be no soul. If there be no soul then, Jesus, You also are not true.' Yet there is no doubt that she inspired tremendous devotion. When she was beatified, hundreds of thousands of pilgrims thronged through St Peter's Square to witness the announcement.

Mother Teresa was an Albanian, born Agnes Bojaxhiu on 26 August 1910 in what is now Skopje, the capital of Macedonia. Her father died when she was just eight years old, and her mother brought her up as a strict Catholic. Apparently, she was fascinated by stories of missionaries from an early age, and by the age of twelve knew that she would become a nun. She left her mother and sister behind forever at the age of eighteen to join the Irish Sisters of Loreto.

After six weeks in Ireland learning English, she was sent to Darjeeling to begin her novitiate and took vows eight years later as Sister Teresa, at the Loreto convent school in Calcutta. She apparently enjoyed teaching at the school, but the horrors of a famine in 1943 and the violence of Partition profoundly shocked her. In 1946, Teresa heard what she was to describe as 'the call within the call' – to leave the convent to live among the poor and help them. That's exactly what she did for the rest of her life, swapping the Loreto habit for a plain blue and white *chira* and wearing Indian clothes while she tended to the needs of the destitute and starving. She founded an order of nuns, which by the time of her death had 4,000 members who looked after 7,000 children and treated 4 million sick people each year.

What left such a profound impression on those who saw Mother Teresa was her willingness to reach out to even the lowest of the low. Her embrace of lepers, for instance, led to a shift in attitudes which went a long way to helping develop more humane treatments for those afflicted by the disease. She had the ability to look at anyone, no matter how badly off, and make them feel special. One nun said her eyes 'were not of a person of this Earth; she belonged to heaven'.

The benefits of Mother Teresa's work were appreciated early on in India, where she became known as the Saint of Calcutta, but her worldwide fame began with a 1969 TV documentary by Malcolm Muggeridge called *Something Beautiful for God*. Thereafter the diminutive nun became an international celebrity, receiving honour after honour – everything from an honorary citizenship bestowed by the US Congress to the Nobel Peace Prize. When asked at the Nobel ceremony what could be done to promote world peace, she answered, 'Go home and love your family'.

# 6 September

## *A Soviet pilot, Viktor Belenko, defects with his MiG-25 jet fighter*

**1976** In 1976 the Mikoyan-Gurevich MiG-25 was a top secret Soviet aircraft, given the name 'Foxbat' by NATO. It was a state-of-the-art jet fighter using advanced materials and technologies. Western leaders couldn't believe their good fortune when Viktor Belenko decided to defect with his aeroplane. He even brought the instruction manual with him, expecting to assist with flight tests.

As it turned out the Western leaders chose to be diplomatic

about the event. They allowed the US Air Force to examine the MiG-25 but not fly it. In fact, the Americans took the plane to pieces, quite literally, and it was eventually shipped back to the Russians packed into 30 crates, just to let them know that every square inch had been inspected. The US was so impressed by the MiG-25 that it used elements of the Soviet design in its modified F-15 Eagle.

As for Belenko, he was debriefed for a few months and then employed as a consultant. He then became an American citizen and worked as an aerospace engineer. His defection caused an enormous tactical shift in the USSR. The administration decided to completely revamp its military aircraft having realised that the West had taken a step ahead in the Cold War arms race.

This didn't prevent further high-profile desertions though. In 1989 a MiG-29 Fulcrum was flown by Alexander Zuyev to an air base in Turkey. He famously defected by using sleeping pills in a cake to drug his fellow officers. Zuyev also became an American citizen. Sadly he was killed in a plane crash in 2001 when his trainer aircraft failed to recover from a stall.

Since the 1950s there have been over 40 cases of pilots defecting to the West. They include some from the USSR, as well as those from countries including Algeria, Iran and Iraq. Relatively few have defected in the opposite direction, but it has happened from time to time, for both political and religious reasons. During the Cold War a number of Western spies opted to live in the Soviet Union when they were exposed as double agents. Kim Philby was a member of British intelligence who had communist leanings and defected to Moscow in 1965.

# 7 September

## Monty Python's Flying Circus *records its first episode*

**1969** Few TV comedy shows are remembered with the same devotion as *Monty Python's Flying Circus*. Almost 40 years on, there are still many people who can quote whole skits word for word, such as the famous 'Dead Parrot' sketch in which a man tries to return a dead parrot to a pet shop; there are many more who have lines such as 'Nobody expects the Spanish Inquisition!' and 'Nudge nudge wink wink' etched indelibly on their consciousness. Even the show's comic use of the brand-name Spam has been co-opted into the internet world as the term for unwanted junk emails.

People often talk about 'ground-breaking' comedy shows, but it was really true of *Monty Python*, and it spawned a whole generation of people who grew up in its shadow. The show sprang from the very clever Oxbridge satire that had emerged in the 1960s, with such shows as *The Frost Report* and *At Last the 1948 Show*. Some of the Python team, notably John Cleese and Graham Chapman, had been directly involved in these shows. But the genius of *Monty Python* was to minimise the satire and allow six very intelligent, funny young men to go off on the flights of comic fancy that boys often indulge in during private moments. The show's favourite word was 'silly' and it was the fantastic silliness of the show that gave it such wide appeal. No other show before or since has been able to cause such mirth with wonderfully silly ideas such as a dance between two men slapping each other with fish.

The Python team got together when John Cleese saw *Do Not Adjust Your Set*, a zany children's TV show in which Michael Palin, Eric Idle and Terry Jones were involved, and decided he wanted to work with Michael. BBC producer Barry Took had the same idea and brought them together. John brought Graham Chapman along to the meeting, and Michael bought Eric and Terry Jones, along with Terry Gilliam, who had done some animations for *DNAYS*. The six hit it off immediately, sharing a love of *The Goon Show* and Spike Milligan. To the BBC's credit, they were given a budget to make thirteen shows, without any brief whatsoever.

The first show was recorded on 7 September 1969, and broadcast on 5 October. The series was buried in the late-night schedules, but developed sufficient word-of-mouth following for a second series to be commissioned the next year. A third series followed in 1972. Soon the show was required viewing for a huge number of young people in Britain.

Before long the team were embarking on a feature-length film, *And Now For Something Completely Different*, with the hope of breaking into the American market. The Americans didn't get it at first, but then suddenly in the mid-1970s Pythonmania took off there in a big way – just as the team were releasing their second film, *Monty Python and the Holy Grail*. It was their third film, *The Life of Brian*, however, which most consider their finest. Following a man called Brian, who is mistaken for the Messiah, it had a brilliant central performance from Graham Chapman, and some outrageously funny moments – but of course it raised the ire of fundamentalist Christians who campaigned, in some places successfully, for the film to be banned.

The team made one more film, the critically acclaimed *The Meaning of Life*, before finally going their separate ways. People often talked about a reunion, but Graham Chapman's death in 1989 put paid to that – though there was a single stage appearance of the team in Aspen, Colorado in 1998 in which Chapman also 'appeared' with his ashes in an urn, until the urn was accidentally kicked over and spilled ... But if the team are no more, their humour has left a lasting legacy.

# 8 September

## *The first episode of* Star Trek *is shown in the US*

**1966** The 80 episodes of the original *Star Trek* series were made between 1966 and 1969. To devout fans – known as Trekkies – nothing compares with this first series, even though there have been no fewer than five subsequent spin-offs. The characters and the plots of the first programmes captured the viewers' imaginations in such a way that the crude sets and props didn't matter.

The long-lasting affection in which the original *Star Trek* is now held is shown in all sorts of ways. 'Beam me up, Scotty!' is now an established part of our vocabulary, and in the US, NASA dubbed its prototype space shuttle the *Enterprise*, in honour of the main vessel in the television show. Despite all this, the early reception of the famous sci-fi series was not all that encouraging, and the original show was cancelled after the third season.

In the years that followed, *Star Trek* was revived with the introduction of CGI effects to make the productions more slick and visually lifelike or realistic. However, the quaint charm of the earlier rickety sets was absent and this, coupled with the fact that new actors and characters were used, led the loyal fans to argue that the new show was only something masquerading as *Star Trek*. Consequently, fans of the later episodes don't usually have a passion for the first series and vice versa. In other words, there are real Trekkies and there are quasi-Trekkies, and never the twain shall meet.

In addition to the original television series a number of *Star Trek* films were also made using the original cast. They are rather more polished than the TV programmes, but the familiar characters maintain the integrity of the movies. *Star Trek I–VI* (1979–91) were made using the original cast, while *Star Trek VII* (1994) sees the original crew of the Starship *Enterprise* meet with the crew of *Enterprise-D* of the *Star Trek: The Next Generation* series.

*Star Trek* also introduced a number of science fiction ideas which many now take for granted as (non-existent) things of fact. The warp drive was a *Star Trek* first, for instance, as was teleportation and spaceship-cloaking devices. In fact, the show's writers were so prolific that many of the weird and wonderful items they conjured up are now very much a part of our modern world: desktop computers, handheld communication devices and laser surgery being just three.

The key characters and actors of the original *Star Trek* series are as follows: Captain James T. Kirk (William Shatner), Spock (Leonard Nimoy), Bones (DeForest Kelley), Scotty (James Doohan), Uhura (Nichelle Nichols), Sulu (George Takei) and Chekov (Walter Koenig). *Star Trek XI*, due for release in 2009, will include these characters played by new actors when young and by the original cast when old.

# 9 September

## Mao Zedong is dead

**1976** Between them Hitler, Stalin and Mao Zedong were responsible for the deaths of countless millions of people in the last century. And more deaths were probably caused by Mao than by Hitler and Stalin combined.

Yet Western history's attitude towards Mao is more ambiguous than it is to either Hitler or Stalin. Indeed, there was a time in the 1960 when Mao was something of a hero among young idealists in the West, who carried around the *Little Red Book* of his gnomic sayings. It maybe that the ambiguity comes the fact that most of the deaths, casualties of Mao's Great Leap Forward, were unfortunate by-products of his policies, not the result of deliberate killings. That, at least, is the official verdict of the Chinese Communist Party today.

Whatever the verdict, Mao and his policies may have killed some 50 million or more Chinese – most as a result of the famine caused by his Great Leap Forward of political and economic reforms in the 1960s, but many millions too by the deliberate targeting of political opponents in times like the Cultural Revolution. Yet Mao was the man who, more than anyone else, reunited China after the terrible times of civil war and Japanese invasion. It was Mao, too, who brought China the communist ideals that would at last lift at least some of its peasants out of the bondage of poverty. This is why many Chinese people still revere him despite the devastating effects of some of his policies.

Mao first came to prominence in the 1920s, when the country was divided after the collapse of the Chinese Empire and in the face of threats from the Japanese. While most leaders of the newly founded Chinese Communist Party worked in the cities, Mao went out into the fields to organise peasants into a Red Army. Mao's peasant army was small and ill-equipped, but with the epic Long March through mountains in the depths of the winter of 1934–35, it escaped the encircling Nationalist Guomindang

(GMD) forces of Chiang Kai-shek. Three-quarters of the Army perished on the March, but the feat turned Mao into a Chinese hero and communist leader. When China emerged from the trials of Japanese occupation after the Second World War, it was Mao who led the final battle against the GMD which ended with victorious communists declaring the People's Republic of China in 1949.

In the communist clampdown that followed, tens of thousands of GMD supporters were executed and many more were tortured or driven to their death. Millions of landlords may have been exterminated to make way for the communists' land reforms. Half a million more intellectuals were 'purged' in 1957, when Mao apparently encouraged the expression of opinions, saying 'Let a hundred flowers bloom, and let a hundred schools of thought contend' – an invitation some commentators later believed was simply designed to flush out Mao's opposition before he launched his next scheme, the Great Leap Forward of 1958.

The Great Leap Forward was the most catastrophic economic policy ever introduced. It turned most farms into 'People's Communes', where party members, not farmers, were in charge. To meet Mao's demand for a massive boost in steel production, farm workers were dragged off the field into village blast furnaces into which they threw their farming tools. When subsequent floods and droughts hit, the result was crop yields so low that more than 30 million (and maybe twice as many) Chinese peasants died of starvation.

Even Mao could not survive this entirely undamaged, and was forced to resign as party chairman. He remained a powerful force, though, and launched the Cultural Revolution as his comeback to destroy his opponents. Although the effect on millions of Chinese intellectuals and on China's heritage was catastrophic, it brought Mao back to the chairmanship in 1971. By now, though, he was ill and in 1973 he died of cancer. For a while, the Gang of Four, led by Mao's widow Jiang Qing, tried to carry on his heavy-handed rule, but with Mao gone they had less of a power base, and within a few years Mao's arch-rival Deng Xiaoping took over the reins, and a new direction for China began to emerge.

# 10 September

## *The noun 'quisling' enters the vocabulary*

**1945** The word 'quisling' is used to describe a traitor and colla-borator. It comes from the surname of Vidkun Quisling, who betrayed the Allies during the Second World War and sided with Germany. Quisling was a Norwegian army officer and diplomat who ruled Norway on behalf of the German occupying forces between 1942 and the close of the war. Worse than that, he had actually assisted the Germans in their invasion of Norway in 1940. Hitler originally intended to set Quisling up as premier, but he was so unpopular that Hitler saw no use in him when the invasion was complete. Josef Terboven, a Nazi officer, was put in charge in 1940, and he eventually named Quisling as Minister President of Norway when he wished to silence the monarchy.

Quisling was arrested for treason in May 1945 when the Allies forced the Nazis out. He was tried and found guilty in September and shot by firing squad in October. The term 'quisling' was actually coined by *The Times* in 1940. In a later reflection on the noun, a journalist from the same publication remarked, 'to writers, the word "quisling" is a gift from the gods. If they had been ordered to invent a new word for "traitor", they could hardly have hit upon a more brilliant combination of letters.'

The reason why Quisling attracted so much attention for his antics was that he had formally been appointed Commander of the British Empire for his services in the Soviet Union. This had raised his public profile so that his betrayal of Norway and the Allies was all the more marked. Although a fascist, Quisling also clearly had delusions of grandeur as he tried to seize the oppor-tunity to appoint himself leader of Norway at the earliest opportunity.

An equivalent to being a quisling is being a 'Judas', after Judas Iscariot. Iscariot was one of Jesus' apostles or disciples, but betrayed Jesus' whereabouts to the Romans. Central to the notion of betrayal is not just the act of betrayal but also the selfish gain to be had by the traitor. In the case of Iscariot he received a monetary bribe. Traditionally betrayal was considered a worse crime than most, sometimes even than murder. In Dante's *Inferno* the deepest tracts of hell are reserved for traitors. There is clearly something about betrayal that affects the primal ability to trust other human beings.

# *11 September*

## *The day that changed everything*

**2001** What made 9/11 so dramatic was that events unfolded on the world's television screens as if the attacks were being staged for optimum visual entertainment. Usually news crews arrive at the scene of a terrorist attack some time after the key moment, but in this case it was all there to see. The sky was clear blue, the Twin Towers of the World Trade Center were perfectly lit and we saw every detail. In fact it looked so much like a movie that it became difficult to believe that it was a genuine terrorist attack.

Broadcasting began with one tower already ablaze, and then a second aircraft arrived to plunge into the other tower. If there had been any doubt that the first collision was a deliberate act, then the second made it quite obvious that we weren't witnessing an unfortunate accident.

Then, as the fires took hold, the horrific plight of those inside the buildings became clear. People began jumping from the blazing floors to certain death below. Just as we all wondered what on Earth anyone could do to save the poor souls trapped above the infernos, the towers began to collapse.

Again, it all seemed almost too dramatic to be real. The fuel from the aircraft had flooded the central storeys of the towers so that the heat was very evenly spread. This caused the towers to collapse vertically under their own weight as if they were being destroyed by controlled demolition. It turned out to be a blessing in disguise. Had the towers toppled over sideways, there is no telling what carnage they would have wrought; they would have taken out many neighbouring buildings and crushed thousands of flee-ing people.

This, the most visual of terrorist attacks, remains so bewildering that it is still difficult to discuss. It is as though people were so affected by what they saw that day that their minds have chosen to blank it out from their memories. One factor that made the attack so remarkable was that it was so easily and simply executed. There was nothing hi-tech about the terrorists' method. They had simply taken a few flying lessons in order to learn how to steer the aircraft and then taken control armed only with knives. People expected terrorists to wield guns and bombs and to stand out in the crowd; these terrorists slipped through unnoticed. A third plane was crashed into the Pentagon. Their only failure was not to crash into the White House, as the crew and passengers of the hijacked plane apparently destined for it overpowered the terrorists upon hearing of the attack on the World Trade Center.

The far-reaching effect of the 9/11 attacks has been to make the West only too aware of the extremes that other cultures will go to in their efforts to be factored into world politics. Until 2001 America had felt relatively immune from terrorist attacks on its own soil. Then came the wake-up call of all wake-up calls and the world was changed forever.

# 12 September

## Stephen Biko dies and becomes a martyr

**1977** Apartheid was a political system used in South Africa where the wealthy whites in power segregated their society so that black Africans and those of mixed race were physically and culturally kept apart from them. It was a form of sanctioned racism, designed to keep the whites in a position of superiority, even though they formed a minority percentage of the population.

Nelson Mandela had been jailed for his efforts in attempting to subvert the white administration, so those protesters who remained free had to tread very carefully to avoid incarceration.

Stephen Biko became a source of irritation for the government and on 18 August 1977 was duly arrested at a road block, on accusations of terrorism.

During 'questioning', which was clearly forceful interrogation, if not torture, he received severe wounds to the head. On 11 September, stripped naked and nearly dead from his injuries, Biko was loaded into a Land Rover. The intention was to finally take him to a prison with hospital facilities – but the one towards which the police headed was in Pretoria, some 1,500 km (930 miles) away. Stephen Biko stood little chance of making the journey without immediate medical assistance, and on this day in 1977 he died as a result of his brutal treatment.

Biko's major contribution towards the struggle against apartheid rule was the founding of the Black Consciousness Movement. Designed to unify the urban black population, he used it to spread his famous slogan, 'Black is Beautiful'. Biko himself explained the egalitarian message behind it: 'Man, you are okay as you are, begin to look upon yourself as a human being.'

After Biko's death, the police attempted a cover-up by suggesting that he had starved himself to death. However, a journalist at the *Rand Daily Mail* named Helen Zille exposed the truth. The story caused international condemnation and served to educate and inform other nations of the apartheid problem in South Africa. Ultimately the situation only resolved itself with the end of white rule in 1994, when the ANC came to power under Mandela.

With hindsight it might be argued that apartheid would have come to an end anyway, due to a general shift of viewpoint in new generations of white South Africans, but Biko is seen as a martyr whose death accelerated the process. Zille went on to become a politician and leader of the official opposition party in South Africa, the Democratic Alliance.

Despite the removal of apartheid there is still a significant social divide between rich and poor in South Africa, which has resulted in demonstrations and unrest, occasionally turning to violence. The country did well to avoid civil war in 1994, but the population comprises such a mix of races and tribes that there is always an undercurrent of tension brought about by various resentments and rivalries.

# 13 September

## *The Battle of Heartbreak Ridge, Korea*

**1951** In the 1950s America had a large chip on its shoulder about communist regimes. The Cold War had been initiated between the US and the USSR, which led to the Americans developing an obsession with 'reds' and 'commies'. So much so that it became an arrestable offence to express communist political leanings on home soil. It is unclear exactly why this situation developed and it seems to have been borne entirely on a wave of paranoia that the American way of life might somehow be undermined by an infestation of socialism.

The Battle of Heartbreak Ridge was essentially fought between the populations of South Korea and North Korea. On the side of the former were the United Nations, the United States and the French. On the side of the latter was China. The war represented an ideological battle of democracy versus communism. Following the removal of the Japanese occupation in 1945, the region had been divided into North and South Korea in 1948. But in 1950 the government of North Korea chose to invade its southern neighbour, thereby beginning a war that would last until 1953 and see millions die. The boundary between the two countries was ultimately redrawn more or less where it had been to start with, at the 38th parallel, making the loss of life seem even more pointless than usual.

Heartbreak Ridge was a geographical ridge that the democratic forces tried to take from the communists. It proved to be a costly mistake, as the communists kept replenishing their numbers so that the attack saw thousands die for no gain. On 27 September, after two weeks of fighting, the attack was called off. Nearly 4,000 democratic troops had perished in the attempt to take the ridge. An incredible 25,000 communists had died defending it. It echoed the way in which the Russians had defeated the Germans in the Second World War, by sending an endless supply of troops to the front line as 'cannon fodder' until the enemy was forced to reconsider its strategy. Perhaps it was that unquestioning devotion to the communist cause that put fear into the hearts of the Americans back home.

# 14 September

## First US saint

**1975** On 14 September 1975, Pope Paul IV gave the USA its first native-born saint, when he canonised Elizabeth Ann Seton, an early-19th-century New York society woman who turned Catholic and devoted her life to the establishment of schools for the poor. St Elizabeth is now regarded as the patron saint of Catholic schools.

America had waited a long time for its first saint. The USA is an unusually religious country for the developed world. A survey of global religious attitudes in 2002 showed that the US was the only major developed nation in which a majority of people said religion played a 'very important' part in their lives. Similar levels of religious life exist in Latin America, and in India, but in no other comparable nation. By far the majority (over 76 per cent) are Christians – compared with just 44 per cent in the UK.

Yet what makes the USA especially different from the rest of the world is the degree of religious volatility. In most religious countries people stay true to the same faith throughout their lives, but in the USA more than half the population switch their allegiances during their life – either switching from, say, Protestantism to Catholicism, or between other faiths, or abandoning their faith altogether.

So Elizabeth Ann Seton was very much in the American tradition when she converted from Protestantism to Catholicism. That was not how many of her contemporaries in society saw it, though. America is generally seen as a Protestant country rather than a

Catholic one. It was the Protestants from Northern Europe who were first to settle in America, and they often formed the upper strata of American society. Catholicism arrived later with the Irish, the Poles, the Spanish and the French, who were generally lower down society's ladder.

Elizabeth Ann Seton was of well-to-do Protestant stock and her embracement of Catholicism caused her to be ostracised by many of her society friends. The conversion happened when at the age of 29 in 1803, she took her husband William Seton, who was dying from tuberculosis, for a health cure to Italy. The trip did little to help William, who died before the Setons were allowed out of the quarantine in which the Italian authorities had held them for fear of yellow fever, said to be rife in New York. But Elizabeth met Antonio Filicchi and his wife, and the Filicchis introduced her to their Catholic faith. As a memoir written for her sister reveals, her route to conversion was long and anguished, but by the time she returned to New York in June 1804, she was both a widow and a Catholic with a mission.

Her husband's death had left her virtually penniless, and many of her former friends shunned her for her change of faith. But she determinedly stepped up her commitment to the charity work she had begun as a Protestant, which had earned her and her sister-in-law Rebecca the name 'Protestant Sisters of Charity'. In 1808, a group of Catholic bodies, including the émigré French Sulpicians, invited her to become the head of America's first Catholic school for the poor in Emmitsburg, Maryland. The Emmitsburg school proved to be the first of many. Saint Elizabeth ran the school until she died aged 46, on 4 January 1821 – the day now considered her saint's day.

## 15 September

### The John Bull keeps on running

**1831–1981** This *John Bull* is a steam locomotive built by Brunel's great rival, Robert Stephenson, in England and shipped to the US.

It was delivered to the Camden and Amboy Railroad, New Jersey, on 4 September 1831 and steamed up the track for the first time on the 15th. It was used until 1866, when it was put into storage, although it was maintained and operated from time to time so that it was kept in good working order. In 1884 the Smithsonian Institute purchased the machine and it was put on display, where it stayed for over nine decades. In 1981 the Smithsonian decided to celebrate the 150th anniversary of the *John Bull*'s first journey by running it once again. On 15 September, the engine ran under its own power amid a fanfare and celebration. In doing so, it became the oldest original steam locomotive still capable of movement.

There is now a replica *John Bull*, as well as a number of other famous trains. The *Rocket*, built in 1829, also by Stephenson, is one such engine. It may not have been the first steam locomotive, but the *Rocket* established the basic design format. The original *Rocket* can be seen in the Science Museum, London.

The first steam-powered locomotive was built by Richard Trevithick in 1802. He converted a stationary steam engine as an experiment and it was never given a name. A replica stands in the entrance to Telford Central Station, England. At that time railroads were made of wood, as opposed to iron, and were only suitable for carriages drawn by pit ponies. Steam locomotives were too heavy, so they didn't catch on until iron rails were manufactured, which were both tough and hardwearing.

The name 'John Bull' was devised as a personification of Britain in 1712 by John Arbuthnot, who was a satirist and polymath. John Bull was the equivalent of Uncle Sam in the US and used to represent Britain in cartoons of the day. As a character he was a rotund country gentleman, in tailcoat and top hat. These days John Bull is largely forgotten as a symbol of a bygone era, but the name was still synonymous with Britain when the locomotive was built.

# *16 September*

## *A fiscal lesson is learnt in Britain*

**1992** Wednesday 16 September 1992 was the day Britain paid for the excesses of the 1980s. The British government had only recently entered sterling into the European Exchange Rate Mechanism (ERM), but things went spiralling out of control. The government withdrew from the ERM at an estimated cost of £3.4 billion. Inflation in Britain was at 15 per cent, which caused the economy to stall and go from boom to bust overnight. It became known as Black Wednesday.

Although shareholders were badly hit by the sudden recession, the population felt the shockwaves too because it triggered a collapse in the housing market. Mortgages became incredibly expensive with inflation so high, and a loss of confidence caused housing prices to plummet by 15–20 per cent.

The Conservatives had actively encouraged people to invest in property during the 1980s and many people had done so, despite the financial stretching this imposed. The collapse meant that many found themselves in negative equity – they owed more on their mortgages than their properties were worth. It was a disastrous situation for the common man. The knock-on effect of the recession was such that homeowners simply couldn't pay their mortgages or sell their homes, so repossession orders were issued left, right and centre. The only people to benefit were those just beginning to enter the housing market from 1993 onwards. They found themselves able to purchase property at very low prices just as the market began to re-inflate.

The Conservatives had the finger of blame pointed fairly and squarely at them for leading the nation towards the recession and luring so many into positions of vulnerability in the first place. Confidence in their government had been irreparably damaged and they duly lost the next general election when it came in 1997 – long overdue in many people's opinion. By the time Labour came to power under Tony Blair there had been a sea change in the mindset of the British nation. People felt a collective sense of shame about the superficiality and simple greed that had culminated in the events of 1992, and a more 'caring and sharing' ethos began to pervade Britain.

# 17 September

## Twins no longer joined at the hip

**1953** Carolyn Anne and Catherine Anne Mouton were conjoined twins, attached to each other at the lower spine. Twins joined in this way are scientifically described as pygopagus twins. They became the first such pair to be surgically separated and survive the operation. The twins were just two months old when the operation was performed at the Ochsner Foundation Hospital in New Orleans, USA. They were found to have connected intestines as well as a shared membrane in the lower spine. Surgery was not, therefore, a simple matter of cutting them apart. A team of fifteen doctors toiled for two hours and fifteen minutes to complete the procedure, which went without complication.

The term 'Siamese' was originally used in describing conjoined twins because the famous Bunker twins – Chang and Eng – actually came from Siam (now Thailand). They were born in 1811 and attracted the attention of the world when Robert Hunter, a British merchant, discovered and then exhibited them. It became politically incorrect to use the term in the late 20th century.

There are several forms of conjunction, because the developing embryos may remain fused in different ways. In many cases surgery is not an option, because too much tissue is shared and any attempt at separation would result in the death of one or both of the twins. However, as surgical technologies and techniques have improved, increasingly difficult operations have been attempted. It has even been possible to separate twins conjoined at the head, which would have resulted in certain death in the 1950s. The twins in question were Mohamed and Ahmed Ibrahim from Egypt. Their skulls were fused together at the crown, but they had separate brains. Reconstructive surgery saw them make a complete recovery following separation in 2003.

Conjoinment is recorded through history in the form of paintings and sculptures. In times before scientific understanding of genetics, conjoined twins were often regarded as divine curiosities. During the 19th century many conjoined twins were forced to make a living by appearing in freak shows. One pair, Millie and Christine McCoy, actually went further and had a successful career as singers. Their stage name was the 'Two-Headed Nightingale'.

# 18 September

## *The world's greatest guitarist is found dead*

**1970** Jimi Hendrix's singing voice could hardly be described as dulcet. In fact, he was encouraged to sing by listening to Bob Dylan, reckoning that if Dylan could get away with it, then so could he. But he could certainly play guitar. In fact, he could play guitar like no one else before or since. Playing left-handed on a right-handed instrument, Hendrix could also play with his teeth, behind his back, and between his legs. Sometimes he set fire to his guitar on stage for good measure. And a chord that he popularised, the 'Hendrix' or 'Purple Haze' chord, has entered the musical lexicon.

Hendrix's background was one of poverty and unemployment. His first instrument was a one-string ukulele that his father had found in a garage, but he soon graduated to a second-hand acoustic guitar. He learnt his trade as a backing musician playing the 'Chitlin circuit' of black music clubs all over the American South in the early 1960s. He developed his flamboyant stage style early on, having been taught how to play with his teeth by a childhood friend in Seattle, his home town. His showmanship sometimes hampered his career, as when he was dumped by Little Richard for playing too ostentatiously for a backing musician. He was also hopelessly unpunctual and slovenly, which turned out to be as much of a handicap in the world of music touring as it had been in the army, where he lasted little more than a year.

He moved to New York in 1964, settling in Harlem, and while playing at the Cheetah Club on West 21st Street in 1966 he was spotted by Linda Keith, girlfriend of Rolling Stones guitarist Keith Richards. After introducing him to the mind-bending 1960s drugs scene, she then brought him to the attention of Chas Chandler, a member of The Animals. Chandler was so impressed with Hendrix's unique style that he flew him to London and teamed him up with two British musicians to form the Jimi Hendrix Experience. They were Noel Redding on bass and Mitch Mitchell on drums.

Hendrix soon cemented a reputation as a virtuoso guitarist, earning instant respect from such established stars of the swinging Sixties as Eric Clapton and Paul McCartney. His fame, helped by his filmed appearances at the Monterey Pop Festival in 1968 and Woodstock in 1969, increased until his untimely death in 1970.

The details of Hendrix's death are uncertain, although he seems to have died from drowning in his own vomit, having consumed a cocktail of alcohol and prescription drugs. He was with a girl named Monika Dannemann that evening, but she apparently fled the scene in panic when he might have been resuscitated.

Within a few months, Janis Joplin and Jim Morrison had also succumbed to drugs, making with Jimi Hendrix a sad triumvirate of wasted lives.

# 19 September

## Ötzi the iceman rears his beautiful head

**1991** When Ötzi was found by a German couple hiking in the Alps, they thought he must have been an unfortunate mountain climber who had died and been frozen. In a way they were correct, but he turned out to be more than 5,000 years old and from the Copper Age or Chalcolithic period, which preceded the Bronze Age as part of the Neolithic period.

The location of his body was a glacier on the border between Austria and Italy. His remains had been frozen into the glacial ice by layers of falling snow and entombed, so that they travelled with the glacier until the ice reached a point where the summer sun was able to melt it. Helmut and Erika Simon found Ötzi in a state of thawing. His head and shoulders were protruding above the ice. They summoned help and the mummified body was crudely removed with ice axes, which caused some damage.

When the authorities realised that Ötzi was not a recently deceased modern man the scientific community got very excited by the find. A team returned to the site and undertook a detailed archaeological dig to rescue everything they could. They discovered that he had died with a complete Neolithic kit of clothing, weapons, tools and materials, and his body was so well preserved that they could even tell what he had for his last meal. Perhaps most valuable to the scientists was his copper axe, which would have been an important status symbol to Ötzi in life. Analysis of trace metals in his hair showed that he had probably made the axe himself by smelting copper ore.

All of the evidence suggested that he had lived locally as part of an Alpine Neolithic culture. The cause of death was uncertain but it initially seemed most likely that he had got caught in a blizzard above the tree line, perhaps while herding livestock or hunting. Then X-rays showed that he had an arrowhead imbedded in his shoulder, with the shaft broken away. He had evidently been shot deliberately or by accident, most likely the former.

Ötzi had eaten chamois and red deer meat before he died, along with some bread and sloes. He was about 45 years old and of small but muscular stature. Chemical analysis of his teeth showed that he had probably always lived within a range of 50 miles or so of where he died. Pollen grains of various plants showed that he had met his death in the springtime. The name 'Ötzi' is derived from the region in which he was found – the Ötzal Alps.

# 20 September

## France is cheered up with the first Cannes Film Festival

**1946** France had a pretty rough deal during the Second World War. It had been invaded by Germany in a matter of weeks and then suffered the indignity of being forced to sign an armistice with Hitler. Throughout the Nazi occupation of France, the famous French Resistance, with the help of the Allies, sought to oppose Hitler as far as they could.

As part of the post-war celebration it was decided that the first Cannes Film Festival should be held. The first one had actually been scheduled to take place in 1939, but the outbreak of the Second World War had forced plans to be put on hold. The idea behind the Cannes festival was that it should be a recognition of international filmmaking, in contrast to the Academy Awards in America which had started in 1929 and were largely about US movies. Prize-winning films came from the USSR, UK, US, Denmark, France, Italy, India, Mexico, Sweden, Switzerland and Czechoslovakia.

Louis Lumière agreed to be president of the first festival. Along with his brother Auguste, he had pioneered filmmaking in the 1890s. In fact they had made the first screening of their short films to a paying audience in 1895, thereby inventing cinema too. Amazingly the Lumière brothers saw no future in cinema and had turned their attentions to developing colour photography at the turn of the 20th century. In fairness, though, they were inventors rather than filmmakers, so they moved on to new things once they felt that their work was done.

The movie industry was originally a marriage of the technology invented by the Lumière brothers and the traditions of stage plays. Actors and actresses in early films used grand speech and gestures to express themselves just as they would in a theatre. Movie makers quickly realised, however, that it was possible to create scenes that the stage had previously left to the imagination. Thus, to shoot scenes 'on location', rather than on a conventional set, became a familiar part of the filmmaking process. At first filmmakers used established stories as their themes, but eventually they began to create their own and at this point the modern movie was ushered into being.

# 21 September

## The 'Hindu Milk Miracle' causes mass hysteria in India

**1995** On 21 September 1995, Hindus all across the world began to flock to temples amid reports that statues were miraculously drinking milk. The miracle is said to have began when an ordinary man, never identified, dreamt that Ganesh, the elephant-headed Hindu god of learning, wanted milk. Waking up, the man apparently rushed to the nearest temple and proffered a spoonful of milk to the statue of Ganesh. To the astonishment of the man and a watching priest, the milk vanished from the spoon, apparently magically drunk by the idol.

Within hours, news of the 'miracle' had spread across India and tens of millions of people of all ages began to flock to the temples to make their own milk offerings. Indian cities came to a standstill as worshippers queued up with milk in everything from waxed cartons to pottery jugs and glass tumblers, and Delhi's vast stocks of millions of litres of milk sold out completely in a matter of hours. Everywhere the story was the same. A teaspoonful of milk offered by touching it to Ganesh's trunk, tusks or mouth would disappear almost instantly.

The Indian Ministry of Science and Technology was called in to investigate. By adding a little food colouring to the milk in a teaspoon, they were able to show that as soon as the milk drained from the spoon, it spread down over the surface of the statue. They concluded that the 'miracle' was a simple effect of capillary action. Such a killjoy explanation did nothing to dampen the enthusiasm of devotees, however, and they continued to flock to the temples, or simply spoon-feed statues in their homes and cars.

Surprisingly, the miracle had stopped in India by the end of the day. It was reported that statues had started to refuse to take any more milk. By that time, though, the news had spread to the rest of the world, and Hindus from San Francisco to Leicester were reporting similar miracles – and having similar effects on milk sales. According to the *Sun* newspaper, which reported the story under the banner headline 'Cow do they do that?', the Gateway store in Southall, England sold 25,000 pints of milk in just a few hours. The *Sun* also reported that 'Even doubting outsiders, including hard-boiled newsmen, had to admit the statues DID seem to be drinking. And they were left wondering "How is it happening?"'

Within a few days, however, reports of milk-drinking statues stopped, and the fervour that greeted the first news of the miracle had evaporated. Nonetheless, *Hinduism Today* was still asserting years later that the milk miracle 'may go down in history as the most important event shared by Hindus this century, if not in the last millennium. It has brought an instantaneous religious revival among nearly one billion people'. Yet it is not just non-Hindus who remain sceptical about the whole event. Even *Hinduism Today* admits that there are many Hindus who prefer the scientific explanation of capillary action combined with mass hysteria. It has also been suggested that the unidentified dreamer who started the craze was a dubious mystic called Nemi Chand Jain or Chandraswami, who was trying to divert public attention away from criminal charges being levelled at him at the time for harbouring a murderer.

# 22 September

## *The Dead Sea Scrolls go on public display*

**1991** The story goes that a shepherd boy discovered the first of the Dead Sea Scrolls when he threw a stone in a cave to evict one of his sheep. The stone struck an earthenware pot, so the boy investigated and found the scrolls wrapped in linen inside the pot. To date, scrolls have been found in a total of eleven caves, which are cut into cliff faces and relatively inaccessible. In fact, about 1,000 documents exist in total. They are written in a number of languages and date from the first millennium. They contain biblical texts and other information relating to the burgeoning belief systems at that time in human history. Some of the scrolls are the oldest biblical texts known and were written before AD 100, so that Jesus would have been in the living memory of people at the time.

The reason why the scrolls were concealed in the caves was primarily persecution. The region was in flux in that era, so the devout felt that they had to document their belief systems and hide them for posterity. It worked, as the climate in Israel is rather dry so the scrolls were preserved from rotting away for the best part of 2,000 years. Nevertheless, many were found to be very fragile upon discovery and photographs taken of them at the time are now easier to read than the originals because the scrolls have deteriorated so much since.

Perhaps the most intriguing scroll is the Copper Scroll. All of the others were made with leather or papyrus, while the Copper Scroll is made from thin sheets of copper. It is not a religious document either. It contains details of treasures that were hidden in the region and made from gold and silver. The treasures were from a Jewish temple and were carefully concealed to prevent the enemies of the Jews from finding them, perhaps during the Babylonian Exile. However, the clues, that seem to be themselves hidden in the text, are open to interpretation and so far no one has had any success in finding the treasures, which may be worth over $1 billion.

# 23 September

## Redgrave wins a record fifth Olympic gold

**2000** When the British team held on to the gold medal position after an incredible late surge by the Italians in the coxless fours at the 2000 Sydney Olympics, Steve Redgrave, the veteran of the team, was quite overcome. Not only had he become the first ever to achieve gold in endurance events in five successive Olympics, but he had overcome an enormous personal setback to get there.

At the previous Olympics in Atlanta, Redgrave had established himself as the greatest rower of all time by winning the coxless pairs with Matthew Pinsent for the fourth time in as many attempts. But at already 34 years old, age was beginning to creep up on him. After Atlanta, he felt maybe he had done enough. 'Shoot me if you ever see me in a boat again', he famously declared. But he did get in a boat again, without being shot. However, soon after announcing that he was going to carry on competing through to the Millennium Games in Sydney, he received a crushing blow to his ambition.

In November 1997, Redgrave felt unusually thirsty after completing a training session and went to see a doctor. Blood tests revealed high blood sugar levels. It was clear that he had diabetes, and he has been taking insulin ever since. With that diagnosis, Redgrave felt his career was over, acknowledging that 'the little I knew about diabetes was that there were few sportspeople with the condition competing at the level I wanted to be at'. But his forward-thinking consultant told him, 'I don't see why you can't achieve whatever you want to achieve'. With a changed diet and carefully adjusted insulin support – and a healthy dose of determination – Redgrave threw himself back into training, and amazingly got himself back to the phenomenal level of fitness needed to bring home the fifth gold at Sydney.

Redgrave was used to battling. At school, he suffered the acute awkwardness of being dyslexic. As Redgrave says, 'I think it would be an oversimplification to say that it was dyslexia that inspired me to do better at sport', but there is no doubt that he became used to dealing with problems. When injury and failure had threatened to halt his career before it had started back in 1983 when he was just 21, he threw himself back into the fray with such vigour that the following year he led the British team to a stunning triumph in the coxed fours at the Los Angeles Olympics, coming out of the mist on Lake Casitas to drive past the Americans in an unforgettable moment. From then on, victory followed victory.

In 1987, Redgrave met Andy Holmes in a cafe in Putney, and the two agreed to race in a pair at Seoul in 1988, a partnership that brought Redgrave his second rowing gold. But Redgrave's greatest partnership was with Matthew Pinsent. The pair won a bronze in the World Championships in Tasmania in 1990, and never looked back. Throughout the 1990s, Redgrave and Pinsent won a World or Olympic title every year. The Olympic golds came in the coxed pairs in Barcelona (1992) and Atlanta (1996), and the coxless fours in Sydney (2000). World Championship victories arrived via coxless pair victories in 1991, 1993, 1994, 1995 and 1997 events, and coxless four victories in 1997, 1998 and 1999.

A giant of a man at over 6' 5" tall – big even for a rower – Redgrave is one of the world's greatest athletes, dominating his sport at the Olympics for sixteen years, a record only rivalled by the German kayaker Birgit Fischer. After the Sydney victory, Pinsent commented, 'He has made himself the greatest Olympian Britain has ever produced and arguably in the world – you can't get better than that. It is an inspiration to all of us'.

# 24 September

## Operation Majestic Twelve enters US folklore

**1947** The so called Roswell Incident of July 1947 led to a great deal of intrigue about the possibility of alien life forms having visited our planet. The idea of alien visitors in flying saucers is, of course, a little far-fetched. Nevertheless, those that wanted to believe *did* believe and so they ignored the more rational explanations that ranged from weather balloons to covert experiments by the US military. Indeed, the term UFO, which was invented around this time, could feasibly apply to terrestrial unidentified objects, rather than just alien spaceships as it is generally interpreted.

Majestic Twelve was an operation supposedly set up by Harry Truman, then US President, on this day in 1947 to investigate these apparent extraterrestrial contacts. Consisting of a group of just twelve individuals – hence the dramatic name – there are documents in existence that seem to provide details of this most secret of projects, although it is difficult to prove their veracity.

The first of these documents, now collectively known as the Majestic Documents, was leaked in 1984. They claim that 'the Majestic Twelve group ... was established by order of President Truman on 24 September, 1947, upon recommendation by Dr Vannevar Bush and Secretary of Defense James Forrestal'.

For the next thirteen years, until 1997, further documents totalling thousands of pages made their way into the public domain. Bound together, some of them form the 'Majestic Twelve Special Operations Manual'. Inside are all kinds of information regarding alien life forms, ranging from details of government cover-ups to the correct etiquette to use upon meeting an extra-terrestrial.

Despite anomalies in style and presentation, there are some, of course, who believe that the Majestic Twelve documents are completely authentic. They claim that the papers point to a wide-ranging conspiracy that involved high-profile names in both politics and science – Albert Einstein's signature appears in the documents.

There are those, however, who are rather more sceptical of the actual existence of the Majestic Twelve, but who nevertheless believe that there are links between the leaked documents and other verifiable government agencies. One such theory is that the Majestic Twelve may actually be associated with the highly secret NSC 5412/2 Special Group. Inaugurated by President Eisenhower in 1954, this agency has been confirmed by the authorities, although little else is known about it other than its name and its first chairman, one Gordon Gray. This same Gray is cited in the Majestic Twelve documents as being one of the group's alleged members.

A similar reasoning also links the Majestic Twelve to an alternative group – the CIA's Office of National Estimates (ONE), now the National Intelligence Council. Formed of twelve figures, the ONE was created by the director general of the CIA, Walter

Bedell Smith. According to the Majestic Twelve documents, Smith was supposedly grafted into the Majestic Twelve organisation after the death of Forrestal.

Many others – some ardent conspiracy theorists among them – are convinced that the Majestic Twelve documents are nothing more than an elaborate hoax. There have been no more leaks since 1997 and official investigations into their authenticity have repeatedly shown them to be fraudulent. The documents are even available on the FBI website, along with proof that they are false.

There is a final school of thought, however, that argues that even if the Majestic Twelve documents are real, it is likely that they are nothing more than a giant smokescreen. Leaked by the US military, they directed attention towards supposed alien spacecraft and created all sorts of false trails that disguised what was really going on at Roswell in 1947: secret military trials which had to be kept from the Russians at all costs. Of course, that in itself, while appealing to the rational mind, still requires a certain appetite for the delicious taste of conspiracy.

# *25 September*

## *Thirty-eight in a mass escape from the Maze prison in Ulster*

**1983** Today, the site where the Maze prison once stood, nine miles outside Belfast, is empty and abandoned. The prison itself was demolished in 2006 and the plans for the cleared site are mired in controversy. Several million pounds have been spent drawing up plans for Northern Ireland's national sports stadium to be built here, along with a conflict resolution centre. But a recent damning report on the financial viability of building a stadium so far from Belfast city centre seems likely to derail the project – especially as Unionists suggest that the conflict resolution centre could become a memorial to the Troubles.

Back in 1983, the Maze (formerly know as Long Kesh) was the

focus of the Troubles. Millions of pounds had been spent making this one of the most secure prisons in Europe, and its role in keeping captured Republican terrorists put it at the centre of the whirlwind. In 1981, the Maze had become the focus of worldwide attention when ten IRA prisoners in one of the prison's H-blocks, led by Bobby Sands, had starved themselves to death in a hunger strike for better conditions. With her characteristic stubbornness, Margaret Thatcher had given few concessions to the strikers, and the Republican movement became determined to get its own back.

Inside the Maze, everything went quiet for a while, convincing prison authorities that the prisoners had at last seen sense. In fact, they were busy laying meticulous plans for what was to be the biggest mass prison breakout in British history, an event still celebrated by Republicans today as the Great Escape.

After months of planning, led by men like Gerry Kelly and Brendan McFarlane, now deeply involved in the political peace process, the escape was launched on this day in 1983. Using six small 'ladies' automatic' handguns that had been smuggled into the prison, the prisoners first took over one of the prison's H-blocks, taking warders hostage. One who tried to resist was shot in the head by Kelly but survived.

When a food delivery lorry arrived outside the H-block, Kelly forced the driver at gunpoint to drive the lorry towards the prison gates with all the prisoners hidden in the back. Despite running into trouble on the way out, when one warder was stabbed and later died of a heart attack, 38 prisoners made it over the perimeter fence. They were supposed to be met by a fleet of trucks supplied by the IRA from over the border in southern Ireland, but due to a miscalculation the trucks had already left five minutes before the prisoners got out.

In the confusion, nineteen of the prisoners simply legged it across the fields and were recaptured within a day. The rest, though, hijacked cars and got away to the Republican stronghold of South Armagh. A few returned to active service with the IRA, but most went to the Republic of Ireland, to the USA or Holland, where they became the subject of long extradition procedures when they were finally captured. Only a few returned to the Maze, and Gerry Kelly was actively involved in the Good Friday Agreement of 2000 in which the Maze was closed and the prisoners released. Kelly is now deputy first minister in the Northern Ireland Assembly.

# *26 September*

## *Russian saves the world from a Third World War*

**1983** There can't be many people who know the name Stanislav Petrov, yet he single-handedly averted a nuclear Armageddon that would have been described as a Third World War. The application of the doctrine known as MAD (Mutually Assured Destruction) was such that the Soviet Union was primed to launch an immediate nuclear missile counterattack if its satellite warning system detected incoming weapons.

In 1983 Petrov was on duty when the warning system indicated that the US had launched an offensive. His intuition told him that such an attack was very unlikely, as recent relations between East and West had been reasonably cordial. He reasoned instead that the warning system must have been at fault. Petrov thus ignored the warning system and failed to set the wheels in motion for a counteroffensive to occur.

Despite his having effectively saved the world from a nuclear winter, Petrov was punished by the Soviet administration for disobeying orders. The Communist Party found itself facing what it saw as an awkward and potentially embarrassing situation. The event was duly swept under the carpet and Petrov was prevented from progressing with his military career on the grounds that he was an unreliable officer. He was eventually sidelined completely and ended up taking early retirement.

In 2004 he was finally given recognition for his actions and was presented with a World Citizen award. It is worth pointing out that having been ignored for so long, he should not necessarily be over-celebrated as he could not have prevented a nuclear war entirely on his own. In truth he failed to report the warning signal to his superiors, who would then have assessed the situation before deploying weapons. Nevertheless, they might well have opted to push the button, so we can certainly credit him with having averted the possibility of nuclear war.

The very fact that Petrov effectively saved the world is in itself a sobering thought. No matter what our ideological, political, cultural or religious differences, humanity has reached a point where conflict could be catastrophically self-defeating. We need to find a way to celebrate our differences rather than hate and fear them; it just remains to be seen whether we can learn to do so.

# 27 September

## Missions to the Moon begin again

**2003** It's a funny thing, but the term 'Space Age' has almost become a euphemism for that brief era when astronauts made visits to the Moon in the late 1960s and early 1970s. All of those intrepid explorers are now well beyond retirement and soon we'll be talking about the last living veterans to have set foot on the Moon, just as we talk of surviving combatants from the two world wars. It's almost as if Moon exploration was a complete waste of time and resources, serving only for the US to get one up on the USSR during the Cold War. Of course, that was essentially true. But at least the US showed that it could be done, just as Columbus had made it across the Atlantic to the Americas nearly 500 years earlier.

Now it is the turn of the next wave of explorers – those with ideas of pioneering settlements. In 2003 the first European mission to the Moon was launched. It was an unmanned probe named SMART-1, whose job it was to survey the Moon's surface in search of signs of water. Water is seen as an essential foundation for establishing Moon bases because it is needed to sustain life, but is impracticable to transport from Earth due to its density. As well as providing drinking water, $H_2O$ can also be used to manufacture oxygen for breathing.

The probe was propelled by an ion drive or ion thruster. Ion thrusters use jets of electrically accelerated ions as their propulsive force. It means that a small amount of fuel can create a relatively large amount of energy. In fact the SMART-1 probe covered a distance of 62 million miles and positioned itself in orbit with only thirteen gallons of liquid gas. Clearly ion thrusters are set to become the primary engines used in deep space exploration. The theory behind them was realised by physicist Hermann Oberth in 1929. The first working prototype was developed in 1959 and different types have been used on Earth-orbiting satellites. They have used xenon, bismuth and caesium as fuels so far, but interestingly hydrogen has been prototyped, which could be obtained as a by-product of oxygen production, as long as water does exist on the Moon.

# 28 September

## *The ferry* Estonia *sinks in the Baltic with the loss of 852 lives*

**1994** In March 1987 a cross-Channel ferry, the MS *Herald of Free Enterprise*, travelling from Zeebrugge, Belgium to Dover, England capsized because the bow door had not been closed properly, allowing water to flood the hull. Many passengers died, but a good proportion were also saved. 193 lost their lives, but the ferry came to rest on its side in shallow water enabling 345 to be saved.

On that occasion human error was to blame, but a similar tragedy that occurred in the Baltic was due to severe weather. The MS *Estonia* was sailing between Tallinn, Estonia and Stockholm, Sweden. A storm caused the bow door to open and the vessel sank within minutes. It was 1:30 am so the event occurred in total darkness. An incredible 852 men, women and children lost their lives.

Just 137 people were saved. They were among the ones lucky enough to be on deck when the ferry suddenly listed. It was all over in about 30 minutes.

Many who fell into the water died of drowning and hypothermia. The water was 10°C in late September, but it was still cold enough to drain vital warmth from those who failed to find lifeboats. Another vessel, the *Mariella*, arrived about twenty minutes after the *Estonia* went down and had difficulty rescuing the survivors due to the high seas. Only 92 bodies were recovered.

As the MS *Estonia* lay in deep water and had so many lost souls on board, it was decided that the best course of action was to declare the wreck an official burial ground. It was sealed up and buried in sand out of respect for the memory of the dead. An investigation showed that mechanical failure had been to blame for the tragedy. It called into question the safety of designing ships with bow doors, as they are an intrinsic point of vulnerability in any sea-going vessel. This fact lead to the meaning of the acronym RORO (roll on, roll off), used to describe the types of ferries involved, being cynically twisted to mean 'roll on, roll over' in allusion to the Zeebrugge and Baltic sinkings.

# 29 September

## Creutzfeldt-Jacob disease is linked to vCJD – Mad Cow Disease'

**1997** Before 1997 scientists knew that certain pathogenic diseases didn't fit the definitions of either bacteria or viruses. They postulated that there must be a nano-organism, smaller than a microorganism, which they dubbed a 'virino'.

Diseases such as scrapie and BSE (bovine spongiform encephalopathy) were clearly caused by something, although it was invisible under the microscope and very difficult to destroy. When humans began suffering from the human form of BSE, known as CJD (Creutzfeldt–Jakob Disease), scientific investigation stepped up a gear. This led to the discovery that the theoretical virinos were in fact protein particles with the ability to self-replicate and corrupt the normal functioning of nerve cells. They were identified by a team of scientists from the University of California in 1982, and given the new name prions, or proteinaceous infectious particles.

The most worrying thing about prions is that they are not organisms at all, nor are they even biological entities. In fact, they are not alive, which means that they cannot be killed. This is why scrapie-infected sheep and BSE-infected cattle have to be burned, as the prions remain intact within their neural cells after the death of the host. On this day in 1997, research was published indicating that this was how CJD had evolved. Prions from BSE-infected cattle entered human digestive systems in cooked meat. Thankfully it was discovered that most humans have a natural immunity to the development of CJD, even though they may be infected with the prion.

CJD in humans is a particularly nasty affliction. It is classed as a degenerative neurological disorder – effectively a disease of the brain – and essentially causes the brain to shut down. Symptoms generally begin with early-onset dementia, which then progresses to memory loss, altered personality and hallucinations. As the brain degenerates, the sufferer also experiences motor problems, which can be expressed as anything from jerky movements, to the inability to balance oneself, to uncomfortably rigid postures or seizures. Cows infected with BSE often lose the ability to stand up. In the end, the nerve cells in the brain all die off until the brain can no longer function and it shuts down, causing death. There is no cure for CJD and while it is very rare, it always ends up in this fashion – although the whole process can take anywhere from several weeks to several years.

Other than CJD, about a dozen diseases have been attributed to prions, including kuru, which is found in Papua New Guinea, and fatal familial insomnia (FFI), where the brain cannot enter a sleep state. FFI eventually results in death as the brain gradually fails to function normally. It is, however, an extremely rare disease and has so far been discovered in only 28 families worldwide.

Prions are the only known disease-causing agents that can be infectious (passed environmentally from one host organism to another), hereditary (passed from one host organism to another in their genes) and sporadic (spontaneously arising in host organisms).

# 30 September

*Hollywood legend James 'Too fast to live; too young to die' Dean is killed in a car crash*

**1955** James Dean is one of those figures who divide opinion. Was he a good actor, or was he just playing himself? He only made three films: *East of Eden*, *Rebel Without a Cause* and *Giant*. The first two were released in 1955, while the latter was released after his death in 1956. In fact he had finished filming *Giant* only the day before he died.

Whether Dean was a good actor or not, he certainly had star quality. He was photogenic and possessed what filmmakers describe as 'screen presence'. In addition, his short career coincided with an era in popular culture which saluted adolescence. In 1951 J.D. Salinger's novel, *The Catcher in the Rye*, had been published. It was the first book to delve into the psychology of the temperamental and disenfranchised teenager, which Dean somehow personified even though he was 24. The words 'teen' and 'teenager' had appeared in American English around that time and were first entered into *Webster's Dictionary* in 1961. Dean was thus one of the first teen idols. One might say that teenagers felt that he understood their burgeoning sense of isolation in ways that no other film star had done before.

The crash that killed James Dean was entirely the fault of the other driver. Dean was driving along a state highway when the driver of the other car came in the opposite direction and decided to turn. He moved into the path of Dean's car without seeing Dean approaching. There was a head-on collision and Dean was mortally wounded. His passenger and the other driver were injured, but survived.

Such was Dean's iconic status that his passenger was blamed by many fans for his death. Wolf Wütherich happened to be a racing mechanic for Porsche, so people presumed that he had encouraged Dean to drive too fast, which wasn't the case. Wütherich was so traumatised by the public reaction that he suffered from bouts of depression and attempted suicide on a number of occasions. He too died in a car crash in 1981. He drove into a building while intoxicated with alcohol, in what may have been a final, successful attempt to take his own life.

# 1 October

*Thalidomide is marketed as a cure for morning sickness*

**1957** Thalidomide was marketed as a sedative for the treatment of morning sickness in pregnant women. Initially it seemed to be a wonder drug, but then babies started to arrive with varying mental and physical abnormalities. Some 10,000 afflicted babies were born before the drug was withdrawn. It was found that thalidomide crossed the placental wall and impeded the normal growth of the foetus. The defects that came to typify the condition were deformed and vestigial limbs. What initially appeared to be a saviour for mothers became responsible for a generation of 'thalidomide children'.

Thalidomide was originally developed in Germany by the drugs company Chemie Grünenthal. Widespread adoption saw it go on sale in nearly 50 countries under a variety of names.

Although it wasn't made available to the public until 1957, thalidomide was stumbled upon in 1953 during research into cheap antibiotics. Prior to its subsequent launch, it was subjected to inadequate levels of testing. As a result, doctors who prescribed it did so in complete ignorance of its devastating side effects.

As a direct response to this, and to prevent anything similar ever happening again, in 1962 the US Congress passed a series of laws outlining specific rigorous tests that prospective drugs must pass in relation to pregnancy. Similar legislation followed in a number of other countries as well.

Since the withdrawal of thalidomide in the 1960s it has been discovered that the drug is useful in treating other, unrelated, health problems. It inhibits the development of MM (multiple myeloma) which is a cancer of plasma cells, and also works as a therapy for skin lesions caused by ENL (erythema nodosum leprosum) which is a type of leprosy. As the effects on developing offspring are well known, doctors try to police the use of the drug. In places like Africa this has proven difficult, however, and a new generation of thalidomide children has resulted. Thalidomide is also used in treating Crohn's disease, which is an inflammation of the bowel.

The classic effect of thalidomide on the foetus is termed phocomelia, which is the shortening or even absence of the long bones in the arms or legs. Despite the obvious crippling nature of this condition, some adults affected by thalidomide have gone on to forge remarkable careers. Briton Mat Fraser has successfully pursued everything from acting, to drumming in a rock band, to martial arts, and American Nicaraguan Tony Meléndez is a multi-award-winning guitarist – born with no arms, Meléndez remarkably plays his instrument with his feet.

# 2 October

## *The results of the first scientific study into cannabis are published in the US*

**1974** As the late 1960s drew to a close, smoking 'pot' had come to be the very epitome of hippy culture – the gentle stimulant that helped the already laid-back to recline even further. It was still an illegal drug, but for the first time in the 1960s more middle-class white people were convicted for its use than black people. By the early 1970s, it became as much an everyday part of university life as drinking, sex and the occasional lecture. When a coffee shop opened in Amsterdam selling pot with its pots of coffee, it seemed that cannabis was on the road to social acceptability, if not legality – no more outrageous than eating a few too many cream cakes.

Even the legal war on cannabis was relaxing. In 1972, the Shafer commission in the USA recommended the decriminalisation of marijuana for personal use. Although President Nixon rejected the recommendation, a number of individual states did decriminalise and most others reduced their penalties. All across the Western world, police began to take a far more lenient attitude to dope. So it may have come as something of shock when scientists began to wage war on the drug, with the release on 2 October 1974 of research that seemed to show that cannabis caused brain damage.

The research has since been discredited, but a campaign to point out the 'Perils of Pot' immediately began to gather momentum, and it was clear that those who opposed the loosening of attitudes to marijuana use had found a new tack – science that highlighted the dangers of the drug. Ever since, there has been continual and heated debate about the merits and dangers of the drug.

There are certainly many who believe taking marijuana is no more harmful than smoking tobacco – harmful, but not harmful enough to require legislation. A study by the British Lung Foundation found that smoking three cannabis joints a day causes the same damage as twenty cigarettes, but those who are pro-cannabis point out that most dope smokers only smoke, on average, one or two joints a day anyway.

More worrying for dope smokers are the constant links found by scientists between cannabis use, psychosis and schizophrenia. The statistical evidence for such links is convincing – but no one has yet been able to demonstrate a causal link, despite repeated efforts. Most researchers believe that cannabis smokers are 20–25 per cent more likely to be psychotic simply because many people with psychotic tendencies tend to smoke cannabis to alleviate their symptoms.

Meanwhile the argument continues on whether to legalise cannabis for medical uses, which it undoubtedly has, in the treatment of such ailments as multiple sclerosis, glaucoma and long-term pain. In 2005, Canada legalised the cannabis-based drug Sativex, while the Medical Research Council began conducting the first UK trials of cannabis for medicinal purposes. In the US, however, the Supreme Court ruled against users of cannabis for health reasons being exempted from prosecution. So the debate goes on, and politicians remain wary about admitting that they indulged in a little pot in their student days. Many, like Bill Clinton, apparently smoked it but didn't inhale.

# 3 October

## *Showman Roy Horn is nearly killed by a white tiger*

**2003** The tragedy of this story is that the tiger, named Montecore, was quite possibly not attacking Roy Horn when the near-fatal injuries resulted. It is suggested that had he been doing so, he would have certainly killed Horn.

Instead, it is argued that the tiger was protecting Horn, who had slipped on the stage. Treating him like one of its own cubs, Montecore reacted by picking him up by the neck. Being human, however, Horn's neck was not equipped with the loose, protective skin of a tiger cub and his throat was crushed by the bite of the tiger as a result.

The official report into the event, by the US Department of Agriculture, however, failed to support this conclusion. Nevertheless, while being rushed to hospital, Roy Horn's main concern was the fate not of himself, but of Montecore, and he apparently urged those involved, 'Don't harm the tiger'.

Horn was critically wounded and almost died of blood loss, which then caused a stroke. He has partially recovered following drastic surgery, which involved the removal of part of his cranium to relieve blood pressure. Intensive physiotherapy has enabled him to stand and walk again, but he will never be fully repaired. Needless to say, the Siegfried and Roy Show, which for so long was a highlight of the Las Vegas entertainment scene, has been cancelled indefinitely.

At the time of the incident, the show had been running for thirteen years and it was Roy Horn's 59th birthday. Both originally from Germany, Siegfried and Roy were hired by the then owner of the Mirage hotel and casino, Steve Wynn. From their Vegas base, their status soared, both in terms of fame and fortune. Their annual earnings from the Mirage were said to be nearly $60 million, and in the year 2000 they were ranked as the ninth-highest-paid celebrities in America. They have also been afforded the recognition of having a star on the famous Hollywood Walk of Fame.

These days, since the cancellation of the show in which they were the stars, Montecore and the other white tigers live in a special habitat within the Mirage complex. Now housed safely away from the casino-goers, it is incredible to think that during their shows, Siegfried and Roy used no safety barriers between their cats and the audience.

As well as affecting both the showmen and their tigers, the cancellation of the Siegfried and Roy Show has had a huge financial impact on the Mirage hotel. The *Las Vegas Advisor* points to the minimum loss of $45 million, which ticket sales to the performances brought in each year. On top of that, it has been suggested that the brand of the Mirage itself was damaged, and with so much competition around, this could have contributed to many more millions being lost in gambling revenues.

However, before one starts to fear that Montecore's actions may have caused an entire Las Vegas casino to crumble, it might be worth pointing out that the annual revenue of the Mirage – or the MGM Mirage as it is now called – amounts to somewhere between $7 and $8 billion.

# 4 October

## The concept of 'satnav' is realised

**1957** When the Soviets put their first *Sputnik* satellite in orbit, American scientists found that they could calculate its position by analysing the Doppler effect in its radio signals. The Doppler effect is when sound waves are compressed or stretched when the source is travelling towards or away from the point of reception. We can hear the Doppler effect in everyday life when a siren-carrying vehicle – police car, ambulance, fire engine – drives past. The pitch of the siren rises when it approaches and then drops as it gets further away.

The scientists reasoned that a satellite in a known position could be used to reverse the phenomenon. In other words, radio signals could be used to determine the location of a receiver on the surface of the planet. This was the origin of satellite navigation and GPS (global positioning systems). The first system used was called Transit and went operational in 1964. It was used by submarines, which operate in conditions where other navigational elements are largely absent.

The satellites that enable modern GPS are described as the GPS constellation. There are about 30 in orbit, forming a positioning matrix above the Earth. This ensures that any GPS device can detect radio signals wherever it happens to be in the world. Personal devices are commonly used in road vehicles, aeroplanes and boats. They can also be carried by hand so that people know exactly where they are while hiking and in other outdoor activities.

Although satnav has, these days, proved to be incredibly useful in a number of ways, it does have a few drawbacks of which van and lorry drivers are all too aware. Portable systems which choose the shortest route without regard for the size of the vehicle they are in have led them into all sorts of tricky situations. There have been reports of vehicles becoming stuck down narrow lanes and demolishing walls in the process of trying to negotiate tight corners.

For all these irate haulage drivers, satnav does have its light-hearted side as well. A nifty game called GeoCaching has become popular in recent years. It involves the use of satnav to locate treasure caches hidden in places all over the world. The idea is that the treasure seeker uses his or her satnav device to locate the first of a series of clues that will then lead them on to the treasure. Once found, the idea is that the successful seeker takes something from the cache and replaces it with something else, ready for the next seeker. New caches are declared on dedicated websites.

# 5 October

## The Guildford pub bombings

**1974** In the early 1970s the Troubles, as they were known, in Northern Ireland had reached a moment of extremely high tension and emotion. The infamous Bloody Sunday shootings of January 1972, where British troops had shot 26 civil rights protesters and killed fourteen, were still present in many minds.

Later that same year a temporary ceasefire was agreed between the British and the IRA. However, talks for a permanent peace agreement broke down when the IRA refused to consider a treaty without a full British withdrawal from Northern Ireland, and the British for their part flatly rejected such a measure. In an attempt to force the British hand, the IRA resolved to take their offensive onto British soil and attack not major political targets, but public houses where the blow would be felt more fully.

The two Guildford pubs singled out by the IRA for attack, the Horse and Groom and the Seven Stars, were both popular with army personnel. The bombs themselves, both six-pound gelignite devices, were manufactured in London by an active service unit of the IRA. In all, five people died in the blasts and a further 65 were seriously injured.

The bombs were exploded on the same evening, half an hour apart. The first target was the Horse and Groom. At 8:30 pm on a Saturday night, military servicemen and local residents were enjoying the atmosphere of the bustling pub when the bomb went off. All five casualties were victims of this initial attack. They included four off-duty soldiers from the Scots Guards and the Women's Royal Army Corps, as well as a plasterer, Paul Craig.

By the time the second bomb went off, at 9 o'clock, the Seven Stars had already been evacuated and while there were some resultant injuries, there were no further deaths.

After the attacks on the Guildford pubs, there were other attacks later in 1974 on similar venues. On 7 November, a bomb was detonated in the Kings Arms in Woolwich, London, killing two. Then on 21 November two bombs were set off in the Tavern in the Town and the Mulberry Bush, both in Birmingham. In this third incident, 21 people died and over 150 were injured.

The British had been rocked by the attacks and they were determined to bring the perpetrators to swift justice. In December 1974, the Guildford Four were arrested. They were three men, Gerry Conlon, Paul Hill and Patrick Armstrong, and one woman, Carole Richardson.

A year after the attacks, in October 1975, all four were sentenced to life imprisonment. In 1989, however, the conviction was reversed and they were all released. Paul Hill, who had also been convicted of the murder of a British soldier, Brian Shaw, subsequently saw that conviction quashed in 1994.

Doubts over the actual guilt of the Guildford Four had been raised earlier on and in 1987 the Home Office issued a memorandum indicating that they were unlikely to be those responsible for the attacks. The evidence that vindicated the dramatic turn of events surfaced two years later when notes were found relating to police interviews with Patrick Armstrong. These notes were shown to have been heavily edited by police hands in order to enhance the case against the suspects. Furthermore, material that weakened the case had been suppressed during the trial.

The story of the Guildford Four has since gone down in the record books as being one of the most significant miscarriages of justice and cases of wrongful imprisonment ever. It is a case made the more poignant by the fact that Gerry Conlon's father, Patrick 'Giuseppe' Conlon, died in prison having been convicted as a member of the Maguire Seven, another supposed IRA group involved in bomb production. Like those of the Guildford Four, however, the convictions against the Maguire Seven were overturned in the early 1990s having been discovered to be another miscarriage of justice. Unfortunately, unlike his son, Patrick Conlon never made it back to the outside world.

# 6 October

## Sadat is assassinated for his conviviality

**1981** Anwar Sadat was president of Egypt. He became a victim of his efforts to improve relations between Israel and his own nation. From 6–26 October 1973, Egypt was at war with Israel, as a part of the larger Arab–Israeli conflict. Egypt and Syria had launched a territorial offensive on Israel, but the Israeli army was too well equipped and well trained. In less than three weeks the Jews had countered the Arab attack and a ceasefire was brokered by the United Nations. Many Egyptians felt humiliated by the outcome of the war and Sadat bore the brunt of the blame.

Sadat had not always suffered such unpopularity with the Egyptian people. He had come to power in 1970 as the successor to President Nasser. Nasser was a powerful leader who had been responsible for, among other things, leading the 1952 Egyptian Revolution which ousted King Farouk I and the Egyptian royal family, and the hugely successful construction of the Suez Canal. The choice of Sadat to replace Nasser was seen in some corners as a move by the pro-Nasser elements in the army and government to continue the same policies and use Sadat as a kind of puppet.

In 1971, however, Sadat split from the wishes of the Nasserites by suing for peace with Israel. Both the Israelis and the United States – who were integral to the peace process – flatly rejected the terms upon which it was offered, and no agreement was reached.

Sadat then turned himself into a national hero by adopting a new aggressive stance towards Israel. In 1973, in conjunction with Syria, Egypt attacked Israel in what became known as the October War (also called the Yom Kippur War in Israel). The objective was to reclaim the Sinai Peninsula, which they had lost during the disastrous Six-Day War back in 1967. This unexpected offensive, and the successful capture of the territory, was greeted with jubilation back home and elsewhere in the Arab world.

Regardless of this development, Sadat continued to hold out hope for achieving a lasting peace with Israel. In 1977, therefore, he became the first Arab leader to make an official visit to Israel. The Egypt–Israel peace agreement followed and Egypt found itself expelled from the Arab League in 1979 as a result. By 1981 tensions between Sadat and his military officers were strained.

Strong displeasure was also expressed by strongly Islamist and nationalist sections of the Egyptian population. Civil unrest known as the 'Bread Riots' had erupted in January 1977. These were nominally in protest against the government's lifting of price controls on basic necessities, such as bread, but they also provided a platform for the Islamist movement to foment its ideological platform.

One group in particular, El-Jihad, that counted military officers among its ranks and operated cells within the army, planned to assassinate the president. In September 1981, having uncovered the rumours of a plot in February, Sadat ordered a highly controversial round-up of potential dissidents. There was no attempt to restrict arrests to members of El-Jihad though, and unrelated activists, as well as intellectuals, homosexuals, Nasserites and many others, found themselves imprisoned.

Despite the best attempts of the authorities, they were unable to collect everyone who opposed Sadat's presidency. The leader of one El-Jihad cell, Lieutenant Khaled Islamboudi, evaded capture and in October 1981 he led the successful assassination attempt on the president.

Sadat was attending a military victory parade when his assassins struck. They opened fire with assault rifles and lobbed grenades in front of an assembled crowd. Although there were clear military connections, a fatwa had been issued against Sadat, so the assassination wasn't technically a military *coup d'état*.

On 14 October 1981, Sadat's vice-president, Hosni Mubarak, succeeded him as leader. Under Mubarak, Egypt was readmitted to the Arab League in 1989.

# 7 October

## The 'dark side' of the Moon is illuminated

**1959** It just so happens that the Moon orbits the Earth at exactly the same rate that it rotates about its own axis. The consequence of this is that we always see the same portion of the Moon's surface. The portion that we don't see is often termed the 'dark side' although it is more correctly called the far side, as it receives just as much light from the sun. In fact, when we see a new moon, the other side would be a full moon and vice versa.

The first images of the far side of the Moon were taken by the Soviet space probe *Luna 3*. It took a total of 29 photographs of the far side, but only seventeen were transmitted back to Earth. Their quality was very poor, but it was nevertheless the first time we had set eyes on this surface.

Intriguingly, the two hemispheres of the Moon are remarkably different. The one facing the Earth that we are used to seeing is characterised by numerous large lunar *maria*. *Maria* is the Latin term for 'seas' and reflects the fact that early lunar observers wrongly took certain features to be expanses of water on the Moon's surface.

The side hidden to us, by comparison, has relatively few of these seas. Instead, its terrain is pitted with impact craters caused by objects and debris speeding through space. In fact, our Moon boasts the South Pole-Aitken basin – the largest known impact crater in the whole of the solar system. This enormous dent in the Moon's surface is an astonishing 2,500 km in diameter, and in some places thirteen kilometres deep.

The information sent back to Earth by *Luna 3* was eagerly received by the renowned USSR Academy of Sciences. In November 1960, after careful analysis, they published the first atlas of the Moon's unseen face. This was followed up in 1961 by the production of a globe showing all the Moon's identifiable features, including those revealed by *Luna 3*.

Further exploration of the dark side was undertaken in 1965 by a second Soviet probe, *Zond 3*. In July of that year, the probe sent back 25 pictures of a much higher quality than the *Luna 3* ones. This new information allowed for the publication of a revised atlas in 1967. Whereas the original atlas had identified 500 lunar features on the far side, this new edition included 4,000. A new globe also followed in the same year.

A year later, and nine years after *Luna 3* transmitted its first historic photographs, human eyes were laid directly upon the far side of the Moon during the *Apollo 8* mission. William Anders, an American astronaut on board the spacecraft, described what he saw as 'like a sand pile my kids have played in for some time. It's all beat up, no definition, just a lot of bumps and holes'.

# 8 October

## *Che Guevara is captured*

**1967** Nowadays Ernesto 'Che' Guevara is familiar as the iconic face staring out of hundreds of posters, t-shirts and badges. To many he is righteous rebellion personified, and his place in history is reinforced by the romantic place he occupies in people's imaginations. There was little that was righteous or romantic, though, about his capture at the hands of US forces.

Che Guevara was an Argentine revolutionary with a strong Marxist political ideology. During his youth he had travelled throughout Latin America. The hardship he had come across, the poverty and deprivation of the peoples and the corruption of the officials profoundly affected him. As far as he could see, the strife that cut his continent deep was the result of the imperialist and capitalist dogmas championed by the United States.

Determined to do something about it, he met Fidel Castro in Mexico in the 1950s and joined him on his mission to depose the US-backed Cuban dictator Fulgencio Batista. In 1959, Castro's 26th of July Movement successfully overthrew Batista and assumed control of Cuba. Guevara duly adopted a role within the new Cuban administration, holding a number of important positions over the forthcoming years.

In 1965, Che left Cuba to continue his revolutionary work elsewhere. First he unsuccessfully attempted to incite rebellion in Congo-Kinshasa (now the Democratic Republic of Congo) in central Africa. Then in 1967 he returned to Latin America to further the revolutionary cause in Bolivia.

At this time, as a prominent part of the Cuban communist movement and a proven Marxist revolutionary, Guevara was a wanted figure within the US administration. The CIA had for years unsuccessfully tried to uncover his whereabouts. Then, in October 1967, a CIA team reportedly led by Félix Rodríguez tracked Guevara down to a guerrilla camp in the Yuro ravine.

On 8 October, the Bolivian special forces had surrounded Che Guevara's position and a gunfight broke out. Guevara himself was hit twice and, wounded, he emerged from his hiding place shouting 'Do not shoot! I am Che Guevara and worth more to you alive than dead'.

Rodríguez duly took him prisoner. However, if Guevara hoped that his status afforded him some kind of bargaining power, the CIA man thought very differently. The following day, Che was tied up and taken to a disused school in the nearby village of La Higuera. There he was shot by one of the Bolivian soldiers. His supposed response, when asked if he was hoping for immortality for himself, was to respond with his final words: 'No, I'm thinking about the immortality of the revolution.'

Following his death, his body was displayed and steps were taken to prove his identity. After that, his remains were buried in an unknown location and remained there for nearly 30 years until they were discovered by his biographer, Jon Lee Anderson. His body, along with those of six other revolutionaries, is now housed within a magnificent white mausoleum in the Cuban city of Santa Clara.

# 9 October

## Meteorite punches hole through car

**1992** Michelle Knapp heard a crash outside and went to investigate. She discovered that her Chevrolet car had a hole clean through it. Beneath the car she found a hot piece of rock that had fallen from the sky. It was part of a meteor that had exploded over the eastern US and scattered its debris. Her car was parked on her drive in Peekskill, New York.

As far as anyone knows, no one has yet been killed by a meteorite in recorded history. Thousands fall on Earth every year, but they seldom cause any harm. There are two cases of people being indirectly hit by meteorites that have ricocheted off other objects. In 1954, Ann Hodges of Alabama, USA, was bruised by a meteorite that punched through the roof of her house and bounced off a piece of furniture. In 1994, José Martin was driving near Madrid, Spain, when a meteorite plunged through the windscreen. It bounced off the steering wheel, breaking his finger in the process.

It seems likely that people have been struck and even killed by meteorites in other places on Earth, but they haven't been reported, perhaps because the cause of injury or death wasn't realised at the time. In densely populated countries like India and China the odds have to be far higher than in the USA and Europe.

Of course, it is fairly well documented that large meteorites have been responsible for mass extinctions in prehistory. Large strikes have caused temporary climatic changes that have wiped out whole groups of organisms, such as the dinosaurs, and consequently completely shifted the evolutionary direction of life on our planet. One only needs to see the craters in the surface of the Moon to appreciate how many large meteorites must have hit Earth over the years.

The meteorite that is held responsible for the demise of the dinosaurs struck the Earth around the Gulf of Mexico. It was several miles across and geological evidence suggests that it filled the atmosphere with dust for months. This would have been sufficient to kill off the world's forests, due to lack of sunlight. As a consequence of this, the large herbivores would have died from starvation with the large carnivores following suit. By the time the dust cleared only smaller species had managed to eke out a living, and the stage was set for the age of mammals and birds.

# 10 October

## The world's highest road bridge is begun

**2001** Not only is the Millau Viaduct a magnificent feat of engineering, but it is also an elegant and beautiful piece of architecture. Were it not for the fact that its purpose is to carry vehicles, it might be viewed as a colossal sculpture. This is especially so when the Tarn valley in the south of France is filled with mist, so that the pylons vanish from view and the bridge appears to float in midair.

Until 2004, when the viaduct was opened for business, vehicles had to travel through the valley and across a bridge in the town of Millau. It was a notorious bottleneck for holidaymakers travelling north and south, with enormous queues of traffic waiting to squeeze their way through the beleaguered town. It was so bad that many preferred to drive hundreds of miles out of their way to avoid the frustration.

The viaduct comprises nine sections of steel roadway, held aloft by seven pylons. The sections don't sit on the pylons but are instead suspended from cables radiating from the tops of the pylons. In effect, each section is a separate suspension bridge. The tallest pylon is 340 metres (1,115 feet), taller than the Eiffel Tower in Paris. The roadway is lined with high, overhanging fencing to prevent people from using the bridge to commit suicide, or otherwise using it for extreme sports such as base jumping.

Although Millau is no longer subjected to invasions of cars en route to and from holidays, it has experienced a new lease of life as many more people now visit the town to stay and admire the viaduct. In fact, it has built a number of new hotels to accommodate the unpredicted influx of sightseers. Of course, the town is also more attractive in its own right now that the streets are not filled with the fumes of idling automobiles.

Perhaps surprisingly, the Millau Viaduct is yet to be included among the 'Wonders of the World'. In July 2007 the 'New Seven Wonders of the World' were identified as follows: Chichen Itza (Mexico), Christ the Redeemer (Brazil), Colosseum (Italy), Great Wall (China), Machu Picchu (Peru), Petra (Jordan) and Taj Mahal (India). One day, surely, Millau will take its place alongside them.

# 11 October

### *The Tudor flagship,* Mary Rose, *is raised from the seabed*

**1982** In the 16th century, during the reign of Henry VIII, sea-going vessels were built intuitively, rather than using any precise mathematical understanding of physics. By and large it worked, but occasionally shipwrights took things too far. That is what happened to the *Mary Rose*, the flagship of the English navy. It had been adapted to carry additional guns and men in 1536 and that proved the vessel's undoing. With so much weight above water, the ship was top-heavy and wildly unstable.

On 15 July 1545, during an engagement with the French fleet, the *Mary Rose* turned sharply and capsized in the Solent, a stretch of water between the Isle of Wight and the southern English coast. The *Mary Rose* had been in active service since 1510 and was used extensively in defending England against potential invasions.

As the ship had rested on her side following her sinking, a good deal of the superstructure was protected from decay by the mud of the seabed. The wooden remains were brought to the surface and carefully preserved as an exhibit in a dedicated museum. Along with the ship itself, marine archaeologists recovered tens of thousands of artefacts that were originally on board. They included weapons, tools, utensils, cutlery, crockery, musical instruments and the remains of crew members. All in all, the wreck provided an interesting insight into the lives of sailors during that period in

English history. A new, purpose-built *Mary Rose* Museum is due to open in 2012.

Investigation with models of the *Mary Rose* has suggested that as she turned for the final time, she listed too far as a combined result of top-heaviness and windy conditions. Her lower gun ports were pushed below the waterline and took on water before she could right herself. Most people on board drowned as they were trapped below decks. In addition, most sailors couldn't swim anyway so only a few above decks were able to save themselves. She had over 400 souls on board when she went below the waves. Although the *Mary Rose* was the flagship of the fleet, there was a far larger and more powerful ship in its ranks, the *Henry Grâce à Dieu* (*Henry Grace of God*). She could carry up to 1,000 men.

# *12 October*

## *Six billion and still counting*

**1999** On Tuesday 12 October 1999, just as the second millennium was coming to a close, the world's six-billionth inhabitant was born. It was a remarkable landmark, revealing the astonishing explosion in the world's population in the 20th century – which was achieved despite two world wars, and famines in both China and Africa that claimed the lives of tens of millions of people.

During the 19th century, the world's population had doubled from well under a billion to 1.65 billion in 1900, reflecting the mushrooming of cities in Europe and America as the Industrial Revolution brought massive urbanisation. Yet that huge rise was nothing compared with the explosive growth of the 20th century, especially during the second half. In 1927, the world's population reached 2 billion. But by 1961, it had reached 3 billion and another billion were added every twelve years or so until reaching six billion in 1999. In June 2008, there were about 6.7 billion people alive, and most experts believe that we will hit the 7 billion mark by 2011.

Back in 1968, when the population boom was just beginning to be felt, Paul R. Ehrlich wrote the bestselling book *The Population Bomb*, in which he predicted disaster as the world's resources were stretched beyond their capacity by the ever-growing population. But there are now more than twice as many people scattered across the surface of the globe.

One reason Ehrlich's anticipated calamity has not yet come upon us is that there has been a revolution in agriculture which has dramatically boosted the world's food output. So although over a billion people suffer from lack of food, the problem is how the world's food is shared, not the total quantity. Another reason is that population growth has gradually slowed.

The developed world was already beginning to see population growth slow down or even stop altogether as families got smaller. What was less expected was how growth slowed in other places, too. Sometimes, this was as a direct result of a deliberate policy, such as in China where the compulsory 'one child per family' rule has dramatically curtailed population growth. Sometimes, though, it has simply come through the education of women about the possibility of contraception. In Africa, tragically, growth has slowed, uniquely in the world, because of rising mortality due to Aids, rather than declining birth rates. The result is that projections for population growth were, until quite recently, being constantly revised downwards. The UN now estimate that the world's population will peak at around 9 billion in 40 years' time and thereafter decline.

Interestingly, current population growth has coincided with a reduced birth rate in most countries. This is because of increasing life expectancy. Consequently, while there are more of us, the world's population is becoming older. In Europe, one in five people are already over 60.

At the same time, the spectre of the population bomb has not entirely vanished. The growth rate in places like Afghanistan has not slowed as much as expected, and the UN is now beginning to revise its projections upward again. Moreover, a global food and energy crisis is beginning to reveal that the world's resources are already stretched. It seems likely that before long, people will begin to talk once more about the problem of the sheer number of people in the world.

# 13 October

## *The world's deadliest disease is given its name*

**1976** Ebola is one of those diseases surrounded by myth in the Western world, because it originates in deepest Africa. It also happens to be a particularly nasty pathogen, as it causes haemorrhaging from areas where the skin is delicate, such as the eyes, nose, mouth and anus. The reason for this is that the virus has a filamentous or worm-like morphology. Consequently, it ruptures the cells in which it grows, causing widespread bleeding in the victim. Of course, the haemorrhaging occurs throughout the body internally, which is why Ebola is such a killer. By the time the body has found a way of combating the virus, it is too late, as the patient's body has broken down to such an extent that it can no longer sustain life.

Ebola has had a number of outbreaks and become famous for having a 90 per cent mortality rate. Thankfully it seems to require specific conditions to cause an epidemic, so it has remained localised so far. Nevertheless, there is always concern that a new strain of the virus might evolve with pandemic capabilities. In fact, it has been postulated that some of the historical plagues may have been caused by an Ebola-type virus. This is because the evidence suggests that transmission of the plague in some places cannot have been due to contact with conventional carriers (i.e. rats and fleas) as symptoms arose too rapidly. Ebola is highly contagious because of the haemorrhaging, which contaminates others with blood and bodily fluids containing the virus. Coughing, sneezing and vomiting can all cause micro-particles to travel through the air, so that they land on new victims or are inhaled. Most new infections, however, come from physical contact where the virus may be ingested or rubbed into the eyes.

One of the big mysteries about Ebola is that the natural reservoir for the virus has not been identified. Scientific investigations have aimed to locate a carrier species, but no one has yet discovered where the virus comes from. It seems that the most likely candidates are bats, as they often roost in the buildings where outbreaks occur and are known to be susceptible to Ebola infection. A disease capable of jumping from animals to humans is called a zoonotic disease.

# 14 October

*Chuck Yeager becomes first man to travel at the speed of sound and Jim Hines becomes the first person to break the ten-second barrier for 100 metres*

**1947 and 1968** To run 100 metres in ten seconds requires an average speed of ten metres per second, which is 36 kph (22.5 mph). In fact the top speed required is nearly 43 kph (27 mph), as the 100 metres has a standing start. Apart from falling, that is the fastest a person can travel without mechanical assistance. Ever since 1968, athletes have continued to shave off fractions of a second from the 100 metres record, so that it now stands at 9.69 seconds. It seems increasingly doubtful whether anyone will improve on that time as each new record over the decades has become ever more difficult to beat.

When people first travelled on locomotives some thought that the air pressure might kill them. Just imagine, therefore, what people must have thought when Chuck Yeager broke the sound barrier, which is about 1,230 kph (768 mph). Beyond this speed, sound waves coming from the vehicles cannot escape forwards and they build up as a funnel-shaped wall of energy as a result. A sonic boom occurs when the vehicle bursts this energy field.

As a unit of velocity, the speed of sound is referred to as Mach 1 and aircraft speeds are duly measured in Machs. When supersonic aircraft are approaching Mach 1 they go through a transitional phase, described as transonic flight. At this point a cone-shaped cloud of water vapour will often surround the vehicle. A sudden drop in the air pressure immediately around the aeroplane causes vapour to condense and become visible. The phenomenon that causes it is known as the Prandtl–Glauert singularity.

When objects, including people, fall from a great height they reach a terminal velocity. This means that they reach a speed at which they cannot go faster due to wind resistance. In fact, they are always decelerating very slightly because the air molecules become more dense towards sea level and create more resistance as a result. In a spread-eagle position, skydivers reach a terminal velocity of about 120 mph (190 kph), but they can increase this by adopting a head-first posture, so that wind resistance is minimised. Parachutes have the opposite effect, by increasing wind resistance and allowing the parachutist to land safely.

# 15 October

## Hermann Goering manages to poison himself with a cyanide capsule

**1946** Hermann Goering had been a flying ace in the First World War. Although he was a Nazi, he was more of a traditional military officer than others under Hitler's command. In fact, he quite fancied himself as Führer and attempted to assume that role when he realised that Hitler had lost control of his nation in the last days of the European campaign during the Second World War. As it turned out, Hitler objected to this idea so much that he appointed Karl Dönitz as his successor.

During the Nuremberg trials, Goering was increasingly frustrated by his portrayal as a war criminal. He didn't feel that it was fair to include him as a true Nazi in the context of having had anything to do with the Holocaust. Footage taken at concentration camps seemed to genuinely shock him when it was screened during the trials, but he began to acknowledge that being a high-ranking Nazi officer meant a burden of responsibility, whether he had had any direct involvement or not.

It seems that he managed to trick those guarding him, so that he was able to acquire a cyanide capsule from his own store of belongings. The day before he was due to be executed by hanging he bit into the capsule and ended his own life. He was determined that he would die on his own terms and he duly succeeded.

The capsule used by Goering contained hydrogen cyanide, an incredibly unpleasant poison that was used by the Nazis in their extermination camps. It is a very fast-acting toxin and nothing can be done once it has been introduced to the body. It prevents aerobic respiration so that the central nervous system and heart are quickly starved of oxygen, leading to death.

Hydrogen cyanide is a naturally occurring compound found in some plants. For example, the leaves of cherry laurel give off its distinctive almond-like aroma when crushed. In fact, entomologists once used crushed laurel leaves in their jars to kill insects without damaging them. Although the dose is sufficient to overcome insects, it is not harmful to humans.

# 16 October

## The heaviest man-made element is discovered

**2006** It may seem odd to use the word 'discovered' when describing something that has been artificially and intentionally manufactured by scientists. The word 'invented' might seem more appropriate, but the idea is that scientific phenomena *can* exist naturally at least somewhere and at some time in the universe, so the fact that some don't on Earth is neither here nor there. Thus it was that element 118 was discovered by a team of scientists from America and Russia. What is more, it only existed for 0.001 seconds before decaying.

The atoms of super-heavy radioactive elements are extremely unstable, so they spontaneously decay to become atoms of other elements in an effort to stabilise themselves. This is why they don't exist in nature, or at least in the nature of our planet. If they ever were created, they have long since decayed into stable elements.

When radioactive decay occurs, the element typically double-steps down the periodic table, so that element 118 becomes 116 and so on. This is how scientists verify their ephemeral discoveries, by tracing the path of decay. So far only three 118 atoms have been produced.

Element 118 has been given the temporary name 'ununoctium', although it has also been dubbed 'eka-radon'. This is because it is a noble gas, along with helium, neon, argon, krypton, xenon and radon. Various permanent names have been suggested now that it officially exists. New elements are traditionally named after places associated with their discovery, or physicists who are no longer living.

It goes without saying that element 118 has no practical use, but then nor do any of the elements above plutonium, which is element 94. The purpose of creating the 24 elements above plutonium has really been to further scientific knowledge, primarily because this informs scientists about the way the universe works and how it was created in the first place. The fascinating thing is that all atoms are constructed out of different combinations of protons, neutrons and electrons, regardless of the type of element they represent.

Protons have a positive charge, electrons have a negative charge and neutrons have a neutral charge, or no charge at all. As opposite charges attract it means that the electrons of an atom are attracted by the protons in the nucleus and vice versa. But, it also means that electrons are repelled by other electrons and protons are also repelled by each other. It is this instability in electrons that enables elements to chemically combine and form compounds. In the case of protons there is a force called the strong nuclear force which holds them together, even though their electrical charge tries to force them apart. It is this force that unleashes so much energy when it is broken during a nuclear explosion. Radioactive decay is when the nuclei of atoms partially disintegrate to form other elements. The radiation emitted is the energy released during this process.

# 17 October

## The world's tallest building is completed

**2003** Far below, in the crowded streets of Taipei, Taiwan's capital, people gazed skywards at the huge and gleaming edifice towering far above them. They were watching the final stages of the completion of the Taipei 101, so called due to its 101 inhabitable floors. With its inverted step sides, the Taipei 101 looked rather like a glass version of an ancient Chinese pagoda, but it had just become, on 17 October 2003, the world's tallest building – at 509 metres – taking the crown from Kuala Lumpur's twin Petronas Towers.

For almost half a century after it was completed in the early 1930s, New York's Empire State Building held the honour, at 381 metres high, and there was only one other building over 250 metres tall, the Chrysler, also in New York. In the 1970s, the Empire State was finally overtaken by Chicago's Sears Tower. All the world's tallest buildings, however, remained in the American homes of the skyscraper, New York and Chicago. Then suddenly, in the 1990s, all that changed.

In the early 1990s, incredibly tall buildings began to spring up in cities all around the world, made of gleaming steel, glass and concrete. There are now over 100 skyscrapers that top 250 metres. New York and Chicago have their share of these mighty new constructions, with towers like the *New York Times* building, completed in 2007 and standing at 319 metres. Yet many more have gone up in the Middle East, in Dubai and Bahrain and, especially, in south-east Asia. Hong Kong alone has eight buildings over 250 metres tall, as many as New York, while Shanghai has seven. What's more, eleven of the very tallest twenty buildings in the world are in China. Three of the rest are in Dubai, three in Chicago, and just one, the Empire State, in New York. The final members of the top twenty are the twin Petronas Towers in Kuala Lumpur in Malaysia, which overtook the Sears as the world's tallest in 1998, reaching 452 metres.

The Petronas's reign at the top, however, lasted just five years as it was overtaken by the Taipei 101. And then the Taipei 101 was itself overtaken in late 2007 by the staggeringly tall 167-floor Burj Dubai in Dubai, which is still under construction. It is thought that the Burj Dubai will be completed sometime around the end of 2009, but the developers are being cagey about just how tall it will be. Some people say 800 metres; some even suggest 900 metres. Yet despite this, there are further rumours afoot that elsewhere in the United Arab Emirates the first building to soar to over a kilometre in height will be started in the next few years.

Building towers this high has required a quiet revolution in construction technology, since skyscrapers 400 metres tall have to withstand wind forces 50 times as strong as buildings just 60 or 70 metres tall do. Earlier, less extreme skyscrapers were built around a stiff backbone of steel and concrete that ran up through the centre to provide the building's strength. The inner core was used as an elevator shaft, while the floors were cantilevered off the core, allowing for plenty of open, airy spaces. But above a certain height, this design becomes unstable and top-heavy. So the new skyscrapers all move the columns and beams of the building away from the core to the perimeter, creating a hollow, rigid tube. Despite this, the monster buildings of today are built with much the same materials as ever, and it is perhaps the computer development and testing of designs that has really enabled architects to climb so far into the heavens.

There is always some dispute over what constitutes a building that can be considered the world's tallest. Most agree that spires and flagpoles don't count, and many also argue that observation and communications towers don't count either, because they don't have habitable living space. The proposed Freedom Tower in New York, the replacement for the destroyed World Trade Center, would have risen higher than the Taipei 101 before redesign work, but much of that would have been a spire.

# *18 October*

## *The first transistor radio is launched*

**1954** Prior to the inclusion of transistors in electronic devices, valves (vacuum tubes) were used as the components of amplification and switching. They were large items, rather like light bulbs, making electronic devices cumbersome goods. The new transistors were made from solid chips of semiconductive material, making them far smaller and more robust. They paved the way for hand-held and personal electronic devices and gadgets.

The first transistor radio was manufactured in the USA by Texas Instruments. As well as being relatively small, it didn't require filaments to heat up, which meant that it could be used instantly. Also, it didn't need nearly so much electrical energy, so a battery could be used to power it.

Despite the advances in microelectronic devices, transistor radios are still very popular today. It is reckoned that there may be one for every person on the planet – around 7 billion. As they are so compact and robust, they last a long time before they stop working. One only needs to see a typical builder's radio to see what kind of abuse they can cope with and still continue operating perfectly well. This is largely due to the fact that they have virtually no moving parts. Only the tuner and volume dials need to turn, and the on/off switch is usually incorporated into the latter. It seems fair to say that most transistor radios are thrown away only because they look shabby and not because they have stopped doing their job.

In Africa the transistor radio has taken on a new lease of life in the form of the wind-up or clockwork radio. In poverty-stricken places where there is little or no infrastructure, people cannot rely on batteries, let alone mains electricity, so radios that provide their own power are ideal. They use a magnet to convert kinetic energy into electrical energy, so that the user simply winds a handle. Without these radios it would be very difficult for governments to inform their scattered populations of important things such as elections, medical advice and weather forecasts. In this respect, the transistor radio is to the developing world what the internet has become to the developed world.

# 19 October

## A Frenchman decides to cross the Atlantic with no provisions

**1952** Alain Bombard was a French biologist who wanted to show that it was possible to endure long periods at sea, surviving only on the resources of the ocean. He sailed from Tangier, Morocco to Barbados. When he arrived at his destination he had lost a couple of stone in weight and was hospitalised for a while due to dehydration and high salt levels. In an attempt to simulate being set adrift after a shipwreck, he had taken virtually no supplies with him. He reported that he ate fish and drank small quantities of seawater for the five-week journey. Subsequent research has suggested that he may have 'cheated' to a certain extent, by drinking rainwater and consuming more supplies than he admitted to.

A genuine story, which replicates Bombard's journey, is that of American sailor Steven Callahan. He set off from the Canary Islands, off north-west Africa, on his way to Antigua in the West Indies. His boat was wrecked by a storm and he found himself adrift in a rubber life-raft for 76 days in 1982. He managed to catch fish and seabirds for food. He also collected rainwater and distilled freshwater from seawater. He was eventually rescued near the island of Marie Galante in Guadeloupe, in the Caribbean.

Following his ordeal he wrote a book describing his survival story titled *Adrift: 76 Days Lost at Sea*. Callahan suffered from similar medical complaints to Bombard and was also hospitalised until his vital functions had restored their equilibrium. Excess sodium was the biggest threat to his life. Callahan subsequently invented a new type of life-raft, called the 'Clam', as a result of what he had learnt at sea. It has a rigid-bottomed, folding design, as he found that inflatable craft are inadequate vessels which are susceptible to both shark attacks and general wear and tear. In essence it is a capsule that protects people from the elements and is equipped with a sail.

One of the most famous cases of survival at sea was that of William Bligh, captain of the *Bounty*. A mutiny aboard the vessel resulted in Bligh being set adrift in a landing boat with eighteen other crew members. The men survived a 47-day ordeal thanks to Bligh's skills as a navigator. They travelled over 4,000 miles (6,700 km) in an open launch with very little to preserve them, yet only five men succumbed to the ravages that they had experienced.

# *20 October*

## *The famous footage of Bigfoot or the Sasquatch is made*

**1967** If that piece of footage were revealed to the press today, it would be laughed off as a hoax without delay. For some reason people were much more gullible in those days. It was the era of the cine camera and stories about other fantastical phenomena, such as alien visitations. It was the perfect combination for playing on the imagination of a society that had a desire to believe in such things.

Anyone with a modicum of common sense could see from the footage that it was a man wearing a fur suit, simply by the gestures and movements. It is also clear to see how easily it could be done: get someone to dress up and make a home movie. Yet people persisted in believing the footage to be a 'real' Bigfoot or Sasquatch for decades until the truth finally emerged. It turned out that a man called Patterson had decided to pull the stunt as a practical joke on a friend named Gimlin. A third, unknown actor wore the suit and waited until Patterson and Gimlin arrived at the location. Because Gimlin was the victim of the prank, he thought the Bigfoot was genuine, which lent the story an air of authenticity when the footage was revealed to the media.

Quite apart from the obvious technical ease with which such a hoax can be set up, there is the question of the ecology of such a supposed creature. The same goes for other legendary creatures, such as the yeti and the Loch Ness monster. In other words, a viable population of animals the size of humans, or larger, would be pretty conspicuous, even if they were behaviourally inclined to hide themselves away.

The largest animal to be added to the scientific list of species recently was a type of deer that happens to live in very dense and remote jungle. In fact, the locals knew it was there all the time and hunted it for food, so they were happily able to provide bones and skins when the scientists came in search of it. The only 'evidence' for Bigfoot, yetis and other monsters comes from dodgy photographs, grainy film footage and footprints that are just as easy to hoax. Although it is true that the reality behind the Kraken – the giant squid – was first filmed only recently, in this case scientists had actually found dead specimens on beaches, and seen scars on sperm whales to know that there was something that existed outside of their imaginations.

# 21 October

## Bicentenary of Nelson's great day

**2005** In fact, for Nelson himself it wasn't such a great day, as he died in excruciating pain following the Battle of Trafalgar from a bullet wound to the shoulder. The reason why Nelson's victory on that day was seen as such a significant event is because it altered the likely course of history. Napoleon Bonaparte had designs on Britain, but the sea battle made him abandon plans for an invasion. Although Trafalgar is now one of those names that sounds quintessentially English, the battle was in fact fought off the southwest coast of Spain, close to Cape Trafalgar, near Cádiz. The word translates as 'the farthest edge'.

The enemy that Nelson faced was a mix of French and Spanish ships. Although the English fleet held considerably fewer ships than the combined force it was up against, Nelson's battle plan was the key to his success. He used his smaller ships to divide the Franco–Hispanic fleet, thereby breaking communications and then taking advantage of the uncertainty among the enemy vessels. The size of the English vessels also meant that they were able to turn and fire at the sides of the enemy ships with much greater efficiency.

After a while the balance of advantage was tipped in favour of the English fleet and the enemy capitulated. They lost 22 ships, while the English incredibly lost none. Nelson was struck by a bullet during the height of battle and taken below decks. A sniper had managed to fire at him when the HMS *Victory* had engaged with the French vessel *Redoutable* at close quarters. The bullet lodged in his vertebrae and severed his spine. He died after about four hours, knowing that the battle had been won.

HMS *Victory* remained in service until 1812 when it was permanently moored at Portsmouth as a depot ship. She then became the Naval School of Telegraphy from 1889–1904. By 1921 the ship was deteriorating badly and a campaign was begun to save her. In 1922 she was moved to a dry dock and restoration work began, but in 1941 the ship was damaged by a German bomb. Today she is fully restored but not seaworthy. She is the oldest ship in the world still commissioned as part of a navy. Her keel was laid in 1759, making her 250 years old in 2009.

# 22 October

## *An ecological disgrace exposes the Soviet Union*

**1990** The story of the Aral Sea is one of short-sighted single-mindedness on the part of the Soviet Union. In its determination to remain self-sufficient, the USSR went about destroying its own internal organs.

The Aral Sea used to be the fourth-largest body of fresh water in the world. It straddles the border between Kazakhstan and Uzbekistan and originally supported a human community of 4 million, as well as a rich aquatic and semi-aquatic ecosystem. The

Soviet administration decided, in the early 1960s, to divert the two main water sources for the sea – the Amu Darya and Syr Darya – for use in irrigating vast cotton plantations. With these lifelines severed, the Aral Sea simply began to evaporate. It is now about 10 per cent of its former volume. The salinity of the water has also risen so that the habitat is barren and lifeless. Needless to say, the actions of the Soviet regime caused an environmental and human-itarian disaster on a scale not matched anywhere else. What remains of the Aral Sea is now so polluted with chemicals that disease and mortality are worse around its shores than in any other place in the developing world.

Efforts are being made to rectify the damage done, but it is too little too late. Even if the flow of the Amu and Syr were fully restored and industries removed from their banks, it would take hundreds of years for the environment to heal itself. To that extent, the efforts being made are rather like dressing a wound without removing the knife. All the Soviet administration cared about was becoming a superpower in the eyes of the world and millions had to suffer for that ambition to be realised. As for the ecology of the sea, it is likely that many unrecorded endemic species were lost forever by the depletion and poisoning of their environment. The plight of the Aral Sea stands as a clear warning to all of humanity of what can happen when governments don't consider the likely consequences of their actions, and do not have the structures in place to allow ecologists to voice their concerns.

# 23 October

## The iPod is born

**2001** When Apple launched its sleek little white music player, the iPod, in October 2001, there were some who thought Apple had made a major mistake. After all, Apple made computers, not music players. But the doubters were proved resoundingly wrong when the 100 millionth iPod was sold some time in 2006. Indeed, such is the extraordinary impact of the iPod that it has brought about a revolution in the way people listen to music.

What the iPod did was to get rid of the music storage devices that made personal music players cumbersome. It wasn't the players themselves that were that bulky, but the stacks of CDs that you had to carry if you wanted a decent selection of music on the move. There had been digital music players before the iPod that stored music on flash drives. The iPod's great breakthrough was to take advantage of the miniaturisation of computer hard drives to allow it to store thousands of tunes in a unit the size of a match box.

But it wasn't simply the storage that was revolutionary; it was the ease of access. With its touch wheel, the iPod allowed you to scan through all the tracks in seconds. Moreover, it enabled people to make their own personalised playlists – and has so created an entirely new way of listening to music that moves away from the album-based culture of CDs and vinyl.

The final piece of iconic design for the iPod was, of course, its stunning white casing and sleek styling, which made it a object of desire. Sales were slow to start at first, with the iPod compatible only with Mac computers, but once it was made to work with PCs as well, sales rocketed. Soon other companies were launching their own 'iPods', known as MP3 players. MP3 files enable the amount of digital data space required to store music to be dramatically reduced. In 2005, even the Queen was said to have joined the iPod revolution.

By 2006, one in five Americans owned an MP3 player and the rest of the developed world was not far behind. The exception was Japan, where most teenagers listened to digital music on their phones rather than music players. The distinction began to blur, of course, with Apple's introduction of the iPhone in 2007.

Psychologist Michael Bull has argued that personal MP3 players like the iPod are a way for people to regain personal space in an increasingly crowded and noisy world. And by choosing the music, he argues, you reclaim some of the world because it is no longer dominated by messages aimed at you.

But there is another side to the digital music revolution started by the iPod. CD sales have plunged dramatically, and legal online sales of music for download have not risen correspondingly. Although sales of digital music rose by 40 per cent in 2007, for instance, overall sales of music dropped by a tenth, mainly, music industry bosses argue, because people can now so easily download and swap music illegally. So the music industry is very concerned about the future of music, though the world is now probably filled with more music makers and listeners than ever before.

Meanwhile, the iPod and its cousins are encouraging another revolution, as people begin to download films and TV programmes to watch on their portable players. And as phones merge with MP3 players and computers, entertainment, information and communication on the move is fast becoming as sophisticated as one can imagine.

# 24 October

## *The lonely murderer goes on trial*

**1983** Dennis Nilsen was an English civil servant who had difficulty in forming lasting relationships. He happened to prefer the company of men and his attempts at bonding had left him hurt and lonely. Eventually his frustrations led him to find a rather bizarre and macabre solution to his need for company.

Nilsen turned to picking up waifs and strays in London and taking them to his house with the promise of a good meal and somewhere comfortable to sleep. He would then kill them and keep the corpse by his side, rather like a doll, until it began to decompose. After disposing of the body, he would go searching for a new victim whenever his craving for company reached a new peak. In this way he managed to kill around fifteen young men. As most were runaways or homeless, their disappearances were not reported.

Nilsen was only found out because he made a mistake one day. He decided to dispose of his final victim by chopping the body into pieces and flushing the remains down the toilet. Some of those chunks of flesh got caught in the sewer and began to rot. The unpleasant aroma caused a neighbour to call the local authorities to sort out the problem, and the workmen discovered what they thought were pieces of chicken blocking the drain. When they returned to clear the blockage they found that the 'chicken' had been removed. Suspicions aroused, they called the police. Had Nilsen left things alone the workmen might have simply removed the flesh, still thinking it was chicken, and then gone on their way to the next job. As it was, the police duly arrived and searched Nilsen's home. They found a number of bodies secreted beneath the floorboards before continuing investigations at his former home.

As with many serial offenders, Nilsen justified his actions as a simple need that had to be fulfilled for the sake of maintaining his own happiness. In addition, he felt that his victims were outside society because they were not missed and that fact, under his logic, made them available to him. What he didn't consider was that they were not missed because they were already missing. It didn't mean that they didn't have parents who yearned to see them again and to know how they were getting on in life.

# 25 October

## Hitler is declared officially dead

**1956** As the Soviet forces closed in on Hitler's bunker in Berlin in 1945, the German Führer found himself backed into a corner. He had seen the Italian fascist leader, Benito Mussolini, captured and executed and he was determined to avoid the same fate. As a final drastic course of action, on Monday 30 April 1945, with the Russian troops less than 500 metres from the entrance to the bunker, Adolf Hitler committed suicide.

His body was discovered by his valet, Heinz Linge. Hitler was sitting on a sofa in his office with the lifeless Eva Braun slumped next to him. A gun lay by his feet and there was a single gunshot wound to his temple. Eva Braun's body was without a mark. Hitler was known to carry cyanide capsules with him, but to be paranoid over their efficacy. Linge and the other Nazi staff deduced that the Führer and his wife had both ingested cyanide, before Hitler had shot himself.

If this should seem to have been the end of the matter regarding the death of Adolf Hitler, it was far from it. Seeking to conceal the suicide of their commander, Hitler's SS bodyguard dragged the two bodies outside where they set fire to them. This not only prevented the Soviets from capturing Hitler's remains, it also triggered a raft of conspiracy theories that Hitler had not died at all in his bunker and had actually escaped from Berlin.

For once in the history of conspiracy theories, these suggestions were not as unlikely as they may sound. Following the German capitulation, a number of high-ranking Nazi officers fled overseas, most often to South America. This give rise to a wave of Nazi-hunting expeditions that sought to track down those who had been convicted of wartime atrocities but had managed to escape. A number of senior Nazis were duly caught, tried and executed, and even into the 21st century investigations continued into a few unresolved cases.

Although the Russian army recovered the charred bodies of a man and a woman from the garden of Hitler's bunker, there was some careful hesitation before the world felt confident enough to draw a line underneath one of the 20th century's most atrocious individuals. Eleven years after he had actually died, West Germany at last pronounced him officially dead.

By this time, the remains of Hitler and Eva Braun were in the possession of the Russian intelligence services, and buried in an undisclosed location. Following their discovery, the Russians had been extremely sensitive about the risks of their whereabouts, if they became known, becoming a neo-Nazi shrine. Consequently, on 4 April 1970, nearly 25 years after he had committed suicide, Hitler's body was secretly burned again by the KGB. Finally reduced to a pile of ashes, these dusty remains were then quietly dumped into the River Elbe, to be washed away forever.

# 26 October

## The last natural case of smallpox is recorded

**1977** Smallpox remains the only disease to have been entirely eradicated by human effort. The disease is caused by two types of virus from the same genus, *Variola*, and is unique to human beings. It is an extremely dangerous infection with a mortality rate of up to 85 per cent in some instances, and many of those who do survive are rendered permanently blind. It has been estimated that perhaps 500,000 Europeans died each year from smallpox in the 1700s.

Eradication was achieved by a campaign of vaccination, so that the virus eventually ran out of host bodies. With no other viral population in the wild, smallpox was officially wiped out following that last case of the disease in 1977. In fact, that date is technically incorrect as the final case occurred in Birmingham, England in 1978 when a medical photographer was accidentally exposed to the virus in a laboratory and died. One or two samples of the virus are now in reference storage under strict security.

In the early 1970s the Soviets rather foolishly experimented with smallpox as a potential biological warfare weapon. The virus escaped the 40 km zone surrounding the experiments and caused an outbreak in a local village. The Soviet authorities only narrowly averted a national disaster by ordering a lockdown on the movement of vehicles until the outbreak had passed.

Smallpox was largely responsible for killing huge numbers of natives in the New World. They had no natural immunity, so when the disease was brought over by European explorers and invaders, it struck a devastating blow. On the Caribbean islands it seems that entire populations were wiped out. Cortés' defeat of the Aztecs was also helped by an outbreak of smallpox which decimated the Mexican population in 1520. All over the Americas, tribes were reduced in numbers dramatically by the killer disease.

Those who were fortunate enough to survive smallpox were often left with disfiguring scars on their skin. Queen Elizabeth I caught smallpox in 1562 at the age of 29. That is reputedly why she used makeup so heavily in later life, in an attempt to cover the pockmarks on her face. The disease was called 'small pox' originally to distinguish it from 'great pox', which was the common name for syphilis in the 15th century. Syphilis is still with us but is now treatable. In those days, however, it caused severe disfigurement of the body by forming lesions, known as chancres, in the skin.

# 27 October

## Death of Allen Schindler

**1992** Throughout history, all too many gay men have suffered or died for their sexuality. The murder of US navy radioman Petty Officer Allen Schindler Junior, however, was especially brutal and highly significant in its timing. As a result, it has played a major part in establishing the current status quo on homosexuality in the American armed services.

In October 1992, 23-year-old Schindler was serving on the US navy ship *Belleau Wood* when it docked in Sasebo, Japan. In the previous weeks, Schindler had been repeatedly harassed for his homosexuality and was severely depressed. Then, while ashore one night, Schindler was attacked by shipmates Terry Helvey and Charles Vinsin in a park toilet. Helvey kicked him and stamped on him so violently that a doctor afterwards said it was as if he had been in a 'high-speed auto accident or a low-speed aircraft accident'.

At first the Navy tried to cover it up and Schindler's staunchly Republican, highly patriotic mother Dorothy Hajdys was happy to accept their explanation of a simple fight between shipmates. But the truth came out during Helvey's trial that he was violently homophobic, and that Schindler 'deserved it'. Gradually, Dorothy Hajdys came to understand the persecution her son had endured, and soon became a major campaigner on behalf of the gay community.

Ever since the beginning of the USA, homosexuality had been banned in the armed forces and servicemen found to be homosexual would be 'honourably discharged' under Section 8 of the rule book. That had not stopped gay men from serving, successfully keeping their sexuality hidden. During the Vietnam War, several men had actually feigned homosexuality to avoid being drafted into the army.

In the 1980s, however, more and more people began to campaign for openly homosexual men to be allowed to serve in the armed forces – and for the protection of gay men in the forces from their fellow soldiers. In his campaign for the presidency in 1992, Bill Clinton announced that he would move on this, and the brutal murder of Schindler fuelled his resolve. Early in his presidency, against considerable opposition, Clinton pushed through a stop-gap measure which came to be called the 'Don't Ask, Don't Tell' bill, and citing the murder of Schindler as one of the main reasons the bill was needed.

'Don't Ask, Don't Tell' effectively gave informal permission for gay men to serve in the armed forces. Army authorities were not allowed to question a serviceman's sexuality, but nor was he allowed to disclose it. This supposedly temporary measure, however, has settled into being the status quo. As a result, hundreds of gay servicemen whose sexuality is revealed, through whatever means, are still discharged every year.

Now sympathies on the situation are very much divided along party lines. Most Republicans agree with the argument that gays in the military pose an 'intolerable risk to national security' by potentially dividing troops. Most Democrats, however, including Barack Obama, believe that it is important that troops can be openly gay as they are in the British army, alongside which American troops frequently serve.

# 28 October

## Nobel Prize awarded for DDT, the worst pollutant of the 20th century

**1948** DDT (Dichloro-Diphenyl-Trichloroethane) was regarded as a wonder chemical when it was invented by Swiss chemist Paul Hermann Müller in 1939. It was used as a universal insecticide on crops and for exterminating disease-carrying mosquitoes. Initially it seemed that it could do no wrong, as crop yields rose and disease levels dropped, which was why Müller got his Nobel Prize. But then things started to go horribly awry.

It was realised that DDT, which is in essence a toxin, collected in the food chains of habitats. Herbivores were concentrating the chemical in their systems by consuming grass and leaves with DDT sprayed on them. Carnivores were eating those contaminated herbivores and concentrating the chemical so much in their own systems that they were dying. It meant that entire ecosystems were collapsing due to the effects of DDT, which wasn't decomposing in the soil or being metabolised. Then there were obvious concerns regarding the accumulation of DDT in livestock being eaten by people. Furthermore, mosquitoes and other insects were evolving immunity to DDT so that it was losing its potency.

An American biologist named Rachel Carson delivered the killer blow in 1962 when she published *Silent Spring*. The book was a catalogue of environmental disasters brought about by the use of DDT, and it caused such a public outcry that a complete swing in public opinion took place. By 1972 DDT had been banned in the US and worldwide bans followed. Since then the world has had time to recover from DDT and species, especially birds of prey, that had become endangered as a result of its use have made healthy recoveries.

One continued area for concern, however, is the lack of a real alternative to DDT when it comes to sheer effectiveness as an insecticide. Other pest control sprays of course exist, but in terms of lethal ability few have really offered as much promise as DDT once did. The main contenders are either the organophosphate and carbamate insecticides promoted by the petrochemical companies that manufacture them, or similar chemical insecticides, including toxins such as pyrethroids.

Neither branch is without its troubles, however. The latter is certainly safe for humans in low-level concentrations – it is used in household products – but there is some doubt as to whether it is strictly suitable for widespread crop spraying. The former brings with it more severe health worries. In either case, their long-term effects are unproven and they are both more expensive than DDT.

DDT is now officially described as a persistent organic pollutant. Yet despite its torrid history, it is still used in some tropical parts of the world – especially in Africa – specifically against the thick mosquito populations in the area. The World Health Organisation estimates that there are around 1 million global deaths every year from malaria. Of these, an incredible 90 per cent are in Africa. As mosquitoes are the most significant carriers of the disease, every affordable measure available is used to try and stamp them out. Unfortunately, this includes the continued use of DDT.

# 29 October

## *Electricity is used to repair a bone fracture in the US*

**1971** When human bone bends or breaks it generates very small electrical currents through something called the piezoelectric effect. This is when tiny crystals within the bone produce electricity as they are squeezed. It is exactly the same principle as is used in the sparking mechanisms of gas ovens and hobs.

What is truly remarkable, however, is that those electric currents stimulate new bone growth, to either strengthen or repair the damaged bone. In athletes, the bones that get the most stress often become tougher as a result of this phenomenon. Tennis players, for example, will often have a more robust skeleton in their racquet arm than in their other one. By simulating the piezo-electric effect, it has been found that the bone-healing process can be accelerated.

The therapeutic effects of electricity on bones and joints have been known since the 19th century, although the science was not understood at the time. In fact the effect wasn't explained fully until 1957. Dried pieces of bone were tested under laboratory conditions and found to issue very small electric currents. The collagen in bone contains micelle crystals that react under a shearing force and produce sufficient electrical charge to prompt healing.

The surgical procedure was carried out by doctors conducting research at the University of Pennsylvania. Although there are some obvious advantages of stimulating *in vivo* (in the body) recovery, the efficiency of the treatment has not triggered widespread application. More often than not, the damaged body part is simply set in plaster and the body is allowed to get on with its own healing process – which still relies upon the naturally occurring piezoelectric effect.

There have, however, been other medical applications for electric currents. Electricity can also be used for pain relief in muscles and joints. TENS (Transcutaneous Electrical Nerve Stimulation) devices deliver low-level electrical pulses through the skin, which cause muscles to quiver. They are used on patients with arthritis and women with pregnancy pains. It is sometimes thought that copper bracelets aid arthritic wrists by generating electrical fields, but this is uncertain. Likewise, acupuncture may have an electrical and scientific basis, but then again it may not.

The ability of piezoelectric crystals to convert mechanical energy into electrical energy is an effect that can also be reversed. This way round crystals will convert electrical signals into physical energy, such as sound waves. Piezoelectric crystals are therefore commonly used in audio devices such as earphones and microphones.

# 30 October

## Quebec almost breaks away

**1995** Quebec is a province of Canada, where the population considers itself to be culturally different from the rest of the nation. Not only is French the sole official language at a federal level, but traditional French civil law also has a strong influence upon the Quebecois legal system.

This Anglo–French division that runs through Canada was created in 1763 when France ceded its colonies in the territory to the British. By this time, a French-speaking culture had become firmly established in Quebec. Quebec, as a part of British North America, continued to fall under British rule until 1867. From then on, it became a self-governing dominion until 1982, when it was finally granted full independence. Even today, however, the British monarch officially remains the Canadian head of state.

Two referendums have been held over the question of an independent Quebec, but both have failed to secure a vote in favour. The first of these, in 1980, was called by the separatist Parti Québécois government, but comfortably defeated by 59.56 per cent against secession and 40.44 per cent in favour.

In 1995, the polls had shifted dramatically and the margin between the two schools of opinion was wafer thin. The originators of the vote were again the Parti Québécois. They had been out of government during the 1990s, but then the provincial election in 1994 swept them back into power. Within a year, their leader, Jacques Parizeau, had ushered in a second referendum.

The question that was asked was simple. 'Do you agree that Quebec should become sovereign after having made a formal offer to Canada for a new economic and political partnership within the scope of the bill respecting the future of Quebec and of the agreement signed on June 12, 1995?'

Amazingly, the resulting decision to remain united was achieved with a majority of just fractionally more than 1 per cent in favour of remaining part of Canada, at 50.6 per cent to 49.4 per cent. Despite coming so close to changing history, the separatists managed to deal with their defeat in a peaceful and dignified manner. In fact, the Canadian House of Commons passed a motion in November 2006 to recognise Quebec as a separate nation within Canada.

Quebec holds about half of the entire Canadian population at 8 million, so if ever it did separate it would be a significant country in its own right. It would also mean the geographical isolation of a number of provinces – Labrador, Newfoundland, Nova Scotia and Prince Edward Island – which lie on the other side of Quebec to the main body of Canada.

# 31 October

## Galileo Galilei is cleared of heresy

**1992** It had taken 360 years, but in 1992 the Catholic Church finally accepted that it had a big mistake in condemning Galileo's insistence that the Earth moves around the sun, not the reverse. In issuing a very belated apology to Galileo, Pope John Paul II admitted, 'The error of the theologians of the time, when they maintained the centrality of the Earth, was to think that our understanding of the physical world's structure was, in some way, imposed by the literal sense of Sacred Scripture'.

Back in the 17th century, the official Church view was that the Earth was fixed at the centre of the universe, as the Bible seemed to imply – and as most astronomers had long agreed. But in the early 1500s, Polish astronomer Nicolaus Copernicus had suggested in his book *De Revolutionibus Orbium Coelestium* (*On the Revolutions of the Heavenly Spheres*) that the sun is really fixed at the centre and the Earth moves, and that a proof of this heliocentric theory would be if Venus could be seen to have phases like the Moon's.

For a while, Copernicus' ideas did not arouse much controversy, since there was no proof that they were true. Then, in 1609,

Galileo turned a newly invented novelty, the telescope, into a powerful scientific instrument – and used it to look up at the heavens. Immediately, he saw not only the phases of Venus, but four moons circling Jupiter, and the Moon's supposedly smooth surface broken with mountains and valleys. Galileo insisted that all this was definitive proof of the heliocentric view.

Galileo's forthright expression of his views soon became a problem for the Catholic Church. Church scholars were willing to admit that Copernicus' ideas were a useful theory for making astronomical predictions. But Galileo insisted that they were not just a theory but the truth. This was a direct challenge to the Church's authority, implying that it was not the sole voice of truth, and it was heretical, since it seemed to imply that those passages in the Bible which said the Earth was fixed were false.

The exact sequence of subsequent events is the subject of controversy, but in essence, in 1616 the Pope withdrew Copernicus' book from publication and warned Galileo not to talk about it. Galileo was not so easily silenced. In 1632, he wrote a book called *The Dialogue* in which clever Sagredo argues with stupid Simplicio about Copernicus. It seemed Simplicio represented the Pope. Galileo was summoned to Rome and forced to deny, maybe under torture, that the Earth moves. Legend has it that as he was led away to be imprisoned in his own house, he muttered, *'eppur si muove'* ('yet it does move').

Of course, as more and more evidence came in on Galileo's side, the Church gradually accepted the truth. Finally, in 1821, it lifted its ban on Copernicus' book. Its condemnation of Galileo still stood, however, until at long last the Pope John Paul II issued his apology in 1992. When in 2000, John Paul issued a general apology for all the Catholic Church's mistakes over the previous two millennia, including the trial of Galileo, it seemed that the controversy was finally over. Yet there was still another twist.

In January 2008, Pope Benedict XVI cancelled a planned visit to Rome's La Sapienza University after a protest from academics against comments he had made when conducting the investigation into the Galileo controversy in 1990 as Cardinal Ratzinger.

In a speech, Ratzinger had quoted Austrian-born philosopher Paul Feyerabend as saying the Church's verdict against Galileo had been 'rational and just'. Many Italians, including Prime Minister Prodi, fulminated against the challenge to free speech created by the protest against Benedict, but the Pope withdrew from the field. The ghost of Galileo is still not yet quiet.

# 1 November

## The threat of thermonuclear annihilation looms

**1952** Even though the atomic bombs dropped on Japan in 1945 caused so much destruction and killed hundreds of thousands of people, they were positively tiny weapons compared with those developed less than a decade later. The world's first hydrogen bomb had an explosive force 800 times as great. The Pacific atoll used as the test site was razed entirely by the explosion and a mile-wide crater was left in its place on the seabed. Thermonuclear weapons were a new cause for deep concern as it was clear that a nuclear war would bring untold devastation.

Atomic bombs work on the principle of fission, which means that the atoms split apart and the energy released by this process is what causes the explosion. The elements used within A-bombs, uranium and plutonium, are costly to produce and very heavy, so atomic bombs are consequently relatively small. Hydrogen bombs, on the other hand, work on the opposite principle of fusion, which means that hydrogen atoms fuse together to become helium atoms and the spare energy causes the resultant explosion. The type of hydrogen compound required is less costly and lighter in weight than the material needed for fission reactions, which means that thermonuclear weapons can be made far larger. The fusion reaction employed by the H-bomb is essentially the same reaction that occurs in the Sun.

Nuclear technology is also used in some power stations where fission reactions are kept under careful control. The holy grail of nuclear energy though is a concept known as 'cold fusion'. This is achieving a nuclear fusion reaction under normal atmospheric temperature and pressure. Fusion reactions in H-bombs and proposed fusion-driven nuclear power stations can take place only under conditions of extreme heat and pressure. Cold fusion could theoretically help solve the world's energy requirements in a cheap and clean way. Unfortunately it has so far eluded scientists and may turn out to be scientifically impossible.

A similar thing happened 200 years ago, when scientists pursued the notion of the perpetual motion machine. The idea was that a machine would perpetually keep moving without needing more energy. It turned out to be a scientific no-no, as it broke the first and second laws of thermodynamics. Of course, in modern times it is possible to build quasi-perpetual motion machines that use the energy of the sun in one way or another. Solar-, wind- and wave-powered machines will all deliver power indefinitely, as long as the energy source is not interrupted.

# 2 November

## *The* Spruce Goose *takes to the air*

**1947** With the war won in 1945, America had much to celebrate in the latter half of the decade. It had been the industrial might of the nation that had turned the war in favour of the Allies, so technology was something to be proud of.

The *Spruce Goose* was the nickname for the Hughes H-4 Hercules, a giant seaplane built by the entrepreneur Howard Hughes. Development began in 1942 with a view to using the plane for transporting troops during the war in the Pacific. The shortage of materials due to the war effort meant that Hughes had to use birch-wood laminate to construct most of the aircraft.

2 November 1947 marks the date when the plane made its one and only test flight. Changes in the post-war environment meant that the *Spruce Goose* was unviable as a commercial machine, and it was put into storage, never to be flown again. Even today, the aeroplane holds a number of records in terms of its size, including largest wingspan and greatest height. Hughes himself was at the controls during that maiden flight. The aircraft is now on display at the Evergreen Aviation museum in Oregon.

The legacy of the *Spruce Goose* was to demonstrate that aircraft could be made much larger than had previously been attempted, provided that they had sufficient power and strength. With the development of the jet engine, airliners could reach fast enough speeds to allow them to be made entirely from metal. Lightweight alloys were developed for building both the subframes and skins of aircraft. Another development was the backswept wing, which gave the modern airliner its distinctive appearance. The idea of landing on water was abandoned in favour of tarmac or concrete runways and landing gear with effective suspension.

Despite their enormous size, modern airliners are statistically the safest form of transport. They use the most sophisticated navigational equipment and safety procedures are strictly adhered too, so that far fewer people perish than they do travelling by road, rail or boat.

Howard Hughes had made his money in oil, but was a pioneering aviator. Unfortunately he was afflicted with obsessive-compulsive disorder which manifested itself as a fear of germs. He grew increasingly eccentric as his condition took over his life, until he was rendered unable to function normally and became a total recluse.

# 3 November

## Frozen peas are added to the Birds Eye range

**1952** The frozen pea has become something of an icon in the modern world. It is an everyday product, yet it symbolises the infrastructure of civilisation. The peas are frozen within hours of being harvested, so that the customer receives a product in optimum condition. Before the advent of the frozen pea, people had the choice of canned peas, dried peas or fresh peas as seasonal produce. Suddenly they had fresh peas all year round.

The company name 'Birds Eye' is derived from the surname of Clarence Birdseye, the man who invented the process of flash-freezing foods. He originally worked as a field naturalist and discovered that the Inuits used a technique for preserving fish by placing them on the ice so that the wind chill factor froze them solid almost immediately. When the cells of plants and animals are frozen rapidly there is no time for ice crystals to form, which would ordinarily destroy the cellular structure. Birdseye experimented mechanically until he managed to duplicate the Inuit technique. He then patented the process and began his company, Birdseye Seafoods, in 1922.

By 1930 he had 26 different fish, meats, vegetables and fruits available in frozen form. Needless to say, his products didn't take off in popularity until people were able to purchase domestic freezers, but trade was initially good with restaurants as it solved their problems with obtaining good-quality produce.

The humble pea had to wait for a mechanised process of harvesting before it became truly popular, as it wasn't cost-effective to shell peas by hand. These days just about any water-based foodstuff can be frozen. There are a few things that have eluded food scientists; most notably the strawberry. It will freeze, of course, but it only barely resembles the fresh product in taste and texture when defrosted. This is because strawberries have a very high water content and their shape gives them a low surface area to volume ratio. Consequently it is impossible to freeze and defrost them quickly enough to avoid cell damage.

One might think that frozen foods are entirely frozen in time too, so that they remain chemically fixed. While this is partly true, it is also the case that frozen foods chemically change and degrade. One thing that commonly occurs is that frozen foods dry out. Even though they are frozen, ice can still evaporate at the surface. In addition, foods with high oil and fat contents don't entirely freeze as the lipids have a lower freezing point than water. Consequently, processes of decomposition still occur, albeit far more slowly and differently than they would above 0°C (32°F).

# 4 November

*Sandinistas win by a landslide in the first free elections in Nicaragua for 56 years*

**1984** For many young Western liberals, the massive triumph of Daniel Ortega and the Sandinistas in Nicaragua's elections in

1984 was a moment of supreme joy. In a turnout of over 85 per cent, the FSLN, the Sandinista Front, won an overwhelming 69 per cent of the vote. It seemed a great victory for the people, a ringing popular endorsement of the 1979 revolution which had booted out the dictator Somoza.

The Sandinistas took their name from August César Sandino, the charismatic leader of the Nicaraguan nationalist struggle against the US occupation in the 1930s. Sandino was assassinated in 1934 by the National Guard run by the Somoza family who ruled the country dictatorially with US backing until the 1979 revolution. The lowest moment for Nicaragua, already the poorest country in Central America, came in 1972 when an earthquake ravaged the country and destroyed much of the capital Managua. Foreign aid was forthcoming but much of it was embezzled by the Somozas. Throughout the late 1970s opposition to the Somozas mounted, and finally in 1979, after a bloody struggle, they were overthrown by the revolutionary forces led by the FSLN, many of whom were young students.

Led by Daniel and Humberto Ortega, the FSLN immediately issued a bill of civil rights and began to run the country as an interim government prior to proper elections. Young Western liberals flocked to the country to help out with this 'people's revolution' as the Sandinistas redistributed land, initiated free health care and embarked on a campaign that raised literacy from barely 40 per cent to nearly 90 per cent in just a few years. Back home in Europe and the USA, many people bought Nicaraguan coffee in solidarity.

Much of the expertise for these changes, and much financial backing, came from Castro's Cuba and also from the Soviet Union. The Reagan government in the US feared that Nicaragua would be a bridgehead for the spread of communism in Latin America and began to pour hundreds of millions of dollars into backing the 'contras', rebel forces mainly from neighbouring Honduras. Although most of the world agreed that the 1984 elections which gave the FSLN victory and made Ortega president were free and fair, the US did not. It began an economic blockade of the country and stepped up its support for the contras.

433

To deal with the economic hardship, the Sandinista government introduced food rationing, and to fight the contras they introduced conscription for children as young as fourteen. By the time the next elections came round in 1990, the Nicaraguan people had had enough and they wanted the battle against the USA to stop. The US-backed centre-right National Opposition Union of Violeta Chamorro convincingly defeated the Sandinistas in the vote, to the horror of the young idealists who had cheered the revolution. Before they left office, though, many FSLN officials took legal title to the luxury homes that they had taken over after Somoza fled – a share-out that Nicaraguans referred to as *piñata*, from the paper animal stuffed with sweets that children get at birthday parties.

Throughout the 1990s and the early 2000s, Nicaragua was governed by a series of centre-right governments, and the changes brought by the Sandinistas were gradually dismantled. Free health care disappeared, education became less of a priority, and the gulf between rich and poor gradually widened.

Amazingly, in 2006, Daniel Ortega and the Sandinistas were voted back into power. It has not been an entirely happy comeback. As well as expected US opposition, international donors such as the UK have threatened to pull out over what they see as Ortega's authoritarian and reckless style of government. In late June 2008, even leftwing intellectuals such as Noam Chomsky and Bianca Jagger, who had always been such fervent champions of the Sandinistas, began to attack Ortega for barring the party of Dora María Téllez, an erstwhile revolutionary heroine, from municipal elections. In July 2008, Ortega's poll ratings were lower than Gordon Brown's in the UK.

# 5 November

### *The quadricentenary of the Gunpowder Plot*

**2005** King Henry VIII had ousted Catholicism from its pre-eminence in Britain during his reign in the 16th century, ostensibly because he needed to establish the Protestant-based Church of England as a way of evading certain divorce laws. There was, of course, the beneficial side effect that as head of a new national Church, he would wield a great deal of additional power. He had rallied support for his anti-Catholic stance by painting the religion as something vulgar and excessive – hence the adjective 'catholic' in the English language, which is a pejorative term equating to disproportionately broad taste.

In 1605 James I had been on the throne for two years following the death of Henry's daughter, Elizabeth I. James wasn't an effective monarch and the Catholics sensed an opportunity to regain a political foothold. The result was the Gunpowder Plot. The idea was to kill the king, his family and all of his cronies in one fell swoop by bombing the Houses of Parliament. A number of Roman Catholic conspirators contracted the help of one Guy Fawkes in preparing the explosives required for the job. Unfortunately for Fawkes, he was caught in the act of priming 30 barrels of gunpowder beneath the Houses of Parliament. He and the other revolutionaries were duly rounded up and executed.

The method of death was being hanged, drawn and quartered, which was a horrendous form of public torture producing a long, agonised demise. Apparently Fawkes jumped from the scaffold and managed to kill himself before the executioners had an opportunity to disembowel, or draw him.

Those who celebrate Guy Fawkes' night today would be forgiven for thinking that Fawkes was burnt at the stake, due to the tradition of placing an effigy atop a bonfire. It isn't clear why this practice began, although his corpse may have been burnt following the execution. In those days cremation was a kind of 'punishment' after death as it was symbolic of sending someone's spirit or soul to the flames of Hell. As for the fireworks, they represent the gunpowder that Fawkes failed to ignite 400 years ago.

Guy Fawkes is sometimes described as Guido Fawkes and consequently thought to have been a French Catholic. In fact he was born in Yorkshire, England, and would have spoken with a broad northern accent. Oppression of Catholics in Britain had been brutal and Fawkes had witnessed a number of atrocities that led him to oppose the state. A woman named Margaret Clitherow, 'The Pearl of York', had been pressed to death in Fawkes' home-town when he was sixteen. Her crime was to have harboured a number of Catholic priests in her house. In those days Catholics had 'priest holes' built into their homes where priests could hide if the authorities caught wind of their presence. Penalties were severe for both the priests and those who hid them.

# 6 November

## Ferret on the comeback trail

**1981** Just occasionally there is a good news story relating to an endangered species. That of the black-footed ferret is one. In Wyoming, USA, the ferret was thought to be extinct due to a combination of habitat loss and disease. Then, in 1981, a colony was discovered alive and well, although obviously at risk. Conservationists had the good sense to capture all of the ferrets in the colony and begin a breeding programme in the early 1980s. By the 1990s a reintroduction scheme had been established and the ferrets began to make their comeback in the wild.

Black-footed ferrets are relatively specialised among ferrets because they feed almost exclusively on prairie dogs. This means that they require a good-sized colony of prairie dogs to sustain a population of their own. Extermination of prairie dogs to use land for farming had an inevitable knock-on effect on the ferrets, which even rely on prairie dog burrows for making their own nests. Ferrets are preyed upon themselves by larger carnivores, so it is vital that they have somewhere to shelter on the prairies, where there are few trees and other places to hide.

Reserves have now been established where large prairie dog colonies – known as 'towns' – can exist, thereby restoring the right kind of ecosystem for the ferrets to survive as well. Most are on ranches, where the owners are paid compensation for leaving the habitats unmolested. Something like 100 acres is required for a prairie dog colony sufficiently large to support a family of ferrets, so it is easy to see ranchers might consider the land wasted as it could support a fair number of cattle. In addition, the prairie dogs graze the grass in adjacent fields.

One of the most remarkable resurrection stories is that of the Mauritius kestrel. In the mid-1970s it was considered to be the rarest bird in the world. As it had an island population it was vulnerable to habitat loss and its numbers had fallen to a critical level. However, after a targeted conservation effort spearheaded by Jersey Zoo, the kestrel made a remarkable comeback. There is now a viable population on Mauritius and backup populations are kept in various sanctuaries.

# 7 November

## *A nanny is murdered; a lord mysteriously vanishes*

**1974** In some ways, there is nothing mysterious about the case of Lord Lucan. It is simply a rather nasty tale of a murderer who got away. Yet the case fascinated at the time and continues to intrigue decades on. It's firstly, of course, because the murderer in question was a lord of the realm, and a quite glamorous one at that, known as 'Lucky' for his gambling habit. And secondly because it's quite surprising that someone so high-profile should vanish so utterly.

The story goes that on the evening of 7 November 1974, a distraught woman, covered in blood, ran into the The Plumber's Arms public house on Lower Belgrave Street in London, crying for help and shouting, 'He's murdered the nanny!' The woman was Lady Lucan, and when police entered her house at 46 Lower Belgrave Square, they found the Lucan's three children sleeping upstairs, unharmed. Downstairs, though, the breakfast room was covered in splashes of blood, and through in the kitchen was a sack containing the body of Sandra Rivett, the children's nanny. She had been battered to death with a blunt instrument, and the bloodstained length of lead piping in the hall seemed to be the murder weapon.

Lady Lucan insisted that her attacker was her estranged husband, who very quickly went on the run. Later that same night, Lucan drove to Sussex and saw his friend Susan Maxwell-Scott. According to her, Lucan said that he had been passing his wife's house, saw her fighting with a man and went to the rescue. Lady Lucan then ran outside shouting 'Murder!' and Lucan panicked and ran. While he was at Mrs Maxwell-Scott's, he wrote one letter claiming that his wife would try to frame him and another with details of an auction that would settle his gambling debts. After writing the letters, Lucan left and was never seen again.

Seven months later, Lucan was found guilty of murder *in absentia*, and the hunt changed from one for a missing person to one for a convicted murderer. The hunt went on for years, with countless land searches and aerial reconnaissance surveys, as well as an intensive international effort by police forces around the globe. Some people think that Lucan committed suicide in Newhaven harbour where his borrowed Ford Corsair was discovered, but an extensive dive found nothing. And there have been numerous sightings in places as far afield as Africa, Australia, France and Italy.

One 'sighting' in Australia in 1974 turned out to be the missing MP John Stonehouse, who had faked his suicide a month earlier. Another in 2003 was 'Jungle Barry' Halpin, a bedraggled drop-out found in Goa, India by former Scotland Yard detective Duncan McLaughlin. BBC Radio 2 presenter Mike Harding immediately identified Halpin not as Lucan but as a Lancashire folk-singer who had gone to India 'as it was more spiritual than St Helens'. As recently as 2007, 35 years on from the murder, another former Scotland Yard detective, Sidney Ball, went to investigate an English recluse living in a Land Rover in New Zealand, who turned out to be an ex-civil servant ten years younger and five inches shorter than Lucan.

Lucan was officially declared dead in 1999, 25 years after his disappearance. In October 2004, Scotland Yard re-opened their investigation into the murder, and looked at both the evidence and DNA profiling to get a new angle on the case. But as yet, the guilty verdict stands, and Lucan – or his body – has never been found.

# 8 November

## Colin Powell pulls out of the Presidential race in fear for his life

**1995** When in late 1995, the *Times*/CNN polled the American public for their choice of candidates for the following year's presidential election, the favourite of nearly a third of all voters was a man who neither belonged to one of the two major parties, nor had even announced he was willing to stand as president. What's more, if this man agreed to stand as the Republican candidate, the polls showed that he would clearly beat the Democrat, Bill Clinton. The man was retired soldier Colin Powell, and he had achieved a unique degree of respect among both politicians and the public in America.

Born in Harlem and brought up in the Bronx, Powell had overcome all the barriers of class and race to rise through the ranks of the military at an astonishing pace. He had become the youngest ever chairman of the army Joint Chiefs of Staff, and the only black man to hold this post. Indeed, only Eisenhower and Haig had risen so far without direct battle experience as a commander. His management of the Gulf War and many other crises earned him widespread admiration. Reagan said of him, 'If you say so, I know it's all right', while ordinary people liked his combination of quiet authority and down-to-earth humour.

There was something inspiring and very American too in his comments about his attitude to racism. When he asked how he dealt with racism when growing up, Powell answered, 'I beat it ... You carry this burden of racism, because I'm not going to'. As a member of the black community, Powell had the support of many of the disadvantaged of society, while his old-fashioned, conservative championing of family values earned him the hearts of many on the right. No wonder, then, that many thought that if Powell stood for president he would break the old two-party hold on American politics. He stood a real chance of winning as an independent, while if he stood as a Republican, there was every chance the Democrats would have been almost wiped out.

So there was huge disappointment when he announced on 8 November 1995 that he was definitely not running for president. Of course, he had never said that he would, but the sense of loss was palpable. He never revealed why he withdrew, but in a 2002 book Bob Woodward (the journalist who played a key role in revealing the Watergate scandal), pointed the finger at his wife Alma. 'If you run,' Alma is quoted as saying, 'I'm gone.'

If Powell hoped for the quiet life by stepping down from the presidential race, of course, he must have been sadly disappointed. As Secretary of State under George W. Bush he was thrown into the eye of the storm over Iraq in 2003. While many in the Bush administration were absolutely determined to invade Iraq, Powell was determined that it should only be with UN backing, and was tasked with the presentation of the case to the UN which showed that Saddam Hussein was armed and dangerous with weapons of mass destruction. It was deeply embarrassing to Powell when afterwards he was forced to admit that the intelligence on which he made these claims was flawed, and even faked. Powell resigned from his position, and since then has taken a back seat in American politics, though he is said to have been advising Barack Obama on his policy over Iraq, urging talks with Syria and Iran, 'You have to talk to the people you dislike most in this dangerous world'.

# 9 November

## Nuclear fusion is first achieved under controlled conditions

**1991** In the arena of physics there is a fundamental principle that states that atoms are naturally inclined to stabilise themselves. As it happens, the element iron (Fe) has the most stable atoms. When conditions allow, such as during the formation of stars, the atoms of other elements attempt to become iron atoms. Those elements above iron on the periodic table try to break apart by a process called fission, while those below iron attempt to come together by a process called fusion. In the normal environment in which we live, most elements are considerably more stable than this suggests, because enormous amounts of energy are required to initiate such nuclear reactions.

The reaction that causes the sun to generate so much energy is nuclear fusion. Hydrogen atoms are pushed together by the force of their own gravity so that they fuse into helium atoms. The heat and light are the by-products of this reaction. This process is very attractive to those involved with the manufacture of power for human consumption because there is no radioactive waste, as is the case with nuclear fission. In 1991 scientists managed to produce a controlled fusion reaction under laboratory conditions – otherwise known as a harnessed reaction. It produced 1.7 megawatts of energy in just two seconds, demonstrating that fusion was a potentially revolutionary power source. The only trouble was that this was 'hot fusion', which essentially meant that it was necessary to create conditions similar to those in the Sun to get the reaction going. This made the reaction costly, difficult and dangerous. Also, to achieve fusion it was necessary to use a substance that *is* radioactive – tritium, which is a concentrated source of hydrogen atoms – in combination with deuterium, also called 'heavy hydrogen'. Nevertheless, it showed that it could be done.

A joint initiative to continue with the development of fusion was begun in 2006. It was called ITER, which comes from the Latin for 'way forward', although it is also an acronym for International Thermonuclear Experimental Reactor. Seven nations have funded the project which expects to begin experimentation in 2016.

This approach to achieving practicable hot fusion is in contrast with other experiments, which hope to achieve cold fusion. Hot fusion works on the fundamental principle that energy is required to initiate and run the reaction, but the reaction then generates a far greater level of energy once in motion. Cold fusion is a hypothetical concept that it might be possible to generate energy under 'normal conditions', so that people would be able to manufacture energy for their own domestic requirements, or perhaps run their cars with cold fusion engines. So far, there is no scientific evidence that cold fusion has been achieved, or that it is even theoretically possible, but the idea is so attractive that some scientists pursue cold fusion with vigour.

# 10 November

## The first ever virus-like computer program is revealed

**1983** Until the 1980s it had not occurred to computer scientists that computer programs could behave like biological organisms and essentially live their own lives. Then Fred Cohen decided to centre his PhD studies on the possibility of writing pernicious programs. In 1983 he demonstrated such a program, which he described as a 'computer virus' because it had the ability to enter other programs and duplicate itself in the same way that real viruses replicate themselves within the nuclei of host cells.

Cohen's virus was written for an early type of computer called a Vax. He hid the malicious code inside the software of VD, a graphics program used by the Vax. When the user opened up VD, the virus was able to escape by piggy-backing upon user permissions. This enabled it to move around the machine and theoretically reach any part of it.

To prove the efficacy of his virus, Cohen timed how long it took for his virus to gain access to each and any part of the computer. In every test he ran, it took the invasive code less than an hour, and at its quickest it had penetrated to all areas in just five minutes.

There was widespread alarm when Fred Cohen presented his work. A program that could operate unnoticed inside its host, move around without being controlled and execute commands unprompted posed a severe threat to computer security. Perhaps more alarming still was the potential ability of viruses to move from host to host, infecting new computers as data was exchanged between machines.

Cohen himself recognised the malign potential of his research. In his thesis he wrote with alarming foresight that 'they can spread through computer networks in the same way as they spread through computers, and thus present a widespread and fairly immediate threat to many current systems'. As a result of Cohen's findings, further tests using viruses were banned in an attempt to stamp them out of existence.

Any such hopes that viruses – and the people who wrote them – could be so easily quashed though, was wishful thinking. As computers became more prevalent and new operating systems grew into being – most notably Microsoft Windows – viruses grew with them. Cohen's work effectively changed computing forever and meant that a whole new industry was required to safeguard machines from viral attacks. This was especially important once the internet got going properly as it created an international high-way for viruses to spread themselves.

The first serious viral attack occurred in 1988, when NASA and various US universities and scientific laboratories were infected. In that instance it was an experimental worm intended to monitor the current size of the internet by sitting in all connected machines. It caused problems though because machines kept being re-infected until they slowed down due to reduced memory capacity.

In fact, most deliberate early viruses were similar to the one suffered by NASA. Largely written in the bedrooms of renegade computer programmers, they sought to either corrupt important websites or cause high-profile computer networks to crash. Some that attacked domestic computer users were purely designed to be extreme irritants as they would cause a hard disk to cease functioning, thereby ruining any information saved upon in.

However, since the turn of the 21st century, viruses have been adopted by a whole new group of people. More and more, techno-logical criminals are employing viruses as tools to seize control of computers from which they send lucrative spam emails, or as programs capable of smash-and-grab raids on databases of valu-able information, such as bank details or credit card numbers.

# 11 November

### Ninety years since the end of the Great War

**2008** The terms 'World War I' or 'First World War' were not invented until the Second World War had run its course. Instead the term 'Great War' was used, as the world had never before seen carnage on such a grand scale. What made the war so horrific was that the theatre of battle was in transition, both in terms of technology and strategy. The accepted orthodoxy of warfare was that the opposing armies gathered together in a suitable field and slogged it out until one side emerged victorious, largely based on the fact that it still had some standing soldiers. Even the uniforms did their best to make the soldiers as visible as possible, thereby removing the risk of killing someone on one's own side.

This general view on how battles should be fought was still prevalent in 1914. The military on both sides had by then cottoned on to the idea of camouflaging their soldiers, or at least not illuminating them in bright colours. Specific tactics, however, had not shown much evolution and the invention of machine guns meant that the ill-fated soldiers simply got mown down in droves each time they made an advance. Consequently, although millions died, the military lines remained more-or-less stationary for four years. In essence, it was old-style warfare on a grand scale. Eventually the Germans capitulated because they happened to be the first side to run out of manpower and supplies, and were thus rendered unable to sustain the daily slaughter.

In hindsight it is abundantly clear that the Great War was really a great game of chess, played out by the high command on both sides – who kept well away from the danger themselves. There was an established mindset throughout Europe that the minions were there to fight for king and country exactly like pawns on a chessboard. There was therefore no incentive to change the way battles were enacted as the loss of life was of no consequence.

The only trouble was that the aristocracy were about to learn their lesson. So many able men died during the Great War that the peacetime infrastructures were forever changed after 1918. There simply weren't enough people to employ and those who survived the war now harboured resentment toward the higher classes. By the time the Second World War began in 1939, things had changed markedly. Few people blindly volunteered to enlist as they had done in 1914, so the government had to issue call-up papers. People knew full well that war was war, and they weren't about to willingly throw their lives away.

# 12 November

## The world's first video recorder is demonstrated

**1952** The first video recorder was developed by Charles P. Ginsburg at the Ampex Corporation in America.

Ginsburg hadn't actually started out to become an electrical engineer – he had originally planned to become a doctor and had begun his university years as a pre-med student. By 1940, however, he had changed tack and was working as a sound technician and then in 1948 he joined the Ampex Electric and Manufacturing Company.

Ampex itself had only started trading in 1944, when its founder Alexander M. Pontiaff set it up to manufacture electric motors and generators to be used by the US troops in the Second World War. After the war, Ampex acquired the services of Jack Mullin who had investigated German radio and electronics equipment captured by the Allies. Soon after that it managed to land a deal to record Bing Crosby, then the most famous star in America, for the television broadcaster NBC. From there, it began to develop new audio visual technologies.

When Ginsburg debuted his video recorder in 1952 it stirred up massive excitement. Here was a way to store, edit, copy, broadcast and distribute film that was so much quicker and easier than what had gone before.

The fundamental idea for video stems back to the first answer machine, which used a spool of magnetised wire on which to store its information. This developed into a metal ribbon and the real breakthrough came when magnetic tape was invented. This tape was essentially plastic impregnated with iron dust, so that it could store electronic information but still be lightweight and flexible. And just as a television signal was emitted in electronic form, so the magnetic tape could store that same information and play it back straightaway. In addition, the tape could be re-used time and time again.

Following its successful demonstration, Ginsbury and Ampex went back to work and set about developing their prototype into a commercial product. Just four years later, in 1956, Ampex sold its first video recorder for an eye-watering $50,000. Two years after that, NASA bought its first Ampex video recorder, and the company has supplied the space agency ever since.

Despite its enthusiastic adoption by television and space exploration, the concept of video only really captured the public imagination once video players and recorders were made cheaply enough for the mass market in the 1970s. By this time Ginsburg had been awarded an Emmy in 1957 from the Academy of Television Arts and Sciences, and in 1960 Ampex received an Oscar for technical achievement. Ginsburg was subsequently elected to the National Inventors Hall of Fame in 1990 for his pioneering work on the video recorder.

Since his death in 1992, videotapes have declined, almost to the point of obsolescence. Their replacements, DVDs, have peaked also and new formats wait in the wings, ready to seize the limelight. As well as other disc-based storage systems, most notably Blu-Ray and HD-DVD, there is increasing digital storage on computers, and engineers are prototyping portable chips capable of holding huge amounts of data.

# 13 November

## The World Wide Web is launched

**1990** The launch of the World Wide Web in 1990 was the day that computers went global and triggered a communications revolution so far-reaching that even now its implications are only just beginning to emerge. There are those who believe that the development of the internet will bring about as profound a change in society as the invention of writing, allowing people to meet, communicate and even inhabit a virtual world.

The first computer networks date back to the 1960s when universities, businesses and the military linked their own computers together to swap data. The US military relied heavily on its computer network, which played a key role in missile guidance and early-warning defence systems. But their computers did not work independently. If any one of them were destroyed by an enemy strike, the whole network would collapse. And the whole network slowed down if just one computer got too busy.

So in 1969, the military set up a network called Arpanet. Arpanet split messages travelling between computers into 'packets'. Packets could be sent separately through the network along any route decided by a computer called a router. If part of the network were damaged or working slowly, the router automatically switched packets along alternative routes.

Packet-switching created a very fast network. Arpanet grew to include more and more computers and users could send e-mails. Soon other computer networks in the United States and Europe wanted to join in. Eventually, huge numbers of networks and individual computers were connected together to form the worldwide internet.

Originally, the internet was for specialists only. Because people used many types of computers and swapped all kinds of data, it was rather clumsy. Then in 1990 Tim Berners-Lee, a computer specialist at CERN, invented a way for scientists to find and retrieve data over the internet. It came to be called the World Wide Web, 'www' for short.

The key to the World Wide Web is its 'sites'. A website is where each computer user puts data for other internet users to see, and each site is divided into a number of electronic 'pages'. Websites are stored on computers called servers where they can be accessed by other internet users. It's a little like putting a book into a library so that other people can read it.

With a large organisation, the server may actually be on the organisation's computers. Home users generally put their websites on the servers of their internet service provider. The idea is that other internet users can only access data on the website, not the rest of a computer – although hackers may try to electronically break in.

All the data on a website is in a standard form that can be read by all other internet users. Originally, data on websites was just text, and the standard form was called HyperText Transfer Protocol, or HTTP. Now websites also have pictures, films, sound recordings and all kinds of other media. These are swapped by hypermedia links or hyperlinks. Whenever you see text under-lined or in a different colour on a webpage, clicking on this usually opens a hyperlink to another page. Using these links, you can 'surf' the Web, jumping from site to site – without knowing anything about the computers running any webpage.

Each webpage has an identifying number or URL (Universal Resource Locator). Numbers are hard to remember, so the URL is translated automatically into people-friendly words or 'domain names'. Typing the domain name into a computer takes you directly to the page.

# 14 November

## No more DC electricity supply for Manhattan

**2007** When Thomas Edison first began supplying electricity some 125 years ago, he favoured the DC (direct current) system over AC (alternating current). During the 20th century AC supply was found to be more reliable, less costly and safer too, so DC was largely phased out as a mains supply. However, in some parts of New York City, there were blocks of buildings reliant on DC because their elevators and other machinery were powered by DC motors. For this reason the Con Edison Company continued to supply DC mains to them by converting AC from its power stations. That practice continued right up to 2007 when the few remaining DC buildings had their own converters installed on site.

With direct current the electrical charge flows constantly in a single direction, while with alternating current the orientation of the flow alternates many times per second. Alternating current is better suited to transporting mains supply over distances, but many electrical devices actually require direct current to operate. Semiconductors, for example, which are found in all microelectronics, rely on a unidirectional current. Converters are used to convert the AC to DC, while transformers are used to change the voltage. In the case of motors it is possible to design machines that run on one form of current or the other.

Edison's original power station was in Pearl Street, Manhattan, close to the blocks of buildings that use DC. Supplying them with direct current wasn't a problem, but it was found to be uneconomical to reach consumers who were further away, due to the loss of energy along the cables. It meant that DC had had its day in New York by 1928. Little did the authorities know that it would take a further eight decades before DC mains supply was completely discontinued.

In a rather macabre demonstration of electricity, Thomas Edison executed an elephant in 1903. The animal, named Topsy, had killed three people. It was viewed as a danger to the public, and the death sentence was passed as a result. Edison suggested electrocution as the most humane way of despatching the animal. He even filmed the execution and released the footage for public viewing. Ludicrously, the first method of execution suggested was hanging, and one suspects that it would have been more humane to have simply shot the animal in the head.

# 15 November

*Britain's most notorious murderess dies of a heart attack*

**2002** Along with Rose West, Myra Hindley is the only female prisoner in Britain ever to have been sentenced to life imprisonment without hope of parole. On 6 May 1966, Hindley and her lover, Ian Brady, were both jailed for life for the murders of Lesley Ann Downey, aged ten and seventeen-year-old Edward Evans. Brady was also found guilty of murdering John Kilbride, aged twelve – a crime in which Hindley was convicted of being an accessory. The killings took place between 1963 and 1964. They became known as the infamous Moors Murders, after the bodies of the victims were discovered in shallow graves on Saddleworth Moor near Oldham.

The public were shocked, not only at the age of those killed, but also at the age of the murderers themselves. Hindley was just 21 at the time of John Kilbride's death. The betrayal of innocence that these crimes represented caused the media to cast Hindley and Brady as incarnations of pure evil, and Hindley especially was entrenched as a hate-figure within British society.

At the age of 23 Myra Hindley was sent to Holloway Prison, and she would remain incarcerated until her death on this day in 2002. The only time she was once again able to breathe free air was during her final days in West Suffolk Hospital. At first, Hindley and Brady kept up a regular written contact, and even attempted to marry each other at one point, a request which was turned down. In 1972, however, Hindley broke off all contact with Brady and never wrote to him again.

In some ways, Hindley's status as a figure of hatred was fuelled by the public's inability to comprehend her actions. Brady was, in some regards, easier to define. He was four years older than Hindley, had previous criminal convictions and had even spent time in prison. In November 1985 he was committed to a secure mental institution after being declared criminally insane. Hindley, however, held strong Catholic beliefs and although there are suggestions that she endured some physical abuse during her childhood, she did not share Brady's criminal background. Her apparent ambivalence during her trial and sentencing was a matter of public outrage for many.

This uncertainty as to her status has led to a great deal of disagreement over her life in prison. Many maintain that she never truly repented; that subsequent claims that she had been controlled by Brady were attempts to shift the blame. Others, however, saw the flickers of a redemptive spirit within her. Towards the early 1990s, she certainly stated that she had reformed during her imprisonment.

However, if she held out a hope that she might be able to apply for parole, she was never to get the chance. As her first parole date approached in 1990, the home secretary, Leon Brittan increased her minimum term by five years to expire in 1995. Then, in July 1990, the new home secretary, David Waddington, decreed that she should never be released. This decision was reiterated the following year by his successor, Michael Howard.

In 1995, despite knowing she would never be free, Hindley did appear to publicly express regret for the murders. A portrait of her, constructed from the imprints of children's hands, was to be displayed at the 'Sensation' exhibition in London. Hindley wrote to the curators, asking for it to be removed and criticising the insensitivity to the 'emotional pain and trauma that would inevitably be experienced by the families ...'

Still, the justice system did not believe that she was ever truly reformed and it is a view shared by the vast majority of people. When she died on this day, from a heart attack at the age of 60, it was a time for neither celebration nor regret; it was instead a stark reminder of one of the most painful crimes of the 20th century.

# 16 November

## The US begins its rocket programme

**1945** While the US had been the first to develop the atom bomb during the Second World War, the Germans had been rather good at other technologies. They had been the first to get a production jet fighter operational and they had also been the first to launch guided ballistic missiles. Immediately following the war, the US found itself in the initial stages of the Cold War with the USSR and realised that it would need missiles with which to launch nuclear warheads, should hostilities escalate. As a result, the US offered 88 former Nazi scientists and engineers the opportunity of working in America in exchange for their expertise and know-how. Included among them was Wernher von Braun, who had been chiefly responsible for the success of the V-1 and V-2 flying bomb projects.

With the Germans onboard, the US quickly began developing rockets in two directions. Firstly there were the nuclear missiles, and secondly there were space rockets. The V-2 had functioned by reaching the very top of the atmosphere and then plunging down to its target, so it was clear that it had the potential to put satellites and manned craft into space. Within a decade, both the US and USSR had advanced their rocket technologies sufficiently to begin experiments with putting simple satellites into orbit. The first was *Sputnik 1* in 1957. By 1961 both nations had put men into orbit and the next objective was reaching the Moon. The Soviets' *Luna 2* unmanned probe had already reached the Moon in 1959, but the American *Apollo 11* delivered the first people there in 1969.

Since 1972, however, there has been something of a hiatus in manned space exploration. Plenty of probes have been sent to explore the other planets in the solar system, but so far there have been no serious intentions to send humans on interplanetary missions. It is possible that people will visit Mars during the 21st century, but the Moon mission taught humanity that there really isn't much point in risking human lives just for the sake of it. It may have been a remarkable and awe-inspiring thing putting people on the Moon but in reality it didn't teach us any more about the Moon than could have been achieved with robotic devices. That is why no one has bothered since the early 1970s.

# 17 November

## The first computer mouse is patented

**1970** The humble computer mouse, so called because it originally resembled a mouse with a long tail, is one of those inventions that are seemingly unremarkable yet incredibly important. What it does is provide the computer user with a physical interface for manipulating the monitor screen. It translates physical movements into movements of the cursor or arrow, thereby enabling the screen to become a virtual desktop.

The first computer mouse used perpendicular wheels to interpret the movements of the user's hand: left–right and up–down. It was developed by an American inventor, Douglas Engelbart. Unfortunately for him, he made no real money from his patent because computer manufacturers used different mechanisms for their own versions and his patent had run out anyway by the time the mouse caught on.

The first successful mechanism used a ball and socket principle. There were still left–right and up–down sensors but they were manipulated by the ball, which had the freedom to move in both directions simultaneously. It was therefore possible to make diagonal and circular movements. The ball was inclined to pick up dirt however, so regular maintenance was necessary.

The next success came in the form of the optical mouse, which had no moving parts at all and therefore required no maintenance to keep it clean. Light emitting diodes and photodiodes sent and received beams of light as they reflected off the mouse pad. Movements are thus electronically detected and translated into data. The final stage in the evolution of the computer mouse was to provide it with radio contact and make it wireless. This, of course, means that the mouse no longer has a tail, making it a new animal altogether: the computer vole perhaps, or computer hamster.

Of course, the other great user-input device, the humble keyboard, had already been invented along with the typewriter in the 19th century. The QWERTY arrangement of letters was devised by Christopher Sholes, who invented the popular typewriter in the 1860s. The arrangement was not an ergonomic consideration, but rather to prevent the mechanical typewriter hammers from jamming. Once adopted by journalists, secretaries and writers it became standard, even though electronic systems meant that it was perfectly feasible to change the arrangement to suit higher speeds of typing and prevent repetitive strain injury.

# 18 November

## The amazing new placebo for the common cold

**1970** It's a funny thing, but people are easily convinced by recommendations made by others whom they view as experts. This is precisely what happened when Linus Pauling proposed a link between the intake of Vitamin C (ascorbic acid) and immunity from the common cold. Pauling was a Nobel Prizewinner, so people took his word for it and began taking Vitamin C supplements like they were going out of fashion. To this day, cold and flu remedies contain Vitamin C as if it is received wisdom.

The thing is that there is no empirical proof of Vitamin C making the blindest bit of difference, either in terms of warding off infection in the first place or accelerating recovery. Because colds are really just an inconvenience and make people feel irritable and lousy, there is an element of choice involved in how people react to them. In other words, some people like to just get on with things, while others like to be self-indulgent and make the most of feeling sorry for themselves. This is why so-called cold remedies are allowed to come into their own. The people who take them aren't interested in whether they actually demonstrate a scientific efficacy. They just like to stuff themselves full with placebos and wallow. Colds only last a few days anyway, so it is very easy to put two and two together to make five.

Pauling's emphasis was, and still is, on using Vitamin C to avoid catching colds in the first place by taking large doses daily. His argument is based on the fact that Vitamin C has a metabolic half-life of 30 minutes, so that the body runs out rather rapidly: after 30 minutes only 50 per cent remains, after 60 minutes it's down to 25 per cent, after 90 minutes there's 12.5 per cent of the original amount, 6.25 per cent after 120 minutes and so on. He used the half-life argument to counter the views of sceptics, by pointing out that mainstream researchers haven't been thorough enough. One is bound to ask though: 'what's the big deal about getting a cold anyway?' Even if there was some truth in his idea, most people would surely prefer to take their chances than vigilantly dose themselves with Vitamin C every couple of hours!

# 19 November

## *The prototype jump jet takes to the air*

**1960** Helicopters have proven themselves very useful in warfare situations where landing fixed-wing aircraft is problematic, but they are not very useful as strike aircraft because they are too slow in the air. This conflict of interests led to the development of the first fixed-wing aircraft capable of vertical takeoff: the Harrier Jump Jet.

To achieve its trick, the fuselage was fitted with rotating nozzles that could direct the jet thrust in any direction. It was thus capable of entirely vertical takeoff, by using the nozzles vertically, or short-runway takeoff by using them diagonally. Unlike helicopters, the Harrier could serve no useful purpose as a personnel carrier, so the applications of the two types of aircraft remained mutually exclusive.

Other interpretations of the vertical takeoff theme are many and varied. The Germans produced the Starfighter, which had a titling jet engine on each wing. The Canadian CL-84 and the US V-22 both had propeller engines that tilted in a similar way, so that they effectively became dual rotor helicopters while in vertical flight mode and twin engine aeroplanes in horizontal flight mode.

In 1996 a competition was launched between Boeing and Lockheed Martin to design a Joint Strike Fighter, which basically meant an aircraft capable of vertical takeoff, short-runway take off, full-runway takeoff and supersonic flight. It was to be a multipurpose fighter/bomber for the 21st century. Boeing came up with the X-32 and Lockheed Martin the X-35. In 2001 the latter was chosen for production because it outshone the former on performance in a number of respects. Its ability to fly supersonically was very important as it placed the aircraft in the same performance league as other jet fighters; something that the Harrier could not claim.

The X-35 achieves vertical lift by using a centralised fan in the fuselage, which is covered by flaps when not in use. It is shaft driven by the jet engine, so that it sucks cold air through the fuselage top to bottom. It removes a need for tilting or rotating parts. In the world of aeronautics VTOL stands for 'vertical takeoff and landing', while STOVL stands for 'short takeoff and vertical landing'.

# 20 November

## Artificial blood is used for the first time

**1979** People are generally aware of artificial limbs, organs and other body components, but artificial blood is less familiar. Blood is, in effect, a fluid organ which performs a number of functions: fighting infection, healing wounds, transporting nutrients and hormones, exchanging gases and transferring body warmth. It would clearly be a tall order to design artificial blood capable of all these functions, so scientists have thus far focused on specific functionality.

There are two key areas of development in artificial blood. The first is as a volume expander. When patients have suffered physical injury and rapid loss of blood it is useful to be able to provide a blood substitute so that the heart can keep pumping and air doesn't enter the system. This is often done in situ, at road traffic accidents for example, to keep the patient alive until it is possible to deal with the injury properly. The substitute is an inert filler, so that the medic needn't worry about matching blood type in the heat of the moment. A blood transfusion can then be carried out in hospital to restore full functionality. Blood fillers also mean that the patient can transfer body heat to and from extremities, thereby avoiding both hypothermia and hyperthermia.

The second type of artificial blood enhances the patient's ability to perform gaseous exchange in the lungs and is known as an oxygen therapeutic. Inhalation of poisonous gases, such as carbon monoxide, destroys the blood's ability to absorb oxygen, so this kind of artificial blood can aid the recovery of patients harmed in this way. The same is true of patients suffering from altitude sickness, where they cannot harvest enough oxygen from the thin air. As it happens, the first patient to receive this kind of artificial blood, in 1979, was a Jehovah's Witness who had refused a real blood transfusion on religious grounds.

With regard to blood's ability to maintain the body on a biological level, scientists have suggested that they may be able to design artificial blood which contains living cells derived from stem cell technology. This is still a long way off, but it is theoretically possible and points to a future where artificial blood may combine the functions discussed in a more complete package. It may even be possible to draw a line under the need for blood donation. This would remove the problems that arise from maintaining supply, matching blood type and accidental infection.

# 21 November

## Piltdown Man is unmasked

**1953** Piltdown Man was the familiar name given to a newly discovered human ancestor, known scientifically as *Eoanthropus dawsoni*. The genus name translates from the Greek *eos* ('dawn') and *anthropos* ('human being'), while the species name alludes to its alleged discoverer, Charles Dawson.

The remains were apparently unearthed in a quarry in England in 1912 near the village of Piltdown, East Sussex and described as fossils. In 1953 a new examination revealed that they were not fossils at all, but modern bones. They were, in fact, the mandible of an orang-utan and the cranium of a modern human. Piltdown Man was a hoax and a rather bad one at that. It was a wonder that it had taken 41 years for the truth to out.

To this day, no one knows for sure who was behind the hoax.

Some people describe it as a 'forgery', but one can only forge a copy of something that actually exists in the first place – and Piltdown Man has certainly never existed. It seems most likely that it was Dawson himself. Perhaps it started as a practical joke or perhaps he had an appetite for scientific recognition at any cost. There is also the possibility that Dawson was hoaxed by someone else, but it is pretty easy to tell the difference between stone and bone, so that seems extremely unlikely, unless he realised too late and had to go along with the hoax for fear of damaging his reputation. Besides, since 1953 a number of other finds associated with Dawson have been exposed as fakes or have else been genuine items planted by him, so there seems little doubt that he was a confidence trickster.

He was an amateur archaeologist with no formal training, but managed to cultivate a considerable name for himself by pulling the wool over the eyes of fellow scientists. He was elected to both the Geological Society and Society of Antiquaries. He beguiled his peers to such an extent that he became known as the 'Wizard of Sussex'. In 1912 he was so highly thought of that he knew people would not question his word on the Piltdown Man. In addition, the subject of human evolution was a hot topic, so he had a captive audience, ready and willing to be taken in by his lies. He died in 1916 at the age of 52, a long time before anyone had an inkling of his skulduggery, to use an uncannily appropriate word!

# 22 November

## JFK is assassinated

**1963** The day that American President John F. Kennedy was assassinated in Dallas, Texas is a day anyone in the Western world who was alive at the time won't forget. The news of this sudden and violent end to the life of the young president in whom Americans saw their hope for the future sent a shock around the world so profound that it is etched firmly on the memories of countless millions of people who can remember exactly what they were doing when Kennedy was shot.

It was a beautifully sunny November day in Dallas and Kennedy was travelling in his open-top Lincoln limousine with his wife Jacqueline, waving happily at the crowds gathered in the streets to greet this most popular of presidents. The visit to Dallas was designed to help generate funds for Kennedy's re-election campaign and to mend fences within the Texas Democrats who had been fighting among themselves. As the president's car turned into Dallas's Elm Street at 12: 30 PM, three shots rang out. The first hit nothing. The second went through Kennedy's neck to hit local Governor Connally, who was in the car with him. The third fatally went right through Kennedy's head.

An official investigation which came to be known as the Warren Report concluded that the shots were fired from a high-power rifle by Lee Harvey Oswald from the nearby School Book Depository. Oswald was apprehended within 100 minutes of the assassination, after killing a policeman who had tried to arrest him. But Oswald never came to trial; he was shot and killed two days later by Jack Ruby as he was being transferred to Dallas County Jail.

Ever since, conspiracy theories have mushroomed, despite the official verdict that Oswald and Ruby both acted alone. Forty years after the event, an opinion poll carried out by ABC showed that 70 per cent of Americans believed the assassination was an undercover plot. Oswald said before he was killed that he had been set up as a 'patsy', and many say the shots came not from the Book Depository where Oswald was stationed but from a nearby grassy knoll. Some say it was all a plot by the Mafia. Some say it was the CIA. Some say it was the KGB. But despite countless investigations, numerous revelatory documentaries, and endless theorising, no one has yet been able to provide convincing evidence of anything beyond the initial lone gunman story of the Warren Report.

The abrupt ending to Kennedy's life, at the height of his powers, has created an aura of lasting glamour around him and prompted many people to pose the question, 'What if?' Where would America and the Cold War have gone if Kennedy had not been shot, for example? Some believe that the Cold War would have ended some twenty years earlier if Kennedy had been re-elected. Others believe it could have escalated into a nuclear war. After all, the Cuban missile crisis of 1962 had brought the USA and the USSR as close to a nuclear confrontation as it had ever been. Kennedy and Khrushchev had stepped back from the brink then. Would they have done so if another crisis had arisen?

# 23 November

## First person to dive to 100 metres without equipment

**1976** One of the oddest extreme sports has to that of free diving. In 1976 Jacques Mayol made the sport fashionable by reaching a depth of 100 metres without any artificial breathing assistance. The art of holding one's breath for long periods is known as apnoea, as it is effectively training the lungs to stop breathing, just as those with sleep apnoea fail to breathe while asleep.

Mayol saw himself as a scientific pioneer and had the idea, along with various anthropologists, that humans may have had an aquatic ancestor, thereby explaining why we have virtually no body hair, for example, and why babies can naturally swim or why some people have webbing between their fingers and toes. He saw his free diving as an experiment in bringing out that aquatic ontogeny, which is known as the aquatic ape hypothesis.

Since Mayol's era, free diving has become a curiously competitive activity. Divers drop to dangerous depths by holding onto weights and then swim back to the surface having endured incredible pressurisation. In fact, it is extremely risky because the air in the lungs is so reduced in volume by the pressure that the organs become fist-sized. Other temporary physical changes occur that can lead to sudden death. Of course, there is also the risk of simply asphyxiating if the body isn't replenished with oxygen before too long. It seems that apnoeists (as divers are technically known) enjoy free diving for the same reason that cavers enjoy pot-holing: it is the challenge rather than the environment that provides the reward.

In some cultures free diving is or was a prerequisite for making a living. Pearl divers, shell collectors and fishermen often use their breathing ability to dive deep and stay down for long periods. It has been found that humans do have a behavioural adaptation to submersion called the mammalian diving reflex. All mammals react to water by lowering their heart rate and adjusting their blood supply in certain ways. It isn't necessarily an indication of an aquatic past but more a means of survival in the event of becoming waterborne. It seems likely that some early mammals were semi-aquatic, but that was a long time before apes had evolved.

# 24 November

## 150 years of evolution by natural selection

**2009** On this day, some 150 years ago, the publishers John Murray released the first copies of Charles Darwin's work, *On the Origin of Species by Means of Natural Selection, or the Preservation of Favoured Races in the Struggle for Life*. Its pages held the now famous theory of evolution. The book shone new light on the origins of life and the development of the species that littered the world and, in particular, the role of man as an evolved animal.

The book was a huge success during Darwin's lifetime, going through some six different editions between 1859 and 1872. It was over the course of these editions that certain revisions entered the work to produce the text we know today. It was not until the sixth edition, for example, that the title was shortened to *The Origin of Species*, and indeed it was only in this version that the term 'evolution' first appeared. In fact, the phrase for which Darwin's *Origin* is now so famous – 'the survival of the fittest' – didn't appear in the book until the fifth edition in February 1869 ... and even then it was lifted from Herbert Spencer's 1864 title, *Principles of Biology*.

However, this does not belittle what Darwin achieved with *Origin* at all. He was formulating his theory in the cauldron of scientific debate and incremental changes were an understandable part of reacting to new information and responding to criticism. When the final edition was ultimately published, it contained within it a theory more solid and robust than what had appeared thirteen years previously.

Charles Darwin himself was a meticulous character. His curiosity regarding the principle of evolution had been sparked by his grandfather, Erasmus Darwin, who had been a contemporary of Jean-Baptiste Lamarck. Charles arrived at his theory of evolution by natural selection after examining evidence in the field and coming to the most rational explanation.

His reasoning was based largely on what he saw when he went on his famous voyage aboard HMS *Beagle* as a young naturalist. He then spent decades gathering evidence, developing arguments and honing his ideas. In fact, he had stalled publishing for so long that he might never have done so had it not been for a letter sent to him by Alfred Russell Wallace, who had chanced upon the same idea and wanted to know Darwin's view on the matter. These days Wallace is recognised as the co-discoverer of evolution by natural selection.

Lamarck's original theory regarding hereditary characteristics had propounded the idea that animals and plants could adapt during their own lifetimes and pass on those adaptations to their offspring. The idea was widely accepted because it made apparent sense, but Darwin could see that the logic fell apart as soon as one considered that injuries must also be seen as developmental adaptations. How could it be then that only desirable adaptations were passed to offspring and undesirable ones were dismissed? Darwin's intuition told him that Lamarck was incorrect. Then he realised the simple truth: all individuals are actually slightly different from one another and the ever-changing environment naturally selects those individuals that are slightly better suited to their surroundings.

Darwin's discovery has been reinforced by science over the past 150 years, so that we now know the genetic mechanism by which the process of evolution by natural selection can work. That mechanism also shows that Lamarck was wrong, as there is no means by which information about developmental adaptations can be conveyed to the genes.

# 25 November

## Cable TV makes its inaugural appearance

**1948** It's one of life's little curiosities that radio started life wired and then became wireless, while television did the reverse. In actual fact, all televisions are cable televisions as the cable runs from the aerial to the television set. It's just that *cable* televisions have cables running from a shared aerial, that's all.

In 1948 Leroy Parsons wanted to watch the first broadcast by the American station KRSC and found that it was necessary to rig an antenna on to the hotel roof in Astoria, Oregon. He then ran a coaxial cable from the hotel to his house in order to watch the programme. Soon his friends and neighbours were cabled to the same antenna and they had created the first cable network.

The advantage of cable was simply that one strategically placed antenna could receive signals and relay them to many different television sets that would otherwise just pick up very poor images or not function at all. For the programme providers it had the advantage that fewer transmitters were needed, so cable networks became the preferred method of providing a television service in certain places, especially those where the terrain caused problems with the transmission of radio and television signals. The first proper cable network, involving provider and consumer, was established in Barrow, Alaska in 1967 by the very same Leroy Parsons.

Since its humble beginnings some 60 years ago, cable TV has proved a driving force in shaping how programmes are consumed. The sheer number of channels that can be accommodated on a cable service – as opposed to the very limited volume of non-cable or non-satellite methods – has enabled many different types of television show to find a foothold.

The home of cable television, the United States, matches this huge output with an avid consumption rate. A study in 2006 found that nearly 60 per cent of US homes subscribed to some form or other of cable.

The continued popularity of cable television, and indeed its ever-increasing rise in customers, has been boosted by the regular improvements made to the broadcasting technology. In this day and age the problem of transmission and reception is largely resolved by actually omitting the cables and using communication satellites. These can bounce signals from transmitters to receiving dishes, thereby avoiding physical obstacles.

Cable systems are still used in some places, although they often use optical fibres to carry multiple digital signals, rather than old coaxial cables to carry analogue signals. Analogue signals are waves of varying frequency and amplitude, which weaken over distance and suffer from interference so that the information can become corrupted. Digital signals, on the other hand, are far easier to send and receive without loss of integrity. That is why broadcasters have opted for digital signalling in recent years, as it provides a more reliable service.

# 26 November

## Tutankhamun's 80th re-birthday

**2002** The archaeologist Howard Carter had actually discovered the passageway to Tutankhamun's tomb some three weeks before, but it had taken that long to remove the rubble and debris in order to reach the entrance. On 26 November 1922 he breached the front door and peered through the hole into the antechamber for the first time. To his great excitement he had discovered the only intact pharaoh's tomb in the Valley of the Kings. All of the others had been raided in antiquity and stripped of their contents.

So it was that Tutankhamun began his afterlife over 3,000 years after he had been buried. The riches and artefacts found in the tomb amazed the world and have been famous ever since.

The search for Tuntankhamun's tomb had been funded by Lord Carnarvon, an English aristocrat with a strong interest in Egyptology. Carter's initial explorations had been discouraging but then, shortly before Carnarvon was about to withdraw his financial support, the archaeologist stumbled across a flight of steps leading to the tomb's entrance.

Carter hurriedly wired his benefactor. Having caught a glimpse of the unrivalled treasures within, he was keen to prepare the tomb for entry as soon as possible. For the next couple of months work continued apace as Carter and his team set about for the official opening of the sealed door.

On 16 February 1923 the last breach was finally made. Among the huge numbers of discoveries that emerged from within was a curse which supposedly threatened to strike down anyone who disturbed the dead pharaoh. Apparently, at the precise moment that the pharaoh's resting place was opened, Carnarvon's dog back in England let out a howl and died. When Lord Carnarvon himself, who had been present at the opening of the tomb, suddenly died just weeks later in the April of 1923, the public imagination went wild. Even Sir Arthur Conan Doyle, the creator of Sherlock Holmes and a great believer in the occult, got involved, publicly stating that he suspected that a great curse had been unleashed.

The truth is all rather more prosaic – Lord Carnarvon had actually been in poor health for the twenty years preceding Carter's discovery, and his death was as a result of pneumonia caught when suffering from an infected cut. Not only this, but Howard Carter, who one might reasonably imagine to have suffered the wrath of the curse more than most, was totally unaffected and went on to live for another sixteen years. In actual fact, there wasn't even a curse inscribed into the hieroglyphics that covered the walls of the tomb, and the apparent translations that appeared in British newspapers were little more than the words of imaginative journalists.

Nowadays, the fame of Tutankhamun reaches far and wide, but in historical terms, he was not a particularly significant pharaoh and he achieved relatively little during his reign. However, the chance survival of his remains and burial goods has since made him into an icon of past civilisation.

# 27 November

## *Two firsts in organ transplantation*

**1989** and **2005** When it comes to the transplantation of bodily organs, things have progressed greatly in recent years. In 1989 the first living donor organ transplant was performed in Chicago. A woman donated a portion of her liver to her two year old daughter.

Alyssa Smith was just a baby when she was diagnosed with biliary atresia. The cause behind this condition is unknown, but it occurs in newborn infants when the bile duct connecting the liver to the small intestine is blocked or absent. In the US it affects only 1 in around 15,000 births, but if undetected it results in fatal liver failure.

Alyssa's mother, Teresa Smith, was well aware of the dangers associated with this pioneering surgery. Her justification for going ahead with the operation though was simple, 'Once you've given someone a big piece of your heart, it's easy to throw in a little bit of liver'.

The operation was a success for both mother and daughter. After a six-week recovery period at the University of Chicago Medical Centre, Teresa carried little Alyssa out into the world.

The persistent trouble with transplant surgery, even with mother–daughter donation, is the risk of incompatibility between donor organs and the recipient's body. For thirteen years after the operation, Alyssa Smith had to take a regular course of immuno-suppressant drugs. It wasn't until she was fifteen that the donated liver had sufficiently established itself and she was able to stop taking the drugs.

Twenty-six years to the day after Alyssa and Teresa Smith were operated upon, Isabelle Dinoire underwent an even more remarkable transplant procedure when she was given the first partial face transplantation. Her face had been mauled by a dog and French surgeons were able to rebuild her features by using the nose, mouth and cheek of a brain-dead donor.

Mme Dinoire had been so badly mutilated before the operation that she could hardly speak or eat. The French surgeons reconnected a multitude of blood vessels and muscle tissue fibres in the hope that Mme Dinoire would be able to gain reasonable muscular control over her new face. Since the operation, she has regained the ability to eat and talk, and over time has increased her ability to move her features as normal. A year after the operation, she reported that she had learned to smile again.

In 2008, again in France, a male patient was given the first complete facial transplant. Pascal Coler suffers from a genetic condition called Von Recklinghausen's disease, which causes tumours to grow on nerve endings and had left his face severely disfigured. It is thought that John Merrick – the Elephant Man – suffered from a similar disease, although his deformities also involved grotesque bone growth.

# 28 November

## *The Polaroid camera begins its 60-year lifespan*

**1948** In early 2008 it was announced that the Polaroid camera would be withdrawn from the market due to a decline in sales brought about by the advent of the digital camera. Untilit came into being, however, the self-developing film of the Polaroid was the only way by which a photographer could see instant results. Amateur photographers loved it because it was instantly gratifying, while professional photographers found it highly useful because it provided a preview of their work.

The science behind the Polaroid principle was patented in 1929 by Edwin Land, who then refined the idea over the next two decades until he had arrived at a product suitable for manufacture. The underlying process involves electromagnetic radiation (light waves) causing the realignment of crystals embedded in the surface of the film. They start life polarised, or all standing parallel to one another, but the light causes electrical fields to realign the crystals according to its strength, so that an image is created. The Polaroid camera took off as a popular product in 1953 when an affordable model was put on the market.

Edwin Land was also responsible for the introduction of Polaroid lenses and filters, which are used in a variety of applications, including sunglasses and ski goggles. They work by only allowing light waves to travel through the glass or plastic in restricted ways. In other words, those light waves that approach from the wrong angles are bounced away. This means that glare is removed, enabling the wearer to see things without discomfort.

Liquid crystal display (LCD) screens work in a similar way to Polaroid photographs. Electronic signals cause distortion in the pixel cells so that the light emitted from them changes tone and colour. As the name suggests, the cells contain liquid crystal. This sounds like a contradiction in terms, but the substance possesses properties halfway between a liquid and a solid crystal, making it perfect for this use. Substances behave in this manner when their molecules are arranged in a regular, crystalline way – but loosely enough to remain liquid. The term 'liquid crystal' was coined by Frenchman Georges Friedel in 1922.

# 29 November

*Mary Whitehouse becomes the prime minister of ethical and moral standards in Britain*

**1965** 29 November 1965 was the day when middle-class, bespectacled housewife Mary Whitehouse announced the launch of the National Viewers' and Listeners' Association (NVLA), and put herself at the head of a campaign to 'Clean Up TV' that made her both the scourge of creative artists and a figure of fun.

Mrs Whitehouse came to the fore at a time when what was described as the 'permissive society' was just getting up a head of steam. The revolution in attitudes that finally allowed people to talk about sex, and portray it on film, on TV and in the theatre was seen by Mrs Whitehouse as the start of a flood of immorality which would destroy society. Her main target was the BBC, and she was particularly offended by the Wednesday Play with its gritty realism, which often had scenes of sex and violence (though very mild compared to today's cinema), and by late-night satire. Another famous target for her wrath was the sitcom, *Till Death Us Do Part,* although for its bad language rather than the racism of its central character, Alf Garnett.

Her greatest triumph came in 1977 when she successfully sued for blasphemy the editor of *Gay News,* Denis Lemon, for publishing a poem by James Kirkup in which a Roman centurion imagined having sex with Christ as he looked at him on the cross. She was less successful in suing Michael Bogdanov in 1982 for gross indecency in the National Theatre play *Romans in Britain,* which featured a Roman soldier buggering a young Celt boy. Her biography claims she withdrew the case having made her point. In fact, it seems likely that she would have lost her case, because she had not seen the play, and her solicitor, the only witness, had only seen it from the back of the stalls.

Mrs Whitehouse died in 2001, and since then some people have remembered her fondly, maybe as part of their youth. A recent BBC television play, *Filth – The Mary Whitehouse Story,* portrayed her as a kindly, dotty provincial mother finally driven to protest by an orgy of sex on the BBC. But to victims of her attacks, she was anything but kindly. Denis Lemon was lucky to escape prison. Michael Bogdanov suffered tremendous stress during the trial. Many other artists had their work quietly altered or dropped altogether.

In a recent article in *The Times* A.A. Gill writes that her very spleen acted as a goad to artists: 'What permissiveness and progress need is something to be permissive about and progress from, something to push against.' When *The Goodies* TV comedy failed to arouse her criticism with their first series, they bent over backwards to offend her in subsequent series.

In some ways, her campaigning failed – and seemed to fail mostly in the face of the market economics espoused by what some describe as the other famous middle-class housewife of the last half century, Mrs Thatcher. What is permissible on film and TV now goes far beyond even the worst nightmares of Mrs Whitehouse in the 1960s. Yet there is a self-censorship within broadcast organisations like the BBC which might have pleased her, and the watchdog Broadcasting Standards Commission (now the Office of Communications) sprang at least partly from her NVLA.

# 30 November

## Lucy is unearthed in Ethiopia

**1974** *Australopithecus afarensis* is the scientific name for the species of possible human ancestor to which Lucy belongs. *Australopithecus* means 'southern ape' because previous hominid fossils had all been found in latitudes farther north, while *afarensis* translates as 'of Afar', alluding to the north-eastern Afar region of Ethiopia where the fossils were found. The name Lucy came about because the anthropologists involved happened to be listening to The Beatles' song, 'Lucy in the Sky with Diamonds', on the evening of her discovery.

Lucy is estimated to be about 3.2 million years old. Current thinking is that the Australopithecines were the precursor to the first Homo species – but several Australopithecine species are recognised, so we can never be sure whether Lucy was a member of our direct lineage or a spur which eventually died out. Nevertheless, she had evolved to walk bipedally (on two legs) and to use her hands for manipulating simple stone tools. In addition, she showed clear signs of cranial growth, indicating that increased intelligence had become an evolutionary trait selected by nature because it aided survival.

The Great African Rift Valley is now regarded as the cradle of humanity as it is clear that our ancestors evolved their fundamental prototype in that region before venturing out across Africa and Asia. From that point onwards it was a matter of evolution honing the human design until it arrived at the form in which we are today.

Inevitably there has been some debate about the future evolution of humans. This subject presents some difficulty as it is almost impossible to identify the characteristics in humans that natural selection favours or disfavours. In addition, we reproduce so slowly that it is equally difficult to notice any evolutionary trends. Popular ideas of the human brain continuing to grow, for example, have no proven scientific foundation. There is nothing to suggest that more intelligent people pass on their genes with a higher frequency than less intelligent people. During our past, evolution improved intelligence because it must have offered a survival advantage, but society and technology have negated any real need for that trend to continue. We may find that we remain virtually unchanged over future millennia because we have already reached our optimum design – much like sharks and crocodiles which look pretty much the same nowadays as they did tens of thousands of years ago.

# 1 December

*Rosa Parks makes her famous defiant stand against racial segregation*

**1955** It is shocking to think that until less than half a century ago, there was still racial segregation in the USA – the country that declared at its outset that 'all men are born equal', and the same country that fought a Civil War 150 years ago to end slavery. Yet the 'Jim Crow laws' of America's southern states were every bit as racially divisive as South Africa's apartheid laws, even though perhaps not quite so brutally enforced. That's why Rosa Parks' quiet act of defiance in refusing to give up her seat on a bus to a white man in Montgomery, Alabama, later made her such a heroine.

The Jim Crow laws, named perhaps after a caricature of black people as Jim Crows, came into force in the 1870s and 1880s, after the withdrawal from the American South of the Republican armies that had protected the civil rights of the freed slaves after the Civil War. While in theory black people had the same rights under the constitution as white people, the Jim Crow laws gave racial segregation legal force. Black people were sent to separate schools, worked separately and travelled separately on trains and buses. And, of course, facilities for blacks were far inferior to those for whites. School buses, for instance, were laid on for white children, while black children had to walk to school.

Rosa Parks, a coloured woman of mixed racial background, had experienced the humiliations of racial segregation all her life. In 1943, for instance, she had got on the bus and paid her fare at the front. She had then been forced back off the bus and told to enter by the 'coloreds' entrance at the rear – only for the bus to move off without her before she could get to the back. She was left to walk five miles home in pouring rain. Such things happened to her and many other coloured people all the time, and the resentment gradually built up.

On this day in 1955, she was asked by the driver – the same

driver who had driven off without her twelve years earlier – to give up her seat in the 'mixed' middle section of the bus that she was travelling on. Rosa Parks politely refused. The driver had her arrested. As she later said, 'People always say that I didn't give up my seat because I was tired, but that isn't true. I was not tired physically, or no more tired than I usually was at the end of a working day. I was not old, although some people have an image of me as being old then. I was 42. No, the only tired I was, was tired of giving in.'

On the day of her trial, black civil rights activists called for a boycott of all the buses in Montgomery. The day's boycott turned into one of the longest and most determined civil rights actions America had ever seen. It went on for 381 days, and the campaign to challenge the constitutionality of the segregation laws that had led to Rosa Parks' arrest brought Martin Luther King to the fore.

The black civil rights movement did not begin with Rosa Parks' refusing to relinquish her seat on the bus, but it gained such momentum that the end of the segregation laws – which finally came to pass ten years later in 1965 – soon became inevitable. And it was no accident that the protest movement against apartheid in South Africa began with a bus boycott. In later years, Rosa Parks was showered with accolades by the very state that had humiliated her and so many other coloured people for so long. When *Time* magazine named her as one of the heroes of the century in 1999, it congratulated America on having produced such a heroine, saying: 'It is no less than the belief in the power of the individual, that cornerstone of the American Dream, that she inspires.' For Rosa Parks, it was not a dream, but a harsh reality that drove her to finally say, 'Enough'.

# 2 December

## *McCarthy gets a dose of his own medicine*

**1954** Senator Joseph McCarthy made a name for himself in the post-war years in the US by running a campaign against public figures suspected of communist leanings. The Cold War began when Joseph Stalin made it evident that the Soviets would not fraternise with the West following the end of the Second World War in 1945. McCarthy had been in the US Marine Corps from 1942 but left three months before the end of the war in the Pacific. He then embellished his war record to get his foot on the political ladder and became a senator in 1947.

McCarthy was very much a career politician in that he enjoyed the power and respect above any political principles. He was academically bright and knew how to manipulate circumstances to his advantage. This seems to have been why he embarked on his crusade against the communists, whom he habitually referred to as 'commies' or 'reds'. It gave him a political mission and was a self-perpetuating spin, because he knew that the US public had a suspicion and fear of communism and he simply made them feel that there was indeed something to worry about.

His mode of operation was to arrest and question any public figure who expressed even the slightest sympathy with communist ideals. The generic charge was that such people were in fact spies for the USSR, who used their position and influence to gain access to top secret information and supply it to the Soviets. McCarthy also seems to have been convinced that communists were trying to rise to power in America and undermine the democratic foundation of the 'land of the free'.

Of course, there were a few real spies here and there, so it wasn't difficult for McCarthy to cultivate the impression that his work was necessary and worthy. Well, at least that was true for the first few years, but then McCarthy began to stretch the bounds of the public's credulity. The rate at which people were being dragged through the courts and then re-emerging without indictment led people to believe that his anti-communist agenda was largely without foundation.

Eventually McCarthy became rather too autocratic for his own good and his fellow senators grew weary of his bullying behaviour. In 1954 he was censured by a vote of 67 to 22 and thrown out of government. An investigation into his financial dealings had led to his verbally insulting and abusing members of the Senate

Committee and he paid the price. He died just three years later from hepatitis exacerbated by alcoholism. He was 48 years of age.

# 3 December

## *Dr Christiaan Barnard performs the first successful human heart transplant*

**1967** The patient concerned was a 55-year-old man named Louis Washkansky. He received his new heart in the Groote Schuur Hospital in Cape Town, South Africa. Although the operation was deemed a success, Washkansky enjoyed only a further eighteen days of life. His immune system had been weakened and he died from double pneumonia. Nevertheless, the transplant was a major breakthrough for science.

As it happened, the donor was a woman named Denise Darvall, who had been fatally injured in a car accident. In addition to this, Washkansky was Jewish, while Darvall was Christian. The theological and gender crossover caused less controversy, though, than the fact that her kidneys were donated to a black boy named Jonathan Van Wyck. The cloud of apartheid still hung heavy over South Africa at that time and the racial issues threatened to overshadow the achievements of Dr Barnard.

At the time of the famous operation, immunosuppressive drugs were in their early stages of development. They are required to prevent the patient's body from rejecting the donated organ, and they work by suppressing the immune system so that it doesn't react to the presence of alien tissue. The trouble is that the drugs also prevent the immune system from recognising and attacking pathogens in the body. This was the reason why Washkansky succumbed to pneumonia. He was in an impossible situation, as he would have died from heart failure had Barnard taken him off the drugs. Current immunosuppressive drugs are more target-specific, so that they still allow the body to fend off diseases. It also helps to find a closer tissue match between patient and donor.

Since 1967 over 40,000 similar transplants have been performed worldwide. Some patients have lived with their new hearts for a quarter of a century and died from unrelated causes, demonstrating that such procedures truly do bring new life to people.

Transplant surgery has become increasingly sophisticated in recent years. Heart transplants are now considered almost routine in a world of medicine where surgeons are perfecting the transplants of lungs, livers, hands and faces. Barnard's groundbreaking procedure was actually just a mid-step in what has been a continued progression since the turn of the 20th century – the first cornea was transplanted in 1905 and the first kidney in 1954.

# 4 December

## An enormous squid is filmed alive in its natural environment for the very first time

**2006** What most people don't consider is the volume of habitat offered by the world's oceans. In terms of area, the oceans already account for over two-thirds of the planet's surface, but in terms of volume the ratio is even more pronounced. Land doesn't offer a three-dimensional living space in quite the same way as water. For the most part, organisms occupy a two-dimensional space on land, except for the depth of soil and the height of greenery, which pales into insignificance when compared to the depth of the seas.

At their greatest extent, the world's oceans reach down a staggering 11 km (almost 7 miles) and have an average depth of 3.7 km (2.5 miles). That is a lot of volume. The surface area of the oceans is 362 million km$^2$, so the volume is approximately 1.3 billion km$^3$. Most of that volume is in complete darkness too, making it even harder for us to see into, even if we could get to it all. To save you the maths, land offers about 296,000 km$^3$ of habitable space. That gives a volume ratio of 452:1 in favour of the oceans.

It's hardly surprising, then, that animals as large as these squid can manage to find somewhere to hide. What is intriguing is that the squid has a life history about which virtually nothing is known. Given the vastness of the oceans it seems reasonable to assume that there are breeding grounds to which the adults migrate each year. Being cephalopods, squid have very short life spans. They mate and then die, leaving their eggs to found the next generation.

It isn't fully understood why these squid have evolved to become so large, but a number of ecological factors have probably played their part. The buoyancy of water naturally supports bodies much bigger than those found on land, and being large will increase the number of potential prey species as well as serve to make the squid less vulnerable to predators.

The squid is not, of course, immune to attack and sperm whales famously prey on them, often bearing the scars of battle in the form of circular marks made by the suckers on the squid's tentacles. It seems that these squid may be scavengers too, as old mariners' tales suggest that they were more plentiful in the oceans when there were more whales. It follows that there would have been a high turnover of whales coming to the end of their lives and more carcasses upon which to feed. Consequently, the decline in whale populations has meant fewer large squid.

There are two families of large squid. *Architeuthis* is the genus name for giant squid, of which there are a number of species. Giant squid are large, but even they are put into the shade by colossal squid of the genus *Mesonychoteuthis*. They can reach 14 metres (46 feet) and are the biggest invertebrates ever to have lived.

# 5 December

## The myth of the Bermuda Triangle begins

**1945** On this day in 1945, five TBM Avenger bombers of the US Air Force mysteriously vanished in a clear blue sky while flying out over the Atlantic on a training flight – or so the story goes. Subsequent investigations have revealed that it was probably no such great mystery, just a tragic accident. It seems likely that inexperienced pilots simply got lost in a cloud, were blown by strong winds further out over the ocean than they realised, and simply ran out of fuel.

However, such a rational explanation was of no interest to the theorists who began in the 1960s to build up the myth of the Bermuda Triangle, a large region of the Atlantic off the Florida coast near Bermuda. Here, allegedly, ships disappear without trace, planes vanish off the radar never to be seen again and strange lights hover in the sky.

Over the years, 'Bermuda Triangulists' have built up a dossier of apparently mysterious disappearances of ships and planes. The fact that very few of these mysteries stand up to much scrutiny does not seem to deter the theorists. They cite the case of the nuclear submarine USS *Scorpion* which disappeared in 1968, ignoring the subsequent investigation which confirmed that it went down near the Azores, not Bermuda, and the cause was an explosion of one of its own torpedoes. They cite the Japanese ship *Raifuku Maru* which vanished in 1925, despite the fact that the ship went down in a storm outside the Triangle, and that another ship, the *Homeria*, witnessed the sinking and tried to rescue survivors. They cite the 1969 disappearance, too, of round-the-world yachtsman Donald Crowhurst's *Teignmouth Electron*. In fact, Crowhurst was in a disturbed state of mind, falsified his position so he wasn't actually in the Triangle, and may have committed suicide.

Despite the lack of genuine mysteries, theorists have come up with all kinds of 'explanations' for the Triangle's dangerous power. Some say it is a natural phenomenon. They suggest that ships are being engulfed by giant bubbles of methane bursting up from the sea floor, or that local variations in the Earth's magnetic field are making compasses go haywire. Or maybe the storms here are extra-violent … Others go for much more outlandish theories. Could it be a time warp? Or abduction by aliens? Or mysterious death rays from the lost city of Atlantis?

But, of course, there is no mystery Triangle at all. The shipping insurers Lloyds of London make it their business to find out if any particular place is a higher insurance risk than others, and ships are not charged extra for going through the Triangle. The US Coast

Guard agrees. In fact, hundreds of ships and planes pass through the Triangle *every day* without mishap.

# 6 December

## *The prototype microwave oven comes into being*

**1945** In this day and age the microwave oven is a commonplace device of the standard kitchen. It took a long time, though, for the technology to be developed into a consumer product, and even then people were suspicious because they confused microwaves with radiation. The microwaves themselves are part of the electromagnetic spectrum, which includes light and radio waves, hence the confusion. It meant that some people had the erroneous notion that they were expected to blast their food with nuclear radiation. Not surprisingly, they had ideas of eating radioactive food.

Microwaves are so called because they have short wavelengths in comparison with other forms of electromagnetic radiation – between 1 mm and 300 mm in length. When they pass through materials they cause the atoms and molecules to jiggle back and forth very rapidly, raising the amount of energy emitted by the material and hence producing heat. They work best on foods containing water, where the atoms are relatively free to move around. As water is evenly spread throughout such foods, they are uniformly heated. In the absence of water, food and materials either melt or burn and microwave ovens are not suitable.

The source of microwaves in an oven is a device called a cavity magnetron. It converts electrical energy into microwaves with an efficiency of about 65 per cent. The rest of the energy converts into waste heat, although this can be used to increase the air temperature in the cooking space, thereby improving the performance of the oven to some extent.

Microwave ovens have acquired something of a bad reputation due to their association with fast foods but in truth they are very useful tools in commercial and domestic kitchens when employed in appropriate ways. They are particularly helpful when it comes to speeding up the preparation of dishes for cooking in conventional ovens. They are also very good at accelerating simple cooking procedures such as boiling and steaming. In addition, many modern microwave ovens come complete with elements so that grilling, baking and roasting are possible. They are effectively multi-functional ovens, which combine traditional and microwave technologies.

# 7 December

## Lethal injection is introduced in America

**1982** While most developed countries, including all those of the European Union, have moved away from the death penalty, even for the worst crimes, the United States clings tenaciously to the ultimate retribution, although it remains the focus of fierce debate.

Even in America the death penalty has always had its opponents, and from 1972 to 1976 it was actually suspended entirely across the country. The suspension, though, was due to concern over methods of execution, rather than the principle. In 1972, the Supreme Court had decided in the case of Furman vs. Georgia that the death penalty in some cases was unconstitutional, on the grounds that 'cruel and unusual punishment' was a violation of the eighth amendment of the US constitution. Most people thought that Furman would be the end of the death penalty in America, but after four years, 37 states reintroduced it after addressing what they considered were the problems with the eighth amendment.

In 1977, murderer Gary Gilmore gained international notoriety when he asked for his death sentence to be carried out. It duly was, and he became the first American to be executed since Furman, when he was shot by a firing squad in Utah. For a few years, though, the Gilmore execution was the only one to take place, partly because of litigation from the condemned, and partly because of worries about infringing the eighth amendment.

But in 1977, the Oklahoma legislature had come up with its way of dealing with the obstacle – lethal injection. Apparently, their reason for favouring lethal injection was nothing to do with humaneness, but simply because Oklahoma's electric chair was too expensive to repair, but it seemed to deal neatly with the nasty side of execution. The first lethal injection, administered to Charles Brooks, took place on 7 December 1982. It seemed that the justices had found a way of killing convicts as painless as putting animals to sleep. Typically, injections begin with a dose of an anaesthetic called sodium thiopental. This is followed by the muscle blocker pancuronium bromide which stops the breathing, and then by the cardiotoxin potassium chloride which stops the heart.

After the Brooks execution, nearly all the states with the death penalty adopted it as their chosen method, and after a long hiatus the number of executions began to creep up, reaching a climax in the 1990s. Since the death penalty was reintroduced in 1976, there have been over 1,000 executions, of which most have been by lethal injection – over a third of these in Texas alone. It seemed to proponents that they had found the perfect 'humane' way of carrying out death sentences, and that the opponents' case against capital punishment was weakened.

Then in December 2006, convict Angel Diaz took 34 agonising minutes to die after a botched lethal injection in a Florida jail. The state governor, Jeb Bush, immediately suspended all executions. Across the USA there was sudden concern that lethal injections might be unconstitutional after all, and executions slowed down almost to a halt once more. A test case from Kentucky, Baze vs. Rees, was brought before the Supreme Court and on 16 April 2008, the Court ruled that lethal injections were constitutional, although not ideal. At once, some states announced that they would soon resume execution. But if the moratorium is over, the debate certainly isn't.

# 8 December

## Dissolution of the Soviet Union

**1991** Such was the astonishing speed and near painlessness of the break-up of the Soviet Union that it is hard to believe that little more than two decades ago the Cold War was very much a reality, that the Berlin Wall was still in place and that the whole of Eastern Europe was still under the military rule of Moscow. In 1983, President Reagan could convincingly scare the world with talk of the 'evil empire'. Yet less than eight years later, that empire had gone entirely.

The transformation began in 1986 when Mikhail Gorbachev came to power in the Soviet Union. Most Russians have little respect for Gorbachev, who, it seems to them, destroyed Russian power and status. In the West, though, his reputation is high, and his Nobel Peace Prize thoroughly deserved. Perhaps in deference to Russian opinion, historians often paint a picture of Gorbachev as a feather blown by events, a symptom of the changes happening rather than a cause.

Whatever the truth, Gorbachev came to power knowing that things had to be altered. All across the Soviet Union, it had become clear that the Soviet economy was stagnating and lives for most were pretty grim. The countless people risking their lives every year to 'escape' over the Berlin Wall to the West told the story clearly. An empire that could hold on to its people only by keeping them prisoners was obviously in deep trouble.

For Gorbachev, the Chernobyl nuclear power plant disaster in April 1986 revealed the 'sickness of our system' with its shoddiness and hushing up. He determined that from then on there would be *glasnost* (publicity and openness) and *perestroika* (restructuring). He came to believe, as American Secretary of State George Shultz told him, that a closed society cannot be a prosperous society.

In December 1988, Gorbachev stunned the UN with a speech in which he stated: 'Freedom of choice is a universal principle.' 'Gorby' began to become something of a hero in the West – and, more significantly, in Eastern Europe where they began to take his words literally.

The following June, the Polish people took the chance and voted out communist leader General Jaruzelski to give a huge majority to Lech Wałęsa and the union Solidarity. A week or so later, the Hungarian prime minister, Miklos Nemeth, decided to take down the barbed wire barrier between Hungary and Austria as 'a health hazard'. At once, thousands of Eastern Europeans, especially East Germans, began to swarm across the border into the West. Hardline East German leader Erich Honecker protested to Moscow, but Moscow said they were powerless to intervene.

When Gorbachev visited East Germany in October that year, young students cheered, saying, 'Gorby help us!' Maybe encouraged by Gorbachev's visit, protesters took to the streets and Honecker's authority evaporated. Just four weeks later, on 9 November, the new East German president Egon Krenz agreed to open the border to the West, and before anyone could stop them, eager Germans from both East and West were tearing down the Berlin Wall.

With the Wall down, the game was on. The following day Bulgarian communist leader Todor Zhivkov stepped down. Within weeks, the communists were gone in Czechoslovakia and Vaclav Havel was president. By Christmas Day, Romania's Ceauşescu had gone, captured after fleeing in a helicopter and brought before a firing squad.

Gorbachev may have thought that would be the end, but once the process had started, the Soviet Union collapsed like a pack of cards. By early 1991, Lithuania, Latvia and Estonia had all declared their independence. The biggest shock, though, was when Boris Yeltsin led the move to make Russia itself independent and to turn it into a democratic capitalist state. This was all too much for the diehard communists, who launched a coup against Gorbachev. Famously standing on a tank outside the Kremlin, Yeltsin announced that the coup would fail. He was right, but Gorbachev's power was gone and Yeltsin became the dominant force in Russian politics.

Yeltsin quickly abolished the Communist Party and recognised the independence of the Baltic states, followed by the Ukraine, Armenia and Kazakhstan. On this day in 1991, on national TV, Yeltsin announced the dissolution of the Soviet Union.

# 9 December

## The first episode of British soap opera Coronation Street

**1960** The British TV soap opera *Coronation Street* has been running for so long now that it is as much a part of the traditional British scene as the London bus or the red postbox. Soap operas originated on radio in the 1930s in the USA as short romantic dramas broadcast for housewives in the afternoon and sponsored by the soap companies that gave them the name. Britain got its own long-running radio soap in 1951 with *The Archers*, but *Coronation Street* was the first TV soap.

It wasn't just being the first soap opera that made *Coronation Street* genuinely groundbreaking, though. It was the setting and characters. It was not set in the Home Counties and peopled by well-spoken characters, as virtually all TV drama until then had been; its drama unfolded among working-class people on a humble street in a fictional Manchester suburb, and the characters spoke with rough and ready northern accents. Phrases like 'chuck' and 'by 'eck' were frequently heard on TV for the first time. In the 1960s, many working-class people were buying their first televisions, and the advent of *Coronation Street* reflected this vast new audience.

Within a few months of its launch on this day in 1960, '*Corrie*', as it became affectionately known, was being watched by 15 million viewers, and by September 1961 it was the most popular programme on British TV. It has remained up there, or nearly so, ever since. One character, Ken Barlow, played by actor William Roache, has been there since that very first episode nearly half a century ago.

The success of *Corrie* quickly inspired many other TV soaps, such as *The Newcomers*, *Crossroads* and *Emmerdale Farm*. But none seemed likely to knock it off the top spot until the arrival of Liverpool-based *Brookside* in 1982, and then BBC's London-based *EastEnders*. With its racy 'modern' storylines, *Brookside* made *Corrie* look old-fashioned, while the raw grit of *EastEnders* threatened to make it look far too cosily northern. Some predicted the demise of *Corrie*, but it survived and continued to vie with *EastEnders* for vast audiences. In the 1980s, these two soaps were frequently watched in key episodes by half the people in Britain, and storylines were discussed on the front pages of the national newspapers – perhaps rather neatly refuting Prime Minister Margaret Thatcher's assertion that the UK was a nation of individuals, not a community.

By the mid-1990s, the British TV audience began to fragment more, and *Corrie* and *EastEnders* were no longer quite such essential viewing. Again, *Corrie* was seen by some as being just too old-fashioned and not reflecting the modern world. New producers tried introducing stronger storylines, such as drug-taking, gay issues, underage sex, and stories based around younger characters. The shift proved unpopular and in 2002, *Corrie* pledged to return to 'gentle storylines and humour'. To this day, *Corrie* remains highly popular and seems likely to pass its half-century in 2010 still going strong.

# 10 December

## Woman's conviction for double infanticide is quashed

**2003** Angela Cannings was sent down in 2002 for the murder of her two infant sons. A third infant had died before them. It was an interesting case because Cannings had always claimed that her children had died suddenly in their sleep. The term for this kind of death is Sudden Infant Death Syndrome (SIDS) or cot death. Scientists are unsure of the causes, but it appears to be a kind of apnoea, where the body forgets to breathe, leading to hypoxia and death.

Cannings was eventually cleared because scientists suggested that a genetic predisposition to SIDS may exist. It meant that the chances of her children all dying naturally rose from virtually impossible in the eyes of the law, to quite likely. In addition, the court heard that the infants of relatives had also died, suggesting a SIDS gene in the family. Earlier in 2003 Sally Clarke had also been cleared of murdering her two infant sons, and Trupti Patel of killing her three babies.

Of course, there now hangs a question mark over how to distinguish between SIDS and infanticide. In effect, SIDS has become a convenient cover for those who actually do kill their own babies, or indeed, those who kill other people's babies. If clear signs of physical injury or tampering are absent, then a conviction will always be regarded as unsafe, unless it becomes possible to identify the gene or genes that have the potential to cause SIDS, and thereby provide definitive proof either way in court. Until then it seems likely that any case requiring expert opinion will have to conclude on the side of the defendant to ensure that wrongful imprisonment is avoided.

As for the reasons why a mother might genuinely kill her babies: it seems the most likely reason would be one or a combination of psychological factors such as fear of responsibility, immaturity, depression, a feeling of being trapped, social isolation, parental incompetence and perhaps plain selfishness. People are certainly capable of the most unlikely behaviour given the right sets of circumstances.

One consequence of the modern trend for giving names to conditions and syndromes is the invention of the term 'post-natal depression'. It is used for describing women, and sometimes men, who suffer symptoms of depression following the birth of a child. It is evidently brought on by the factors associated with adjusting to caring for a newborn baby: sleep deprivation, learning curve stress, worry of responsibility, social isolation and loss of personal space and relaxation.

Of course, new parents have always suffered from these factors, but the modern age seems to have heightened them in some regards. For one thing there has been a decline in extended family support, so that new parents often have no one to turn to for practical help and advice. Secondly, people are seemingly encouraged to abdicate their common sense about childcare issues, so that society tells them to turn to books written by so-called experts. Why this should be is something of a mystery. After all, humans have successfully reared children to adulthood for around 100,000 years.

# 11 December

## Scientists unravel the DNA of the first organism

**1998** Although DNA comes in incredibly long molecules it uses only four types of base pairs to store the code for every organism on the planet. This means that it is simply a case of unravelling the DNA and deciphering the code. It may take a long time, but it is the same for any organism, be it a human or a worm.

The first organism to have its entire DNA blueprint recorded was a nematode worm, scientific name *Caenorhabditis elegans*. The nematode worm is a tiny parasitic creature, no bigger than a pinhead. For something so small and seemingly simple it still has a surprising number of base pairs, or 'genetic letters' as they are referred to. In fact it has 97 million and they comprise about 20,000 genes.

It took eight years and two teams of researchers – one at Washington University in the US, and the other at the Sanger Centre in Cambridge, England – to decipher the genetic make-up of the worm. Over this time, more than 100 million different chemical sequences were identified, recorded and analysed.

Compared to the nematode worm, the human genome is constructed from about 3 billion base pairs. Despite this vast discrepancy, there is still an awful lot that the worm's genes can teach us about ourselves and other more complex animals. Indeed, around 40 per cent of the worm's genes match those found in other species. As Robert Waterston, who led the US effort, explained: 'It's got muscles, it reacts to touch ... It faces the same challenges other animals do.'

It is certainly true that the techniques developed by the research teams helped to significantly advance the Human Genome Project. Ongoing since 1990, this study undertook the mammoth task of discovering exactly what you and I are made of. After the announcement of some draft results in 2000, an almost complete version of the genome was unveiled in 2003.

The speed of progress made by the HGP may seem staggering when placed against the eight years it took to unravel the nematode worm. However, while there were two teams studying the worm, a huge number of scientists from the UK, US and Canada collaborated across the $3 billion human project.

The sequencing data they uncovered is now freely available to academics and the public on internet databases. For a while, though, it seemed as if the fruits of the billions of dollars of public money might be kept out of general reach. At the same time that the HGP was launched, a private initiative funded by an American company called Celera Genomics began their own $300 million attempt to find the same thing.

In 1999, Celera attempted to make the human genome their intellectual property by filing a series of preliminary patents on 6,500 human genes. Their case was destroyed in March 2000 when US President Bill Clinton declared that no part of the human genome sequence could be patented.

With all the information now open to further study, the aim of the scientists working with the human genome is to uncover the causes of, and find cures for, genetic diseases such as Alzheimer's, cystic fibrosis and even some forms of cancer. The difficulty now, though, as expressed by Waterston after the publication of the nematode worm data, is that 'before us we have all the pieces of the puzzle ... Now we need to figure out how it works'.

# 12 December

## Computer programs become copyrightable in the US

**1980** Until the late 1970s computers hadn't been perceived as a means of making any serious money. As their potential revealed itself and the market for computers began to burgeon, those involved with writing computer programs wanted to copyright their ideas to prevent others from simply plagiarising their work.

Copyright in this case is a contentious area of law, though, because scientific phenomena are not regarded as ideas in the same way as creative ideas. Mathematical formulae, for example, are not invented but discovered. In other words, they have always existed in nature, so the scientist merely roots them out.

As computer programs essentially use mathematical formulae as their basis, this caused a problem with copyright law. It was decided, therefore, that the programming method was the copyrightable component. That is to say, all of the mathematical formulae are freely available, but the way they are arranged can be protected by copyright. The same is true of writing. All of the words are freely available in a dictionary, but the order in which they are used becomes a copyrightable document.

12 December 1980 marks the date at which the US Congress adopted the Copyright Act of 1976 into public law. Prior to this, computer programs had actually been protectable by the Copyright Act of 1909, but understandably the precise legal workings of this protection were a bit of a grey area. Back in 1961, North American Aviation submitted a roll of magnetic tape holding computer software to the US Copyright Office. Although protection was eventually granted, such was the uncertainty during the processing of the claim that it took three years to reach a decision. The 1976 Act was a deliberate updating of the law to accommodate the technological advances of the preceding 65 years.

Copyright law in the UK is enshrined in the Copyright, Designs and Patents Act 1988. On both sides of the Atlantic some important legal battles have been fought over the exact nature of the copyright protection extended to computer programs. One of the most famous was filed in 1988 by Apple against Microsoft. The California company took the Seattle giant to court amid allegations that Microsoft's new Windows operating system had significantly copied elements of Apple's existing Lisa and Macintosh software packages.

The central claim made by Apple was that Microsoft had recreated the 'look and feel' of their system, and that taken as a whole, the 'look and feel' constituted a critical part of the copyrighted work and, therefore, was a copyrightable element in itself. After a trial lasting four years, and an appeals process taking a further two, in 1994 Apple were defeated in their legal argument.

The ramifications of the judge's decision in this case were momentous for the developing software industry. By denying Apple's 'look and feel' thesis, the judge blocked a potentially far-reaching legal precedent. In doing so, he effectively confirmed that copyright law for computer programs was restricted to what it had originally been intended to protect – the specific organisation of the programming code from which the software was built.

If this ruling looked to have laid many of the digital copyright issues to rest, it did not last for long. The extraordinary rise of the internet swiftly opened up new areas of computer programming not considered by either the 1976 US act or the 1988 UK law. Consequently, America introduced the Digital Millennium Copyright Act in 1998, and the UK embraced the 1996 WIPO Copyright Treaty as laid out by the World Intellectual Property Organisation.

There have also been increasingly diverse ways of licensing computer software and allowing others to make use of it. The collaborative nature of the internet and Web 2.0 has led, in some corners, to a much more open approach and laws have been focused around what you can do with software, rather than what you can't. This development has perhaps been best observed in the increasingly ubiquitous Wikipedia, in which any user may edit, adapt or enter content without fear of stepping on anyone else's copyright-protected toes.

# 13 December

*First large mammal brought to official extinction*

**2006** On this day in 2006, scientists announced that China's Yangtze river dolphin, or baiji, was finally extinct, after 20 million years. The loss was described by the scientists who made the announcement as 'the first large mammal brought to extinction as a result of human destruction to their natural habitat and resources'.

As it turned out, news of the baiji's demise may have been premature. The following August, a businessman in China's Tongling City took a picture of a 'big white animal' in the Yangtze that was later confirmed by experts to be a baiji. And the baiji was probably not the first large mammal to be driven to extinction by humans. Prehistoric creatures such as the mammoth and the Irish elk may have shared the same fate. Indeed, North and South America and Australia lost up to 86 per cent of large mammals and birds soon after humans arrived – species such as giant wombats, killer ducks, ground sloths, mammoths, sabre-tooth cats and moas.

Nevertheless the point the scientists were making about the apparent loss of the baiji was all too clear. The escalating impact of human activity on the natural environment is having a dreadful effect on many wild creatures.

In 2007, the World Conservation Union estimated that 40 per cent of all species of life are endangered. Potential casualties among the higher-profile creatures include the blue whale, snow leopard, African wild dog, tiger, albatross, and crowned solitary eagle. They are on the endangered species list, which means they face a high risk of extinction in the very near future. Recently, the polar bear was put on the list, too. But beyond these, there are countless smaller creatures that are falling by the wayside with barely anyone noticing.

The most important reason for this decimation is habitat loss. Some habitats are destroyed directly, as they are developed for farmland, or urban and industrial expansion. In the Amazon rainforest, an area the size of New York's Central Park is cleared every hour. Round the world, almost four times this area of rainforest is being lost. In 54 of the world's countries, 90 per cent of the forests have been destroyed. Even those habitats not directly destroyed are damaged by climate change, the main threat to polar bears.

Another major threat is the introduction of exotic species by humans. In Australia, rabbits and foxes have had a devastating effect on native marsupials. In Britain, the grey squirrel has virtually eliminated the native red. In Maryland, USA, the Asian snakehead fish is chewing its way through native fish and wildfowl.

Thirdly, there are direct human attacks on animals – hunting, fishing and collecting. All too well-known is the tragedy of the American bison, which was reduced after the Europeans arrived from a population of 30 million to just 750 by 1890. Many whales are now facing extinction after 200 years of mass hunting.

Finally, there is that stealthy killer, pollution. Some species are poisoned by pesticides applied by farmers, others by industrial chemicals allowed to escape into the environment. In countless rivers, life has become almost unsustainable because of the waste chemicals that have been dumped – and this may be the one of the causes of the baiji's demise.

There are those who say that mass extinctions are an inevitable part of life on Earth. Others argue pragmatically that the loss of biodiversity could be disastrous for humans. Many more, however, think we have a moral obligation to do our utmost to save each one of these endangered animals, and preserve the wonderful richness and variety of life on Earth.

# 14 December

*Teenager John Paul Getty III is set free by his kidnappers*

**1973** In 1973, everyone knew that John Paul Getty was one of the world's richest men, if not the richest. Born into a wealthy Oklahoma oil family, he had turned his small fortune into a much,

much bigger one. He began by buying up oil companies, but then bought the oil rights to large areas of Saudi Arabia and Kuwait in 1949 before anyone knew just how rich in oil they were. Getty was probably the world's first billionaire, so it may be no surprise that Italian gangsters thought they were on to a winner when they kidnapped his sixteen-year-old grandson John Paul Getty III in Rome, where he was living, on 10 July 1973.

But Getty senior proved a harder nut to crack than perhaps the gangsters had anticipated. When the first ransom note arrived, demanding $17 million for the safe return of the boy, the family simply ignored it, thinking it was one of the wayward teenager's pranks to get cash from his stingy grandfather. The kidnappers sent a second demand, but this got delayed by a postal strike. When it finally got through, the boy's father, John Paul Getty II, asked his father for money to pay the ransom, since he hadn't got that amount of cash. Getty senior turned him down.

By now, having had John Paul III for almost five months, the kidnappers were getting desperate. In November, a daily newspaper received an envelope containing a lock of hair and a human ear, along with a note demanding $3.2 million: 'This is Paul's ear. If we don't get some money within ten days, then the other ear will arrive.' The boy's father persuaded Getty senior to lend him the money to pay the ransom.

Even then, Getty senior was not satisfied. He bargained with the kidnappers, and got the ransom demand down to $2 million. Finally, the ransom was paid, and John Paul Getty III was found alive, but in a sorry state, in southern Italy. The boy never really recovered from the trauma of the kidnapping, and although he married two years later and has a son called Balthazar who is a successful actor, he turned to drugs and alcohol and by 1981 he had become speechless, blind and paralysed. His father, Sir John Paul Getty II, went on to become one of the greatest philanthropists to have lived in the UK, making huge donations to places like the National Gallery.

After the teenager's safe return, Getty senior justified his tough stance with the kidnappers in two ways. First he insisted that giving in to their pressure put his other fourteen grandchildren at risk from copycat kidnappers. It was also, he claimed, a moral stance: 'The second reason for my refusal was much broader-based. I contend that acceding to the demands of criminals and terrorists merely guarantees the continuing increase and spread of lawlessness, violence and such outrages as terror-bombings, "skyjackings" and the slaughter of hostages that plague our present-day world.' The kidnappers were never caught.

# 15 December

## Shintoism is outlawed in Japan

**1945** When the final surrender of Japan ended the Second World War, the Allies had to decide what to do with the defeated nations. Most Allied leaders were determined not to repeat the mistakes after the First World War and exact the harsh reparations which drove Germans into the arms of the Nazis. In the Potsdam Declaration, the leaders asserted: 'We do not intend that the Japanese shall be enslaved as a race or destroyed as a nation.'

It was determined that the Allies, led by the US General Douglas MacArthur, would occupy Japan until it could be trusted again. The Japanese military establishment was quickly demobilised and some generals put on trial as war criminals, but the central government and even Emperor Hirohito were allowed to stay, with MacArthur merely giving 'suggestions' and 'advice' from behind the scenes.

In Japan, the Shinto religion had been an integral part of the militaristic state machinery, and Emperor Hirohito was believed to be descended from the Kami, the Shinto spirits or gods. Moreover, the ancient Shinto slogan *Hakko ichiu*, 'the world under one roof', had been a justification for Japan's aggressive expansion. MacArthur, believing that democracy went hand-in-hand with Christianity, began to wage war on Shinto. On this day in 1945, he cut all ties between the Shinto religion and the state and banned the teaching of Shinto in schools. On New Year's Day 1946, at MacArthur's prompting, Hirohito publicly announced that his descent from the Kami was a myth. Some stories say MacArthur thought of converting Hirohito to Christianity but thought better of it. But he did draft in thousands of Christian missionaries to try to convert the Japanese people.

Very few Japanese converted to Christianity, though. They politely listened, and when the Allied troops left Japan, returned to their Shinto traditions. To calm any fears of renewed aggression, Shinto leaders carefully removed any militaristic tone in the religion, reinterpreting the phrase *Hakko ichiu* as a spirit of peaceful world government.

The tone of Shinto religion shifted away from the big myths and emperor-worship to a more practical folk religion, which is how it had begun long ago. Shinto shrines focused on helping ordinary people improve their fortunes. Far fewer Japanese people now admit to following the Shinto religion than before the war but, interestingly, many of those who say they are not religious have a Shinto altar at home or wear an *omamori* bracelet which is supposed to bring the Kami's protection. And every New Year, more than 45 million Japanese people still flock to the shrines to watch girls in red and white robes perform the stately traditional Kagura dance.

# 16 December

## *Heathrow airport is opened*

**1955** In the years before the Second World War, travelling by plane was strictly for the elite. Long-distance flights were leisurely, elegant affairs in flying boats such as Pan Am's Clipper service, which could glide in to land wherever there was smooth water. But during the war a multitude of runways were built for the military all around the world, and afterwards they were turned over to commercial use, allowing a new breed of huge four-engine passenger planes like the Douglas DC-8 to carry not just a dozen or so but over 100 passengers on each flight to countless destinations.

As the cost of flying came down, passenger numbers rose, and London's Heathrow was just one of many ex-military fields around the world to make the most of the new post-war flying boom. Heathrow originated as a military airfield in the First World War and between the wars was used as a commercial test facility. It was still tiny, though, when the Air Ministry commandeered it in 1943. In 1944, they took over a vast stretch of land that included the hamlet of Heath Row and began to build a big new airfield for the Royal Air Force.

Commercial flights from Heathrow began in 1946. Soon it became clear that Croydon, which had been London's main commercial airport in the 1930s, was just not big enough for the increasingly large passenger planes that were coming into service. In 1952, the decision was made to close Croydon and expand Heathrow as London's major airport instead. The following year, the young Queen Elizabeth II laid the first runway slab. Two years later everything was complete and the airport officially opened on this day in 1955.

Now Heathrow is used by 67 million people each year, including more international passengers than any other airport in the world. Atlanta-Hartfield-Jackson and Chicago's O'Hare handle more passengers by volume, but most of these are just moving around the US.

But Heathrow is running out of space. In March 2008, the new Terminal 5 was opened to accommodate the extra people, but now it faces an even bigger challenge over its runway capacity.

At present, Heathrow has just two runways and has virtually no room for expansion. The airport authorities want to take more local land and build a third runway. They insist that the third runway is essential for Heathrow's – and the UK's – future commercial success.

Opponents of the third runway point out that an increase in flights at Heathrow will bring devastating noise pollution to local residents and that encouraging air travel is irresponsible at a time when the world is threatened by climate change. They also point out that more than a third of Heathrow's passengers are 'transfer' passengers, who simply change planes and bring nothing to the UK economy.

# 17 December

## *The world celebrates 100 years of powered flight*

**2003** The key problem with getting a machine airborne was achieving the appropriate power to weight ratio. The first locomotive machines were steam engines, and although they drove the industrial revolution they were wholly unsuitable for powered flight. Not only were they incredibly heavy, but they also required large quantities of water and fuel. It wasn't until the invention of the internal combustion engine that inventors saw the potential for leaving the ground.

As for the principle of lift, well, plenty of aviators had already worked out that the aerofoil was the secret. They didn't understand the science, but they simply copied the design of a bird's wing and experimented with different shapes and sizes until they got it right. It was now a matter of fitting an engine to a glider and prototyping the first aeroplane.

In December 1903 the Wright brothers wrote their names in the history books by becoming the first to achieve a sustained powered flight. It is conceivable that, with so many inventors pursuing the same aim, others achieved it before them, but the Wrights achieved official recognition by filming their efforts and inviting the press to watch.

Perhaps the most remarkable thing about powered flight is how quickly things progressed from 1903. By the beginning of the First World War in 1914, the aeroplane had evolved from an ungainly kite into the elegant biplane. By the end of the war, in 1918, the monoplane was emerging into dominance, and by the start of the Second World War the aeroplane had been developed into a range of designs for specific purposes: bomber, fighter, troop-carrier and reconnaissance. By the close of the war the first jet-powered aeroplanes had been flown – only four decades on.

Jet engines revolutionised aeroplanes because they made it possible to fly at high altitudes. Propellers cannot work where the air gets too thin, because they don't have enough air molecules to pull through. Jet engines, however, take in and compress the air molecules before issuing thrust from the exhaust. It meant that planes could fly above the clouds and at much faster speeds. The age of globetrotting had begun by the 1950s.

# 18 December

## Drug traffickers' appeal against the death penalty is rejected

**1985** Cambodia, China, Vietnam, Laos, Thailand and Burma are all major sources of opium and heroin, while Singapore is a major hub for the heroin trade. In an effort to keep trafficking under control, many of these countries impose the harshest of all sentences on anyone caught – the death penalty.

Between 1991 and 2005, 420 people were hanged in Singapore for drugs trafficking. Vietnam sentenced nearly 50 people to death for drugs offences in 2004 alone, while Indonesia has over 50 people on death row for drugs offences at any one time.

The quantity of drugs needed to trigger the death sentence can be tiny. In Thailand and Singapore, being caught with just 15 grams of heroin is punishable by death. What's more, the death sentence is mandatory for drugs offences in many countries, so judges have no option but to apply it, even when there are extenuating circumstances.

However, most of those hanged are south-east Asian nationals, so their deaths don't arouse much controversy abroad. Only when there are foreign nationals involved does the spotlight get turned on properly. This is what happened in 1985, when two Australians, Kevin Barlow and Brian Chambers, were convicted of drug smuggling in Malaysia and sentenced to death. They were arrested at Penang International Airport with 180 grams of heroin. Few contested that they were guilty, but many Australians were shocked by the severity of the sentence for an offence which in Australia carried an average of three years in prison.

At first the pair, with the backing of Australian officials, tried to appeal against the sentence. But on this day in 1985, their appeal was rejected. Australian foreign minister Bill Hayden at once appealed to Malaysia for clemency, but no avail. Barlow and Chambers were hanged on 7 July 1986 and became the first non-Malaysians to be hanged in Malaysia for drugs offences.

Despite efforts by Western governments and human rights groups to persuade south-east Asian countries to reduce their use of the death penalty, they remain as committed to it as ever. Another Australian national, Vietnamese-born Van Nguyen, was hanged in Singapore in 2005, amid international appeals for clemency. In defending the decision to carry out the death sentence, Singapore's foreign minister George Yeo pointed out to his Australian counterpart Alex Downer that Nguyen was carrying enough heroin to provide 26,000 doses.

Interestingly, when in 2006 two more young Australians, Andrew Chan and Myuran Sukumaran, were convicted in Bali of smuggling heroin, Australian prime minister John Howard did not attempt to challenge the death sentence imposed, saying, 'the warnings have been there for decades, and how on Earth any young Australian can be so stupid as to take the risk is completely beyond me'.

# 19 December

## Titanic *is released in cinemas*

**1997** After two years of solid production work, James Cameron's epic film, *Titanic*, was unleashed to the general public. Starring a fresh-faced Leonardo DiCaprio and a young Kate Winslet, the story, based upon the sinking of the eponymous ship in 1912, followed their two characters, Jack Dawson and Rose DeWitt Bukater, falling in love during the ship's ill-fated maiden voyage.

The film, which was produced by Paramount Pictures and 20th Century Fox, set a number of impressive records. Costing $200 million to make, it subsequently grossed around $1.8 billion worldwide – both figures which top the tables. It was also nominated for a record-equalling fourteen Oscars, and alongside *Ben-Hur* (1959) and *The Lord of the Rings: Return of the King* (2003), shares the record for the most Oscars won, with eleven.

To generate the right feel and look for the film, Cameron had a full-size replica of the RMS *Titanic* constructed. Although much of this was an immobile model, the key areas were working sets, faithful to the design of the original. In order to ensure accuracy, the production team had worked with Harland and Wolff, the builders of the real *Titanic*. The blueprints from their archives were followed with exacting detail.

The ship, along with smaller models designed for use in the sinking scenes, was built on hydraulic arms that could be tilted in any direction required. This allowed the film crew to accurately simulate sailing on a stormy ocean, as well as the dramatic footage of the liner disappearing beneath the waves.

For all the care and attention they took to getting the look absolutely perfect, however, Cameron and his production team could do nothing to prevent the schedule slipping as they filmed. There were numerous issues to contend with, notably a staircase becoming dislodged during a flooding scene and slamming across the set (fortunately no one was injured), and several of the cast, including the lead actress, succumbing to colds and flu after spending so long in cold water. Indeed, at one point, Kate Winslet supposedly came close to drowning on set. When everything is considered, it is perhaps quite an achievement that the schedule was ultimately delayed by less than a month.

However, although Winslet is quoted as saying that she would work with Cameron again only for 'a lot of money', the troubled filming was worth it for her, the film's director and everyone else involved. Just two days after the movie went on general release on this day in 1997, cinemas in America were declaring that they had sold out of tickets. On its opening weekend, it made nearly $30 million in box office sales. It soared straight to number one in the box office charts and stayed there for an incredible fifteen weeks. In total, *Titanic* was screened in US cinemas for nine months following its initial release.

# 20 December

## *The Housing Bill is introduced in Britain*

**1979** The Housing Bill is one of those things that divide opinion. Margaret Thatcher believed that 'an Englishman's home is his castle'. She saw that, by giving the tenants of local authority properties the right to buy their homes from the council, she would have a loyal and aspirational foundation of voters over the years to come. It was a clever ploy, as this demographic had been traditional supporters of Labour – the Housing Bill aimed to switch their vote to the Tories. Call it an incentive, call it bribery, but it worked, and the Tories remained in power for another eighteen years.

Ironically it was the Housing Bill that drove the largest nail into the Tory coffin during their fall from power in the 1990s. With the emphasis on home ownership, the housing market became a bubble of fiscal celebration. The value of property rose so much that people began using their equity by drawing down on their mortgages to release the cash. Then the bubble burst. Property values dropped by 15 per cent – enough to bring many homeowners into negative equity. Interest rates soared and people owed more to their lenders than their properties were worth. It spelled financial disaster and inevitably many pointed the finger of blame at the Tory party. They felt that they had been beguiled by the good times in the 1980s and now the electorate were paying the price for the politicians' foolishness.

As the dust has settled, though, the Housing Bill is now perceived as generally a good thing. It is still in force and it does provide people with a chance of long-term investment. It works by allowing those who live in authority-owned housing to purchase their homes if they so desire. That way their money is invested rather than being frittered away as rent. Furthermore, such people can seldom afford to purchase privately-owned properties as their first-time buys, so it allows upward mobility, which is one of the core principles of democracy. In this light, Thatcher can be thanked for introducing the Bill, even if her original motive was thoroughly devious. The jury remains out on that one.

With the threat of a second housing crash in 2008, the Labour party tried their utmost to prevent history repeating itself. Properties purchased for capital gain were subject to a capital gains tax, which began at 40 per cent of profit from the sale of investment property and tapered down to 0 per cent over a 30-year period. The Labour party scrapped the tapering system and introduced a flat rate of 18 per cent. The idea was that as owners no longer had to wait fifteen years to lower their capital gains to 18 per cent, they therefore had less reason to keep hold of properties. In effect they were no longer being penalised for an early sale. The knock-on effect would be to free up properties at the lower end of the housing market and keep some fluidity in house sales, thereby warding off a crash.

# 21 December

## *The Lockerbie terrorist attack*

**1988** The fuselage of a Boeing 747 ploughed into the middle of a residential area in the village of Lockerbie in Scotland. A bomb in a suitcase had ripped the airliner apart at altitude, so the debris scatter was enormous. The cockpit was found some distance away from the fuselage in a field. All of the crew and passengers, 259 in total, were inevitably lost. A further eleven residents of Lockerbie died too.

Pan Am Flight 103 was en route from Heathrow, London, to JFK International, New York. The bomb had been planted by Libyan terrorists. Just 1 lb of plastic explosive was enough to destroy the jumbo jet, because it tore a hole in the cargo bay while the aircraft was at cruising speed, causing it to disintegrate. Debris and casualties were found over an 80-mile (130-km) swathe of southern Scotland.

The man eventually convicted for the Lockerbie disaster was Abdelbaset Ali Mohmed Al Megrahi, a former Libyan intelligence officer. The trial took place at a special Scottish court convened at Camp Zeist in the Netherlands. At the trial, Al Megrahi's co-accused, Al Amin Khalifa Fhimah, was acquitted. On 31 January 2001, though, Al Megrahi was sentenced to life imprisonment. He has always maintained his innocence, but his first appeal in 2002 was rejected and he was denied a second attempt at an appeal in 2007.

Despite the fact that there remains some uncertainty, at least in some quarters, over the conviction of Al Megrahi, there is no doubt that the attack itself was perpetrated by a party with Libyan interests. Libya itself has stopped short of formally admitting responsibility, but in a letter to the United Nations it 'accepted responsibility for the actions of its officials'.

This rather tentative wording, however, was a clear acknowledgement of its role, at whatever level, in the disaster. Subsequently, in May 2002, the Libyan government offered $2.7 billion – $10 million for each of the victims – by way of compensation to the victims of the bombing.

As for the motive for the attack, it is most likely that this arose out of a prolonged period of antagonism between Libya and the United States. Between 1981 and 1986, the US armed forces shot down Libyan military planes and sank their boats during disagreements over territorial waters in the Gulf of Sidra. During this time, Colonel Gaddafi, the Libyan leader, allegedly sponsored the hijacking of another Pan Am flight on its way to JFK International by the terrorist group the Abu Nidal Organisation.

Today there are a number of memorials in America and Scotland for the victims lost on Pan Am Flight 103. A sculpture on Long Island, New York by Susan Lowenstein, whose 21-year-old son died in the bombing, shows 43 nude women, representing the wives and mothers whose husbands and children were victims of the terrorists. Each statue contains a personal memory of the victim. There are two further dedications in the US, one at the

Arlington National Cemetery and another at Syracuse University. Scotland also has two memorials, at Dryfesdale Cemetery, near Lockerbie and in Sherwood Crescent in Lockerbie itself.

# 22 December

## *Fourteen survive an air crash in the Andes*

**1972** The story of Uruguayan Air Force flight 571 was one of the great survival epics of the last century. When the plane crashed high in the Andes, survivors managed to stay alive in freezing cold for ten weeks with no food but the bodies of their dead companions until two of them made an extraordinary ten-day hike across the mountains to get rescue.

It all began to go wrong when the Uruguayan Fokker Fairchild plane, carrying members of a rugby team with their friends and relatives, was flying through the Andes to Chile on 13 October. The plane had to fly south before turning right to slip through a pass in the mountains. With visibility very poor, the only way to guess when to turn right was by their flying time – but a strong headwind slowed them down more than the pilots thought, and the Fokker was not nearly far south enough when it turned towards the mountains. Suddenly, a mountain peak loomed out of the mist before the plane had time to climb. Both wings were ripped off by hitting first one peak then another, and the fuselage cannoned on over the top of a ridge and hurtled down the other side like a horrific toboggan before coming to rest in a snow drift.

Amazingly, 33 out of the 45 people aboard survived the crash. But many were badly injured and the conditions on the mountain peak well over 4,000 metres up were unbelievably cold. Five of the survivors died very soon after. The rest of them huddled inside the plane, and with great ingenuity found ways to keep warm, melting snow for drinking water and sharing out the few bits of chocolate and other items of food they had. Search parties hunted for days for the missing plane, but in the snow of the mountains the white plane, far from its expected flight path, was impossible to spot. On the eleventh day, the survivors heard on a transistor radio that the search had been called off. Extraordinarily, a young survivor called Gustavo Nicolich saved them all from despair by saying, 'That's good news ... because it means that we're going to have to get out of here on our own.'

Food stocks quickly dwindled to nothing, and the survivors were left with a terrible choice: either eat the bodies of their dead companions or die. It was a decision that none of them took lightly, but before long they made the choice that was to shock the world when the truth came out some time after their rescue.

An avalanche on the sixteenth day after the crash killed eight more of the survivors, and those left alive realised that someone would have to go over the mountains for help. On 12 December, two months after the crash, nineteen-year-old Roberto Canessa and 21-year-old Fernando Parrado set off over the mountains to the west. After ten days of arduous hiking in bitter cold, they spotted a Chilean *huaso* (cowboy) and hailed him. Hours later a rescue team and helicopter arrived and the two lads guided the rescuers back to the crash site, where the fourteen remaining survivors were airlifted to safety on this day in 1972.

# 23 December

## *The unmagnificent seven go to the gallows*

**1948** The Nuremberg Trials were such a significant event in Europe that many forget about their equivalent in Japan: the Tokyo Trials. Just as there were war criminals in Germany, so Japan had its own. The doctrines of racial supremacy that characterised both regimes resulted in the most barbaric and inhumane treatment of prisoners and occupied populations.

The trials, officially known as the International Military Tribunal Far East, were convened at the Ichigaya Court. The choice of venue was a powerful bolt of symbolism; the Ichigaya building had previously been the HQ of the Imperial Japanese

Army. Sitting in session were eleven judges, one from each of the victorious Allied countries.

For each defendant, the prosecution set out to prove one of three classes of crime. These ranked from Class A (crimes against peace), through Class B (war crimes), up to the most severe of all, Class C crimes, or crimes against humanity. Class A crimes were aimed at those who were accused of being complicit in Japan's original plans to wage war. The latter two were reserved for the gross atrocities committed by Japanese troops. These included, notably, the Nanking Massacre in which Japanese soldiers obliterated the inhabitants of Nanking, then the capital city of the Republic of China, in a sustained six-week campaign of rape, looting, arson, murder of civilians and execution of war prisoners.

The main problem encountered by those prosecuting in the Tokyo Trials was much the same as that met by their counterparts at Nuremberg. Soldiers who had been in the lower ranks of the Japanese army typically, and often truthfully, pointed the finger of blame at their superiors, explaining that they themselves would have been executed had they not carried out orders. For the prosecution it was a matter of deciding where the buck stopped and then apportioning blame accordingly.

Quite aware of their guilt, many of the Japanese high command had committed suicide with the capitulation of their nation and before they could be hauled before the court. Nevertheless, a few stood up to be counted and in 1948 were convicted and executed for their roles in the atrocities.

Among them was Hideki Tojo, the former prime minister. He was in a compromised position as he had been acting on behalf of the Japanese emperor. However, the Americans decided to grant the emperor immunity from prosecution, largely because he was perceived as a god by the Japanese people and there was a real danger of chaos erupting if he were to be prosecuted. It isn't entirely clear just how involved the emperor was anyway, due to his courtly lifestyle which kept him removed from everyday Japan. As the individual, therefore, with the final responsibility for overseeing all that happened in the name of Japan during the Second World War, Tojo was sentenced to death at the trials.

# 24 December

## *The world's first solar-heated house*

**1948** This story puts paid to any ideas that solar energy is something new. Maria Telkes was a Hungarian-born American who pioneered solar technology to such an extent that she became dubbed the 'Sun Queen'. Her house was situated in Dover, Massachusetts and used devices called heat bins to store thermal energy collected from the rays of the sun. This was done by using black sheets of metal to absorb and conduct the heat, with the help of a substance called sodium sulphate decahydrate. The stored heat was then used to warm the house by using an air duct system. This kind of solar heating is useful overnight when temperatures drop below a comfortable level. It is a form of storage heating.

Telkes also made inroads into thermoelectric technology, by experimenting with semiconductor materials to convert photons (light energy) into electrons (electrical energy). This is what is known as photovoltaic technology today. She made a thermoelectric generator and a thermoelectric fridge, among other things.

Despite her best efforts, though, it would take half a century before ideas on sustainable energy sources were taken seriously. These days there are all kinds of devices for using the energy from the sun, from the environment, from wind and from water. As supply and demand increases, such devices are likely to become ubiquitous in households around the world. They may never entirely replace the need for electricity from coal, gas or nuclear, but they will certainly reduce the need for so many power stations.

One significant area of sustainable energy technology is heat exchange. The basis for this technology is that the environment contains ambient energy. For example, the soil beneath a lawn always stores energy, even though it is not warm to the touch. It helps to realise that anything contains heat energy if its temperature is above absolute zero, which is a chilly $-273\,°C$.

A heat exchanger runs a fluid through pipes buried within the storage medium, which absorbs this heat. The heat is then condensed using the same process as that used in a fridge or an air conditioning unit. By condensing the heat energy it becomes much more useful. For example, if the heat available in an entire lawn is condensed into a single radiator, then it will feel hot to the touch. However, as the available energy level is not especially high, it is usually used for background heating, so that it raises the general temperature within a property and means that a conventional heating system doesn't need to work so hard.

# 25 December

## The Stone of Scone is pinched from Westminster Abbey

**1950** In June 2008, Scotland's famous Stone of Scone hit the headlines again. Scotland's first minister Alex Salmond claimed that the stone, which has been on display in Edinburgh Castle since 1996, is a medieval fake. The timing of his comments, of course, was no accident, since the film *Stone of Destiny*, about the famous theft of the stone from Westminster Abbey on Christmas Day 1950, was about to be released.

The stone, known in Gaelic as the *Lia Fail*, is believed to have been used in the coronation of Scottish kings since the 8th century and is a potent symbol of Scottish nationalism. In 1296, it was looted by Edward I from Scone Abbey in Perthshire and taken to England. Salmond thinks that the Abbot of Scone hid the real stone, which he believes to be a piece of black meteorite said to have been used by the biblical Jacob as a pillow, and let Edward have a fake version made of local Perthshire sandstone. Whatever the truth, the stone that Edward took back to England was installed beneath a wooden chair, known as the Coronation Chair, in Westminster Abbey, where it remained another 650 years until the theft.

The theft was the work of a group of Scottish nationalist students from Glasgow University, Ian Hamilton, Gavin Vernon,

Alan Stuart and Kay Matheson. Their plan was to steal the stone to revive the idea of Scottish independence, then almost forgotten. On Christmas morning in 1950, the four went to Westminster Abbey. 'This was before the days of high security', Hamilton explained later. 'We took a jemmy with us to get through the door, and although there was a guard floating around he spent most of his time making cups of tea'.

Unfortunately the stone broke in two during the theft, and after hiding the pieces in Kent for a few weeks, the four skipped past the road blocks in two cars and made it into Scotland. In Glasgow, the stone was repaired by stonemason Bailie Gray. Finally, on 11 April 1951, the students ceremonially laid the stone before the high altar of Arbroath Abbey on the grave of King William, the Lion of Scotland, along with a declaration demanding Scottish independence. After a night or two in a police cell in Forfar, the stone was returned to Westminster Abbey until 1996, when the government decided to let it go back to Scotland.

None of the thieves were ever charged, although their identity was known. On 24 June 2008, First Minister Alex Salmond took Hamilton, now 83, to see the stone in its current resting place in Edinburgh Castle. Afterwards he said: 'It's nearly 60 years since I last saw the stone. It was well worth the wait to see it again.' Salmond, meanwhile, said: 'The moment of that rescue attempt in 1951 marked the reawakening of a sense of Scottish nationhood.'

# 26 December

## The Great Tsunami

**2004** Somewhere between 250,000 and 300,000 people perished when the Boxing Day Tsunami struck the Indian Ocean. A submarine earthquake caused massive waves to radiate outwards like enormous ripples on a pond. When they struck land they swept away everything in their path, and so quickly that most people didn't even see what was coming. If they had just been carried away by water then many more might have survived, but the water carried vast quantities of debris against which they were thrown and battered. Every cubic metre of water had a force of more than a ton, so the debris was pushed forwards like a bulldozer, razing settlements to the ground as it went. Most of the destruction occurred in south-east Asia, as the earthquake's epicentre was to the east of the Indian Ocean. Other waves hit India, Sri Lanka, Madagascar and Africa.

With no early warning system in place at the time of the tsunami, there were few people who expected the wave to come. Although an earthquake out at sea brings with it certain inherent risks, tsunamis form several hours after the quake has struck, and without sophisticated sensors it is impossible to predict when, and if, they will do so.

As the first waves spiralled away from the quake's epicentre, gathering speed and height, the waters retreated from many of the beaches in their path. All around the Indian Ocean, exposed sand was covered with stranded fish, struggling in the calm sun. Not recognising this as a highly typical sign of an impending tsunami, and curious to examine this oddity closer, many people flocked to the shoreline.

Some present did understand what the vanishing sea meant. At Maikhao Beach in Thailand, ten-year-old Tilly Smith, who had learnt about tsunamis in a geography lesson at school, raised the alarm to nearly 100 people. The aboriginal populations on the Andaman Islands were also familiar with the workings of nature. Despite initial fears that their lack of scientific knowledge might have left them hopelessly exposed to the wave, it was found that they had retreated far from the shore at the first sign of a potential tsunami.

In many other places, though, people weren't so fortunate. The earthquake itself, with a magnitude of somewhere between 9.1 and 9.3, shook the world for ten minutes – the longest tremor on record. The rumbling waves that spread outwards had reached up to 30 metres (100 feet) in height by the time they reached the shore. Tragically, the natural coral reefs that might have afforded some protection by breaking the waves before they got close to land, had in many places been destroyed to allow free access to the shipping industry.

The immediate humanitarian response to the devastation wrought by the sea was vast. Food supplies, relief workers, medical aid and charities descended on south-east Asia and the other affected areas. Nations from across the world donated $7 billion to help care for the survivors and start the rebuilding of damaged infrastructure. Much of the money was raised via the public; in the UK alone the people gave over £300 million, in addition to the money pledged by the UK government.

Across the whole of the Indian Ocean, the United Nations started the construction of an early warning system. The system came on stream in June 2006 and has since been monitoring the state of the sea, always on the lookout for signs of disaster.

All efforts to respond to the human cost of the Boxing Day Tsunami remain ongoing, some years now after the waves struck. Nearly 10 million people were left homeless as a result of the destruction and former-UN Secretary General Kofi Annan predicted that it could take up to ten years before everything has been put right.

# *27 December*

## *The Soviets take Afghanistan*

**1979** During the Cold War the USSR had concerns about coastal accessibility. It had plenty of shoreline to the north, but none to the south. It was a strategic move therefore to invade and occupy Afghanistan. That way, in the event of any future conflict the Soviets could reach the Indian Ocean by piercing through Pakistan.

Soviet forces had officially allied themselves with the governing Marxist People's Democratic Party of Afghanistan (PDPA). In recognition of the shared communist ideals of the two countries, the Russian and Afghan administrations had signed a bilateral treaty of friendship in December 1978.

Prior to the Soviet invasion, the Afghan government had requested Russian military assistance in suppressing small armed rebellions throughout the country. In 1975, militants from the Jamiat Islami party had attempted to oust the government. Factions of the mujahedeen were also causing difficulties for the Afghan army.

However, if the Afghans had hoped for domestic assistance from their fellow communists, they were quickly disabused. Moscow had for some time been concerned about the path being followed by the Afghan president, Hafizullah Amin. Although he was a member of the PDPA, he had sought to expand Afghanistan's political standing by conducting a dialogue with the US. After declining to come to the aid of the Afghan government, the Red Army launched an offensive attack not in support of the president, but directly against him.

Three weeks before the attack, Soviet advisors within Afghanistan recommended that the Afghan armed forces conduct a full maintenance cycle for all their crucial equipment. With much of the Afghan army temporarily demobilised, on 27 December Russian troops donned Afghan uniforms and marched virtually unopposed across the Afghan borders.

Within hours the Soviets had penetrated to Kabul, where they killed Amin. In his place they installed Babrak Karmal as the new president. The USSR now thought it had secured a tactically essential piece of territory, as well as pushing out any American connection to Amin and shoring up the communist government under a carefully chosen leader.

The significance of all this, however, did not go unobserved by the United States. Determined not to allow the Soviets such an important gain within the icy conflict of the Cold War, Jimmy Carter, the US president, publicly condemned their actions as 'the most serious threat to peace since the Second World War'. Privately, though, he was delighted. The US had been backers of the mujahedeen rebels before the Russian invasion and now they upped their level of support. As Carter's political advisor Zbigniew Brzezinski later wrote, it was the perfect opportunity to give 'the Soviet Union its Vietnam War'.

For the next nine years, the American government routed funds via Pakistan's military ruler, General Muhammad Zia-ul-Haq, to the Afghani mujahedeen. These militant rebels achieved exactly what the US hoped they would. Rather than being able to consolidate its position, the Red Army was drawn into running battles with urban guerrilla fighters.

Eventually the Soviets were forced to concede that they simply couldn't contain the mujahedeen any longer. The cost, both in financial and military terms, was unsustainable and Russia's political image was taking a severe battering. On 15 May 1988 the last Russian soldier withdrew from Afghanistan. The Soviet invasion had been a disaster, and just four years later communist rule collapsed completely within Russia's former ally.

# 28 December

## The 900th birthday of Westminster Abbey

**1965** Westminster Abbey actually took many years to be built, but was finally completed in 1065, just in time to see the advent of modern Britain. There had been shrines on the site for hundreds of years, but King Edward the Confessor had it constructed in stone somewhere between 1045 and 1050. It was consecrated just a week before the king's death and became the site of the coronation of King Harold, the last pre-Norman king, on 5 January 1066.

The first evidence that the ground upon which the Abbey rests was of special holy interest stems from 616. Then in the late 10th century Saint Dunstan formalised the site by establishing a community of Benedictine monks there. After the initial completion of the stone building, the Abbey has been significantly revised over the years. Beginning in 1245, Henry III completely rebuilt it, and this fresh construction work took place over nearly 300 years until 1517. The two western towers were built in the 18th century and further renovations and appendages were added during the

Victorian era. More recent plans to update the western front in the 20th century were drawn up by Sir Edwin Lutyens, but the project was eventually shelved.

Since Harold's coronation in 1066, Westminster Abbey has been the home of coronations for almost all British monarchs. Having deposed Harold after just a few months of rule at the Battle of Hastings, William the Conqueror cemented the Norman invasion of England by receiving the crown at the Abbey on Christmas Day 1066.

Kept within the Abbey is the throne upon which monarchs-to-be sit as they are crowned by the Archbishop of Canterbury. For 700 years between 1296 and 1996, the Stone of Scone, upon which the monarchs of Scotland receive their coronation, was housed underneath the throne. Nowadays, though, it is stored in Edinburgh Castle in Scotland.

Westminster Abbey is the last resting place of many past kings and queens, and there have also been a number of non-royals interred in the Abbey's crypts. Buried beneath the nave are political and scientific figures, including Clement Attlee, Charles Darwin and Sir Isaac Newton. In the southern transept there is a patch known as Poet's Corner where the likes of Charles Dickens, Geoffrey Chaucer and Thomas Hardy, among others, all lie at rest.

It is not surprising for a building that has been standing, in one form or another, for nearly 1,000 years that Westminster Abbey has come close to destruction on more than one occasion. During the upheaval of the English Reformation, at the time when Henry VIII was sacking abbeys and monasteries due to their Catholic connections, Westminster Abbey was saved by being relabelled as a cathedral of the Church of England. On 15 November 1940, a German bomb hit the roof of the Abbey, causing severe damage. But the building survived and it continues to play a major role in Britain's religious and royal heritage.

# 29 December

## Avian flu alarms the world

**1997** In an ever more overcrowded world there is a genuine fear that a new plague will sweep through humanity, leaving only a small percentage alive. Apart from the obvious misery of death, such an event could threaten to bring about a collapse in the infrastructure of the modern world.

In 1997 Hong Kong killed 1.25 million chickens – the entire chicken population of the island – in an attempt to prevent the spread of an influenza mutation of avian flu that had already infected a number of people. A similar influenza outbreak in 1919 had killed more people than were lost in the First World War. The Hong Kong authorities had good reason to be terrified of the potential for such a plague.

Worryingly, a number of infected people had boarded planes and flown to other parts of the world before their symptoms had developed. Their movements were traced back to a single elevator in a Hong Kong building, where an influenza victim had sneezed in the confined space. As it turned out, the influenza strain of the bird virus was not as virulent as feared and the outbreak was brought under control.

Unfortunately bird populations in Asia now act as reservoirs for the avian flu virus, which is known as subtype H5N1. This form can still infect people and often proves lethal, although direct contact with a diseased bird is necessary to contract influenza. As wildfowl are capable of flight and migration it has been necessary for scientists to remain vigilant in preventing outbreaks whenever isolated human infections occur.

The last pandemic of influenza occurred in 1968. With four decades having now passed, the World Health Organization (WHO) is currently concerned that humanity is due a major outbreak. So far over 200 million birds have been slaughtered in an attempt to contain H5N1. The virus continues to thrive, though, and a level-3 phase of threat is recognised. This means that lethal strains of influenza are known to be infecting populations, but that a strain has yet to develop with a level of contagiousness capable of sweeping the globe. The worry is that it is only a matter of time.

# 30 December

## Anti-abortion campaigners carry out a terrorist attack

**1994** It is wholly unfortunate that people obsessed with the idea of preserving life should resort to murder in their campaign to be heard. That is what happened at the Planned Parenthood Clinic in Brookline, Massachusetts in 1994. Two women were shot dead in an act of terrorism by activists who described themselves as pro-lifers.

The women, Shannon Lowney and Lee Ann Nichols, were receptionists at the clinic. Their murderer was identified as John Salvi, an activist who worked on behalf of Human Life International. On 19 March 1996 he was found guilty of the double charge of murder (a conviction that was later overturned on a technicality). Later that same year, Salvi was found dead in his prison cell, having apparently committed suicide.

The December killings followed on from two other murders in the June of the same year. Outside another abortion clinic in Pensacola, Florida, Paul Jennings Hill shot an abortion practitioner, Dr John Britton, and his clinic escort James Barrett. Hill was convicted on 4 December 1994, just over three weeks before Salvi struck in Brookline. He sat on death row for seven years before being executed by lethal injection on 3 September 2003.

Of course, the issue of abortion is a contentious subject on more than one level. On the one hand, there are those who disagree with abortion entirely. On the other, there are those who disagree about the developmental stage at which a foetus becomes a human with human rights. There are reasonable arguments for and against abortion, which is why people will never concur, but what matters is that people argue and campaign in a civilised manner.

There are currently more people in favour of abortion being available in one form or another than not. It isn't necessarily that they are pro-abortion, but that they recognise a practical requirement for abortion because societies are complex and people make mistakes or become the victims of circumstance. In that context, abortion might be seen as a necessary evil, because those in favour of its availability consider it better that a child is not born into an environment where it is not wanted and will consequently live an unhappy life. Those against abortion make an equally valid point that society should be geared to cope with unwanted births, so that those children are given the opportunity of having happy lives whatever the circumstances of their conception.

The usual way of determining the cut-off point for abortion is to identify a stage of foetal development when a baby will not be able to survive unassisted. Inevitably advances in medicine have meant that this foetal age has moved progressively, because incubators can increasingly provide premature babies with the life support they need.

# 31 December

## New millennium's eve

**1999** Quite a few people had a genuine fear that the world would literally come to an end at the stroke of midnight on 31 December 1999. As well as a few over-zealous concerns regarding Armageddon, it turned out that computer scientists were not entirely convinced that all would be well come 1 January 2000. They imagined that the global technological infrastructure might go haywire at the stroke of midnight due to computers losing their ability to communicate with one another, or indeed, communicate with themselves.

The crisis was dubbed the 'Y2K Problem'. The US and UK spent millions of pounds in anticipation of the apocalyptic outcome, but as it turned out not much happened. People's home computers simply ticked over to the new millennium without a hitch, which demonstrated that all other computers would have done the same had they been left alone.

In truth there were one or two minor issues that crept into some systems. In Onagawa, Japan, for example, an alarm at a nuclear power plant was set off, while in France a weather map displayed the new date as the year '19100'. Perhaps the biggest problem in the US, where so much anxiety had built up, was experienced by gamblers in Delaware where 150 slot machines suddenly stopped working.

The total cost of the preparations taken to prevent a worldwide computer meltdown has been estimated at over $300 billion. And what was the root cause of this frenzied spending? The fact that digital dates were often abbreviated to just two figures, and it was not clear how computers would react when the year rolled back to '00'.

This isn't actually as inconsequential as it sounds. The argument that predicted the Y2K Problem claimed that as computers cannot interpret dates in a human fashion, breaking the linear progression made by the date figures would disrupt other more important operations within the computer, potentially disabling the whole system.

That this doomsday really failed to materialise has led many to claim that the vast amount of money spent on fixing the problem was a complete waste. Voices seeking to defend the amount spent, however, claim that nothing happened precisely because so much had been spent on correcting all the potential glitches out there. There is a degree of contention to this view, particularly when it is pointed out that Italy, which spent virtually nothing on the panic, and the UK, which spent millions, experienced the exact same benign outcome.

Despite the apparent unfounded nature of the infamous Y2K Problem, computer experts continue to have palpitations about other potential disaster dates. The Year 2007 Problem was an actual issue caused by changes to US daylight saving time. There is also the projected Year 2038 Problem, when the binary code that sets the date for 32-bit computer systems will switch back to a long line of zeros; the Year 2070 Problem, which is again to do with dates being stored as two-digit figures; and the Year 10,000 Problem which wonders how computers will cope when the need for a five-digit date arises. The history that will shape our lives 8,000 years in the future starts now.

# Index

521

**Bermuda Triangle** 5 December 1945
**Bernardini, Micheline** 5 July 1946
**Berners-Lee, Tim** 30 April 1993
**Beslan (North Ossetia, Russia)** 3 September 2004
**Best, George** 22 January 1983
**Best, Pete** 10 April 1970
**Bethlehem, star of** 14 March 1986
**Bevan, Nye** 26 July 1945
**Bhabha Atomic Research Centre (BARC)** 18 May 1974
**Bible, the** 5 January 1982; 31 October 1992
**Big Bang, the** 8 February 1969
**Bigfoot** 20 October 1967
**Biggs, Ronnie** 8 August 1963
**bikini bathing suit** 5 July 1946
**Biko, Stephen** 27 April 1950; 12 September 1977
**Biosphere Project** 6 March 1994
**Birdseye, Clarence** 3 November 1952
**Birmingham** 5 October 1974; 26 October 1977
**Black Consciousness Movement** 27 April 1950; 12 September 1977
**Black Wednesday** 16 September 1992
**Blair, Tony** 16 September 1992
**Blige, Mary J.** 21 May 1972
**Bligh, William** 19 October 1952
*Blood On The Tracks* **(album)** 19 March 1962
**Bloody Sunday** 5 October 1974
**'Blue Moon of Kentucky' (song)** 16 August 1977
**Boeing** 12 January 1970;

19 November 1960; 21 December 1988
**Boer War** 12 March 1958
**Bogdanov, Michael** 29 November 1965
**Bohlen, Nils** 10 July 1962
**Bolivia** 8 October 1967
**Bombard, Alain** 19 October 1952
**Bonatti, Walter** 31 July 1954
**Bopp, Thomas** 4 March 1997
**Borg, Björn** 22 January 1983; 24 June 1968
**Borglum, Gutzhon** 3 March 1972
**'Born in the USA' (song)** 4 August 1966
**Bose, Satyendranath** 24 August 2000
**Botany Bay** 26 January 1988
*Bounty,* **HMS** 19 October 1952
**Bourn Hall Clinic** 25 July 1978
**Bowie, David** 8 January 1947
**Boxing Day Tsunami** 22 May 1960; 26 December 2004
**Bradbury, Ray** 8 June 1949
**Bradley, Tom** 29 April 1992
**Brady, Ian** 15 November 2002
**Braque, Georges** 8 April 1973
**Braun, Eva** 25 October 1956
**Braun, Wernher von** 16 April 1946; 16 November 1945
*Brave New World* **(book)** 8 June 1949
**BRAVO (nuclear bomb test)** 12 August 1953
**Brazel, William** 8 July 1947
**Brazil** 18 June 1993; 10 October 2001
*Breitling Orbiter* **(balloon)** 3 July 2002

**Congo, Democratic Republic of**
8 October 1967
**Conlon, Gerry** 5 October 1974
**Conlon, Patrick 'Giuseppe'**
5 October 1974
**Cook, Captain James** 26 January
1988
**Copernicus, Nicolas** 31 October
1992
**Cornell, Eric** 24 August 2000
*Coronation Street* **(TV show)**
9 December 1960
**Cortés, Hernán** 26 October 1977
**Cosans, Jane** 25 February 1982
**Costa Rica** 15 May 1989
**cot death** *see* **Sudden Infant Death**
**Syndrome (SIDS)**
**Côte d'Azur** 8 April 1973
**Cox, Lynne** 7 August 1987
**Crary, Albert** 3 May 1952
**Crick, Francis** 21 February 1953;
25 April 1953
**Crohn's disease** 1 October 1957
**Croix, Félix du Temple de la**
29 July 1953
**Crosby, Bing** 12 November 1952
*Crossroads* **(TV show)** 9 December
1960
**Crowhurst, Donald** 28 May 1967;
5 December 1945
**Crowley, Aleister** 31 July 1954
**Croydon airport** 16 December
1955
**Crump, Martha** 15 May 1989
**Crutzen, Paul** 23 January 1978
**Cuba** 3 January 1961; 19 August
1960; 8 October 1967;
4 November 1984
**Cuban missile crisis** 3 January
1961; 19 August 1960;

30 August 1963; 22 November
1963
**Cubism** 8 April 1973
**Cultural Revolution (China)**
16 May; 9 September 1976
**Cunningham, Sir Alan**
29 February 1948
**Czechoslovakia** 20 August 1963;
20 September 1946

**Dachau** 11 April 1961
**Dalai Lama** *see also* **Tenzin Gyatso**
31 March 1959
**Dallas** 22 November 1963
**Dannemann, Monika**
18 September 1970
**Dante, Alighieri** 10 September
1945
**Darvall, Denise** 3 December
1967
**Darwin, Charles** 5 January 1982;
21 February 1953; 24 February
1989; 2 April 1982; 25 April
1953; 2 June 2003; 29 June
1994; 4 July 1976; 24 November
2009; 28 December 1965
*Datebook* **(magazine)** 13 January
1964
**Davis, Jefferson** 3 March 1972
**Dawkins, Richard** 14 April 2003;
4 July 1976
**Dawson, Charles** 21 November
1953
**Dawson, Jack** 19 December 1997
**'Day In The Life' (song)** 19 March
1962
**Dayr-yasin (village)** 29 February
1948
**D-Day** 10 March 1949; 28 August
1963

**Kasparov, Garry** 10 February 1996

**Kazakhstan** 22 October 1990; 8 December 1991

**Keegan, Kevin** 12 July 1974

**Keenan, Brian** 9 June 1985

**Keith, Linda** 18 September 1970

**Kelley, DeForest** 8 September 1966

**Kelly, Gerry** 25 September 1983

**Kennedy Space Centre** 11 February 2006; 21 July 1969

**Kennedy, John F.** 21 July 1969; 5 August 1962; 22 November 1963

**Kennedy, Ludovic** 15 July 1953

**Kennewick Man** 28 July 1996

**Kensington Gardens** 31 August 1997

**Keynes, J.M.** 26 July 1945

**KGB** 13 April 1953; 3 August 1988; 25 October 1956; 22 November 1963

**Khan, General Ayub** 14 August 1947

**Khmer Rouge** 7 January 1979

**Khomeini, Ayatollah** 16 January 1979; 7 March 1989

**Khruschev, Nikita Sergeyevich** 19 June 1963; 12 August 1953

**Kidd, Eddie** 30 May 1967

**Kiebold, Dylan** 1 August 1966

**Kieffer, Dimitri** 7 August 1987

**Kilbride, John** 15 November 2002

**King David Hotel** 29 February 1948

**King, Billie Jean** 24 June 1968

**King, Martin Luther** 1 December 1955

**King, Rodney Glen** 29 April 1992

**Kirkup, James** 29 November 1965

**Kligman, Ruth** 11 August 1956

**Knapp, Michelle** 9 October 1992

**Knievel, Evel** 30 May 1967

**Knott's Berry Farm** 17 July 1955

**Koenig, Walter** 8 September 1966

**Kohlhase, Charles** 25 August 1981 and 1989

**Kokura** 9 August 1945

**Kola Peninsula** 24 May 1970

*Kon-Tiki* (raft) 28 April 1947

**Koon, Stacey** 29 April 1992

**Koran** *see* Qu'ran

**Korea** 13 September 1951

**Korean Airlines** 3 August 1988

**Korolyov, Sergey** 19 June 1963

**Krafft, Katia and Maurice** 3 June 1991

**Krasner, Lee** 11 August 1956

**Kremlin, the** 3 August 1988; 12 August 1953; 8 December 1991

**Krenz, Egon** 8 December 1991

**Kreuzberg district (West Berlin)** 17 August 1962

**Kroc, Ray** 15 April 1995

**Ku Klux Klan** 3 March 1972

**Kuala Lumpur** 17 October 2003

**Kulbeik, Helmut** 17 August 1962

**Kurdistan** 16 March 1988

**Kurds, the** 16 March 1988

**Kuwait** 10 June 1967; 2 August 1990; 14 December 1973

**Kuznetsov, Aleksandr** 3 May 1952

**L.A.P.D. (Los Angeles Police Department)** 29 April 1992

**La Higuera** 8 October 1967

**Labrador** 30 October 1995

**Lacedelli, Lino** 31 July 1954

New Orleans 29 August 2005;
17 September 1953
New South Wales 27 January 1988
New York 13 January 1964; 2
February 1987; 28 February
1985; 9 March 1952; 18 April
1949; 21 May 1972; 4 June
1973; 13 July 1977; 5 August
1962; 11 August 1956;
1 September 1972; 14 September
1975; 18 September 1970;
9 October 1992; 17 October
2003; 14 November 2007;
21 December 1988
*New York Daily News* (periodical)
9 March 1952
*New York Times* (periodical)
4 March 1997; 3 April 1996;
2 August 1990; 5 August 1962;
17 October 2003
*New Yorker* (periodical) 11 April
1961
New Zealand 31 January 1968;
22 May 1960; 29 May 1953;
29 July 1953; 7 November 1974
*Newcomers, The* (TV show)
9 December 1960
Newfoundland 30 October 1995
Newton, Sir Isaac 30 March 1953;
28 December 1965
Niagara Falls 20 April 1961
Nicaragua 1 October 1957;
4 November 1984
Nichols, Lee Ann 30 December
1994
Nichols, Nichelle 8 September
1966
Nicolich, Gustavo 22 December
1972
Nigeria 26 March 1953

Nilsen, Dennis 24 October 1983
Nimoy, Leonard 8 September
1966
*Nineteen Eighty-four* (book)
8 June 1949
Nixon, Richard 9 May 1974;
5 June 1989
Nobel Prize 23 January 1978;
22 March 1960; 27 May 1994;
28 October 1948; 18 November
1970
North Africa 5 March 1946; 1 May
1945; 30 June 1973
North American Aviation
12 December 1980
North Atlantic Ocean 21 January
1954
North Pacific 21 July 1969;
7 August 1987
North Pole 3 May 1952; 28 May
1967
Northern Ireland 18 April 1949;
4 June 1973; 23 September
1983; 5 October 1974
Norway 3 August 1988; 19 August
1960; 22 August 2004;
10 September 1945
Notorious B.I.G. 21 May 1972
Nova Scotia 30 October 1995
Nuclear Non-Proliferation Treaty
18 May 1974
Nuremberg Code 13 April 1953
Nuremberg trials 23 December
1948
Nureyev, Rudolf 6 January 1993
Nyos, Lake 21 August 1986

Obama, Barack 29 August 2005;
27 October 1992; 8 November
1995

**Pearse, Richard** 29 July 1953
**Peary, Robert** 3 May 1952
**'Penny Lane' (song)** 17 February
   1967
**Perry, Fred** 24 June 1968
**Persian Empire** 16 January 1979
**Peshawar** 19 August 1960
**Peters, Martin** 30 July 1966
**Petronas Towers** 17 October 2003
**Petrov, Stanislav** 26 September
   1983
**Phelps, Michael** 4 September 1972
**Philby, Kim** 6 September 1976
**Philippines, the** 24 January 1972;
   22 May 1960; 10 August 1990
**Phillip, Captain Arthur** 26
   January 1988
*Phoenix* **(spacecraft)** 26 May 2002
**Phoenix, Arizona** 18 June 1993
**Piaggio and Co.** 26 August 1959
**Picasso, Pablo** 8 April 1973
**Pilos, Greece** 23 February 1980
**Piltdown Man** 21 November 1953
**Pinsent, Matthew** 23 September
   2000
*Pioneer X* **(space probe)** 2 March
   1972
**Pisa** 27 February 1964
**Piscine Molitor, Paris** 5 July 1946
*Playboy* **(magazine)** 5 August
   1962
**Pleasant Island** 31 January 1968
**'Please Please Me' (song)** 10 April
   1970
**PLO** 7 June 1981
**Pluto** 18 February 1980; 2 March
   1972
**Plymouth** 28 May 1967
**Poet's Corner** 28 December 1965
**Pol Pot** 7 January 1979

**Poland** 27 January 1996; 13 May
   1981; 2 September 1945
**poliomyelitis** 26 March 1953
**Pollock, Jackson** 11 August 1956
**Polynesia** 28 April 1947
**Pompeii** 4 March 1997
**Pons, Stanley** 23 March 1989
**Pontchartrain, Lake** 29 August
   2005
**Pontiaff, Alexander M.**
   12 November 1952
**Potsdam Declaration**
   15 December 1945
**Powell, Colin Luther** 8 November
   1995
**Powell, Laurence** 28 April 1992
**Powers, Francis Gary** 19 August
   1960
**Prague** 20 August 1963
**Prandtl–Glauert singularity**
   14 October 1947 and 1968
**Presley, Elvis** *see also* **Graceland**
   **Mansion** 21 April 1956;
   16 August 1977
**Price, Vincent** 9 April 1953
**Prince Edward Island** 30 October
   1995
**Prince, The Artist formerly**
   **Known As** 4 August 1984
*Principles of Biology* **(book)**
   24 November 2009
**Prodi, Romano** 31 October 1992
**Pulitzer Prize** 2 July 1961
**Punxsutawney 2 February 1987**
   *see also* **Groundhog Day**
**'Purple Rain' (song)** 4 August
   1984

**Qin Dynasty** 11 July 1975
**Qin Shi Huang** 11 July 1975

**Shute, Nevil** 8 June 1949
**Siam** 17 September 1953
**Siberia** 27 May 1994; 6 June 2002;
  20 June 2005; 7 August 1987
**Sichuan, China** 22 May 1960
**Sidra, Gulf of** 21 December 1988
**Sikorsky, Igor** 8 March 1946
*Silent Spring* **(book)** 28 October
  1948
**Silvia, Rhea** 11 March 1986
**Simjian, Luther George** 4 June
  1973
**Simó Orts, Francisco** 17 January
  1966
**Simon, Helmut and Erika**
  19 September 1991
**Sinai Peninsula** 10 June 1967;
  6 October 1981
**Singapore** 18 December 1985
**Sinhala** 20 July 1960
**Sinn Féin** 18 April 1949
**Sino–Japanese War** 2 September
  1945
**Six-Day War** 6 October 1981;
  10 June 1967
**Slave Trade Act** 25 March 2007
**Slavery Abolition Act** 25 March
  2007
**Slipper, Jack** 8 August 1963
**Slovenia** 1 January 2002
**SMART-1 (space probe)**
  27 September 2003
**Smith, Alyssa** 27 November 1989
  and 2005
**Smith, Teresa** 27 November 1989
  and 2005
**Smith, Walter Bedell**
  24 September 1947
**Smokejacks Pit** 19 July 1983
**SNORT (Supersonic Naval**

**Ordnance Track)** 19 February
  1959
**Sobell, Morton** 5 May 1951
**Sofia** 13 May 1981
*Sojourner* **(Mars probe)** 6 July
  1997
*Solar Challenger* **(solar-powered
  aircraft) see also** *Gossamer
  Penguin* 7 July 1981
**Solidarity (trades union)**
  8 December 1991
**Solzhenitsyn, Alexander** 27 May
  1994
**Sorensen, Gunar** 22 August 2004
**South Africa** 24 February 1989;
  27 April 1950; 2 May 1952;
  12 September 1977; 1 December
  1955
**South America** 21 March 1963;
  2 April 1982; 28 April 1947;
  28 July 1996; 7 August 1987;
  2 September 1945; 25 October
  1956; 13 December 2006
**South Sea Islands** 31 January
  1968
**Soviet bloc** 7 February 1992
**Soviet Union (USSR)** 3 January
  1961; 7 February 1992;
  20 February 1956; 12 April
  1961; 13 April 1953; 16 April
  1946; 26 April 1986; 12 May
  1949; 7 June 1981; 19 June
  1963; 8 July 1947; 3 August
  1988; 6 August 1945; 12 August
  1953; 15 August 1945;
  19 August 1960; 30 August
  1963; 3 September 2004;
  6 September 1976; 10 September
  1945; 26 September 1983;
  22 October 1990; 22 October

**Van Gogh, Vincent** 11 August 1956

**Van Nguyen** 18 December 1985.

*Vanity Fair* (film) 4 August 1966

**Varivax** 17 March 1995

**Varro, Marcus Terentius** 11 March 1986

**Vatican City** 1 January 2002; 13 May 1981

**VaxGen** 23 April 1984

**VE Day (Victory in Europe)** 7 May 1945; 14 May 1948

**Velvet Revolution, the** 20 August 1963

**Venus** 1 March 1966; 29 March 1974; 30 June 1973; 10 August 1990; 31 October 1992

**Verne, Jules** 24 May 1970

**Vernon, Gavin** 25 December 1950

**Vespa** 26 August 1959

*Victoria* (ship) 10 August 1990

**Victoria and Albert Museum** 26 July 1945

**Victoria, Queen** 12 March 1958

*Victory*, HMS 21 October 2005

**Viet Cong** 15 January 1973

**Viet Minh** 7 January 1979

**Vietnam War** 15 January 1973; 13 July 1977; 27 October 1992; 27 December 1979

*View from the Summit* (book) 29 May 1953

**Vinsin, Charles** 27 October 1992

**Virginia Tech** 1 August 1966

**VJ Day (Victory in Japan)** 15 August 1945; 7 May 1945

**Volvo** 10 July 1962

*Vostok* (satellite) 1 March 1966; 12 April 1961

*Voyager* (space probe) 2 March 1972; 25 August 1981–1989

**Waddington, David** 15 November 2002

**Wade, Virginia** 24 June 1968

**Waite, Terry** 9 June 1985

**Wakefield, Dr Andrew** 17 March 1995

**Wałęsa, Lech** 13 May 1981; 8 December 1991

**Walker, William** 19 July 1983

**Wallace, Alfred Russell** 24 November 2009

**Walter, Natasha** 4 May 1979

**Wankel, Felix** 1 February 1957

**Wannsee conference** 11 April 1961

*War and Peace* (book) 27 May 1994

**Warner Brothers** 9 April 1953

**Warsaw Pact** 20 August 1963

**Washington** 3 April 1996; 23 April 1984; 26 July 1945; 28 July 1996; 30 August 1963; 11 December 1998

*Washington Post* (periodical) 3 April 1996

**Washkansky, Louis** 3 December 1967

**Watergate scandal** 9 May 1974

**Waterston, Robert** 11 December 1998

**Watson, James** 21 February 1953; 25 April 1953

**Watts, Charlie** 10 May 1963

**Weise, Jeffrey** 1 August 1966

**Wells, H.G.** 8 June 1949

**West Africa** 19 July 1983; 25 March 2007